E. K. Hunt and
Jesse G. Schwartz

Penguin Modern Economics Readings

General Editor

B. J. McCormick

Advisory Board

K. J. W. Alexander
R. W. Clower
G. R. Fisher
P. Robson
J. Spraos
H. Townsend

A Critique of Economic Theory

Selected Readings

Edited by E. K. Hunt and Jesse G. Schwartz

Penguin Books

Penguin Books Ltd, Harmondsworth,
Middlesex, England
Penguin Books Inc, 7110 Ambassador Road,
Baltimore, Md 21207, USA
Penguin Books Australia Ltd,
Ringwood, Victoria, Australia

First published 1972
This selection copyright © E. K. Hunt and Jesse G. Schwartz, 1972
Introduction and notes copyright © E. K. Hunt and Jesse G. Schwartz, 1972

Made and printed in Great Britain by
Richard Clay (The Chaucer Press) Ltd
Bungay, Suffolk
Set in Monotype Times

Contents

Introduction

The following collection of essays brings together recent criticism of academic economics. This is part of the insurgence now sweeping the social sciences – in literature, political science, sociology, history and economics – which can only be understood as an aspect of the general crisis of cold-war liberal ideology.[1]

The increasing elaboration of administrative edifices, the sedimentation of layer upon layer of organizational hierarchies coupled with the sophisticated mechanization of production meant large numbers of 'silent' compliant technostructure replacement parts had to be produced. And they were. During the bleak fifties an endless, faceless stream rolled off the educational production line. A generation allowed themselves to be cowed by the spectre of a relentless monolith besieging the 'free world'. Liberal newspapers lamented student apathy.

Something has gone wrong. Young people everywhere are no longer automatically adopting the overall perspectives of commodity society as the unquestionable limits of their own aspirations. The knowledge machine is no longer able to produce and reproduce. At the annual meetings – confrontations, counterconventions and counterpresences. Members of the American Economic Association, for example, were told that 'the economists are the sycophants of inequality, alienation, destruction of the environment, imperialism, racism and the subjugation of women . . .'.[2]

Once more those fuzzy, 'non-objective' hoary old battle-scarred words – imperialism, exploitation, alienation, commodity fetishism – dog the professors at every turn as they elaborate endlessly, 'utility', 'consumer sovereignty' and 'marginal products'.

1. The opinions expressed in the Introduction are those of the editors. They do *not* necessarily reflect even in part the views of the contributors to this volume.
2. From a statement read during a meeting of the American Economic Association, New York, December 1969.

Economics: a respectable science

The academic social sciences are fragmented and compart-mentalized into history, economics, sociology, political science, etc. Each discipline or even subdiscipline, an overwhelming literature, a specialized jargon. A professionalism abandoning itself in a desert of detail while remaining utterly indifferent to the whole. In the case of economics we find an extraordinary gradation into 'pure' theory, monetary economics, fiscal economics, international economics, welfare economics, in-dustrial economics, labour economics, 'development' economics and so on. These categories all seem to have a set of assumptions in common:

1. Acceptance of the socio-economic institutional structure. Capitalism defines the constraints – the economist's task is clearly delimited within these bounds.

2. The premise of social harmony. Aside from a few 'frictions' and difficulties, there are no irreconcilable conflicts of interest between social groups.

3. A bombastic, antiquated individualism.

4. The State is an impartial arbitrator, not committed to any particular class or group.

5. Total lack of historical perspective – capitalism is accepted as for all time – its past evolution from feudalism is dealt with summarily, other systems are discussed only to underline the superiority of capitalism.

These assumptions do not merely limit, they overwhelm academic economics. These are the premises not of the scientist but of the corporate manager devoted to keeping the industrial motor running and proclaiming a few platitudes about why it is the best there is. After all, no system can maintain itself by force exclusively; some sort of ideology is needed to show how things fit into place, to reproduce within each new generation a particular conception of the world, a framework of values within which in-dividuals can define their goals.

The first assumption rigidly limits inquiry to the 'ongoing' system and it is indeed a very unreal model of the 'ongoing' system. A monotonous recitation of 'free choice', 'competition' and the Market. Private property is taken as a beneficial socio-logical 'fact'. Everything outside of this absolute 'efficient' productive engine, every aspect of human relations is taken as outside 'economics'.

Despite protestations as to its 'value-free' character as 'a positive science', production and exchange as they exist within capitalism are taken as a normative standard. According to Myrdal (1953, p. 4):

Even when the claim is not explicitly expressed, the conclusions unmistakably imply the notion that economic analysis is capable of yielding laws in the sense of *norms*, and not merely laws in the sense of *demonstrable recurrences and regularities of actual and possible events.*

Thus the theory of 'free competition' is not intended to be merely a scientific explanation of what course economic relations would take under certain specified assumptions. It simultaneously constitutes a kind of proof that these hypothetical conditions would result in maximum 'total income' or the greatest possible 'satisfaction of needs' in society as a whole. 'Free competition' thus on logical and factual grounds becomes more than a set of abstract assumptions, used as a tool in theoretical analysis of the causal relations of facts. It becomes a political *desideratum.*

He furthermore points out (p. 10):

the whole theoretical objective of J. B. Clark may be summed up as an attempt to prove the thesis that, given free competition, price formation will meet the requirements of equity, inasmuch as each man's income must then correspond to the value to society of his productive contri-bution. Yet Clark, too, took it upon himself to stress that economic science as such had nothing to do with the question of the relative justice or injustice of existing institutions, laws, or customs. The same dual attitude is apparent in the majority of neo-classical theorists.

Even today one still finds: 'The economist's value judgements doubtless influence the subjects he works on and perhaps at times the conclusions he reaches. . . . Yet this does not alter the funda-mental point that, in principle, there are no value judgements in economics' (Friedman, 1967, p. 86).

The social harmony premise has been insisted upon in every crisis-ridden *ancien régime.* In its current sophisticated form each individual is endowed with an initial set of 'factors' – land, labour power, etc. – and exchanges these for an alternative set of factors such that his 'utility' is maximized. Everyone is happy. The system is stable and self-reproducing. No conflict, no social classes, no exploitation, no imperialism, no wars. The 'invisible hand' has cleared the Market. The mechanism of exchange has been reified into the political ideology of Western society as a whole.[3] So when confronted by explosive social conflict, all that the academics can do is to discover a few unrealized 'externalities', make a case for 'black capitalism', reduce racism to the employers' 'disutility' for hiring black workers, propose a few reforms in health, education, welfare to augment 'human capital'. Yes, there are conceptual difficulties here – the blurred ragged edges of those 'value-laden' concepts – class, exploitation, alienation – so difficult to quantify, to work up into an exact analysis.[4]

Closely associated with social harmony is ' "Individualethik" ... the sublimated expression of crude bourgeois egoism' (Mészáros, 1970, p. 258). All statements about society are reduced to those about privatized, self-seeking individuals. There is no recognition that social class exists, that class origins may be an influence in an individual's development, that the interests of different classes may be contradictory, perhaps irreconcilable. Even in academic sociology and political science the concept of social class has long since become respectable. But in economics we still have the unending celebration of the instalment-plan Robinson Crusoe, the sovereign consumer guiding the economy as he maximizes his satisfaction. 'Using the medium of money,

3. This bears a remarkable resemblance to the 'vulgar economy' that Marx castigated a hundred years ago: 'which deals with appearances only, ruminates without ceasing on the materials long since provided by scientific economy and there seeks plausible explanations of the most obtrusive phenomena, for bourgeois daily use, but for the rest, confines itself to systematizing in a pedantic way, and proclaiming for everlasting truths, the trite ideas held by the self-complacent bourgeoisie with regard to their own world, to them the best of possible worlds' (Marx, 1867a, p. 81 of 1961 edn).

4. Today it is claimed that imperialism cannot be studied, it is not a 'scientific' term, cannot be 'operationally defined', etc. Several decades ago there were those who had 'come near to claiming that all abstract words are meaningless, and have used this as a pretext for advocating a kind of political quietism. Since you don't know what Fascism is, how can you struggle against Fascism?' (Orwell, 1946, p. 157 of 1968 edn).

consumers cast their votes in the market to determine what gets produced and by whom' (Homan, Hart and Sametz, 1958, p. 68).

As Veblen puts it:

[This] conception of man is that of a lightning calculator of pleasures and pains, who oscillates like a homogeneous globule of desire of happiness under the impulse of stimuli that shift him about the area, but leave him intact. He has neither antecedent nor consequent. He is an isolated definitive human datum, in stable equilibrium except for the buffets of the impinging forces that displace him in one direction or another. Self-imposed in elemental space, he spins symmetrically about his own spiritual axis until the parallelogram of forces bears down upon him, whereupon he follows the line of the resultant. When the force of the impact is spent he comes to rest, a self-contained globule of desire as before (Veblen, see Lerner, 1948, pp. 232–3).

That social mediation produces needs and wants, that the consumer may possibly be as much a mass-produced product of the system as cornflakes or Coca-Cola, is not even remotely hinted at. These issues are discussed in several of the articles in Part Two, in particular, Reading 3 by Marx.

There is a curious dualism in economic theory concerning the State. In 'microeconomics' it exists in a shadowy, unreal form. Its primary function is to intervene only in the case of external economies or diseconomies and to provide 'public goods' – the usual example being 'Defence'. Now the Keynesian Revolution meant the overthrow of the doctrine of automaticity. It was realized that there were strong tendencies for stagnation and large-scale unemployment. It became theoretically valid for the State to intervene. So in 'macroeconomics', in contrast to 'micro', the State is regarded not as a foreign entity but as an active participant in the economy.

In Part Five we have included articles critical of both of these approaches. O'Connor (Reading 15) discusses the standard neoclassical view of the State. Much closer to the ideological frontier is Galbraith's conception of the rationalized corporate State and this is discussed by Fitch (Reading 20). Rosen (Reading 16) outlines the emasculation of liberal elements in Keynesian theory and Nuti (Reading 18) emphasizes that the 'new' economics has only ameliorated the basic contradictions, it is still the same Capital–Labour conflict though its outward forms have changed somewhat. The article by Kalecki (Reading 17), written in 1943, presages with remarkable insight the 'political business cycle' of post-war capitalist economies – that full employment, 'labour discipline' and stable prices are basic incompatibilities. Goodwin (Reading 19) presents an economic model which, among other things, attempts to explain why reformist political parties probably have very little effect on the distribution of income in a capitalist economy, but also shows why the working class enjoys an unsteady, persistent rise in its standard of living – a possible clue to its lack of revolutionary commitment.

Academic economics: a form of alienation

By means of productive activity, man transforms his environment and, in the process, himself. Man must produce to satisfy physical needs and in doing this he necessarily creates a complex hierarchy of non-physical needs. 'The *entire so-called history of the world* is nothing but the begetting of man through human labor' (Marx, see Struick, 1970, p. 145).

Through purposeful activity, basic physical needs are overcome and a unique, specifically human mode of existence is produced. This is a process of self-mediation in which man, by productive activity, manufactures a world of objects and is himself produced. However under capitalism a peculiar set of artificial barriers are interposed in this self-development process. In effect man's 'inorganic body', the world of objects and institutions that he himself has produced, becomes 'reified', becomes something alien and external to him.

We speak of price trends, stock exchange prices, and by so doing we acknowledge the inhuman, autonomous movement of objects, a movement that carries human beings along as a stream carries twigs of wood. In a world governed by commodity production, the product controls the producer, and objects are more powerful than men (Fischer, 1959, p. 82 of 1964 edn).

What has happened is that useful material objects have taken on a very peculiar and special form – they have become commodities. A commodity is an object of utility produced for exchange on an autonomous market. Its properties are due to its twofold character. First, it is a useful object; secondly, when brought to the market it acquires a definite social status, as a value. Value is a sort of 'social hieroglyphic'. It is only in a very special, historically specific form of social organization that useful and in many instances necessary items (food, clothing, etc.) are values. 'To stamp an object of utility as a value, is just as much a social product as language' (Marx, 1867a, p. 74 of 1961 edn). In this state of affairs, human relations are subordinated to relations between external objects; the quantitative manifold produced by exchange assumes the aspect of unchangeable, natural reality.

Once the world of commodities has, so to speak achieved its independence and subjected the producers to its sway, the latter come to look upon it in much the same way as they regard that other external world to which they must learn to adjust themselves, the world of nature itself. The existing social order becomes in the apt expression of Lukács, a 'second nature' which stands outside of and opposed to its members (Sweezy, 1942, p. 36).

Furthermore, this reduction of all things to commodities by no means stops with material objects. 'With the *increasing value* of the world of things proceeds in direct proportion the *devaluation* of the world of men' (Marx, see Struick, 1970, p. 107). Rather than the world producing realization of human potentialities, labour becomes a mere material fact of production. Rather than man and nature we find Wage Labour and Capital. Human activity becomes a private property cakewalk. The worker's 'human qualities only exist in so far as they exist for capital *alien* to him' (Marx, see Struick, 1970, p. 120).

At this point a new historic entity emerges, commodity-man, the Anglo-Saxon maximizing Robinson Crusoe of the textbooks; but a reflection of the heavily armoured, mortgaged individuals of the present 'war of all against all' epoch; one-dimensional, alienated expressions of the property–labour relationship.[5] In

5. Alienation and its commodity-fetish manifestation, under capitalism, go well beyond the strictly 'economic' sphere. Berger and Pullberg (1966, p. 60) explain how in Marxian thought this is conceived to extend through all human experience: 'the autonomization of the economic is paradigmatic of the autonomization of the whole range of social relations. . . . In other words, there are not only fetishized commodities, but there is also fetishized power, fetishized sexuality, fetishized status. Just as the fetishism of commodities finds its theoretical expression in a reified political economy (or,

this situation,

man experiences himself as a thing to be employed successfully on the market. He does not experience himself as an active agent, as the bearer of human powers. He is alienated from these powers. His aim is to sell himself successfully on the market. His sense of self does not stem from his activity as a loving and thinking individual, but from his socio-economic role . . . If you ask a man 'Who are you?', he answers 'I am a manufacturer', 'I am a clerk', 'I am a doctor'. . . . That is the way he experiences himself, not as a man, with love, fear, convictions, doubts, but as that abstraction, alienated from his real nature, which fulfills a certain function in the social system. His sense of value depends on his success: on whether he can sell himself favorably, whether he can make more of himself than he started out with, whether he is a success. His body, his mind and his soul are his capital, and his task in life is to invest it favorably, to make a *profit* of himself. Human qualities like friendliness, courtesy, kindness, are transformed into commodities, into assets of the 'personality package', conducive to a higher price on the personality market. If the individual fails in a profitable investment of himself, *he* feels that he is a failure; if he succeeds, he is a success. Clearly, his sense of his own value always depends on factors extraneous to himself, on the fickle judgement of the market, which decides about his value as it decides about the value of commodities. He, like all commodities that cannot be sold profitably on the market, is worthless as far as his exchange value is concerned, even though his use value may be considerable (Fromm, 1965, pp. 129–30).

Academic economics is the algebraization of this ethos, a historically limited arithmetic of prices, physical aggregates, etc., with the underlying social relations given, accepted and taken as for all time. In place of human beings, community, etc. we find only conglomerations of labour and capital. The conditions of the worker are treated only as they relate to the undisturbed functioning of the process of production.

In Marx's day, pre-capitalist, feudal vestiges were much nearer at hand; one could still observe Western societies in which the relations between individuals were primarily political. Given our total immersion in a thoroughly commercialized world, a world

to use a more contemporary term for this science, in reified economics), so the other species of fetishization are theoretically formulated and thereby mystified in reified political science, reified sociology, reified psychology and even scientistic philosophy.'

that has become so alien to its inhabitants that social reality is exceedingly difficult to grasp, it is more necessary than ever to differentiate between what is ontologically and what is capitalistically necessary. Such a viewpoint is most 'embarrassing'. The transitory nature of Private Property and Wage Labour is its first premise. Indeed, the importance of the Marxian theory of value is that it enables us to see through the fetishism of commodities and that it poses in an unmistakable way the qualitative questions 'What are Profits?' 'How is it that Profits exist?', and this is beyond the purely quantitative question of the level of profits under various conditions. (Medio discusses this in Reading 13.) Nothing so clearly shows the fetishism of conventional economics as the recent 'capital controversy', which we will now discuss.

The marginal productivity theory of distribution, the marginal utility theory of consumer behaviour and the arrested development of scientific economics

The traditional theory of distribution states that distribution is simply a special case of price theory. The income of any factor of production (and hence the amount of the national product that it is able to command) depends on the price that is paid for the factor and the amount that is used. If we wish to build up a theory of distribution we thus need a theory of factor prices and quantities. Such a theory is a special case of the theory of price. . . (Lipsey, 1963, p. 407 of 1966 edn).

This is typical of the attempt to locate distribution entirely in the exchange or market process as part of the general pricing mechanism for commodities. That is, to explain by exchange, by supply and demand for factors, who gets what share of the cake. In this way the impersonal forces of the market, not human relationships, purport to govern the distribution of wealth.

The United States Social Security Administration declared that in 1966 any urban family of four persons living on an income of $3150 or less was living in poverty. Nearly twenty-five million persons fell into this category. But the $3150 figure was based on an economy diet which could sustain humans only for short, temporary emergency situations. Over a longer period persons in this category could not meet even minimal nutritional requirements and their health would deteriorate. Any reader familiar with price levels in the American economy of that year can use his own knowledge of the price of rental units, clothes, entertainment and medical and dental expenses to imagine how truly dismal the general style of life of these people would be as their health deteriorated from malnutrition. Undernourished, insufficiently clothed against the weather, living in rat-infested slums. Who is to blame? The Market! 'Impersonal', 'impartial', 'competitive' – each 'factor' remunerated according to the value of its marginal product. A man gets what he is worth.

Back in the 1890s this was a potent stupefier: '. . . what a social class gets is, under natural law, what it contributes to the general output of industry' (Clark, 1891, p. 313). Present-day economists abstain from anything so blatant as declaring whether this is 'fair' or 'right'. But the import is still the same – social harmony prevails, class struggle, exploitation, dissent and conflict are made to dissolve in a whirl of factor substitutability, isoquants and marginal products.

Let us see briefly how this works. The textbooks begin invariably with a very sharp dichotomy – the theory of the consumer and the theory of the firm. First, we meet commodity-man, with fixed budget, intent upon choosing commodities so as to maximize his utility. This results in commodities being chosen in such proportions that the marginal rate of substitution between any pair, the number of units of one commodity that a person is willing to exchange for one unit of another, will be equal to the ratio of their prices. Furthermore, these marginal rates of substitution between any pair of commodities will be the same for all consumers since they are confronted by more or less the same prices. We will call this the 'Consumer's Condition'.

Next an individual firm is considered, confronted by given prices in a competitive market. Now with specified prices for both inputs and outputs, the firm will, in order to maximize profits, arrange its production so that the price of any factor (including labour) is equal to the value of its marginal product. The marginal rate of substitution between any pair of factors is equal to the ratio of their prices, the marginal rate of transformation between any two outputs is equal to the ratio of their respective prices. These rules will be followed by all firms since they all face the same input and output prices. We will call this the 'Production

Condition'. In equilibrium, since the prices facing the individual firm and the individual consumer are the same, an individual consumer's marginal rate of substitution is equal to any firm's marginal rate of transformation. At which point the academics ecstatically proclaim 'Consumer sovereignty!', 'Pareto optimality!' Every resource is being used, every commodity is produced, in accordance with consumers' wants – it is not possible to reallocate without decreasing someone's 'utility'.

This basically is the microeconomic exposition that is repeated endlessly (more hollow-sounding every day), the 'neo-classical' wisdom that prevails with bland uniformity at nearly all American and British universities. Some radicals, perceiving at a glance that something is missing – namely private property, capitalists, workers, imperialism – have regarded the whole thing as an apologetic without, it must be said, a complete understanding of much of the argument. But ... they have been quite right! Others have accepted this view of how capitalism works, have claimed it to be, however, a counsel of perfection and have emphasized real world 'imperfections' and 'rigidities'.

Now the Consumer's Condition is an expression of the simple fact that the consumer will adapt his expenditures to prevailing prices. Regardless of what prices he is confronted with, maximizing his 'utility' with these given prices will result in his choosing commodities such that 'marginal utilities' are proportional to their prices. All this is largely a tautology, yet a remarkable conclusion is drawn from it: according to Dorfman (1967, p. 91):

Since all consumers purchase at the same (or at least similar) prices, all consumers will have the same marginal rate of substitution between every pair of commodities. We are therefore justified in saying that there is a community marginal rate of substitution between every pair of commodities, and that it is equal to the ratio of their prices.

The implication here is that (quite independently of the distribution of income) there is a sort of social or community consensus in what is produced, that it makes no difference to social welfare whether more of one commodity or more of another is produced. This, as Dobb (1969, p. 51) points out, amounts to illicit aggregation:

Different persons will consume commodities in very different proportions, for a variety of reasons including differences in their incomes. A rich man may consume much wine and relatively little bread, a poor man may consume them in opposite proportions; and the benefit to the latter from the last shilling spent on bread will be very much greater than to the former. It would be quite absurd to conclude . . . that to produce additional wine costing a shillingsworth of productive resources and additional bread costing the same amount represented equal increments of *utility to the community* [italics added]. The fact is that if more bread were produced and less wine, there would be an effect, *ceteris paribus*, on relative prices favourable to bread consumers, and hence to the poor; and conversely if more wine were produced and less bread.

Furthermore, while the consumer is indeed absolute tsar over whether to put brand X or Y toothpaste into his shopping basket, he and his fellow-consumers do not decide, *qua* consumers, the amount and pace of investment and its sectoral pattern – the primary determinant of the overall level of employment. This is the outcome of decisions taken by the managers of national and international capitalist firms. The sovereignty of five million American consumers today is the sovereignty of being unemployed.

The other objective 'efficiency' rule, the Production Condition, specifies, as we have mentioned, the choice of optimum methods of production and the relative scale of output. Now the first problem, the choice of techniques, is one of finding a means of production–labour ratio in each industry such that there is no further gain in output in any industry when labour or equipment is swapped between the different industries. This will occur when the marginal rate of substitution of 'capital' for labour is equal over all industries. The second problem is one of allocating the total amount of resources (say, iron, coal, etc.) among industries. If any factor is more profitable in one industry than in others, there is a gain to be made in transferring it to this industry – at the optimum the value of the net product of any factor is the same among all industries. In this Walrasian equilibrium system both of these criteria are met – from this follows the neo-classical argument that this will result in the most efficient allocation of resources for society as a whole.

The Walrasian schema, however, is only tenable for a society in which particular natural resources or skills (i.e. mineral deposits, soil and climate or special skill or knowledge) are owned by individuals. Each person's income depends upon the price in terms of other commodities that a day's output of his commodity will fetch. Obviously the distribution of real income is highly arbitrary, depending upon the nature and extent of each individual's 'factor endowment'. It is postulated that an equilibrium will be reached and this is taken to be the optimum in the sense that no one consumer could be made better off, by changing the composition of output, without making someone else worse off.

This is all very well for a society of self-employed artisans or small farmers. But modern capitalist economies are characterized by the fact that the overwhelming majority of the population own neither land, minerals, special knowledge nor skills. They own nothing except their labour power and are confronted with the concentration of the ownership of the means of production in a very few hands. Since there is a great deal of mobility of both labour and resources, a more or less uniform rate of profit and pattern of wage rates prevails. Regardless of what a worker is producing, he receives the same wage – the income of an individual depends upon his type of occupation and amount of labour and whether he owns any capital. Wages are fixed in terms of money, and prices of products are established in terms of money. Clearly this type of industrial price system is very different from the Walrasian Consumer Condition/Production Condition price system where there is no mechanism to establish a uniform rate of profit and an individual's income depends upon what commodity he owns. Furthermore, in an industrial price system, the rate of profit cannot be ascertained from the technical conditions of production and exchange. It cannot be taken as the 'marginal product' of a 'quantity of capital' because it is necessary to know the rate of profit in order to aggregate capital into a single quantity to determine the effect on output of varying it by a unit amount, i.e. its marginal product or rate of return. 'One has to assume a rate of interest in order to demonstrate how this equilibrium rate of return is determined' (see Dobb, page 207). The point is that the value of capital depends on the rate of return. This cannot be used in turn to determine the rate of return. It is seen that either the rate of profit or alternatively the share of wages must be determined exogenously, and the explanation of 'who gets what' set in terms of 'relative bargaining power' or class struggle, not marginal productivity.

So we see that both the Consumer and the Production Condition cannot explain relative prices or income distribution in industrial capitalism and are in fact irrelevant. Once this is admitted, capitalism, the Market, etc. can no longer be said to allocate resources, to produce, in some objectively 'efficient' manner. The consumer sovereignty apparatus is seen to be nugatory. All sorts of questions never dreamt of in Samuelson's *Economics* come to mind: is the cake 'distributed in proportion to the productive contribution of the participants in production (in proportion to the share of each in the cost involved), or is some class which has made little or no productive contribution successful in annexing it, and if so, how and why?' (Dobb, 1937, p. 32 of 1940 edn).

What accounts for the persistence of the remarkable state of affairs in which an individual can 'own' factories and natural resources, can privatize forests, fields, seashore, etc.?

Neo-classical theory was largely a response to certain 'unsettling' conclusions drawn from labour theory of value arguments current in the last century. It is the stock-in-trade of most academics. The origins and ideological impact of neo-classical theory are discussed at length by Dobb and Meek in Readings 1 and 2, its basic structure is challenged in Part Two, a fundamental error in its internal consistency and logic is analysed in Part Three and an alternative explanation of 'who gets what' is offered in Part Four.

The neo-classical conception of capital is an outstanding example of fetishism, the process in which men project upon outside objects, upon reified abstractions, those powers which are truly their own. 'Since profit is calculated as a return on total capital, the idea inevitably arises that capital as such is in some way productive' (Sweezy, 1942, p. 129). So a 'quantity of capital' is postulated and this rather than human labour is attributed with the power of producing wealth. This is an ideological cornerstone:

A free private enterprise system . . . also rests on *private property*, meaning that most productive property (capital goods) is owned directly or indirectly by individuals who reap a 'return' based on the fact that capital goods can be used to create goods where no goods existed before. This is the essential meaning of 'capitalism' (Homan, Hart and Sametz, 1958, p. 68).

Marx (1867b, p. 814 of 1967 edn) thundered against this sort of reasoning:

Capital is not a thing, but rather a definite social production relation, belonging to a definite historical formation of society which is manifested in a thing and lends this thing a specific social character. Capital is not the sum of the material and produced means of production. Capital is rather the means of production transformed into capital, which in themselves are no more capital than gold or silver is money.

That was written in 1867.[6] In 1908 Veblen (see pages 181–2) asserted:

The continuum in which the 'abiding entity' of capital resides is a continuity of ownership, not a physical fact. The continuity, in fact, is of an immaterial nature, a matter of legal rights, of contract, of purchase and sale. Just why this patent state of the case is overlooked, as it somewhat elaborately is, is not easily seen. . . . This would, of course . . . upset the law of 'natural' remuneration of labor and capital to which Mr Clark's argument looks forward from the start. It would also bring in the 'unnatural' phenomena of monopoly as a normal outgrowth of business enterprise.

Maurice Dobb (1937, see p. 9 of 1940 edn) argued this same point:

When, however, one is dealing with the generality of commodities, or even with large groups of commodities, or with a long instead of a short period of time . . . one is no longer justified in using the level of wages, of profit and rent as determining constants, for the reason that these will be influenced by the value of commodities as well as influencing them. It follows, therefore, that an essential condition of a theory of value is that it must solve the problem of distribution (i.e. determine the price of labour-power, of capital, and of land) as well as the problem of commodity-values; and it must do so not only because the former is

6. As far back as 1823 we find Ricardo well aware of the meaninglessness of measuring a 'quantity of capital' independent of distribution. See Sraffa (1951, p. xlix).

an essential, indeed major part of the practical inquiry with which Political Economy is concerned but because the one cannot be determined without the other. In other words, neither Distribution nor Commodity-Exchange can be properly treated as 'isolated systems'.

The neo-classicals further mystified their theory of capital and distribution via the formalism of an aggregative production function. In 1953 Joan Robinson (see 1960, p. 114) remarked:

the production function has been a powerful instrument of mis-education. The student of economic theory is taught to write $O = f(L,C)$ where L is a quantity of labour, C a quantity of capital and O a rate of output of commodities. He is instructed to assume all workers alike, and to measure L in man-hours of labour; he is told something about the index-number problem involved in choosing a unit of output; and then he is hurried on to the next question, in the hope that he will forget to ask in what units C is measured. Before ever he does ask, he has become a professor, and so sloppy habits of thought are handed on from one generation to the next.

Of course the neo-classicals paid no heed. In article after article, treatise after treatise, we have the confusion of capital as machinery, buildings, i.e. the technical means of production, with its existence in monetary value terms. Nothing shows the stagnation of academic economics better than that it was necessary at this late date to enter into a controversy with the neo-classicals (the majority of academic economists) as to what 'capital' is.

The new criticism, inspired by Piero Sraffa, does not merely mock at orthodoxy. It penetrates into its theoretical system and exposes its weakness from within. The debate is carried out on the plane of logical analysis; when the logical argument has been refuted, the orthodox ideology is left floating in the air deprived of what it used to claim was its scientific basis (Robinson, 1971, p. 30).

In Part Three we have gathered a set of essays about the 'capital theory controversy' which will enable the reader to grasp the essentials of this critique. We suggest that the articles be read in the order in which they appear. Those by Robinson, Dobb and Nuti summarize the issues. We have, in addition, included an important article by Garegnani, though it may prove difficult for most readers. We recommend that the reader consult the survey by Harcourt (1969), a logical starting point for further research. Advanced students should also consult Sraffa's (1960) book, as it remains the basis for most of the formal arguments.

Conventional economics, to this very day, does not have a theory of profit. This has led naturally enough to renewed interest in other conceptualizations of how capitalism works, in particular that of Karl Marx. Most recent work, has found that the Marxian system provides the methodological tools for a depth of inquiry beyond that of any other approach. In Part Four we have included articles by Medio and Johansen which support the Marxian view. Sherman (Reading 14) expresses the dissenting opinion that while neo-classical theory is thoroughly ideologically tainted and useless for political economy, it is logically compatible on a purely formal plane with the labour theory of value.

Training the new economic mandarins

Learning economics in the United States is a conditioning process that often systematically weeds out the more inquiring, curious or radical student. Endless reading lists, mid-term and final exams. No time to stop and think, to evaluate, to consider alternative arguments. So the students are kept mindlessly accumulating and busily competing for grades. All that is required is to reproduce the course material successfully. This is as much an aculturization process as an educational one. At every turn the students' fields of thought are rigidly prescribed. The staggering fees, on one hand, plus the irregular, highly subjective meting out of financial aid, function quite repressively. But the basic mechanism is simply that the students are being programmed to be the efficient mandarins of corporate capitalism and they must master an enormous body of material specific to this – the positive transcendence of political–economic estrangement is not on the reading list!

And not only students. Modern capitalism has reduced all things to universal saleability – even economics professors! Every year, the spectacle of thousands of academics, in the cavernous AEA 'job market', treated precisely as the commodities they so assiduously analyse.

The job market for people in the social sciences is saturated.[7] This, plus the pressures on department chairmen to hire docile, article-producing automata, means that anyone putting down 'Marxian economics', 'radical economics', 'political economy', etc., on his *curriculum vitae* will most probably be by-passed for a 'respectable' econometrician. Of course, getting hired is just part of the story. What happens when Professor A addresses an anti-war demonstration, Professor B participates in a building take-over, or Professor C goes to Cuba, returns and gives an enthusiastic report? All too often there are suddenly budget problems. It is always a 'budget problem' – 'funds' spontaneously evaporate with every trespass of the institutionally defined limits of discourse.

The feudal organization of economic indoctrination directly affects the form and nature of the research work being carried on. In the physical sciences and especially in engineering or physics the virtuoso or lone innovator is totally anachronistic – more and more problems are tackled by teams or groups. Yet medieval craftwork methods still prevail in economic research. Each harassed academic remains an isolated part-time research entrepreneur, part-time pedagogue. That an insurgent tide of radical criticism has appeared is all the more remarkable . . . and the greatest cause for optimism.

Marx: a minor post-Ricardian!

At the December 1966 American Economic Association meeting the Professors held a celebration of the hundredth anniversary of *Das Kapital*.[8] Marx's great work breaking through the mountain chain of years, ponderous, crude, intangible, confronts them at every turn. Here was a chance to get back. So the Professors exuding erudition overwhelming, confronted *Das Kapital*. A swarm of problems was perceived. Professor Letiche (1967, p. 598) began with something about 'co-existence of the different intellectual traditions' and how 'the exploration of new fields of experience in economics may disclose unsuspected application of

7. In the United States, for example, during the academic year 1967–8, a total of 23,091 Ph.D.s were turned out – an increase of 12 per cent from the previous year (of which 600 were in economics). See US Department of Health, Education and Welfare (1969).

8. We will only discuss some of the more remarkable events.

our economic concepts both to market and to centrally planned economies'.

Rather than continuing with these tepid platitudes the *wunderkind* of American economics, Professor Paul A. Samuelson, started by subtitling the first section of his paper with the query 'Genius or crank?' (Samuelson, 1967, p. 616). The trouble, it seems, is that Marx was an autodidact – he did not have a degree in economics. 'Too bad Marx could not have done systematic graduate work at Harvard under John Stuart Mill, and then been given a good chair at Columbia!' Yes, if only Marx had been taught proper economics – rigorous, scientific, exact, and had never taken up those rabble-rousing, fuzzy notions!

Professor Samuelson further remarks: 'Many a newly published fragment by Marx would be of no interest at all if known to be the work of some 1844 John Doe.' This scholarly allusion to the *Economic and Philosophical Manuscripts of 1844* could only have been manufactured at MIT!

At this point Professor Samuelson breaks off this most enlightening line of inquiry and proceeds hurriedly to turn his 'microscope onto aspects of Marxian economics that can be fruitfully discussed'. That is, he introduces the usual false polarity between Marx's economic concepts and those pertaining to history, sociology, philosophy. Only the former are, of course, respectably dealt with and Marx's contribution in this respect is rated by Professor Samuelson as that of 'a minor post-Ricardian'.

So we are immediately plunged into the scholastics of relative prices and an age-old textbook refutation argued as follows.

Marx's labour theory of value is construed to be the proposition that the prices of commodities are proportional to the amounts of direct and indirect labour going into their production. Once this straw man is set up it is easily shot down. Suppose a scarce factor, say, land is introduced or suppose that the proportions of labour to means of production are not equal in the various industries.[9] Prices will deviate from values in either case. Hurrah! *This* labour theory of value is refuted.[10]

9. It is interesting to note that in the 'capital controversy' so critical to bourgeois ideology, Samuelson rested his case for the marginal productivity theory of distribution upon this very assumption he criticizes in Marx. 'Samuelson, in a Centenary appreciation of the *Capital*, remarked that the

But not Marx's theory. Prices will, of course, deviate from values in these two cases, as both Ricardo and Marx were well aware.[11] However, the functional determinant of prices remains the quantity of labour expended. Prices will indeed diverge from values. But, given the rate of surplus value, this divergence can be calculated. In Readings 12 and 13 by Johansen and Medio, this problem is discussed in greater detail.

The explanation of relative prices is only a first step in the account of how an amount of surplus labour over and above that corresponding to the wage bundle is extracted from the actual producer, the labourer, and realized as profit, rent and interest, 'which different persons, under different pretexts, share amongst themselves' (Marx, 1867a, p. 220 of 1961 edn). This enables one to see through, at a glance, the textbook sophistry where the factors 'land and capital' spontaneously 'produce' an income for their owners. Alas Marx muddled his argument with that exploitation stuff. He should have waited a hundred years till armed with matrix algebra and 'systematic graduate work at Harvard' he could have 'proven' the same thing by showing that since land is a non-produced means of production, it can be eliminated from

assumption of equal factor proportions in all lines of production and therefore labour-value prices, provides an "impeccable model" "even though not defensible as a general theory of markets". But if he gives up the labour-value assumption it is *his* system that collapses. Marx, taking the rate of exploitation to be governed by the balance of forces in the class struggle, can derive from it the rate of profit and so find the appropriate "prices of production", whether proportionate to labour-values or not, but Samuelson is at a loss when the value of capital is not independent of the rate of profit. A "quite ordinary theory of cost of production" is just what the neo-classics and the neo-neo-classics have not been able to find' (Robinson, 1968, p. 335). Dobb (Reading 8) and Garegnani (Reading 11) also discuss this.

10. 'The Marxian labour theory of value does *not* say, as is commonly supposed, that the equilibrium prices of commodities are always proportionate to the quantities of labour required to produce them. It affirms, certainly, that this statement is true of an economy where "the whole produce of labour belongs to the labourer"; but it agrees – indeed emphasizes – that equilibrium prices do not normally follow this simple rule in a capitalist economy where part of the net product goes to profits. In a capitalist economy, it is demonstrated, relative prices normally deviate from relative quantities of embodied labour' (Meek, 1967, p. 175).

11. See 'Some notes on the transformation problem' in Meek (1967).

the price system without relative prices or the rate of profit being affected and that a 'marginal product of capital' cannot be defined independently of the rate of profit.

Anyway, after polishing off 'its inferior statics', Professor Samuelson considers its 'dynamics'. Again we find an old textbook refutation. Marx is said to have predicted the immiseration of the working class. This has not occurred. Now, nowhere in his mature economic writings does Marx state that real wages *per capita* have a long-run tendency to fall. An absolute increase in the wage level is at least implied in the fully elaborated model of volume 3 of *Das Kapital* where a constant rate of exploitation combined with rising productivity will result in a rising real wage (alternatively if the organic composition of capital is rising, the rate of profit will fall). Furthermore, if we consider capitalism as a whole, *both* industrialized countries and neo-colonial hinterland, a strong case can be made for increasing relative impoverishment. Next it is doubted whether Marx's prediction of the increasing concentration of monopolies is occurring and whether this follows formally, analytically, from the theory of value model or was just a guess. Then the ultimate refutation – 'the successful development of the Mixed Economy'. [No mention, of course, of the dismal record of the US economy – deficiencies of aggregate demand, simultaneous recession and price inflation, a 1·6 rate of growth (*per capita*) during the fifties, palpable social dissolution, and the familiar palliative of imperialist war . . . every day in Vietnam – the Neoclassical Synthesis!]

Finally, Professor Samuelson proclaims: 'the cash value of a doctrine is its vulgarization'. He cites the treatment of Western economies in Soviet textbooks as the pay-off of Marxian economics. By this criterion neo-classical theory has been indeed lucrative!

The consumer is, so to speak, the king . . . each is a voter who uses his money as votes to get the things done that he wants done (Samuelson, 1948, p. 56 of 1964 edn).

To understand what determines labor and property's share in national product, and to understand forces acting on the degree of equality of income, distribution theory studies the problem of how the different factors of production – land, labor, capital, entrepreneurship, and risk taking – are priced in the market place or how supply and demand

interact to determine all kinds of wages, rents, interest yields, profits and so forth. . . .
the Clark neoclassical theory of distribution, although simplified, is logically complete and a true picture of idealized competition (Samuelson, 1948, pp. 525–6 of 1964 edn).

Under perfectly perfect competition, where all prices end up equal to all marginal costs, where all factor-prices end up equal to values of marginal-products and all total costs are minimized, where the genuine desires and well-being of individuals are all represented by their marginal utilities as expressed in their dollar voting – *then* the resulting equilibrium has the efficiency property that 'you can't make any one man better off without hurting some other man' (Samuelson, 1948, p. 621 of 1964 edn).

Consumer sovereignty! Distribution by supply and demand! Pareto optimality! These textbook truisms once so profitable, are now heavily mortgaged.

Next it was Bronfenbrenner's turn at the conference 'to consider what bourgeois economics owes to Marx'. He does go on to present an interesting symbolic interpretation of some aspects of Marxian theory though no conclusions, no forecasts, no generalizations are made. To Samuelson Marx is 'a minor post-Ricardian', to Bronfenbrenner 'an embryonic general equilibrium theorist in advance of Léon Walras'. The Professors, it seems, are somewhat at variance as to which anaesthetizing category Marx belongs.

A discussion followed. Professor Donald F. Gordon (1967, p. 637) couldn't understand all the fuss about the labour theory of value – 'the definition of value by labor seems to be an unnecessary detour in an attempt to understand modern capitalism'. Right on! Why bother with a theory that poses in the most unmistakable terms the question of whether the economic categories, wages, profits, interest, rent, must be taken as eternal truths – that views these categories rather as abstractions of real historical social relations between men, specific to a particular historical development every bit as permanent as the categories: king, nobility, serfs.

He agrees with Samuelson that Marx was a 'minor post-Ricardian' and this is a really shattering indictment because, Professor Gordon goes on to tell us 'that overwhelmingly the largest part of his [Marx's] intellectual work was in economics, not other social sciences'. This splendid sanitizing characterization as 'economics' of perhaps the most ample conceptualization of society yet devised is really paying 'economics' a compliment it hardly deserves. Professor Gordon (1967, p. 639) is deeply puzzled:

Why does half the world regard him as a patron saint? Why in particular do we witness the ironic spectacle of the underdeveloped world embracing Marx and socialism so unreservedly, while we know that in his praise for the productive powers of capitalism Marx had few if any peers? Far from being hidden in an obscure passage of a weighty tome, this praise was trumpeted in the Communist Manifesto which people do in fact read.

Alas for the academics, Marx did not confine his remarks to contrasting the positive advance of capitalism over feudalism. Just after the section to which Professor Gordon refers, Marx impertinently declares, 'the history of industry and commerce is but the history of the revolt of modern productive forces against modern conditions of production, against the property relations that are the conditions for the existence of the bourgeoisie, and of its rule' (see Feuer, 1959, p. 13) and furthermore, social progress necessitates 'the most radical rupture with traditional property relations' (ibid., p. 27). Apparently, to Professor Gordon the existence of machines, factories, technology in any form other than as bourgeois private property is inconceivable. The 'underdeveloped world' is under no such illusion.

Next Professor H. Scott Gordon (1967, p. 641) expresses his concern. Just can't find a proper pigeon-hole: 'it would be a mistake, in my opinion, to approach it [*Das Kapital*] solely in terms of modern analytical economics, for a fundamental purpose of the book is to do something that modern economists rule out of economics altogether – the making of normative judgements'. (All the Readings here, especially those by Dobb, Veblen, Hunt, Robinson, Meek and O'Connor, assess the ideological content of 'modern economics' as somewhat more colourful.)

So . . . what attraction does Marxism have? H. Scott Gordon (1967, p. 641) is baffled.

The deep mystery that surrounds *Das Kapital*, however, is not really its content, but its influence. . . . In attempting to understand its leverage, we can probably get more assistance from Durkheim and Frazer and Freud, than from Walras and Keynes, for we are faced here with the influence that such things as totem and myth and fantasy have on human thought and action, not with anything that is as severely rational as modern economics.

We think that 'anything as severely rational as modern economics' will in the years ahead become increasingly difficult to maintain. Conventional economics simply refuses to consider basic social problems, to which Marxism is addressed. It is the systematic exclusion of these problems and the smothering of criticism by a conspiracy of silence that requires explanation from Durkheim, Frazer or Freud.

Cost–benefit analysis: the highest stage

During the fifties and on to the present there has been a tremendous upswing in the development of theories of 'public finance' and 'cost–benefits'. In Prest and Turvey (1965) we find cost–benefit analysis applied to transportation, water resources, urban renewal, public health, education and 'defence'. The procedure is to enumerate and quantify, as far as possible, all of the benefits and costs associated with each project. That with the highest benefit/cost or net present value is chosen.

So what happens: a motorway is to be built through a city displacing thousands of families, inflicting noise, dirt, fumes on nearby residences. Land acquisition, and construction costs are astronomical. Given that the poor and very rich are concentrated, for the most part, in the town centres with middle-income groups in the suburbs and that the latter will constitute overwhelmingly the majority of users, we are in the peculiar situation of spatially distributed class struggle. Nevertheless the valiant quantifiers impute monetary values for user time savings, reductions in accidents, increases in comfort and convenience based upon empirical studies of how much the middle-class suburbanites would be 'willing to pay' for improved transport. This is justified theoretically by linking 'willingness to pay' to social benefit via the maximizing individual metaphysic. A pious remark is made to the effect that income effects may be involved – the matter is left at that. A ratio of benefits to costs is found – this is taken to be the gain to society as a whole. The project is trumpeted to be 'economic'. 'It pays.' An answer from the computer! Exact! Efficient! Objective! Beyond challenge – incomprehensible to the average citizen whose home is about to be bulldozed.

Take health for example. A certain project will reduce illnesses and deaths due to disease. How much is this worth? Or education. What's it worth to keep a person in college busily accumulating his 'human capital'? The value of education is taken simply as the difference between the lifetime wage earnings of those who receive additional education and those who do not. This is a measure of Human Capital. The academics are quite serious. And they are right! The concept of human capital (which goes back at least to Ricardo) is a logically inescapable conclusion of economic theory. This merely reflects, quite correctly, the reduction under capitalism of human beings and all their potentialities to instruments of gain.

And finally Defence:

An alternative interpretation of the differential between military pay and alternative pay requires a significantly different time frame. This interpretation would look upon the differential as an investment, albeit an involuntary one. This investment is partly in income generating capital; that is, military experience is productive in the market sector. . . . For example, the urban Negro or rural white who becomes a policeman, console operator, or mechanic as a result of the military is advantaged by the military, and this addition should be evaluated in estimating the draft's cost (Weinstein, 1967, pp. 66–7).

The draft produces several types of resource-allocative changes within the military sector. First, as noted above, one potentially important allocative effect of a draft system results from the availability of military manpower at wage rates that fail to reflect opportunity costs. Among the decisions which the military services must make are choices between the degree of manpower utilization and the degree of 'hardware' (capital) utilization. Since the latter is generally bought in private, uncontrolled markets while the former is obtained at below market prices through the draft, an incentive exists for the services to substitute labor for capital equipment to a superoptimal extent, or at least to substitute highly skilled, highly trained labor—having large amounts of human capital – for less skilled labor (Hansen and Weisbrod, 1967, pp. 401–2).

Thank you, Professors, for your rigorous demonstration of the 'cannon-fodder' supposition.

This projection of all social institutions and practices back upon the market logic of exchange is now worse than irrelevant. For it is utter folly in a society rife with social conflict to repeat with every kind of sophisticated flourish the smug, well-fed hypocrisy that proclaims business as usual, let's go ahead and internalize a few externalities, equate a few margins.

As Professor Samuelson said, 'The cash value of a doctrine is in its vulgarization.'

Political economy again!

Why do thousands of workers, secretaries, clerks still rationalize their almost unbearably dehumanized existences with 'a man gets what he's worth', 'wages determined by supply and demand', 'the consumer is king'? How is it that generations of students have accepted unquestioningly Robinson Crusoe aphorisms as descriptive of advanced capitalism?

The entire school of economic theory going back to the 1870s is now under attack. There is little the academics can counterpoise except a shallow consumerism and a fetishized theory of production. 'Severely rational modern economics', the austere science, is being seen to function essentially as a pseudo-sophistication proclaiming the greatest beneficence while the wretched of the earth are starved, clubbed, gassed and bombed into submission.

In a period of drastic social change the first and most fundamental changes are in the intellectual sphere. Intellectuals are highly trained, can work with complex ideas, can relate seemingly disparate phenomena to discover new facets of social reality. For most, industrial society is a treadmill of ceaseless work and interminable bills, time payments, etc. Only intellectuals, and of these a small number, have the time to go through the long and grinding process of learning ... and unlearning ... and dialectically transcending. All things cry out give us new forms, new ways of thinking: a new political economy!

A New Political Economy that encompasses economics, sociology, history, art, literature, poetry. The negation of the atomistic compartmentalization of development economics, labour economics, industrial economics, statistical economics, business economics . . . of the bureaucratic lattice of qualifications, examinations, degrees, dissertations. An approach – a frame of mind – not a formal degree. A science of the purely human, universal basis of the production of material wealth for human needs.

Political economists see their task as demystifying Modern Economics, helping young people everywhere to discover a world of passionate possibilities.

References

BERGER, P., and PULLBERG, S. (1966), 'Reification and the sociological critique of consciousness', *New left Rev.*, vol. 35, pp. 56–71.

CLARK, J. B. (1891), 'Distribution as determined by rent', *Q. J. Econ.*, vol. 5, pp. 289–318.

DOBB, M. (1937), *Political Economy and Capitalism: Some Essays in Economic Tradition*, Routledge & Kegan Paul, 2nd edn, 1940.

DOBB, M. (1969), *Welfare Economics and the Economics of Socialism: Towards a Commonsense Critique*, Cambridge University Press.

DORFMAN, R. (1967), *Prices and Markets*, Prentice-Hall.

FEUER, L. S. (ed.) (1959), *Karl Marx and Friedrich Engels. Basic Writings on Politics and Philosophy*, Anchor Books.

FISCHER, E. (1959), *The Necessity of Art: A Marxist Approach*, trans. A. Bostock, Penguin, 1964.

FRIEDMAN, M. (1967), 'Value judgements in economics', in S. Hook (ed.), *Human Values and Economic Policy*, New York University Press.

FROMM, E. (1965), *The Sane Society*, Fawcett Premier Books, Greenwich, Conn.

GORDON, D. F. (1967), 'Discussion. *Das Kapital:* a centenary appreciation. Papers and Proceedings, 79th Annual Meeting of the American Economic Association, San Francisco, 27–9 December 1966', *Amer. econ. Rev.*, vol. 57, pp. 637–40.

GORDON, H. S. (1967), 'Discussion. *Das Kapital:* a centenary appreciation. Papers and Proceedings, 79th Annual Meeting of the American Economic Association, San Francisco, 27–9 December 1966', *Amer. econ. Rev.*, vol. 57, pp. 640–41.

GRAAF, J. DE V. (1957), *Theoretical Welfare Economics*, Cambridge University Press.

HANSEN, W. L., and WEISBROD, B. A. (1967), 'Economics of the military draft', *Q. J. Econ.*, vol. 81, pp. 395–421.

HARCOURT, G. C. (1969), 'Some Cambridge controversies in the theory of capital', *J. econ. Lit.*, vol. 7, pp. 369–405.

HOMAN, P. J., HART, A. G., and SAMETZ, A. W. (1958),
The Economic Order: An Introduction to Theory and Policy,
Harcourt Brace Jovanovich.

LERNER, M. (ed.) (1948), *The Portable Veblen*, Viking Press.

LETICHE, J. M. (1967), 'Introductory comments. *Das Kapital:* a
centenary appreciation. Papers and Proceedings, 79th Annual Meeting
of the American Economic Association, San Francisco, 27–9
December 1966', *Amer. econ. Rev.*, vol. 57, pp. 597–8.

LIPSEY, R. G. (1963), *An Introduction to Positive Economics*,
Weidenfeld & Nicolson, 2nd edn, 1966.

MARX, K. (1867a), *Capital: A Critical Analysis of Capitalist
Production*, vol. 1, Foreign Languages Publishing House, Moscow,
1961.

MARX, K. (1867b), *Capital: A Critique of Political Economy: III. The
Process of Capitalist Production as a Whole*, International Publishers,
1967.

MEEK, R. L. (1967), *Economics and Ideology and Other Essays: Studies
in the Development of Economic Thought*, Chapman & Hall.

MÉSZÁROS, I. (1970), *Marx's Theory of Alienation*, Merlin Press.

MYRDAL, G. (1953), *The Political Element in the Development of
Economic Theory*, trans. P. Streeten, Routledge & Kegan Paul.

ORWELL, G. (1946), *Politics and the English Language. Inside the
Whale and Other Essays*, Penguin, 1968.

PREST, A. R., and TURVEY, R. (1965), 'Cost–benefit analysis: a
survey', *Econ. J.*, vol. 75, pp. 683–735.

ROBINSON, J. (1960), 'The production function and the theory of
capital', *Collected Economic Papers*, vol. 2, Blackwell.

ROBINSON, J. (1968), 'Value and price', Symposium on the Influence
of Karl Marx on Contemporary Scientific Thought, International
Social Science Council and International Council for Philosophy and
Humanistic Studies, Paris, 8–10 May 1968.

ROBINSON, J. (1971), 'The relevance of economic theory', *Month. Rev.*,
vol. 22, pp. 29–37.

SAMUELSON, P. A. (1948), *Economics: An Introductory Analysis*,
McGraw-Hill, 6th edn, 1964.

SAMUELSON, P. A. (1967), 'Marxian economics as economics. Papers
and Proceedings, 79th Annual Meeting of the American Economic
Association, San Francisco, 27–9 December 1966', *Amer. econ. Rev.*,
vol. 57, pp. 616–23.

SRAFFA, P. (ed.) with the collaboration of M. H. Dobb (1951), *The
Works and Correspondence of David Ricardo*, vol. 1, Cambridge
University Press.

SRAFFA, P. (1960), *Production of Commodities by Means of
Commodities*, Cambridge University Press.

STRUICK, D. J. (ed.) (1970), *Karl Marx. Economic and Philosophic
Manuscripts of 1844*, trans. M. Milligan, Lawrence & Wishart.

SWEEZY, P. M. (1942), *The Theory of Capitalist Development: Principles of Marxian Political Economy*, Monthly Review Press.

US DEPARTMENT OF HEALTH, EDUCATION AND WELFARE, OFFICE OF EDUCATION (1969), *Earned Degrees Conferred: 1967–1968: Part A. Summary Data*, catalog no. FS 5.254:54013–68, US Government Printing Office, Washington.

WEINSTEIN, P. A. (1967), 'Discussion. Papers and Proceedings, 79th Annual Meeting of the American Economic Association, San Francisco, 27–9 December 1966', *Amer. econ. Rev.*, vol. 57, pp. 66–70.

Part One
Historical Descriptions of the Rise of the Neo-Classical School

By the late nineteenth century, capitalism appeared to have triumphed everywhere in Europe and North America. Economists shifted their focus of attention from fundamental social issues to 'efficient resource allocation'. The essential social and economic institutions of capitalism were assumed, generally with very little argument or justification, to be 'natural' and eternal social forms.

In Reading 1 Maurice Dobb outlines the development of neo-classical economics. This sets in perspective the recent 'capital controversy' by showing how, after Ricardo, academic attempts to explain profit fell 'broadly into two main types: on the one hand . . . in terms of some creative property inherent in capital, namely, in terms of its productivity; on the other hand . . . in terms of some species of "real cost", analogous to labour, which the capitalist contributed and for which profit was not a surplus-value but an equivalent'.

Ronald Meek (Reading 2) discusses the impact of the so-called 'marginal revolution'. With this new approach, put forward as an alternative to the theories of the classical economists and Marx, the rather unsettling notion of social conflict disappeared.

Part One
Historical Developments of the Neo-Classical School

1 Maurice Dobb

The Trend of Modern Economics

Maurice Dobb, 'The trend of modern economics', in *Political Economy and Capitalism*, Routledge & Kegan Paul, 1937, 2nd edn, 1940, revised 1944, reprinted 1960, pp. 127–84.

Once the formal question of internal consistency is settled, the acceptance or rejection of a theory depends on one's view of the appropriateness of the particular abstraction on which the theory is based. This is necessarily a practical question, depending on the nature of the terrain and the character of the problem and the activity to which the theory is intended to relate. One frequently hears the claim made for a theory that it has a greater generality than some rival formula; and on the face of it this plea seems cogent enough. But one would do well to be somewhat sceptical of such a claim, at least until one was sure that the greater generality had not been purchased too dearly at the expense of realism. In making abstraction of particular elements in a situation, there are, broadly speaking, two roads along which one can proceed. In the first place, one may build one's abstraction on the exclusion of certain features which are present in any actual situation, either because they are the more variable or because they are quantitatively of lesser importance in determining the course of events. To omit them from consideration makes the resulting calculation no more than an imperfect approximation to reality, but nevertheless makes it a very much more reliable guide than if the major factors had been omitted and only the minor influences taken into account. So it is that one creates the abstraction of a projectile which moves in a vacuum – as it is never found to do in reality – in order to estimate what are the dominant factors which will govern the trajectory of an object propelled through a resistant medium. The correctness or otherwise of the particular assumptions chosen can only be determined by experience: by knowledge of how actual situations behave, and of the actual difference made by the presence or absence of various factors.

The method as a whole yields valid results (provided the assumptions are rightly chosen), so long as the presence of the minor factors introduced in the subsequent approximations has the effect merely of adding certain additional parameters to the original equations and not of altering the structure of the equations themselves.[1]

Secondly, one may base one's abstraction, not on any evidence of fact as to what features in a situation are essential and what are inessential, but simply on the formal procedure of combining the properties common to a heterogeneous assortment of situations and building abstraction out of analogy. This is akin to what an early scientific writer described as a 'general definition of the things themselves according to their universal natures . . . (relying) on general terms which (have) not much foundation in knowledge', and used to 'build most subtle webs' from 'themes not all collected by a sufficient information from the things themselves'.[2] Within limits, of course, such a method is not only perfectly valid, but is an essential element in any generalization: a generalization is no generalization but an imaginary hypothesis unless what it generalizes is something common to the phenomena to which it refers. The danger of the method is of its being pushed too far, beyond the point where the factors which it embraces cease to be the major factors determining the nature of the problem which is in hand. What the abstraction gains in breadth it then more than loses, as it were, in depth – in relevance to the particular situations which are the focus of interest. And the danger is the greater in that this point may be passed without any awareness that this is so. Frequently this method of progressive refinement of analogy has led to little but confusing sophisms. In a sphere where generalization can take a quantitative form the method can have a greater show of reason and is doubtless less subject to abuse. And it may be the case that, even in its most abstract forms, the method can yield some element of truth; since so long as the abstractions it employs retain any elements which are common to actual situations, the relations which are

1. This, I believe, is the case which J. S. Mill called one where the principle of the composition of causes applies. Cf. for further reference to this, p. 190 [of *Political Economy and Capitalism*].

2. Sprat, quoted by Hogben (1936).

postulated must represent *some* aspect of the truth in each particular problem. One may instance, perhaps, the theory of probability applied to features which are common to all games of chance; or, as probably a more barren example, attempts which have been made to develop general rules of language which shall be valid for all particular languages. As a yet more barren example, one might add the attempt of the economist Barone to frame a set of equations which would demonstrate that the same law must prevail in a collectivist economy as rules in a *laissez-faire* world. But in all such abstract systems there exists the serious danger of hypostatizing one's concepts; of regarding the postulated relations as the determining ones in any actual situation, instead of contingent and determined by other features; and hence of presuming too readily that they will apply to novel or imperfectly known situations, with an abstract dogmatism as the result. There is the danger of introducing, unnoticed, purely imaginary or even contradictory assumptions and in general of ignoring how limited a meaning the corollaries deducible from these abstract propositions must have and the qualifications which the presence of other concrete factors (which may be the major influences in this or that particular situation) may introduce. All too frequently the propositions which are products of this mode of abstraction have little more than formal meaning and at most tell one that an expression for such-and-such a relation must find a place in any of one's equational systems.[3] But those who use such propositions and build corollaries upon them are seldom mindful of this limitation and in applying them as 'laws' of the real world invariably extract from them more meaning than their emptiness of real content can possibly hold.

It does not seem a bad rule in a subject so wedded to complex practical issues as is political economy to keep one's feet firmly planted on the ground, even if this be at the sacrifice of some logical elegance of definition and of some of the impressive, but often misleading, precision of algebraic formulation. In general the abstractions employed by the classical economists and by Marx were of the

3. Such pursuits are sometimes defended on the ground that they are 'tool-makers' for subsequent analysis. Perhaps it is true that this is their principal use. But even tools are better made when their manufacture is fairly closely subordinated to the uses which they are intended to serve.

first of the two types that we have mentioned. The concept of the perfect market, of homogeneous labour, of equal compositions of capital were intended to generalize what were in actuality the most essential factors in determining exchange-values. Patten (1893) has remarked that Ricardo was essentially a concrete thinker, and Marx was specially anxious that his theory should embrace those features which were characteristic of capitalist society rather than of any other. While a disturbing influence, even a reflex influence, was admittedly exerted by other and neglected factors in the situation, this was regarded as being of secondary importance in determining the larger shape of actual events. Interest was focused on what was peculiar to a particular system of economic relations, even at the expense of a wider, but perhaps more barren, generality. Since their time, however, I think it is not incorrect to say that the efforts of economic analysis have been predominantly directed along the second road. In abstracting phenomena of exchange from the productive relations and the property and class institutions of which they are the expression, an attempt has been made to arrive at generalizations which will hold for *any* type of exchange economy. Marshall (1890, p. 824) remarks of J. S. Mill that he seemed to attribute to the laws of exchange 'something very much like the universality of mathematics', even while he admitted distribution to be relative to transitory institutions. From the general relations of an abstract market we pass to yet more perfect abstractions and today are introduced to the relations which will necessarily prevail in any situation where 'scarce means which have alternative uses serve given purposes'. Something of the real world doubtless still lingers even in this tenuous definition. But hardly enough to make one believe that the resulting propositions can hold anything at all imperative for the problems of the actual world. If an economic law is a statement of what actually tends to happen and not a mere statement of a relation between certain implicitly defined variables, then such propositions can surely be precious little guide to the 'laws of motion of capitalist society' – or, indeed, to any of the other matters on which they are intended to pass an economic judgement.

It was an important element in Marx's theory of ideology that in a class society the abstract ideas which were fashioned from a given society tended to assume a phantom or fetishistic character in the sense that, being taken as representations of reality, they came to depict actual society in an inverted or a distorted form. Thereby they served not merely to hide the real nature of society from men's eyes, but to misrepresent it. The examples which he cited were mainly drawn from the concepts of religion and of idealist philosophy. Thus it came about that ideas and concepts, which in their day may have played a positive role of enlightenment as weapons of criticism turned against the system both of ideas and of institutions of a previous epoch, later became reactionary and obscurantist, precisely because they were treated as constituting the real essence of contemporary society, not merely its abstract and partial reflection; with the result that reality was veiled. In the realm of economic thought (where one might at first glance least suspect it) it is not difficult to see a parallel tendency at work. One might think it harmless enough to make an abstraction of certain aspects of exchange-relations in order to analyse them in isolation from social relations of production. But what actually occurs is that once this abstraction has been made it is given an independent existence as though it represented the essence of reality, instead of one contingent facet of reality. Concepts become hypostatized; the abstraction acquires a fetishistic character, to use Marx's phrase. Here seems to lie the crucial danger of this method and the secret of the confusions which have enmeshed modern economic thought. Today, not merely do we have the laws of exchange-relations treated in abstraction from more fundamental social relations of production, and the former depicted as dominating the latter, but we even have the relations of exchange treated purely in their *subjective* aspect – in terms of their mental reflection in the realm of individual desires and choices – and the laws which govern actual economic society invertedly depicted as consisting in the abstract relations which hold in this ghostly sphere.

The dividing landmark in the history of economic thought in the nineteenth century is usually placed in the seventies with the arrival of the new utility theories of Jevons and the Austrian School. But if we fix our attention less on the change of form and instead on the shift towards subjective notions and towards the study of exchange-relations in abstraction from their social roots, we shall see that essential changes came earlier in the century, or at any rate the commencement of tendencies which later assumed a more finished shape. Marx, indeed, mentioned 1830 as the year which closed the final decade of 'classical economy' and opened the door to 'vulgar economy'[4] and the decline of the glories of the Ricardian School. This was the period when the new industrial capitalism, both economically and politically, was coming into its own, and when at the same time (as the events of the thirties were witness) the proletariat and its criticism of capitalist society was emerging as a coherent social force for the first time. Thenceforward, no statement concerning the nature of the economic system could remain 'neutral'.[5] Economists, becoming increasingly obsessed with apologetics, had an increasing tendency to omit any treatment of basic social relationships and to deal only with the superficial aspect of market phenomena, to confine their thought within the limits of the 'fetishism of commodities' and to generalize about the laws of an 'exchange economy', until in the end these were made to determine, rather than be determined by, the system of production and of productive relations. In his Preface to the second edition (1873) of volume 1 of *Capital*, Marx

4. This term, of course, was not used by Marx simply as a term of abuse, as is commonly supposed, but in a descriptive sense, familiar to continental philosophy, as contrasted with 'classical'. He states that 'by classical political economy I understand that economy which, since the time of W. Petty, has investigated the real relations of production in bourgeois society, in contradiction to vulgar economy, which deals with appearances only . . . and confines itself to systematizing in a pedantic way, and proclaiming for everlasting truths the trite ideas held by the self-complacent bourgeois with regard to their own world' (Marx, 1867, p. 53). Marx seems particularly to have had in mind McCulloch, Senior, Bastiat, and if not Say at any rate Say's 'interpreters' and followers. Professor Gray (1933) is clearly wrong in implying that Adam Smith and Ricardo were included under the title of 'vulgar economy'.

5. This, of course, was specially true of the theory of profit. Here it is interesting to note that Böhm-Bawerk refers to the position of Adam Smith on the subject of interest as one of 'complete neutrality' and adds that 'in Adam Smith's time the relations of theory and practice still permitted such a neutrality, but it was not long allowed to his followers' (Böhm-Bawerk, 1884, pp. 74–5). On the other hand, Cannan's statement that 'James Mill . . . showed a desire to strengthen the position of the capitalist against the labourer by justifying the existence of profits' (Cannan, 1893, p. 206 of 2nd edn) seems more questionable. James Mill was capable of some

speaks of English political economy as belonging 'to the period in which the (proletarian) class struggle was as yet undeveloped'. Of the period from 1820 to 1830 he says that it 'was notable in England for scientific activity in the domain of political economy. It was the time as well of the vulgarizing and extending of Ricardo's theory, as of the contest of that theory with the old school. Splendid tournaments were held. The unprejudiced character of this polemic . . . is explained by the circumstances of the time.' But this, though it was reminiscent of the intellectual vigour prior to 1789 in France, was no more than 'a Saint Martin's Summer'. After 1830 'the class struggle practically as well as theoretically took on more and more outspoken and threatening forms'. This 'sounded the knell of scientific bourgeois economy. . . . In place of genuine scientific research, the bad conscience and the evil intent of apologetic.' Even honest inquirers were limited by the general atmosphere to evasive compromises and to eclectic attempts 'to harmonize the political economy of capital with the claims, no longer to be ignored, of the proletariat'. The product was 'a shallow syncretism, of which John Stuart Mill is the best representative'. Of that new departure in economic thought which marked the last quarter of the century neither Marx nor Engels seem to have made more than cursory mention or to have taken much notice.[6] If they had done so, it seems probable that they would have regarded it as a continuation of tendencies already latent in the 'vulgar economists', rather

exceedingly frank characterizations of the nature of capitalist production, which one can hardly imagine being made twenty-five years later. One of the best examples of the change was the subsequent attitude to Ricardo's 'lapse' in his third edition. Ricardo was frank enough to add a chapter in this edition on 'Machinery' in which he stated his conversion to the view that the introduction of machinery was capable of being harmful to the interests of labour. This shocked McCulloch, and his followers hastened (and for most of the century succeeded) to draw a veil over this breach of good taste.

6. Engels, in his Preface to volume 3 of *Capital* in 1894, refers parenthetically to the new theory of Jevons and Menger as the 'rock' on which Mr George Bernard Shaw was building a new kind of socialism and 'the Fabian church of the future' (p. 20). But apart from this they seem to have made no mention of it. This would seem surprising in view of the importance it had for the new Fabian socialism: a fact of which, as this single reference shows, Engels was perfectly aware. Jevons's *Principles* appeared in 1874; Marx died in 1883; *The Fabian Essays* appeared in 1888; Engels lived until 1895.

than as the revolutionary novelty in economic thought which it has generally been regarded as being. After all, the new departure consisted more of a change of form than of substance, as Marshall always emphasized. That so many of the economists of the last quarter of the century should have advertised their wares as such an epoch-making novelty, and tilted their lances so menacingly at their forebears, seems to have an obvious, if unflattering, explanation: namely, the dangerous use to which Ricardian notions had been recently put by Marx. It is, I think, significant of the temper of economists that Foxwell once declined to deliver a Presidential Address to the Royal Economic Society on Ricardo on the ground that his denunciation of the author of the heresy of a conflict of interests between capital and labour would have been too violent (see Keynes, 1936, p. 592); and among the leaders of the Austrian School the desire to refute the socialists was a greater preoccupation than in England.

The essential problem for Marx, as we have seen, was the explanation of surplus-value; and it was because the successors of Ricardo either evaded this problem entirely or provided quite inadequate solutions that they provoked his condemnation and his scorn. The 'cost of production' theory of J. S. Mill he regarded as a superficial evasion of the issue. Treating value as being governed by the price of labour (wages) *plus* an average rate of profit, it was not a refinement of Ricardo's theory, but, since it included no explanation of profit, represented an abandonment of the crucial problem which Ricardo's system had presented without ever having solved. The 'cost of production' theory of value solved nothing, because it left the determination of the 'cost of production' unexplained.[7] But there were others who were less

7. With regard to J. S. Mill's attitude, Cannan (1893, p. 214) has said: 'Senior is at least entitled to the credit of having seen that profits had not been satisfactorily explained. . . . J. S. Mill, on the other hand, seems to have been totally unaware that anything was lacking.' Böhm-Bawerk (1884, pp. 286, 498, etc.) classed J. S. Mill (along with Jevons and Roscher) among the eclectics in their interest theory, who did little more than add an element or two to Senior's unsatisfactory theory. To his credit, Mill (1844, p. 90) rejected the productivity theory of profit, stating that 'the only productive power is that of labour'. In his *Principles* (book 2, ch. 15) he seemed to adopt Senior's abstinence theory without examination or further analysis of the problem.

innocent of recognizing the crucial difficulty than was J. S. Mill and attempted to supply an explanation of profit, even if it was one which was shallow and untenable. These attempts fall broadly into two main types: on the one hand were those who sought to explain profit in terms of some creative property inherent in capital, namely, in terms of its productivity; on the other hand were those who sought to explain profit in terms of some species of 'real cost', analogous to labour, which the capitalist contributed and for which profit was not a surplus-value but an equivalent.

The attempt to explain profit in terms of the 'service' rendered by capital to production had already been made by certain of Ricardo's contemporaries, in particular by Lauderdale and Malthus and also by Say, 'that master of polished and rounded sentences', as Böhm-Bawerk called him. Labour which was aided by machinery, said Lauderdale, could produce a larger sum of values in an hour than could labour which was not so aided. 'The moment he places a portion of capital in the acquisition of a spade, one man must obviously, in the course of a day, be able, with his spade, to prepare as much land for receiving seed as fifty could by the use of their nails.'[8] The difference represented the 'productivity' of capital. The fundamental objection to this, as to any form of productivity theory, was that, as Marx pointed out, it included the illicit link of imputing to the owner the 'productivity' of the things he owned. 'A social relation between men assumes the fantastic form of a relation between things'; and the behaviour of things is not only represented animistically as due to some innate property in them, but imputed to the influence of those individuals who exercise rights of ownership over them. On this level there could be no distinction between the 'productivity' of a capitalist and of a landlord – to deny which, indeed, seems partly to have been the intention of the theory. But neither could there be any distinction between the income of the employer of

8. Lauderdale (1804, p. 163). Lauderdale admitted, however, that profit may 'in some cases be more properly said to be acquired than produced' (p. 161). Say (1821, p. 19) said: 'The capitalist who lends, sells the service, the labour of his instrument.' Say (1819, p. 60 of 1821 edn) spoke both of 'labour or productive service of nature' and 'labour or productive service of capital'!

'free' labour and the income of the slave-owner: the 'productivity' of the latter, indeed, was presumably the greater of the two since it was derived from the productivity of his animate as well as his inanimate chattels. A further difficulty has been expressed by Cannan (1893, p. 205) as follows:

If the income of England without any capital would be but one instead of a hundred, it does not necessarily follow that the whole ninety-nine hundredths is profits at present. The weak point in the explanation of profits given by Lauderdale and Malthus is that, while they show clearly enough that the use of capital is an advantage to production . . . they fail to show why the advantage has been paid for at all, why the 'services' of capital are not, like those of the sun, gratuitous.

Böhm-Bawerk (1884, pp. 179–80) trenchantly summed up the productivity theories of interest thus:

What the productive power can do is only to create a quantity of products, and perhaps at the same time to create a *quantity* of value, but never to create *surplus* value. Interest is a surplus, a remainder left when product of capital is the minuend and value of consumed capital is the subtrahend. The productive power of capital may find its result in increasing the minuend. But in so far as that goes it cannot increase the minuend without at the same time increasing the subtrahend in the same proportion. . . . If a log is thrown across a flooded stream the level of water below the log will be less than the level of water above the log. If it is asked why the water stands higher above the log than below, would anyone think of the flood as the cause? . . . What the flood is to the differences of level, the productive power of capital is to surplus-value.

The truth is that if a number of factors are jointly necessary to a given result, there is as little meaning in comparing the degree of 'necessity' of these factors in the creation of wealth as in asking whether the male or female is the more necessary to the creation of a child. Even if it were possible to give a meaning to such separate 'productivity', it would have no necessary relation to the emergence of *value*. For the latter one must inevitably look to characteristics affecting the supply; and any differentiation between incomes must necessarily be sought, not in terms of 'service', but in terms of cost.

The attempt to find an explanation of profit which would make it analogous to wages as payment for a necessary cost involved in production, and at the same time contrast it with the rent of land, is represented by Senior's notorious 'abstinence' theory. This constituted an important landmark in economic thought, because it introduced a species of 'real cost' which was purely subjective and so shifted the whole context of the discussion – shifted it more radically than was apparently recognized at the time or has been recognized since. 'Abstinence' is capable of being defined, it is true, objectively in terms of the things abstained from; but such abstaining could have no significance as a cost – no more than any other act of free exchange – unless one were to suppose that some special 'pain' to the owner was involved in parting with these things. And if 'abstinence', as the subjective equivalent of profit, was to be conceived in a psychological sense, then so presumably must labour be: labour as a cost for which wages were paid being regarded not as a human activity, involving a given expenditure of physical energy, but as the strength of the psychological disinclination to work. Abstraction was to be made of human activity, its characteristics and its relationships, and only the reflection of them in the mind to be taken as the data for economic interpretation.

Already among previous writers there had been signs of an inclination, if shown only in ambiguity, to conceive the notion of 'real cost' as something subjective rather than objective. Adam Smith had used the phrase 'toil and trouble'; while McCulloch (1825, pp. 216–17) referred to the fact that things which cost the same 'toil and trouble' to acquire would involve 'the same sacrifice' and hence be held in similar 'esteem' and be 'of precisely the same real value'. With the introduction of Senior's 'abstinence' there could be no mistaking that such a shift of meaning had occurred. Both question and answer had thereby been subtly moved to a quite different context. But as an explanation of profits, even within its restricted sphere, the theory met with an essential difficulty. Marx was quick to point out that there was no discoverable connection between the capitalist's 'abstinence' and the profit which he earned, and that if they were connected at all, it was apparently in inverse relation. He had only to contrast the profit and the 'abstinence' of a Rothschild to feel that the so-called 'explanation' required no further refutation.

This defect was one aspect of a fundamental dilemma which faces any attempt to cast a theory of cost in subjective terms, and to which we shall later return. Where was one to set the limit to such 'abstinence', short of including in it the sale or hire of every sort of property and so imputing a 'real cost' to any means by which an income could be acquired in an exchange society? If 'abstinence' was to be allowed to the capitalist who owned a factory which he had inherited, or owned a dock or a canal, how could it reasonably be denied to the owner of land who leased his property for a rent? Of this difficulty Senior was aware; since he pointed out that, if the revenue to the owner of a dock or canal is regarded as 'the reward of the owner's abstinence in not selling the dock or the canal, and spending its price in enjoyment', the same remark applies to every species of transferable property and 'the greater part of what every political economist has termed rent must be called profit' (Senior, 1850, p. 129 of 1863 edn). Accordingly, he decided to exclude all *inherited* capital from his definition. But this, of course, is to leave one on the other horn of the dilemma; namely, that in this case abstinence could not be regarded as an explanation of profit at all. As Cannan (1893, p. 198) has said, Senior's theory ended by 'reckoning as rent "the greater part of what every political economist has termed" profit'.

Marx's retort to Senior remained unchallenged until, towards the end of the century, the concept of marginal increments, a concept borrowed from the differential calculus, was introduced as an attempt to give greater precision to economic notions. Jevons's 'disutility' and Marshall's 'effort and sacrifice' were merely the subjective 'real cost' of McCulloch or of Senior in a more finished guise. Marshall, it is true, was careful to discard the discredited term 'abstinence' for the more neutral term 'waiting'; but as a designation of a subjective real cost the concept would seem in essentials to have retained the character of its sire.[9] But

9. Marshall (1890, pp. 232–3), noting Marx's objection to the abstinence concept, defined the term 'waiting' as applying, not to 'abstemiousness' but to the simple fact that 'a person abstained from consuming anything which he had the power of consuming, with the purpose of increasing his resources in the future'. This seems to imply that the concept was not limited by Senior's qualification, excluding inherited property, and that it could equally well be applied to land – to the fact that a landlord leased his land for cultivation, instead of using it for his own enjoyment or subjecting it to

with the introduction of the concept of marginal increments, the new treatment had this difference. A relation between 'efforts and sacrifices' and their price only existed *at the margin*; and while interest paid and sacrifice involved were regarded as tending towards identity for the *marginal* unit of capital supplied, there was no necessary relation between the *total* income received by the capitalist and the *total* 'sacrifice' incurred, either in any individual case or for the whole class. The rich man who inherited his wealth, and having more than he could conveniently spend saved it, might get an income quite disproportionate to any 'sacrifice' that he incurred. But an equality, nevertheless, would *tend* to prevail between the price of capital and the disutility involved in the saving of the marginal £ invested and added to the existing stock of capital; since, if the former was greater than the latter, capital accumulation would increase, while if the former was less than the latter, capital decumulation would set in until equality was restored. Hence, interest was a necessary price to maintain the requisite supply of capital. Labour and wages were treated by a similar method. Wages would tend to equality with the disutility involved in the most burdensome unit of a given supply of effort, even though the worker who loved work and hated leisure might be fortunate enough to suffer little psychic pain from his day's labour and yet received the normal wage for

---

'exhaustive' cultivation himself. In which case, as a category of 'real cost', it was clearly so general as to lose any distinctive meaning. If it was *not* intended to imply the existence of any psychological 'pain' associated with the act of postponement (as the remark about 'abstemiousness' seems to suggest), then it seems to remain a mere description of the act of investment which adds little to our knowledge of the nature and cause of profit. Elsewhere, however, Marshall speaks of 'postponement of gratifications' as 'involv(ing) *in general* a sacrifice on the part of him who postpones, just as additional effort does on the part of him who labours', this sacrifice justifying 'interest as a reward to induce its continuance' (Marshall, 1890, p. 587). A recent writer in the *Quarterly Journal of Economics* claims that Marshall identified 'two wholly different things under the term real cost'; but considers that the hedonistic element – the positive 'pain' – was not intended to figure prominently in either his concept of work or of waiting (Parsons, 1931, pp. 121–3). Whether intended, however, to figure prominently or not, it seems, according to the evidence of several passages, to have been an important part of the background of Marshall's theory of value and of distribution.

his work.[10] The landlord, however, remained in a different category, since no disutility presumably was involved, even at the margin, in the supply of land, since *ex hypothesi* land as a free gift of nature did not depend on any human will or action for its existence. Yet even the natural powers of the soil could be sapped by exhaustive cultivation and land be reclaimed from the sea; while, on the other hand, in the supply of capital there was room for a substantial element of what Marshall termed 'savers' surplus'. Hence, the difference between the reward of capital and the return to land was only one of degree. 'Rent of land', in a famous phrase of Marshall, 'is not a thing by itself, but the leading species of a large genus.'

The influence of this theory over half a century has undoubtedly been to discredit the Marxian theory of surplus-value and to imply that interest was as 'necessary' a category of income as wages and essentially similar in its origin; even though a writer such as J. A. Hobson attempted to give a different twist to the theory by making it the basis for an elaborated concept of 'social costs' and 'surpluses' which has been hailed in some quarters as an attempt to dress Marxian 'surplus-value' in up-to-date clothes. But the dilemma which confronted Senior's theory is not

10. Cf. 'The exertion of all the different kinds of labour that are directly or indirectly involved in making it, together with the "abstinence" or rather the "waitings", required for saving the capital used in making it: all these efforts and sacrifices will be called the *real cost of production* of the commodity. The sum of money that has to be paid for these efforts and sacrifices will be called either its money cost of production or its expenses of production; they are the prices which have to be paid in order to call forth an adequate supply of the effects and waitings that are required for making it; or, in other words, its supply-price' (Marshall, 1890, p. 339). The essential dualism of this theory of real cost was admitted by Marshall when, in an article in 1876, he referred to the fact that it was only possible to measure 'an effort and an abstinence . . . in terms of some common unit' through the medium of some 'artificial mode of measuring them' – namely, through their market-values (Marshall, 1876, pp. 596–7). This difficulty he considered to apply similarly to the measurement of 'two diverse efforts'. While the difficulty in this latter case is much *less* than in the case of two quite dissimilar things such as 'effort' and 'abstinence', it remains a much greater problem when effort is conceived in subjective terms than when it is conceived objectively in terms of output of physical energy. The ratio of different types of subjective real cost could only be regarded as equivalent to the ratio of their money measures, if the *same persons* supplied both types.

avoided by this more generalized concept of disutility; and only some vagueness in its enunciation seems to have prevented its inadequacy from being appreciated much earlier and more widely than has been the case. Either the concept is too narrow, if strictly defined, to afford any complete explanation, or else it is too wide, if more generally defined, to give much meaning to subjective 'real cost'. If the 'sacrifice' involved in 'waiting' is to have any meaning, at least a meaning analogous even to the subjective cost involved in work, then it must apply only to acts of postponing consumption with which is associated some positive psychological loss or pain over and above the temporary loss of the goods the consumption of which is forgone. It may well be said that some such additional loss is involved for the man who starves himself in order to educate his children, or in any case where a *greater* present utility is sacrificed for a *smaller* future utility. But how it can be said to be involved in most ordinary acts of saving and investment, where an act of exchange of utilities today for at least an equal quantity in the future is generally involved, is hard to see. To do so is to assert that there is some unique loss attaching to postponement, which attaches only to choices made in time and to no other choices. But does one's experience suggest that mere waiting for one's fruit ever causes positive discomfort unless one is either uncertain of getting it or one is suffering pangs of hunger in the interval?[11] Unless 'waiting' does indeed imply 'abstemiousness' one finds difficulty in discovering what, positively, it means. On the other hand, if *mere* postponement is all that 'sacrifice' is held to represent (as Marshall's statements in *some* places suggest), then it is hard to see where to draw the line short of any and every act of choice involving alternatives, one of which must be 'sacrificed' whatever choice is made. As Marx (1867, pp. 608 ff.) retorted to Senior and Mill, 'every human action may be viewed as "abstinence" from its opposite'. At any rate, if postponement of consumption occurs in an act of *new* saving, it must surely be held also to occur in the postponement of consumption of existing and of inherited capital; and if in the case where the property is inherited from history, why not also in

11. The answer to this question is not necessarily the same as the answer to the question: would one decide to have the fruit now or to wait for it, if the free choice were offered?

the case where property is inherited from nature as well as history, namely, in the case of land? (For the landowner to sell his land and live on the fruits of this sale as much reduces the total capital of society as for a capitalist to live on his capital, even though the supply of land itself is unaffected.) Marshall, indeed, seems here to have adopted the empirical solution of taking all cases of post-ponement for which a recompense was in fact demanded by individuals as identical with cases where a 'sacrifice' was involved in the act – taking individual attitudes towards saving at their face-value and assuming the empirical fact of resistance to the act of postponement as evidence that a real 'sacrifice' attaching to the act existed and was a fundamental cause.[12] This line of dis-tinction may be both convenient and plausible. Nevertheless, the crucial dilemma remains. If a 'something more' is postulated as lying behind the mere empirical fact of resistance to postpone-ment, one finds difficulty in giving it any precise meaning or even in believing that it exists. If, on the other hand, no more than the empirical fact of resistance is postulated, then this solution rids the notion of 'real cost' of any content: it is to make it in-distinguishable from what later came to be called 'opportunity cost' – the cost of sacrificed alternatives (that 'arithmetical truism', as Mr Durbin has called it).[13] Such a quantity by itself affords no explanation, because it is itself not independent, but something dependent on the total situation; and all that has been done by this definition is to shift the inquiry back to the nature of the total situation of which both profit and this so-called 'cost' are simultaneously resultant. Whether a person *does* demand pay-ment for a certain act (i.e. whether it has a 'supply-price')

12. Marshall admitted, however, that there was no reason to suppose that the ratio of real cost in two cases was identical with the ratio of their money measures or even to suppose (as we have already noted) that there was any meaning to be attached to a *quantity* of 'real cost' (Marshall, 1876, pp. 596–7).

13. It remains formally distinguishable from the doctrine of 'opportunity cost' as customarily stated to the extent that the latter usually represents the supply of factors of production as given quantities, while the former postu-lates that the supply of them is (in part) a function of their price (and hence that they have a 'supply-price'). But in neither case is a more fundamental cause of their supply or non-supply (in the shape of a real cost 'inevitably' requiring reward) any longer postulated.

depends on whether he *can* demand payment; and this depends on the total situation of which he is a part. To adopt this criterion is to make the existence or non-existence of a 'sacrifice' depend, not on the nature of the action, but on the nature of the circumstances surrounding the individual or the class in question. A 'sacrifice' can only be incurred in the measure that one has the luxury of alternatives to forgo. No opportunities, no sacrifices! Only Lazarus can sacrifice nothing; while Dives, with the world and its fullness before him, can sacrifice daily enough to wash away the sins of mankind. Conceived subjectively, any cost concept must lose its identity amid a world of choices and alternatives, where one facet of every choice is a utility and the other facet a 'sacrifice' or 'opportunity cost', and disutility retains no meaning except as utility forgone.

Let us, however, suppose a subjective loss or pain to be assumed to attach to the mere act of postponement. Even so, there seems no convincing reason for identifying such a real cost with the receipt of interest: no reason to presume that the incidence of this cost rests (save in a sense so superficial as to rid it of meaning) upon the class to which interest accrues as income. The reason by which this identification is customarily defended is that the recipients of interest are those who take the immediate decision on which the act of 'saving' depends. Yet it is by now a commonplace that the *ability* to save (in the shape of an income of a certain size) is the major factor in determining the volume of saving; while it is frequently those who claim the rich to be the bearers of abstinence that are the loudest in their assertions that if incomes were less unequally distributed and the consumption of the poor were raised, capital accumulation would decline. If the latter be true, then it would seem that the final incidence of this cost of saving must lie, not upon the rich, but upon the restricted consumption of the poor, which alone permits those high incomes to be earned from which the bulk of investment is drawn. If we were defining the result of investment in an egalitarian socialist economy, we should have no doubt what to say: we should say that one of its results was a relative restriction of present consumption, the incidence of which fell on the community at large. Yet in the unequal society of today the pedlars of abstinence theories would have us believe that the restriction of present consumption which results from this investment falls upon the rich and not upon the poor, upon whose restricted consumption the high saving ability of the former depends. If abstinence can be held to exist as a 'real cost' at all, it must, surely, be regarded as being borne by the proletariat which receives no recompense for its pains, rather than by the capitalist who draws interest as price of the restricted consumption of others? To assert the contrary is, surely, to be guilty of the circular reasoning of assuming the income of the capitalist to be in some sense 'natural' or 'inevitable' in order to show that what he invests of this income is the unique product of his individual abstinence in refraining from doing what he likes with his own?

Apart from these fundamental difficulties in the concept of subjective real cost, there is a further reason why any cost theory of this type is incompetent to explain interest as a concrete phenomenon in the actual world. The actual world is one in which capital accumulation is a continuing process and not one in which production is carried on with a constant stock of capital, the interest earned on which is in 'equilibrium' with a certain 'supply-price of waiting'. If there were, indeed, such an equilibrium, then no *new* capital accumulation would take place. Hence the 'surplus' element in interest, even in the restricted sense in which the term 'saver's surplus' is employed, is actually much greater than Marshall's theory on the face of it represents: for any existing stock of capital there is, in fact, not even an equality between the reward of capital and the 'supply-price of waiting' *at the margin*.[14]

14. Cf. Ramsey (1928, p. 556): if the rate of interest exceeds the rate of discounting the future 'there will not be equilibrium, but saving, and since a great deal cannot be saved in a short time, it may be centuries before equilibrium is reached, or it may never be reached, but only approached asymptotically. . . . We see, therefore, that the rate of interest is governed primarily by the demand price, and may greatly exceed the reward ultimately necessary to induce abstinence.' Cf. also Pigou (1935, pp. 259–60). Of course, there is *an* equilibrium at the margin; but this applies only to *new* investment, current income being eaten into by 'saving' until equilibrium is achieved (at the margin) between the restricted present expenditure and the (discounted) anticipated future income. This is what Pigou calls a 'subordinate equilibrium'. But there is never an equality between the interest currently received and the 'marginal supply-price' of the existing stock of capital – if there were, there would be no *new* investment.

Neither these ambiguities nor these special difficulties were involved in the interest theory of Böhm-Bawerk. He had explicitly abandoned any attempt at explaining values in terms of cost and for him a cost was always a determined, not a determining, element, representing simply an opportunity cost or displaced alternative, dependent on the strength of competing demands. Thereby costs were all ultimately traceable back to demand and to utility. He was not concerned, therefore, with what he regarded, in that form, as the meaningless question as to whether any subjective real cost was involved in the supply of capital. He was concerned only with the question, on the one hand as to whether the act of postponing consumption, in other words an act of choice through time, had any peculiarity attaching to it which would cause a given quantity of present utility generally to be treated as equivalent to a *larger* quantity of utility in the future and, on the other hand, whether the fact of time had any significance for the productivity of labour. He concluded that there was this peculiarity attaching to choices made through time: that the dimness of will and imagination, which was a general psychological trait of human beings, caused objects and events at a distance in time to be permanently discounted when balanced subjectively against equivalent objects and events which were close at hand; while, on the other hand, time had a significance for production in that labour expended on productive processes which took time ('roundabout' or long or indirect methods of production) was generally more productive than labour expended directly to produce immediate output. These two influences were principally responsible for the fact that a competitive market always placed a premium on present goods as against future goods, both because in the individual estimation the former were valued more highly and because the possession of goods in the present (e.g. subsistence for labourers) enabled labour to be employed on 'roundabout' or long processes of production which would yield a larger final product than labour employed at short notice on immediate and current production. The one factor operated on the side of supply and the other factor on the side of demand, to produce a permanent discount, *ceteris paribus*, of the 'future' price of anything over its 'spot' price. This premium or *agio* on present goods was the phenomenon of interest, which had given rise to the problem of 'surplus-value'. Not 'human prospectiveness', as Marshall put it, but the prevailing weakness of human prospectiveness – or what Professor Pigou has aptly termed 'a deficiency of the telescopic faculty' – was the explanation of the mystery which had perplexed economists for half a century.

It can hardly be denied that this ingenious theory contained positive elements which afford insight, descriptively and analytically, into certain aspects of the process of capital accumulation. Even though time or 'roundaboutness' was clearly not the only, or even major, condition of the productivity of technical processes, it was clearly an important element; and since time was irreversible, the time-dimension of different productive processes assumed a particular significance in determining the order in which such processes were successively adopted. Moreover, the concept of 'stored-up labour', as represented by an additional time-dimension (the length of time over which it was designed to be stored), was an objective one which was independent of the subjective theory of value in which the remainder of the theory was cast. But, viewed as a whole, as an explanation of surplus-value, the theory depended for its validity on the subjective theory of value of which it was simply a part and a particular application. Given the adequacy of this wider theory, its own adequacy seemed to be implied; since it showed that interest was simply the product of a general subjective estimation, as was any other value: in this case a subjective estimation of things separated through time. If the former was valid as a general explanation of value, so was the latter as the explanation of a particular value; if the former is invalid, then so also must the latter be.[15]

15. True, Böhm-Bawerk claimed that each of the factors of which he treated was alone sufficient to explain the phenomenon of interest. For this reason it might be held that his theory did not depend upon the subjective theory of value, since subjective underestimation of the future was only *one* of the reasons for the emergence of interest. Without the influence of this subjective factor, however, the mere 'technical superiority of roundabout methods' would clearly be incapable of explaining interest as an *enduring* phenomenon and hence as a necessary consequence of permanent elements of the economic problem. By itself, it would rank no higher than any other of the productivity explanations which Böhm-Bawerk himself condemned. The higher productivity of 'roundabout methods' would not suffice to explain why labour applied to this particular use yielded a surplus-value, in

Yet, after his impressive critique of previous theories of interest, it is strange that the weakness of his own theory – its inability to answer essential questions – should not have been plain to its author and particularly strange that he should have imagined that it afforded a sufficient answer to the problem as it was posed by Marx and hence a refutation of the answer which Marx gave. In what sense did this theory explain the phenomenon of interest? Hardly in any sense which could assimilate interest to wages in its origin or in the character of its determination or in its universal 'necessity' as a category of income. It amounted to an explanation in terms of the relative scarcity, or limited application, of labour applied to particular uses – namely, in the form of stored-up labour embodied in technical processes involving a lengthy 'period of production': a scarcity which persisted by reason of the short-sightedness of human nature. As a result of this underdevelopment of the productive resources, the ownership of money-capital, which in existing society provided the only means by which lengthy production processes were able to be undertaken, carried with it the power to exact a rent of this scarcity. As a landlord could exact the price of a scarcity imposed by objective nature, so, it would seem, the capitalist could exact the price of a scarcity imposed by the subjective nature of man. If there was any significance in such analogies within the limits of this theory, it was, surely, between interest and rent, rather than between interest and wages? Like Ricardo and Marx, Böhm-Bawerk had condemned the inadequacy of mere 'supply and demand' explanations.[16] But, confined as it was in the main within the limited circle of exchange-relationships between factors of production abstracted from more fundamental social relationships, was his own theory any more competent to explain? True,

the absence of some additional reason to explain why the application of labour to this use was restricted and hence was relatively scarce. It might suffice to explain the surplus-value as a temporary and disappearing phenomenon due to the time required for the construction of these more productive 'roundabout methods', but not as a phenomenon consistent with full equilibrium.

16. 'The man who, when asked what determines a certain price, answers "Demand and supply", offers a husk for a kernel' (Böhm-Bawerk, 1884, p. 66).

he introduced into his theory one significant assumption about production: a technical fact, associated with the dimension of time. But why should he have chosen this technical fact in isolation from the rest and neglected the social relations which determined the place of man in production and his association with technique? The decisive factor in the supply of capital, according to his theory, was the subjective underestimation of the future. Not only is this a factor which would not necessarily exist outside an individualist society, and the existence of which even in an individualist society has been denied by some; but the degree of this subjective underestimation is itself dependent on the distribution of income, and hence on the class relations in society. Interest is, therefore, dependent on the latter in a double sense: in that the size of incomes among the capitalist class, relative to their accustomed standards of consumption, determines their attitude to saving and investment, while the poverty of the masses determines the price at which they are willing to sell their labour power in return for immediate income. Hence, interest depends for its determination precisely on the type of social relations and institutions, historically determined and not universal, with which Marx was concerned. As will be seen in a subsequent chapter [ch. 8 of *Political Economy and Capitalism*] in a socialist society there would be no reason for the underestimation of the future which gives rise to interest as a persistent phenomenon to prevail and no reason for the emergence of interest as a category of income at all. As a solution of the interest-problem in any sense which would be relevant to questions such as these, this theory is empty and deceptive. Moreover, it is not possible to say that its author had no intention of claiming it to be a solution in this more fundamental sense and that he merely intended his theory to assemble descriptively some of the relevant variables of which any determinate explanation would have to take account. Böhm-Bawerk (1888, pp. 361 and 371) explicitly adduces as important corollaries of his theory that 'the essence of interest is not exploitation', but that, on the contrary, interest is 'an entirely normal phenomenon; is, indeed, an economic necessity', is 'not an accidental "historico-legal" category, which makes its appearance only in our individualist and capitalist society' and 'would not disappear even in the socialist State'.

But in this very application of the notion of utility a strange contradiction appears which takes us at once to the centre of the problem of the subjective theory of value. To be sufficient anchorage for a determinate theory of value, even formally viewed, it was necessary that utility should be conceived as an expression of some fairly permanent and consistent aspect of human psychology. This is not to say that human preferences had to be assumed to be unchangeable; but that they must not be so contingent and fickle as to make it improbable that they were independent of other variables in the system which they were intended to determine.[17] In so far as utility could be hedonistically treated as a fundamental 'satisfaction', then, as we have seen, it could reasonably be held to fulfil this condition. A process of rational selection among the objects of choice could then be held to make economic choice conform to certain fundamental traits of human psychology. Even though the *translation* of such choices into economic action was dependent on the distribution of income, the actual choices themselves might be treated as independent of market prices. But if one can no longer link 'desire' (the immediate volition or act of choice) with 'satisfaction' (the more fundamental psychological event), then the validity of such an assumption of independence becomes very doubtful. Why should we not regard such 'behaviour-reactions' as continually conditioned and modified by the market conditions which they meet? Böhm-Bawerk makes no attempt to maintain that the preference for present goods which lies at the basis of his theory of interest represents any superior 'satisfaction' attaching to present goods: a holiday next year will give us as much happiness when it comes as a holiday next month, only we see the former more dimly in our imagination. If we grasp the present in preference to the future, it is a matter simply of the imagination, of defective rationality and ephemeral desire. Professor Pigou has indeed singled out this case of subjective overestimation of present

17. Clark (1927, p. 54) states his belief 'that this type of theory acquires meaning just so far as there is attached to it some premise as to how choices actually do behave'. But it is not sufficient, for this purpose, to premise merely their behaviour: it is necessary to premise that this behaviour (or certain determining elements underlying it) is independent of the movement of market prices.

utilities as the most important instance where 'desire' and 'satisfaction' diverge, to the detriment of economic welfare. In a very direct sense this subjective attitude to present and future is dependent on, and not independent of, the structure of market prices: namely, that it admittedly varies with the income of the individual or class in question, since the latter will condition the degree of urgency of present wants and the strength with which they excite and obsess the imagination. An example of this is the fact that a group or a community may become cumulatively poorer because, having a high preference for the present, it becomes progressively less capable of providing for the future. In terms of its subjective attitudes, therefore, nothing determinate can be postulated or forecasted. Moreover, this attitude may vary in such a number of ways with such a number of influences as to throw almost as many doubts on its universality as on its constancy. It clearly may vary with the type of commodity offered for sale and the manner in which commodities are sold; it may vary according as the person is an impressionable youth or of more mature experience; it may vary according as the individual is making his choice *qua* isolated individual, or *in loco parentis familiae*, or *qua* collective person in the capacity of a member of a college, a club or a business company. Yet it was an application of subjective notions where their weakness was most evident that Böhm-Bawerk chose in order to provide a solution for the crucial problem of surplus-value. But the weakness which is specially manifest here serves to draw our attention to a defect which attaches to the whole structure.

When Bailey had said that value implied 'a feeling or a state of mind which manifests itself in the determination of the will', he was expressing a notion which by the end of the century was to be woven into a system. The utility theory interpreted the value of a commodity and, by derivation, that of all the constituent factors required to make it, in terms of the service rendered in satisfying consumers' desires. But the relation was not directly between value and *aggregate* service (or total utility): these stood frequently in inverse ratio, as the early economists had observed. The direct relation was between value and utility *at the margin*; the crucial factor being the increment of satisfaction rendered to consumers by the final or marginal increment of a given supply.

A housewife who pursued the motive of maximum satisfaction would achieve her aim by distributing her money so that the satisfaction yielded by the final penny spent in every direction was equal; since, if this equality was not achieved, she would have gained by spending less in one direction and more in another. This is a case of what Jevons called the 'principle of indifference'. There can be seen to follow from this simple principle another one: namely, that the prices of various commodities on a market must stand in the ratio of their marginal utilities – of the satisfaction yielded to consumers by the final or marginal unit of each. If prices do not stand in this ratio, it will profit consumers to demand more of some commodities (those where the ratio of marginal utility to price is relatively high) and less of others (those where this ratio is relatively low), until equilibrium is achieved.

But this leaves the question: what fixes the position of the margin itself? To this the answer is that it is fixed by the available supply; which in turn raises the further question: what determines the limitation of supply? If the supply of all things was unlimited, there would be no unsatisfied desires, no marginal utility and no price. A price can, therefore, only arise because of the limitations imposed on the supply of commodities by the limitation of the factors of production required to produce them – a limitation expressing itself in the form of costs.

In the manner in which they have assumed these limits to be determined, two variants of the subjective theory of value are distinguished. On the one hand, the Austrian School assumed that, in any given set of conditions, the supply of such ultimate productive factors was fixed.[18] Being limited by an unalterable (for the moment) scarcity, these factors, like any commodity, would acquire a price equal to the marginal service which they could render in production; these prices formed the constituent elements of cost. On the other hand, Jevons and Marshall assumed that (with the exception of natural resources) these basic factors of production could be varied in supply, but that their variation was conditioned by the disutility, or the 'effort and

18. Strictly speaking, the Austrians did not assume, or need to assume, that the supply of basic factors of production was unchangeable: merely that the quantity of them was determined by conditions external to the market, and hence could be treated as independent.

sacrifice', which their creation cost. Hence in equilibrium they must receive a price equivalent to the disutility (at the margin) involved in the supply of them. As Jevons put it: 'Cost of production determines supply; supply determines final degree of utility [or "marginal utility"]; final degree of utility determines value'; and again, 'Labour is found to determine value, but only in an indirect manner, by varying the utility of a commodity through an increase or limitation of the supply' (Jevons, 1871, p. 165). Pareto has summarized this notion in the phrase that value is the resultant of a conflict between desire and obstacles – obstacles which preclude the full satisfaction of desires. But the ultimate determinants of both sets of forces – both 'blades of the scissors', in Marshall's phrase – are conceived as subjective in character, products of states of mind.

This structure seems to rest on a crucial assumption: namely, that the individual will is autonomous and independent, in the sense that it is not influenced by the market relations into which the individual enters or by the social relations of which he is part. No one, of course, would deny at least some influence of this kind. If it is of a minor character and confined to a few special types of influence, this can easily be allowed for without impugning the validity of treating the individual will and its characteristics as the determinant of economic relationships. But if this influence of social interaction is considerable, the validity of the assumption is shaken; and this atomistic treatment necessarily breaks down. Not only is it then likely that the fallacy of composition will be involved in any attempt to pass from the individual to the whole; but states of will or of mind will be incapable of being treated as 'independent variables' in the determination of events.

Doubtless such an assumption seemed natural enough to a century of individualism and may today seem natural enough to the isolated bourgeois individual, priding himself on his independence from social influences and social dependence. But anything more than a superficial analysis of the texture of society will show in what numerous ways the individual will, on the contrary to being autonomous or independent, is continually moulded by the complex of social and economic relations into which it enters. In the first place, the actual nature of the preferences which the individual exhibits, as well as the form in which they are translated into money, will be influenced by his position in society and the income he receives. For instance, his preference for present against future, as we have seen, or for leisure as against commodities, and hence the 'sacrifice' which he incurs in working or saving, will depend upon his income; with the circular result that the nature of the fundamental costs which affect both the values of commodities and the rewards of the factors of production will be determined in turn by the distribution of income. A man who is landless will estimate the 'sacrifice' or 'disutility' involved in hiring himself to a master at much less than will a peasant farmer possessed of land and instruments of his own, since the destitute position of the former causes him to place a lower subjective valuation on his own labours in terms of the necessaries of life. The same will be true of workers backed by a trade union, as contrasted with unorganized workers with a traditionally low standard of life. Hence to postulate any normal values requires the prior postulation of a certain income distribution and hence a certain class structure. To give a precise form to the exchange-relationships of a given society requires as data not merely the mental disposition of an abstract individual, but also the complex of institutions and social relations of which the concrete individual is a part. In the search for a spurious generality, such factors are 'taken for granted' in the modern theory of value: in a formal sense you are at liberty to assume about them whatever you please. At best this seems akin to framing the laws of physics or astronomy without the 'gravitational constant'. But in practice a more positive error emerges, when the assumption as it stands is taken to be a description of actual economic society. As a positive descriptive statement, it is false by reason of its very partiality. It implies that economic phenomena are ruled by a series of contractual relations freely entered into by a community of independent individuals, each of whom knows well what he wants and has access to and knowledge of all the available alternatives. And since by unnoticed sleight of hand harmony has been introduced into the premise, harmony emerges in the conclusion.

As we have said, however, it may be maintained that the essential elements out of which human choice is constructed are capable of being postulated independently of the distribution of income and of the social position of the individual. The actual schedule of preferences – the fundamental 'indifference curves' of Pareto – are not affected by the state of the individual, whether he be rich or poor, starving or satisfied. Hence subjective attitudes, in this sense at least, are capable of being postulated as an independent basis for a determination of the value-problem. But, firstly, it is to be remarked that, even if this is so, such factors are not sufficient of themselves to determine the problem; and something additional requires to be postulated concerning the *position* of the individual if we are to know how these basic attitudes will be translated into actual choices and actual demands – what sort of demand curves are constructed from given sets of indifference curves.[19] Secondly, it is precisely these basic mental attitudes which it seems impossible to postulate, short of a hedonistic definition of utility or of some similar assumption. Otherwise what meaning can be given to these schedules of preferences which define the individual's attitude to any conceivable set of alternatives whether he may ever have experienced these alternatives or not – preference schedules written presumably somewhere on the mind which would tell us, if we could discover them by introspection, how the millionaire would value leisure and income if he happened to be beggared or how the means-test victim would behave if he suddenly acquired a fortune? If, as earlier notions of utility implied, 'desires' which prompt immediate acts of choice coincide with some more fundamental 'satisfaction' yielded by the object of choice, then probably some meaning can be given to the assumption of a constant set of mental attitudes of this kind. But if 'desires' diverge from 'satisfactions', the latter, even if they exist, will not rule behaviour and so will have little relevance to the economic problem; while 'desires' alone, divorced from any deeper roots that they may or may not have, can certainly not be held to display any such constancy or independence.

19. This is simply an example of the fact, expressed in Marshall's famous barter-case, that, given a system of indifference curves, it is necessary to postulate the *position* in the plane from which each individual commences to conduct exchange-transactions before one can construct the actual demand or offer curves which will shape the course of the bargaining. Marshall defines this position in terms of the *stock* of each commodity held; but the principle has a wider application than to this simple case.

This brings us to a second reason which impugns the assumption that the individual will is independent: namely, the influence of convention and of propaganda. Both of these factors, to judge by the powerful influence which they so evidently exert on acts of choice, seem to be responsible for considerably greater divergence between 'desire' and 'satisfaction' than has been traditionally admitted by economists. Among the former are to be included all those complex influences which the desires and tastes of others exert on the individual, including the influence of class standards and of social emulation, to which Thorstein Veblen so forcibly drew attention. Among the latter are to be included all those devices of advertisement, suggestion and selling artifice, which have become such a dominant characteristic of the present age. Their success depends on the extent to which they can mould and create desire; and in the degree of their success consumers' choice becomes a variable dependent upon the actions of producers. Moreover, consumers' desires are clearly open to the influence of suggestion in a variety of ways. The mere existence of a supply, if appropriately brought before the public gaze, may create a desire which did not exist before; while the amount and cunning of the sellers' propaganda may be decisive in determining whether people give books at Christmas or gloves or handkerchiefs or umbrellas; whether the public diet shall be composed more largely of bananas or fish or milk; whether the 'drier side of England' or the Cornish Riviera is preferred as a holiday centre. When such propaganda can influence group conventions, the marriage of these influences can exert redoubled power in shaping individual choice, as is fully exemplified in the slavery of fashion, where least of all can the individual be said to have a will of his or her own. In the sphere of world trade today one can see the rising influence, both direct and indirect, of propaganda upon demand. 'Buy British', 'Buy Empire', 'Buy German' campaigns shape consumers' preferences to moulds into which they would not otherwise fit. Apparently a paramount, and neglected, economic influence of the spread of national cultures beyond national frontiers is to create the taste for those things which bulk large in that nation's habitual consumption because that nation has some special facility in producing them. When one takes full account of the extent of such influences as these in the world today, there seems to be little doubt that they are a significant factor in the determination of demand in the case of nearly every commodity other than the prime necessaries of food and shelter.

Nor can the influence of convention be regarded as of minor importance. Human taste, beyond the most primitive level, has clearly been developed by a process of education in which custom and convention have played a principal role, together with other factors in the social environment. The most that can be postulated as innate to the 'natural' individual is certain primary desires or tendencies of a not very differentiated kind. In the history of each individual, the precise configuration of that complex scale of preferences (even assuming such an entity) with which he is supposed to embark on life as an adult is clearly acquired from the influence of the society around him, and is afterwards subject to continual modification by such influence. Artificial silk becomes cheap and every girl factory worker finds silk stockings to be a necessary element in her life because others wear them. The tailored suit becomes a necessity for the gentleman, who would suffer much loss of satisfaction if deprived of it, because a given station in life is conventionally marked by a given standard and style of dress. Most of the expenditures on house decoration, furnishings and social entertainment are clearly controlled by the exactions of certain social standards. People drink afternoon tea or cocktails and would be deprived of satisfaction if individually they had to abstain from them. Men enjoy the austere discomfort of the boiled shirt and starched collar because emulation demands. Their wives collect silver for the sideboard, and, a few years back, muslin curtains, palms or aspidistras for the parlour as symbols of bourgeois respectability. Even a motor-car seems often to be desired as much for the status as for the use it gives. Some years ago a discussion took place in the pages of *Economica* as to whether any meaning could be given to the 'total utility' of boots as measured by what a gentleman would pay if compelled to – perhaps £10 or £20 or £30 – rather than walk barefoot to his office or his club. The answer was given that the question had no meaning, since, if boots were universally priced at £10 a pair or more, none but the very rich would wear them and the average man would find little hardship in being seen in sandals, or even barefoot, when all his neighbours and equals were accustomed to do likewise.

That this assumption of the autonomous individual will, independent of social relations, was fully intended to be taken as a descriptive statement about economic society is evidenced by a significant corollary which the utility theory was held to imply. And the evident zeal with which this corollary was emphasized reveals how far from innocent of apologetic obsessions the economists' choice of assumptions clearly was. This corollary was hailed as a decisive reinforcement of the case for *laissez-faire* and consisted in the demonstration that a regime of free exchange achieved the maximum of utility for all parties. The argument was a plausible one, given its concealed assumptions; and even today, when part of its fallacy has been frequently pointed out, the fallacy seems to die hard and continually to reappear in altered guise. The clearest form of its demonstration is in the simplified case of the exchange between two sellers of two commodities, A and B. It follows as an alternative version of the principle which was referred to above that exchange between them will continue up to that rate of exchange at which the utility of *both* commodities (the amount of the commodity parted with and the amount of the commodity acquired in exchange) is equal for *each* of the two parties. Up to this point each party will gain more utility than he parts with by continuing to exchange A against B. Beyond it any rate of exchange must deprive one or both of the parties of more utility than he acquires in exchange and consequently there can be no agreed rate of exchange which will satisfy both. The point of equilibrium, therefore, in the bartering – the rate of exchange which will be established on a free market – will be the point (as Jevons put it) where 'both parties rest in satisfaction' and where 'each party has obtained all the benefit that is possible'. If this price is one which brings the greatest benefit to each, it must, therefore, be that which brings the greatest benefit to all: prices established under conditions of a free market maximize utility for all concerned. This corollary, which is implied rather than explicitly enunciated in Jevons's presentation of the theory, is emphasized more clearly by Walras and Pareto, and by Auspitz and Lieben (1914).[20]

20. Walras's interest in economic theory, indeed, appears to have been prompted by discussion with a Saint-Simonian and the consequent desire to

Some doubt should have been cast on the significance of such a maximum when subsequent discussion elicited the fact that there was, not one, but a number of rates of exchange where this condition (the equal utility of both commodities to each of the two parties) was fulfilled. Under the simple barter conditions cited by Jevons, equilibrium might be reached at any one of these points, according to which party secured the advantage in the preliminary stages of the bargaining; and any one of these points could equally well be a position of 'satisfaction'. But any such position of 'satisfaction' is clearly relative to the situation of the individual at the time when the bargain is undertaken. In any given situation the resources and the choice of alternatives which lie before the individual are restricted and in a capitalist society most notably restricted by the class to which the individual belongs. In this given situation in which the individual finds himself there may be one path consistent with his best advantage, which it will profit him to take; but that path is determined for him by external circumstances and is not the path he would have trodden had his situation been different. A relative maximum of this kind could only approximate to a *maximum maximorum*, possessed of any absolute significance, on the assumption that each individual had free range of opportunities and had only taken the road he had after surveying and estimating the range of extant alternatives. This is what can*not* be postulated of capitalist society; and it is the absence of this assumption – indeed, the existence of the direct opposite, namely, class division – which forms the necessary starting point for any understanding of the specific character of capitalist society. Yet this was precisely the assumption which the originators of the Utility School had illicitly introduced. That the assumption is still apt to pass unnoticed is indicated by the fact that it still forms the tacit basis today of most of the comparisons of the effects of a competitive and of a monopoly regime, or of a capitalist and a socialist regime, which are made in economic writing.[21]

---

furnish a simple proof that free exchange on a competitive market yielded an *optimum* result. (Cf. Wicksell, 1901, pp. 73–4.)

21. Professor Pigou (1920, p. 24) states that 'all comparisons between different taxes and different monopolies, which proceed by an analysis of their effects upon consumers' surplus, tacitly assume that demand price is also the money measure of satisfaction'. Cf. also von Hayek (1935).

Aware of the difficulties in the conception of utility, economists have been increasingly inclined in recent years either to abandon the concept of utility or else to define it anew in a purely empirical sense. The empirical fact that individual desires express themselves in observable *choices* on a market is postulated and equations to determine economic events are constructed with such choices as the given data; irrespective of what either the psychological or the social roots of these choices may be. Thus Pareto (1909, p. 157) started with the use of the concept of *utilité* and later abandoned it for *ophélimité*; and Cassel, who was fond of parading familiar ideas in novel wording, eschewed the word 'utility' altogether. Professor Robbins denies that utility can ever be compared for two individuals (characteristically using the denial to rebut certain implications of the Law of Diminishing Marginal Utility as to the damage done to economic welfare by inequalities of wealth), and asserts that all that economics as a 'positive science' is right in assuming is that each individual arranges the objects of choice according to a certain scale of preference (Robbins, 1932, pp. 137 ff. of 2nd edn).[22] Economics becomes a sort of theory of 'catallactics', in which 'there is no penumbra of approbation round the theory of equilibrium. Equilibrium is just equilibrium' (Robbins, 1932, p. 143 of 2nd edn).

It might appear as though this was to evade the essential problem by retreating into pure formalism and that a theory defined in this way, and so emptied of real content, had reached a level of abstraction at which it was impotent to deliver any important judgement on practical affairs, at any rate on the problems peculiar to a particular system of economic society. If all that is postulated is simply that men *choose*, without anything being stated even as to how they choose or what governs their choice, it would seem impossible for economics to provide us with any more than a sort of algebra of human choice, indicating certain rather obvious forms of interrelationship between choices, but telling us little as to the way in which any actual situation will

22. Professor Robbins (1932, p. 20 of 2nd edn) claims for modern economic theory this superiority over the Ricardian system, that the former has 'press(ed) through to the valuations of the individual'. Can one not complain of it that it has pressed through *no further* than the valuations of the individual?

behave. Moreover, as we have already seen, if the 'demand schedule' of individuals is not conceived to rest on something ultimate or fundamental, it cannot be very solid anchorage for a system of market equilibria. If demand may change with every wind that blows over the face of the market, as it may if we postulate nothing but empirical desires, what entitles us to assume that such desires are not entirely creatures of price movements? Indeed, if for this theory 'equilibrium is just equilibrium', it looks very much as though a mere generalized definition of equilibrium is all that we are provided with. Such a clarification of definitions may be a highly useful, indeed an essential, task. But can it provide any more than the empty shell of a theory of *political* economy, in the sense of a study of the problems of actual economic society and the type of question which they raise? In the first edition of his *Essay*, Professor Robbins (1932, p. 75), indeed, declared that the corollaries of economic theory depended, not upon facts of experience or of history, but were 'implicit in our definition of the subject-matter of Economic Science as a whole': a statement which seemed sufficiently to characterize the theory as a system of tautology. In his second edition this revealing admission is abandoned: instead, it is pleaded that economic theory is by no means 'merely formal', that it rests on postulates which are, in fact, elementary generalizations about any and every type of economic activity and that its corollaries represent 'inevitable implications' which, far from being 'historicorelative' in character, hold true of any and every type of economic society (Robbins, 1932, pp. 80, 105 and 121 of 2nd edn).[23] But it must be difficult for many to be reassured by this re-statement when they learn that the slender substratum of fact on which these laws of universal application are made to rest still consists simply in the postulate of individual choice. Choice is, of course, not confined to the type of activities which are traditionally known as 'economic'; and it transpires that we are being furnished with an abstraction so general as to embrace features common to *any* type of human activity. This, indeed, Professor

23. Henderson (1922, p. 17 of 1932 edn) has also claimed that economic theory postulates laws which rule whether 'merchant adventurers, companies and trusts; Guilds, Governments and Soviets may come and go', operating 'under them, and, if need be, in spite of them all'.

Robbins (1932, p. 14 of 2nd edn) frankly admits. 'Every act which involves time and scarce means for the achievement of one end involves the relinquishment of their use for the achievement of another (and) has an economic aspect.' Professor von Mises (1922, p. 124 of English trans.) is even more definite: 'It is illegitimate to regard the "economic" as a definite sphere of human action which can be sharply delimited from other spheres of action. Economic activity is rational activity. . . . The sphere of economic activity is co-terminous with the sphere of rational action.' The principles here enunciated, and their 'inevitable implications', consequently refer, and refer only, to *an* aspect of every type of human activity – to cooking and housekeeping, to games and recreation, to the planning of a holiday, to the choice between being a philosopher or a mathematician, as well as to what are usually known as the specific problems of production and exchange. But if this is the case – if economic principles are admittedly so tenuous an abstraction of one aspect of human affairs from all the rest – one is surely justified in doubting whether the imperative character of the corollaries which such a theory is competent to yield can be of any high order of importance for the specific problems to which the specific characteristics of this or that type of economic society give rise.

The search for logically concise definitions of one's subject-matter, which is so popular today, must generally be barren, and when pushed to an extreme must result in emptying ideas of real content and attaining little but an arid and scholastic dogmatism. This tendency would seem to be the product, not merely of a passing fashion, but of a more fundamental defect. What so many apparently ignore today is the lesson which Marshall was primarily concerned to teach in the Hegelian Principle of Continuity which he reiterated in the classic Preface to the first edition of his *Principles* (by comparison with which so much modern economic writing appears shallow and unsophisticated):[24] that in

24. 'If the book has any special character of its own, that may perhaps be said to lie in the prominence which it gives to . . . applications of the Principle of Continuity. . . . There has always been a temptation to classify economic goods in clearly defined groups, about which a number of short and sharp propositions could be made, to gratify at once the student's desire for logical precision, and the popular liking for dogmas, that have the air of being profound and are yet easily handled. But great mischief seems

the real world there are no hard and fast boundary lines, as there are in thought, and that discontinuity and continuity are inevitably entwined. It is doubtless true that in Marshall's work certain aspects of continuity received exaggerated and one-sided emphasis – that his motto, *Natura non facit saltum*, was given a conservative emphasis. Yet by comparison with most modern writing, his approach to intellectual problems at least bore the stamp of a healthy realism: a virtue to which is, I think, traceable much that has appeared as eclecticism and obscurity to his critics; and which owed its origin to the fact that he had sufficient philosophic background to appreciate something of the complex character of the relation between abstract ideas and reality and to be anxious to keep his feet planted on the ground. It is only at the sacrifice of any comparable realism that precise definitions of the type which is fashionable today can be attained. Clearly, any realistic definition of a study like economics must run primarily in terms of the concrete problems which it adopts as its subject-matter (as is the case with any science): it must be a definition by type rather than by delimitation. The definition of economics must be given by the slice of the real world which it handles, and the generalizations it creates, to be adequate, must represent the essential features of its real terrain. Whether it is successful or not in achieving this appropriate blend of generality and realism is a question of *fact*: through worship of epigram to abstract certain *aspects* only of events and enshrine them in isolation from the rest may win an appearance of superb generality, but only at the expense of reality. Precision may be a most desirable, even an essential, ingredient of the process of thought, as is sharpness of steel in cutting. But when sharpness of the tool and of its product are confused, when precision is sanctified as the end of thought and made the touchstone of truth, thought is rendered flat and sterile, and ideas become husks lacking the substance of life.

But the most abstract of economists, of course, intends to state considerably more about the real world than simply that human

---

to have been done by yielding to this temptation, and drawing broad artificial lines of division where nature has made none. The more simple and absolute an economic doctrine is, the greater will be the confusion . . . if the dividing lines to which it refers cannot be found in real life' (Marshall, 1890, pp. viii-ix).

beings make choices. As Professor Robbins tells us there are 'subsidiary postulates'; and these postulates, as he admits (a trifle reluctantly), are 'drawn from the examination of what may often be legitimately designated historico-relative material'. The truth seems to be that it is with these 'subsidiary postulates' that political economy properly begins. At any rate, it is on such postulates that the realistic corollaries drawn by economists depend. Least of all could one charge Professor Robbins with a disregard for the practical implications of economic theory, however abstract his definition of the latter may be. But it is precisely with these 'subsidiary postulates' that assumptions about economic society are implicitly introduced which are substantially similar to those of earlier economists, and which are of the type that we have referred to as that of the autonomy and independence of the individual will. Indeed, the very form in which abstract postulates about individual choices are put constitutes them a distorted description of the actual forces which control economic phenomena in capitalist society, unless they are radically qualified by statements concerning the social relations by which individual choices are governed and the choices of *classes* are differentiated in capitalist society. The mere absence of any such qualification means that the statement that individuals *choose*, as soon as it is made concrete in the form that individuals choose *in a particular way*, becomes the false statement that individuals choose *freely* and that the events which are the outcome of these individual actions are unaffected by those basic productive relations – class relations connected with ownership of economic property – which are the distinguishing characteristic of capitalist society. Assumptions which are concealed are stubborn; and despite Wicksteed's hope that mathematical statement might serve as a reagent to 'precipitate the assumptions held in solution in the verbiage of our ordinary disquisitions', the increasingly mathematical economics of today still rests substantially on the same basic premises. The difference, so far as its apologetic influence is concerned, is that the conjuror's skill is now improved, so that the corollaries which he produces with much patter about 'ethical neutrality' and with considerable elegance of technique seem to his audience to be created *a priori* from scientific principles of universal validity. Yet the secret assumptions are there all the time, implicit in the very formulation of the question; and even though out-moded 'utility' may be banished from the forestage, the desires of a free-acting individual are still conceived as ruling the market, and this 'sovereignty' (as one writer has recently called it)[25] of the autonomous consumer is still the basis of any laws that are postulated and any forecasts that are made. So it is that econ-omists will continue to contrast the autonomy of the consumer under capitalism with the 'economic authoritarianism' of a socialist economy.[26] The fact is, of course, that the valuations of the market under capitalism represent a very high degree of authoritarianism. This assumption which rules subjective econ-omics today – rules it, not simply as an incidental 'additional assumption', but by virtue of the very form in which the whole problem is necessarily set – is parallel to a similar assumption which underlies the traditional theory of politics and of the State: namely, that the State is the expression of some kind of general will constructed out of the multitude of autonomous wills of free and equal individuals. In the economic sphere, as in the political, the facts of a class society belie the idyllic picture. What the power of a capitalist Press is in the one case, that of the advertiser is in the other. What class influence is in the one, class convention is in the other. In both spheres, differences of economic status and the economic dependence of ownerless upon owners are dominating factors. Moreover, in the economic realm 'plural voting' is the

25. See Hutt (1934) where he declares that the principle is fundamental to economics. Cf. also Hutt (1936, pp. 257 ff.).

26. A particularly naïve example of this occurs in the following passage: 'That the consumption of the rich weighs more heavily in the balance than the consumption of the poor . . . is in itself an "election result", since in a capitalist society wealth can be acquired and maintained only by a response corresponding to the consumers' requirements. Thus the wealth of success-ful business men is always the result of a consumers' plebiscite, and, once acquired, this wealth can be retained only if it is employed in the way regarded by consumers as most beneficial to them' (von Mises, 1922, p. 21 of English trans.). If in a certain community where plural or proxy voting was permissible a group of ambitious gentry managed to accumulate, by fair means or foul, a majority of the votes, and at successive elections there-after proceeded to vote the retention of plural voting, von Mises would presumably pronounce this a consistent democracy since the whole process was an 'election result', and approve the actions of the self-appointed rulers on the ground that they reflected the decisions of a plebiscite as to what was beneficial to the majority.

rule and not an exception; and it is a plurality which extends to some casting a thousand or ten thousand votes to another's one. Yet the majority of economic writings refers to the rule of the consumer, because there is a market, as naïvely as Herr Hitler will speak of his totalitarian State as a product of popular will because he has held a plebiscite.

As one might be led to expect, it is in the so-called 'theory of distribution' that the most direct evidence of abstract concepts framed to apologetic purposes is to be found. It would hardly be incorrect to say that modern economics contains no theory of distribution worthy of the name. But that is not to deny that there have been pretentious claimants to this office. Outstanding among these has been the theory of marginal productivity. What is instructive is that this theory, which most strikingly bears the stamp of the mathematical method, has seen most practical service as a reply to critics of the capitalist system; and while the significance of the theory, when properly stated, is generally admitted today to be purely formal in character, it has been and continues to be used as an answer to the type of problem to which Marx's theory of surplus-value was framed as an answer, and hence as a refutation, or at least a sufficient substitute, for the latter. This theory is clearly a lineal descendant of the older theories of productivity of capital; but rid of the more obvious crudities of the older theories by the application to the 'productivity' of different factors of the concept of differential increments. Yet it was this very refinement which, in fact, robbed it even of the slender claim to answer the practical problem of surplus-value which the crude productivity theory had had. By stating that the price of a factor of production (whether land, labour or capital) tended on a competitive market to equal the difference made to the total produce (measured in value) by the addition of a marginal unit of that factor (as the price of a final commodity was equal to the utility of a marginal unit), it was providing no more than a more precise formulation of traditional supply and demand explanations. And as Marshall hastened to point out, it could not constitute 'a complete theory of distribution', since it left unanswered the problem as to the nature and determination of the supply of the various factors of production. Virtually it represented a further step towards treating not only commodities, but also the animate and inanimate instruments of production, simply as objects of market exchange, in complete abstraction from even the concrete activities of production, not to mention the basic social relations of which they were part. Yet the theory was immediately hailed as a complete reply to the classical problem of profit, rendering Ricardo and Marx obsolete. J. B. Clark hailed it as a newly discovered 'law of nature'; and although few economists today are to be found to agree with him in so rash a statement, an important number of them, I believe, would subscribe to the view that there is some significant sense in which the theory could be said to show that the rule of competition 'gave to each factor of production the equivalent of what it created'. At any rate, whatever the private beliefs of professional economists, it seems not untrue to say that 99 per cent of their audience understand some such conclusion to be implied.

The action of critics of the new doctrine at first tended to greater confusion rather than to clarity, owing to their concentration on what proved to be a purely formal problem – the so-called 'adding-up problem'. The question which they asked was whether, if each of the factors was priced according to its 'marginal productivity' as defined, the price of all of them when added together would equal the total product, no more and no less. In pursuing this largely scholastic inquiry they implied that, if this condition could in fact be fulfilled, the theory would have significance as a theory of distribution. This was the line of criticism adopted by Hobson, when he claimed that a factor of production could not be rewarded at a value equivalent to its *marginal* productivity, but must be rewarded at its *average* productivity. Unless the latter were true, the sum of the earnings of factors of production could not equal the total product. The reply to this criticism was simply to define the situation in more precise, and more abstract, terms; and to show that when competition was fully defined, 'normal equilibrium' must imply that marginal costs for each enterprise were equal to average costs (at a point where average costs are a minimum), so that the crucial condition was accordingly fulfilled by the very definition of competitive prices.

It is not, I think, without significance that Wicksteed, to whom so much of the mathematical refinement of this theory is traceable, principally used it to attack the Ricardian theory of rent and to demonstrate that any concept of surplus-value was untenable. What he failed to emphasize, or apparently to see, was that the very form of statement which made a concept of surplus meaningless in terms of this theory, simultaneously rendered meaningless any of those practical corollaries which justified its claim to be a realistic theory of distribution and which he apparently held to be implicit in the theory. Wicksteed pointed out that the Ricardian theory of rent, formally regarded, was a 'residual theory'. Expressed in mathematical terms, it stated that 'the whole produce being $F(x)$, and $F'(x)$ being the rate of remuneration per unit which satisfied capital-plus-labour, the whole amount which capital-plus-labour will draw out will be $x \times F'(x)$, and the remaining $F(x) - x \times F'(x)$ will be rent. Now this is simply a statement that when all other factors of production have been paid off, the "surplus" or residuum can be claimed by the landowner' (Wicksteed, 1894, pp. 17–18). If $S = x+y+z$, and $x+y$ are given, it must necessarily follow that z is determined as equal to $S-(x+y)$. Such a mathematical truism, said Wicksteed, could equally well be applied to x and to y, as to z. On the same line of reasoning the price of capital or the price of labour could be treated as a 'residual surplus': it was all a matter of which factor was taken as 'given' and which as the residual variable to be determined. But Wicksteed (like his present-day disciples) failed to notice that what renders the theory of rent a mathematical truism is the purely formal mode of stating it which he adopted; and that this formal mode of statement also makes the whole theory, as a theory of distribution, a truism, once the concept of competition is fully defined.[27] Naturally, no distinction between factors of production can exist

27. Wicksteed clearly thought otherwise. He thought that the theory could furnish 'suggestions as to the line of attack we must follow in dealing with monopolies, and with the true socializing of production' – suggestions 'magnificent in their promise' (1894, p. 38). Elsewhere he considers it a significant criticism of monopoly to say that it gives the monopolists 'more than their distributive share in the product as measured by their marginal industrial efficiency'. Actually, as 'marginal industrial efficiency' is defined by this theory, the statement is equivalent to saying that the monopolists receive more than they would receive under competition, and is capable of meaning no more than this.

Maurice Dobb 79

on the purely formal plane: x, y, z are symbols which have no differentia except their notation. Rent and profit are not differentiated from wages by the rules of algebra: if they are to be distinguished it must be by characteristics introduced from the real world – characteristics associated with the actual activities which lie behind these price phenomena. Wicksteed (1894, p. 7), indeed, declares that the theory as he expounds it seeks the laws of distribution 'not in the special nature of the services rendered by the several factors, but in the common fact of *service* rendered'; which apparently amounts to an admission that the principal differentiating qualities in factors of production have been, *ex hypothesi*, excluded and the theory erected simply on the premise that the factors in question are essential to production and hence are in demand. On this basis, to affirm an essential harmony of interests between classes, to deny the existence of 'surplus-value' and 'exploitation', and so forth, is a simple case of *petitio principii*.[28] To inquire whether a factor of production is being paid more or less than its 'marginal productivity' has substantially the same meaning (and no more) as to ask whether conditions of competition prevail in the market or not. Moreover, by appropriate re-definition the concept can be made to apply to the pricing of factors of production under conditions of monopoly (cf. Robinson, 1934b).

What has here been said in criticism is not intended to deny that mathematical economics may have much to contribute to the refinement of implications and the clarification of assumptions. Nor is it to deny that the subjective attitudes of individuals play a role as links in the chain of economic events and hence have a

28. How purely formal the difference between factors of production has become is well expressed by the fact that Wicksteed, in addition to suggesting that ploughs, manure, horses, foot-pounds of power must be treated as separate factors of production, also suggested the inclusion (for purpose of formal completeness) of 'the body of customers and their desires' and even 'commercial pushing', 'goodwill' and 'notoriety' as factors of production, each priced according to its marginal productivity (Wicksteed, 1894, pp. 33–5). Mrs Robinson has defined a separate factor as anything which has any technical difference at all from any other requisite of production, i.e. something which has no perfect substitute — a definition applauded by Professor Robbins for its formal elegance and economy (cf. Robinson, 1934a, pp. 108–9). Such definitions are certainly elegant, but they are also very attenuated.

place in any complete analysis of economic phenomena. But it is to say that so long as mathematical technique retains its servitude to a particular mode of thought, the concepts which it fashions are calculated to veil rather than to reveal reality. For this mode of thought, which is enshrined in the subjective theory of value, first creates for us a realm where disembodied minds hold communion with etherealized objects of choice and then, unmindful of the distance between this abstract world and reality, seeks to represent the relations which it finds in this realm as governing the relations which hold in actual economic society and as controlling the shape which events must have under any and every system of social institutions. This is to confuse thought and to distort reality. It is to have everything standing on its head. To emancipate economic thought from this heritage is a task that is long overdue.

References

AUSPITZ, R., and LIEBEN, R. (1914), *Récherche sur la théorie du prix*, Giard & Briére, Paris.

BÖHM-BAWERK, E. (1884), *Capital and Interest*, Macmillan, 1890.

BÖHM-BAWERK, E. (1888), *Positive Theory of Capital*, Macmillan, 1891.

CANNAN, E. (1893), *History of Theories of Production and Distribution*, King, 2nd edn, 1903.

CLARK, J. M. (1927), *Essays in Honour of J. B. Clark*, ed. J. H. Hollander, Macmillan Co.

GRAY, A. (1933), *Development of Economic Doctrine*, Longman.

HENDERSON, H. D. (1922), *Supply and Demand*, Cambridge University Press, rev. edn, 1932.

HOGBEN, L. (1936), 'Our social heritage', *Sci. Soc.*, vol. 1, pp. 137–51.

HUTT, W. H. (1934), 'Economic method and the concept of competition', *S. Afr. J. Econ.*, vol. 2, pp. 3–23.

HUTT, W. H. (1936), *Economists and the Public*, Cape.

JEVONS, W. S. (1871), *The Theory of Political Economy*, Macmillan.

KEYNES, J. M. (1936), 'Herbert Somerton Foxwell', *Econ J.*, vol. 46, pp. 589–611.

LAUDERDALE, Lord (1804), *Inquiry into the Nature and Origin of Public Wealth*.

MCCULLOCH, J. R. (1825), *Principles of Political Economy*, Tait & Longman.

MARSHALL, A. (1876), 'On Mr Mill's theory of value', *Fortnight. Rev.*, vol. 19, pp. 591–602.

MARSHALL, A. (1890), *Principles of Economics*, Macmillan, 8th edn, 1920.

MARX, K. (1867), *Capital*, vol. 1, Sonnenschein, 1896.

MILL, J. S. (1844), *Essays on Some Unsettled Questions*, John W. Parker.
PARETO, V. (1909), *Manuel d'économie politique*, Giard, Paris.
PARSONS, T. (1931), 'Wants and activities in Marshall', *Q. J. Econ.*, vol. 46, pp. 101–40.
PATTEN, S. N. (1893), 'The interpretation of Ricardo', *Q. J. Econ.*, vol. 7, pp. 322–52.
PIGOU, A. C. (1920), *The Economics of Welfare*, Macmillan.
PIGOU, A. C. (1935), *The Economics of Stationary States*, Macmillan.
RAMSEY, F. P. (1928), 'A mathematical theory of saving', *Econ. J.*, vol. 38, pp. 543–59.
ROBBINS, L. (1932), *Essay on the Nature and Significance of Economic Science*, Macmillan, 2nd edn, 1935.
ROBINSON, J. (1934a), *The Economics of Imperfect Competition*, Macmillan.
ROBINSON, J. (1934h), 'Euler's Theorem and the problem of distribution', *Econ. J.*, vol. 44, pp. 398–414.
SAY, J. B. (1819), *A Treatise on Political Economy*, vol. 1, Longman, 1821.
SAY, J. B. (1821), *Letters to Mr Malthus*, Sherwood, Necly & Jones.
SENIOR, N. (1850), *Political Economy*, Griffin, 5th edn, 1863.
VON HAYEK, F. A. (ed.) (1935), *Collectivist Economic Planning*, Routledge & Kegan Paul.
VON MISES, L. (1922), *Socialism: An Economic and Sociological Analysis*, Cape, 1936.
WICKSELL, J. G. K. (1901), *Lectures on Political Economy*, vol. 1, Routledge & Kegan Paul, 1934–5.
WICKSTEED, P. H. (1894), *Co-ordination of the Laws of Production and Distribution*, Macmillan.

2 Ronald Meek

The Marginal Revolution and its Aftermath

Excerpt from Ronald Meek, *Studies in the Labour Theory of Value*, Lawrence & Wishart, 1956, pp. 243–56.

'The critique of Marx's book', wrote Pareto (in Lafargue, 1893, p. iii), 'no longer remains to be carried out. It is to be found not only in the special monographs which have been published on this subject, but also and above all in the improvements made by Political Economy in the theory of value.' The best reply to Marx's theory of value, Pareto believed – and many others from Böhm-Bawerk onwards have shared his belief – was constituted by the new theories of value which arose as the direct or indirect result of the 'marginal revolution' of the 1870s.

I think it may be useful, therefore, before proceeding to discuss the problem of the reapplication of the Marxian labour theory, to give a short account of the 'improvements' of which Pareto speaks. If the new theories are in fact improvements on the old ones, if they are more 'scientific' and give a more useful and meaningful explanation of economic reality, then obviously there is no need to bother our heads about the problem of reapplying the Marxian theory. If, however, the apparent advance in the understanding of economic reality is actually a retreat, if the superiority of the new theories is merely technical and formal, then it is evidently the duty of economists to re-examine some of the older tools which have perhaps been too hastily discarded.

The so-called 'marginal revolution', as every student knows, was ushered in by Jevons, Menger and Walras in the early 1870s. But the term 'revolution' here is something of a misnomer. The change in the general atmosphere was real enough, but the leading ideas of the 'revolutionaries' were by no means as novel as they sometimes liked to contend. Many of these ideas had already been put forward – often in a surprisingly 'advanced' form – in the years before 1870, particularly in the course of the debates on the Ricardian theory which took place in the 1820s and 30s. And, even more important, the work of certain writers like John Stuart Mill, who believed themselves to be writing in the broad Ricardian tradition, had paved the way for the later developments to a far greater extent than the 'revolutionaries' themselves suspected.

Under the influence of Jevons (1871, p. 11), Marshall (1890, app. 1), Keynes (1936a, pp. 32–3) and others, the idea has grown up that the Ricardian system was taken over more or less in its entirety by John Stuart Mill, whose amendments and additions allegedly related only to inessentials. But this is so only if we regard the theory of value as an inessential, since nothing is more certain than that Mill decisively rejected Ricardo's concept of real or absolute value and the theory which he had based upon it. And we surely cannot regard the theory of value as an inessential. The particular theory of value with which an economist begins is almost invariably a sort of shorthand expression of the basic attitude which he is going to adopt towards the phenomena he seeks to analyse and the problems he seeks to solve.[1] This was as true of Mill as it was of Ricardo and Jevons. Mill's role in relation to the opponents of Ricardo was actually very similar to Marshall's role in relation to the opponents of Mill half a century later. From the point of view of the development of economic thought, the real significance of Mill's system lay in the extent to which the ideas of Ricardo's opponents were in fact absorbed into it, thereby clearing the path for the subsequent development of these ideas.

1. Cf. Mill (1848, pp. 264–5 of 1868 edn): 'In a state of society . . . in which the industrial system is entirely founded on purchase and sale . . . the question of Value is fundamental. Almost every speculation respecting the economical interests of a society thus constituted, implies some theory of Value: the smallest error on that subject infects with corresponding error all our other conclusions; and anything vague or misty in our conception of it, creates confusion and uncertainty in everything else.' Cf. also Wieser 1889, p. xxx of 1893 edn): 'As a man's judgement about value, so, in the last resort, must be his judgement about economics. Value is the essence of things in economics. Its laws are to political economy what the law of gravity is to mechanics. Every great system of political economy up till now has formulated its own peculiar view on value as the ultimate foundation in theory of its applications to practical life, and no new effort at reform can have laid an adequate foundation for these applications if it cannot support them on a new and more perfect theory of value.'

Let us examine Mill's theory of value with this point in mind. To begin with, Mill (1848, p. 290 of 1868 edn) insists in the first of the propositions constituting his 'summary of the theory of value' that 'value is a relative term', thus implicitly acknowledging the correctness of Bailey's criticism of Ricardo's concept of absolute value.[2] Then again, although his own theory of value cannot properly be described as a supply-and-demand theory, Mill did on occasion use expressions which suggested that 'the law of demand and supply' was in fact (as he put it in one place) 'a law of value anterior to cost of production, and more fundamental' (Mill, 1848, p. 345 of 1868 edn). So far as the utility theory of value was concerned, Mill cannot be said to have given much encouragement to its development, except to the extent that his emphasis on the role of demand was greater than that of most of his 'Ricardian' predecessors; and he explicitly rejected the theory that profit 'depends upon the productive power of capital'.[3] If he protected the Ricardian fortress against this attack, however, he yielded it completely to another, that of the 'cost of production' theorists. Having begun his analysis of value in the *Principles* by accepting the traditional idea that the equilibrium price of a commodity tends to be equal to its money cost of production, including profit at the average rate, Mill (1848, pp. 277 ff. of 1868 edn) went on to undertake what he called the 'ultimate analysis of cost of production'. This, however, turned out to be little more than a statement to the effect that costs of production consisted of wages, profits and (occasionally) taxes. It could still be said that 'the value of commodities . . . depends principally . . . on the quantity of labour required for their production' – but only, it appeared, in the absurdly restricted sense that wages usually made up the principal part of money costs.[4] This was clearly not Ricardo's theory of value, but an out-and-out rejection of it.

It would be wrong to suggest, however, as some have done, that Mill's analysis of cost of production was couched exclusively in money terms. A real cost underlies the money cost in Mill's system. Behind wages, of course, lies the expenditure of labour – but what lies behind profits? 'As the wages of the labourer are

2. Cf. Mill (1848, pp. 266–7 and 278–9 of 1868 edn).
3. Mill (1844, p. 90). Cf. Mill (1848, p. 252 of 1868 edn).
4. Mill (1848, pp. 277–8 of 1868 edn; cf. p. 291).

the remuneration of labour', Mill (1848, p. 245 of 1868 edn) replies,

so the profits of the capitalist are properly, according to Mr Senior's well-chosen expression, the remuneration of abstinence. They are what he gains by forbearing to consume his capital for his own uses, and allowing it to be consumed by productive labourers for their uses. For this forbearance he requires a recompense.

It is clear that the distance is not so very great between this rather vague labour-plus-abstinence theory of Mill's and the 'real cost' theory put forward by Marshall.[5] And it is also clear that the very juxtaposition of labour (which Ricardo had always regarded as something purely objective) and abstinence (which had necessarily to be regarded as something subjective) must have encouraged the growing tendency to conceive economic categories in subjective terms, in abstraction from the relations of production (cf. Dobb, 1937, pp. 140–41) – if, indeed, it was not itself an expression of this tendency.

Two other features of Mill's work which paved the way for the subsequent developments may be briefly described. The first of these, his well-known distinction between production and distribution, was of course made for the very best of reasons (Mill, 1873, pp. 246–8). But the idea that 'the laws and conditions of the production of wealth, partake of the character of physical truths', whereas the distribution of wealth is 'a matter of human institution solely' (Mill, 1848, p. 123 of 1868 edn), can be taken to imply (as Marx put it) that 'distribution exists side by side with production as a self-contained, independent sphere' (Marx, 1859, p. 276). Smith, Ricardo and Marx, as we have seen, tended to visualize production and distribution as two aspects of a single economic process in which production was regarded as the dominant and determining factor (cf. Marx, 1859, p. 282). Once the ties binding production and distribution together have been broken, however, it becomes much easier to escape from the classical tradition in this respect and to begin to consider the laws of distribution in abstraction from the relations of production.

5. Cf. Schumpeter (1954, p. 604, fn. 33): 'It would be almost though not quite correct to say that Mill (and Cairnes) transformed the Ricardian labour quantity theory into the Marshallian "real-cost" theory.'

Second, there was Mill's (1848, p. 421 of 1868 edn) famous distinction between statics and dynamics, and his analysis of the stationary state (1848, book 4, ch. 6). To Smith and Ricardo, the distinction between static and dynamic analysis would probably have seemed an arbitrary and unnecessary one. The main topic with which Ricardo (1816, p. 24 of 1952 edn), for example, was concerned, was 'the progress of a country in wealth and the laws by which the increasing produce is distributed'; and in his analysis of this essentially dynamic problem the static parts could hardly be separated out from the other parts. Reading Ricardo's work with Mill's distinction in mind, one becomes very conscious of the fact that the distinction cannot really be applied at all to Ricardo's analysis. The fact that Mill (1848, p. 421 of 1868 edn) isolated 'the Dynamics of political economy' in a special section of his book and contrasted it so sharply with 'the Statics of the subject' can no doubt be explained by his passion for logical systematization; but the fact that the section dealing with dynamics constitutes only about one-tenth of the *Principles* requires further explanation. The basic reason for Mill's preoccupation with statics, I think, is that he believed that it would not be very long before the advanced countries arrived at the stationary state,[6] in the analysis of which dynamics would naturally be of little use. In this state, Mill believed, 'the mere increase of production and accumulation' which now unfortunately 'excites the congratulations of ordinary politicians' (p. 453) would by definition be no longer a matter of concern and men would be able to concentrate upon securing something which in the advanced countries is much more needed – a 'better distribution' (p. 454). It would, of course, be too much to say that Mill is here delineating that problem of the distribution of a given set of scarce resources among competing ends upon which so many of his successors have concentrated. By 'better distribution' Mill clearly meant a better distribution of *income*. But it at least seems very probable that Mill's general approach helped appreciably to bring this problem to the forefront.

6. Mill was careful to refrain from making any concrete prophecies, but the whole tone of his argument (see particularly p. 452 of 1868 edn) suggests that in his opinion the end of material progress in the advanced countries could not be long delayed.

That this is so can perhaps be seen from the example of Jevons, who appears to have started with a somewhat similar set of presuppositions concerning the progress of society – except that for him the main obstacle to further advance was the impending exhaustion of Britain's coal reserves rather than the law of diminishing returns. 'The momentous repeal of the Corn Laws', he wrote in his early work on *The Coal Question* (Jevons, 1865, p. 173 of 2nd edn), 'throws us from corn upon coal', and this is bound to mean sooner or later 'the end of the present progressive condition of the kingdom' (p. vi of 2nd edn). Now a man who displays such a 'readiness to be alarmed and excited by the idea of the exhaustion of resources' (Keynes, 1936b, p. 522) as Jevons did is quite likely to visualize the fundamental economic problem as one of making the best possible use of these scarce resources; and a man whose 'vigorous individualism' (Hutchison, 1953, p. 46) and fear of the working-class movement[7] are as manifest as Jevons's were will not be likely to envisage the proper solution of this problem as involving any fundamental change in the relations of production or even in the distribution of wealth and income.[8] 'The problem of Economics', wrote Jevons (1871, p. 267),

may, as it seems to me, be stated thus: *given, a certain population, with various needs and powers of production, in possession of certain lands and other sources of material: required, the mode of employing their labour which will maximize the utility of the produce.*

The problem with which Jevons thought economics ought to be mainly concerned, then, was how to allocate a given set of

7. Anyone who reads Jevons (1866) will not, I think, feel inclined to question this phrase. Jevons was acutely aware of the fact that 'erroneous and practically mischievous' (p. 32) views on political economy were becoming popular among the lower orders. It is worth while reading some of the edifying works whose diffusion he recommended in order to stop the rot setting in, particularly Whateley (1842), which is interesting not only in itself but also because Jevons himself was brought up on it and praised it very highly. It is only fair to add, however, that a much more moderate view was expressed by Jevons (1882).

8. Cf. Jevons (1865, p. xxv of 2nd edn): 'Reflection will show that we ought not to think of interfering with the free use of the material wealth which Providence has placed at our disposal, but that our duties wholly consist in the earnest and wise application of it.'

resources among competing uses so that a given set of desires (or demands) would be most effectively satisfied.[9]

Jevons himself did not carry this through. In particular, his optimum-allocation formulae did not quite extend to the problem of the entrepreneur's demand for producers' goods. But he did at least manage to outline the basic features of the new type of analysis which was soon to be developed to deal with the new problem of 'scarcity'. In the first place, he made it clear that this was essentially a static rather than a dynamic problem (Jevons, 1871, pp. vii and 93–4). In the second place, he established once and for all that it was a problem in which marginal techniques might be expected to be useful. And in the third place, he pointed out that since the problem was one of satisfying a given set of individual demands 'the theory of Economics must begin with a correct theory of consumption'.[10]

It seems to me that the increasing popularity of the new type of analysis in the years which followed can be at least partly explained by the fact that the basic problem of 'scarcity' with which it was designed to deal actually began to emerge to prominence in the real world. In the 1870s and 1880s, as Wesley Mitchell (1949, p. 59) pointed out, 'on the whole the rate of progress was believed by contemporaries to have been checked'; and in spite of the subsequent recovery the general situation has still apparently been such as to induce many economists to begin by assuming (at least provisionally) that 'there is no further possibility of increasing the total quantity of resources' and therefore to concentrate on 'the possibilities of increasing economic welfare by a more efficient allocation of the *given* resources'.[11] In addition, of course, the new type of analysis was found to be particularly useful in connection with the task of opposing the labour theory of value – a task which became more and more

9. Cf. Hutchison (1953, pp. 34–6) for an interesting discussion of certain other factors which may have led Jevons to see 'pure economic problems as optimum-allocation problems'

10. Jevons (1871, p. 40). Cf. also, on the same page, the statement that 'human wants are the ultimate subject matter of Economics'.

11. Myint (1948, p. xii). If my interpretation is correct, it follows that Bukharin (1919) was wrong in characterizing the theory of marginal utility as the ideology of a new *rentier* class, but right in associating it with a particular stage in the development of capitalism.

urgent as Marxist ideas began to grow in popularity.

The marginal utility theory of value, of course, was much more than an alternative method of explaining price ratios. It also expressed an alternative general approach to economic phenomena. First and foremost, it was an expression of the idea that the whole of economics ought to be based on the investigation of 'the condition of a mind'. 'The general forms of the laws of Economics', wrote Jevons (1871, p. 15),

are the same in the case of individuals and nations; and, in reality, it is a law operating in the case of multitudes of individuals which gives rise to the aggregate represented in the transactions of a nation.[12]

What we must start with, Jevons in effect argued, was the mental relation between the individual and finished goods, rather than the social relation between men and men in the production of commodities.[13] And this implied that the basic laws and techniques of economics had a much greater degree of generality than had usually been assumed: they were in fact adequate to deal not only with the optimum-allocation problems to be found in all forms of exchange economy, but also with those of the isolated individual.[14] This amounted, of course, to a complete rejection of the classical idea that economic phenomena could only be properly understood if one started with the relations of production peculiar to the particular economic formation under consideration. It was widely contended, however, that because of its 'scientific' character[15] the new type of approach was capable of giving a much more satisfactory answer to all the main economic problems which the classical economists had tackled.

The chief developments ushered in by the Austrians proceeded within this framework. Indeed, most if not all of these developments are to be found (at least in embryo) in the work of Jevons himself. It is true that Jevons never worked out at all fully any-

12. Cf. Mill (1843, p. 573 of 1891 edn).

13. Cf. Jevons (1871, p. 43): 'Utility, though a quality of things, is *no inherent quality*. It is better described as a *circumstance of things* arising out of their relation to man's requirements.'

14. Cf. Jevons (1871, pp. 75 and 222).

15. The belief that the new developments had at last turned political economy into a real science was expressed (*inter alia*) by what Jevons (1871, p. xiv) described as 'the substitution for the name Political Economy of the single convenient term *Economics*'.

thing which could properly be called a marginal productivity theory of distribution and that he still tended to think in terms of some sort of independent 'real cost' lying behind supply. But there is some justification for the view that his theories of interest and wages were essentially 'in agreement with the modern theory of marginal productivity';[16] and in his preface to the second edition of *The Theory of Political Economy* the foundations of a coordinated marginal productivity theory of distribution and a generalized doctrine of opportunity cost were quite clearly mapped out (Jevons, 1871, pp. xlvi ff. of 2nd edn). And Jevons made it clear from the beginning that the 'real cost' lying behind supply, although it could often be said to be the 'determining circumstance' in the process whereby values were fixed, could never be said to be so directly, but only through the medium of its effect (through supply) on marginal utility – a view summarily expressed as follows in his famous table (Jevons, 1871, p. 165 of 2nd edn):

Cost of production determines supply:
Supply determines final degree of utility:
Final degree of utility determines value.

If he had ever had time to reformulate this argument in the light of the ideas put forward in his preface to the second edition, there is little doubt that Jevons would have come much closer to the Austrian approach, with its rejection of the whole concept of 'real cost'.

To many of the later writers in this new tradition, the refutation of the Marxian version of the labour theory appeared as a particularly urgent task. There seems little doubt, for example, that Böhm-Bawerk set out more or less deliberately to provide alternative solutions to the problems of value and surplus value which Marx had dealt with in so unpalatable a fashion.[17] Wieser, again, was well aware of the fact that in Germany 'there has of

16. Jevons (1871, app. 1, p. 279). It is certainly true, at any rate, that Jevons's theory of interest substantially anticipated that of Böhm-Bawerk.
17. There is an interesting parallel here between Böhm-Bawerk and Schumpeter. Both men agreed that Marx had posed a particular problem correctly (in Böhm-Bawerk's case the problem of surplus value and in Schumpeter's case the problem of economic development) and both set out to give an alternative answer to the problem as posed by Marx.

late years been a widening acceptance of the labour theory', and that many socialists were basing their 'crusade against interest' on Ricardo's system; and he therefore found himself, as he put it, 'obliged again and again to speak against the socialists'.[18] The 'key fact' about J. B. Clark's marginal productivity theory of distribution, as his son has recently reminded us, was probably that 'his statements are oriented at Marx, and are best construed as an earnest and not meticulously qualified rebuttal of Marxian exploitation theory'.[19] Cassel and Pareto, again, wrote extensively on the Marxian system and there can be little doubt that many of their leading theoretical statements, too, were 'oriented at Marx'. And Wicksteed, in 'coordinating' the laws of distribution and attacking the Ricardian theory of rent, was well aware of the fact that 'any diagram of distribution that represents the share of the different factors under different geometrical forms is sure to be misleading and is likely to be particularly mischievous in its misdirection of social imagination and aspiration' (see Wicksteed, 1910, p. 792 of 1933 edn).

For obvious reasons, the desire to use the new theories to attack Marx was not nearly so manifest in the case of the British writers as it was in the case of their continental colleagues.[20] To Marshall, for example, it was evidently a very minor consideration indeed. Marshall's main aim, so far as the theory of value

18. Wieser (1889, pp. xxxi, xxix and 64 of 1893 edn). The extent to which *Natural Value* was, in intention and effect, a sustained polemic against the Marxist and Rodbertian systems has not been sufficiently commented upon. See, e.g., book 2, ch. 7, on 'The socialist theory of value'; book 3, ch. 3, on the socialist approach to the 'problem of imputation'; book 5, chs. 8–10, on 'labour' theories of cost. It is worth noting, I think, that Wieser's most important and distinctive contributions to economics, the theory of imputation and the 'law of costs', were put forward, at least in this work, as arguments against and alternatives to the Ricardian and Marxian theories. Cf. Hutchison (1953, p. 157), who speaks of Wieser's 'constant preoccupation' with attacks on the labour theory.

19. J. M. Clark, in Spiegel (1952, p. 610). Cf. p. 605: 'The readiness of thinkers to accept such a theory [as the marginal utility theory of value] at this time is probably explainable as a result of the use Marx had made of the Ricardian theory, turning it into a theory of exploitation and leaving liberal economists predisposed to adopt a theory of a basically different sort.' Cf. also p. 599.

20. But the example of Sir Louis Mallet (1891) shows that the desire did indeed exist, particularly in Cobdenite circles.

was concerned, was to correct certain excesses of Jevons and the Austrians (notably their overemphasis on the 'demand side' and their dilution or rejection of the concept of real cost) and, while accepting what he regarded as the important element of truth in their doctrines, to emphasize the essential continuity between these doctrines when so corrected and those of the classical economists. The appearance of continuity was maintained by Marshall on the basis of a somewhat shallow interpretation of Ricardo's value theory. Setting the modern fashion for 'generous' interpretations of Ricardo, Marshall (1890, p. xxxiii of 8th edn) argued that Ricardo's theory of value, 'though obscurely expressed . . . anticipated more of the modern doctrine of the relations between cost, utility and value than has been recognized by Jevons and some other critics'. Marshall's own theory of value, however, was not in fact very much closer to Ricardo's than Jevons's had been. It is true that Marshall (1890, p. 90) argued that the theory of consumption was *not* the scientific basis of economics; but his theoretical exposition in the *Principles* nevertheless began with an outline of what was in effect such a theory.[21] It is true, too, that he insisted on the 'real' character of costs and the importance of their role in the process whereby values were determined, much more strongly than Jevons had done, and that he specifically attacked the Austrian idea that cost could be better explained in terms of forgone utilities than in terms of 'real' sacrifices (Marshall, 1890, pp. 527–8, fn.). But it must be emphasized that the elements of 'real cost' in terms of which Marshall's analysis was framed were essentially subjective and therefore very different from Ricardo's (cf. Schumpeter, 1954, p. 924, fn. 10); and also that certain important ambiguities in his concept of waiting brought his analysis of cost rather nearer to that of the Austrians (at least in a formal sense) than he himself probably suspected (cf. Dobb, 1937, pp. 143 ff.). Indeed, as we shall shortly see, there is an important sense in which Marshall's theory of value was actually further away from Ricardo's than Jevons's had been.

21. Similarly, although Marshall always insisted on the importance of dynamics (upon which his numerous incidental comments were often very valuable) and although he was suspicious of 'stationary state' models, his own analysis remained essentially static.

From the point of view of the subsequent development of value theory, the most important feature of Marshall's *Principles* was possibly the encouragement which it gave to the general equilibrium approach to value theory and that preoccupation with form at the expense of content which is today so often associated with it. This encouragement was given in part directly, by means of Marshall's Mathematical Note 21 and the 'intermittent attention' given to 'the wider conception of the general interdependence of all economic quantities' in the *Principles*;[22] and in part indirectly, by means of his insistence on the principle (which he ascribed to Cournot) that

it is necessary to face the difficulty of regarding the various elements of an economic problem – not as determining one another in a chain of causation, A determining B, B determining C, and so on – but as all mutually determining one another. Nature's action is complex: and nothing is gained in the long run by pretending that it is simple, and trying to describe it in a series of elementary propositions.[23]

Nothing is indeed gained by pretending that nature's action (or the action of men in society) is simple or that there is not an important sense in which everything can be said to be determined by everything else. But unless it is held possible to isolate some particular factor in a given situation and to treat it in some significant sense as a 'cause' or 'determinant', it is difficult to see how any science can ever advance very far beyond the classificatory stage. Jevons's *catena* of causes was not quite as silly as Marshall made it out to be. Marshall's attitude, however, would – and in fact did – encourage economists to believe that it was neither possible nor necessary to make any causal statements at

22. Schumpeter (1954, p. 836). Cf. Pigou (1925, p. 417): 'My whole life has been and will be given to presenting in realistic form as much as I can of my Note 21.'

23. Marshall (1890, pp. ix–x). This principle was of course the basis of what Marshall described as his 'greatest objection' to Jevons's tabular statement of his doctrine – that 'it does not represent supply price, demand price and amount produced as mutually determining one another (subject to certain other conditions), but as determined one by another in a series. It is as though when three balls A, B and C rest against one another in a bowl, instead of saying that the position of the three mutually determines one another under the action of gravity, he had said that A determines B, and B determines C. Someone else however, with equal justice might say that C determines B and B determines A' (Marshall, 1890, p. 818).

all in the field of value theory (cf. Cassel, 1925, pp. 93–6). The classical economists and the leaders of the 'marginal revolution', it began to be said, had alike been misled into a false inquiry. There was in fact no need whatever to seek for an 'independent' determining constant. All that was really necessary was that the conditions of the mutual interdependence of economic quantities should be expressible in a mathematically determinate form – i.e. roughly, in the form of an equational system in which the number of unknowns was equal to the number of equations. It will be clear that the particular idea of 'determinateness' which lies behind this approach is radically different from that which lay behind the Classical, Marxian and Mengerian theories of value. To solve the value problem in this way is to solve it only in a purely formal sense – i.e. it is not to solve it at all.

To Walras, who is generally regarded as the founder of this type of approach, utility was still a significant factor – although its role appeared by no means as important to him as it did to Jevons and the Austrians. To his followers, however, it gradually began to appear less and less important. Pareto, for example, noted that 'the whole theory of economic equilibrium is independent of the notions of *utility* (economic), use value or ophelimity'. He himself, like most of his immediate predecessors, had started by establishing the theory of economic equilibrium on the basis of these notions, but he later came to the conclusion that it was possible to do without them and to develop instead 'the theory of choice, which gives more rigour and more clarity to the whole theory of economic equilibrium'.[24] Utility gradually became more and more suspect, partly because of the hedonist presuppositions allegedly involved in the concept, partly because under certain circumstances it was unmeasurable and partly, no doubt (in some instances), because in certain hands it had proved more capable of lending support to equalitarian proposals than many of its progenitors had expected or desired. In any event, utility began to be regarded as an unsatisfactory and superfluous concept. Its place came more and more to be taken by the concept of preference schedules, from which all hedonist presuppositions had allegedly been expelled. To some economists this latter concept at first appeared capable of fulfilling the same function

24. Pareto (1909, p. 543 of 1927 edn). Cf. Schumpeter (1954, p. 918).

as utility had previously done, i.e. the function of serving as the 'independent' factor which could in the last analysis be regarded as determining value. Today, however, the preference schedules have increasingly come to be interpreted as simply reflecting a consumer's empirically observed behaviour in the market place, and it is widely held that all that needs to be postulated concerning the mental attitudes of the consumer is that his choices should be *consistent*, i.e. that in a given price-and-income situation he chooses to buy in a way that is uniquely determined. In effect, this has meant giving up entirely the search for a value theory properly so-called. 'The theory of price', says Little (1950, p. 52), 'can begin on the demand side quite legitimately with the demand curve. That one's "ultimate" data should be statistical can no longer be considered a shocking idea.' Prices can be made formally 'determinate' by setting up an equational system in which the number of equations is equal to the number of unknowns; and the ground has been so well prepared by men like Pareto, Cassel, Fisher and Barone that this type of approach has come to command a wide measure of approval without the majority of economists realizing that anything at all is missing. Modern economists, like modern artists and poets, seem all too often to feel quite at home in

. . . a world where the form is the reality,
Of which the substantial is only a shadow.

The fact that value and distribution theory has developed in this direction does not in itself give grounds for complaint: one cannot properly object to people engaging in a pleasing aesthetic activity. But the new approach is often quite solemnly put forward as an alternative to the classical theory and is used to give answers to the same vital questions with which that theory was designed to deal. Indeed, it is frequently claimed that the new doctrines, being more 'scientific' and precise than the old, and less limited to particular economic formations, are much more capable of giving useful answers to these questions than the 'crude' classical theories were. Thus the fact that the classical theories of distribution gave 'separate' accounts of rent, wages and profits has been widely held to be evidence of their 'unscientific' character.[25] If

25. Cf. Bell (1953, p. 424), Schumpeter (1954, p. 934) and Stigler (1946, pp. 1–3).

one objects that a theory which explains the origin of the wages of labour and the rent of land on precisely the same basis is not likely to be a very useful guide to practice, the upholders of the theory may concede that it is in fact purely formal, but insist that this does not matter because there is nothing at all to stop an economist going on to distinguish between these two forms of income on moral or political grounds if he wishes. Was not Walras a land reformer? All one can really say in reply to this is that it used to be conceived as a major task of economic theory to give information which people concerned with economic practice would at least regard as *relevant* to the decisions they were obliged to reach; and that if economic theory has now ceased to regard this as part of its function, so much the worse for it.

The real point here, I think, is that the expulsion of utility from value theory has not meant the expulsion of the presuppositions which were brought in with the utility theory. So far from meaning a return to the classical emphasis on relations of production, the expulsion of utility has usually if anything meant a further retreat from it. Welfare economics and the so-called 'economics of socialism' remain to a large extent in the grip of the old presuppositions and even Keynes was by no means unaffected by them. And the theory of distribution, broadly speaking, is still weighed down by the notion – the first-fruit of the utility approach – that no 'factor' which is customarily regarded as necessary for production can possibly receive (at least in the absence of monopoly or development) anything in the nature of a true surplus as part of its income.[26] The Marxian labour theory of value is not a magic wand which needs only to be waved to transform the barren desert of 'pure theory' into fertile land. But it is, I think, a signpost pointing to the direction which must be followed if a way out of the desert is to be found.

References

BELL, J. F. (1953), *A History of Economic Thought*, Ronald Press.
BUKHARIN, N. I. (1919), *The Economic Theory of the Leisure Class*, Lawrence, 1927.
CASSEL, G. (1925), *Fundamental Thoughts in Economics*, Fisher Unwin.

26. 'That one cannot get something for nothing' has recently been described by Harrod (1948, p. 36) as 'the most basic law of economics'.

DOBB, M. (1937), *Political Economy and Capitalism*, Routledge & Kegan Paul.

HARROD, R. F. (1948), *Towards a Dynamic Economics*, Macmillan.

HUTCHISON, T. W. (1953), *A Review of Economic Doctrines*, Clarendon Press.

JEVONS, W. S. (1865), *The Coal Question*, Macmillan, 2nd edn, 1866.

JEVONS, W. S. (1866), *Introductory Lecture on the Importance of Diffusing a Knowledge of Political Economy*, Sowler.

JEVONS, W. S. (1871), *The Theory of Political Economy*, Macmillan, 2nd edn, 1879.

JEVONS, W. S. (1882), *The State in Relation to Labour*, Macmillan.

KEYNES, J. M. (1936a), *General Theory of Employment, Interest and Money*, Harcourt Brace Jovanovich.

KEYNES, J. M. (1936b), 'William Stanley Jevons, 1835–1882', *J. Roy. Stat. Soc.*, part 3, vol. 99, pp. 516–48.

LAFARGUE, P. (ed.) (1893), *Extracts from Karl Marx's 'Capital'*, Guillaurin, Paris.

LITTLE, I. M. D. (1950), *A Critique of Welfare Economics*, Clarendon Press.

MALLET, L. (1891), 'The law of value and the theory of the unearned increment', in B. Mallet (ed.), *Free Exchange*, Routledge & Kegan Paul

MARSHALL, A. (1890), *Principles of Economics*, Macmillan, 8th edn, 1920.

MARX, K. (1859), *Critique of Political Economy*, International Library Publishing Co., New York, 1904.

MILL, J. S. (1843), *System of Logic*, Longman, 1891.

MILL, J. S. (1844), *Essays on Some Unsettled Questions of Political Economy*, John W. Parker.

MILL, J. S. (1848), *Principles of Political Economy*, Longman, 1868.

MILL, J. S. (1873), *Autobiography*, Longman.

MITCHELL, W. C. (1949), *Lecture Notes on Types of Economic Theory*, vol. 2, Kelley.

MYINT, H. (1948), *Theories of Welfare Economics*, Longman.

PARETO, V. (1909), *Manuel d'économie politique*, Giard & Brière, Paris, 1927.

PIGOU, A. C. (ed.) (1925), *Memorials of Alfred Marshall*, Macmillan.

RICARDO, D. (1816) 'Letter to Malthus, 23 February 1816', in P. Sraffa (ed.), *Works*, vol. 7, Cambridge University Press, 1952.

SCHUMPETER, J. A. (1954), *History of Economic Analysis*, Allen & Unwin.

SPIEGEL, H. W. (ed.) (1952), *The Development of Economic Thought*, Wiley.

STIGLER, G. J. (1946), *Production and Distribution Theories*, Macmillan.

WHATELEY, R. (1842), *Easy Lessons on Money Matters*, John W. Parker.

WICKSTEED, P. H. (1910), *The Common Sense of Political Economy*, vol. 2, ed. L. Robbins, Routledge & Kegan Paul, 1933.

WIESER, F. (1889), *Natural Value*, Macmillan, 1893.

Part Two Mystification and the Evasion of Social Reality: Criticisms of Conventional Academic Economic Theory

Reading 3, from Karl Marx's *Economic and Philosophic Manuscripts of 1844*, sets forth his concept of alienation, the progressive dehumanization of labour and the struggle between capital and labour. This goes beyond the conventionally accepted limits of academic discourse into the social meaning of property, wage labour and capital. István Mészáros (Reading 4) discusses the structure of Marx's system; his diagrammatic exposition is illuminating.

On a less general plane, Thorstein Veblen (Reading 5) mocks at J. B. Clark's trumpeting of the market as the Economic Order of Nature. E. K. Hunt (Reading 6) shows that even if we grant its premises, academic economics has so restricted itself as to be unworkable.

3 Karl Marx

Estranged Labour[1] and Capital

Excerpt from Karl Marx in D. J. Struick (ed.), *Karl Marx. Economic and Philosophic Manuscripts of 1844*, Lawrence & Wishart, 1970, pp. 106–27.

Estranged labor

We have proceeded from the premises of political economy. We have accepted its language and its laws. We presupposed private property, the separation of labor, capital and land, and of wages, profit of capital and rent of land – likewise division of labor, competition, the concept of exchange-value, etc. On the basis of political economy itself, in its own words, we have shown that the worker sinks to the level of a commodity and becomes indeed the most wretched of commodities; that the wretchedness of the worker is in inverse proportion to the power and magnitude of his production; that the necessary result of competition is the accumulation of capital in a few hands, and thus the restoration of monopoly in a more terrible form; and that finally the distinction between capitalist and land rentier, like that between the tiller of the soil and the factory worker, disappears and that the whole of society must fall apart into the two classes – the property *owners* and the propertyless *workers*.

Political economy starts with the fact of private property, but it does not explain it to us. It expresses in general, abstract formulas the *material* process through which private property actually passes, and these formulas it then takes for *laws*. It does not *comprehend* these laws, i.e. it does not demonstrate how they arise from the very nature of private property. Political economy does not disclose the source of the division between labor and capital and between capital and land. When, for example, it defines the relationship of wages to profit, it takes the interest of the capitalists

1. Estranged labor, *Die Entfremdete Arbeit:* as to the term 'estranged', see *Entfremdung* in 'Note on terminology' and the Introduction [to *Economic and Philosophic Manuscripts of 1844*].

to be the ultimate cause, i.e. it takes for granted what it is supposed to explain. Similarly, competition comes in everywhere. It is explained from external circumstances. As to how far these external and apparently accidental circumstances are but the expression of a necessary course of development, political economy teaches us nothing. We have seen how exchange itself appears to it as an accidental fact. The only wheels which political economy sets in motion are *greed* and the war *amongst the greedy – competition*.

Precisely because political economy does not grasp the way the movement is connected, it was possible to oppose, for instance, the doctrine of competition to the doctrine of monopoly, the doctrine of the freedom of the crafts to the doctrine of the guild, the doctrine of the division of landed property to the doctrine of the big estate – for competition, freedom of the crafts and the division of landed property were explained and comprehended only as accidental, premeditated and violent consequences of monopoly, of the guild system and of feudal property, not as their necessary, inevitable and natural consequences.

Now, therefore, we have to grasp the essential connection between private property, greed and the separation of labor, capital and landed property; between exchange and competition, value and the devaluation of men, monopoly and competition, etc. – the connection between this whole estrangement and the *money* system.

Do not let us go back to a fictitious primordial condition as the political economist does, when he tries to explain. Such a primordial condition explains nothing; it merely pushes the question away into a gray nebulous distance. It assumes in the form of a fact, of an event, what the economist is supposed to deduce – namely, the necessary relationship between two things – between, for example, division of labor and exchange. Theology in the same way explains the origin of evil by the fall of man; that is, it assumes as a fact, in historical form, what has to be explained.

We proceed from an economic fact *of the present*.

The worker becomes all the poorer the more wealth he produces, the more his production increases in power and size. The worker becomes an ever cheaper commodity the more commodities he creates. With the *increasing value* of the world of things proceeds in direct proportion the *devaluation* of the world of men. Labor produces not only commodities: it produces itself and the worker as a *commodity* – and this in the same general proportion in which it produces commodities.

This fact expresses merely that the object which labor produces – labor's product – confronts it as *something alien*, as a *power independent* of the producer. The product of labor is labor which has been embodied in an object, which has become material: it is the *objectification*[2] of labor. Labor's realization is its objectification. In the sphere of political economy this realization of labor appears as *loss of realization*[3] for the workers; objectification as *loss of the object* and *bondage to it*; appropriation as *estrangement*, as *alienation*.[4]

So much does labor's realization appear as loss of realization that the worker loses realization to the point of starving to death. So much does objectification appear as loss of the object that the worker is robbed of the objects most necessary not only for his life but for his work. Indeed, labor itself becomes an object which he can obtain only with the greatest effort and with the most irregular interruptions. So much does the appropriation of the object appear as estrangement that the more objects the worker produces the less he can possess and the more he falls under the sway of his product, capital.

All these consequences result from the fact that the worker is related to the *product of his labor* as to an *alien* object. For on this premise it is clear that the more the worker spends himself, the more powerful becomes the alien world of objects which he creates over and against himself, the poorer he himself – his inner world – becomes, the less belongs to him as his own. It is the same in religion. The more man puts into God, the less he retains in himself. The worker puts his life into the object; but now his life

2. Objectification, *Vergegenständlichung*: the process of becoming an object.

3. Loss of realization, *Entwirklichung*. A better translation might be 'devaluation'. Marx, in true Hegel fashion, opposes *Verwirklichung*, here translated as *realization*, to *Entwirklichung*, the taking away of reality. Here *realization* is meant as accomplishment, performance, making something real. Marx states that the accomplishment of labor turns into its opposite.

4. Alienation, *Entäusserung*. See *Entäusserung* in 'Note on terminology' and the Introduction [to *Economic and Philosophic Manuscripts of 1844*].

no longer belongs to him but to the object. Hence, the greater this activity, the greater is the worker's lack of objects. Whatever the product of his labor is, he is not. Therefore the greater this product, the less is he himself. The *alienation* of the worker in his product means not only that his labor becomes an object, an *external* existence, but that it exists *outside him*, independently, as something alien to him, and that it becomes a power on its own confronting him. It means that the life which he has conferred on the object confronts him as something hostile and alien.

Let us now look more closely at the *objectification*, at the production of the worker; and in it at the *estrangement*, the *loss* of the object, of his product.

The worker can create nothing without *nature*, without the *sensuous external world*.[5] It is the material on which his labor is realized, in which it is active, from which and by means of which it produces.

But just as nature provides labor with the *means of life* in the sense that labor cannot *live* without objects on which to operate, on the other hand, it also provides the *means of life* in the more restricted sense, i.e. the means for the physical subsistence of the *worker* himself.

Thus the more the worker by his labor *appropriates* the external world, hence sensuous nature, the more he deprives himself of *means of life* in a double manner: first, in that the sensuous external world more and more *ceases* to be an object belonging to his labor – to be his labor's *means of life*; and secondly, in that it more and more ceases to be *means of life* in the immediate sense, means for the physical subsistence of the worker.

In both respects, therefore, the worker becomes a slave of his object, first, in that he receives an *object of labor*, i.e. in that he receives *work*; and secondly, in that he receives *means of subsistence*. Therefore, it enables him to exist, first, as a *worker*; and second, as a *physical subject*. The height of this bondage is that it is only as a *worker* that he continues to maintain himself as a *physical subject* and that it is only as a *physical subject* that he is a *worker*.

(The laws of political economy express the estrangement of the worker in his object thus: the more the worker produces, the less

5. Sensuous, *sinnlich*: what can be observed by means of the senses.

he has to consume; the more values he creates, the more valueless, the more unworthy he becomes; the better formed his product, the more deformed becomes the worker; the more civilized his object, the more barbarous becomes the worker; the more powerful labor becomes, the more powerless becomes the worker; the more ingenious labor becomes, the less ingenious becomes the worker and the more he becomes nature's bondsman.)

Political economy conceals the estrangement inherent in the nature of labor by not considering the direct relationship between the worker (labor) *and production*. It is true that labor produces for the rich wonderful things – but for the worker it produces privation. It produces palaces – but for the worker, hovels. It produces beauty – but for the worker, deformity. It replaces labor by machines, but it throws a section of the workers back to a barbarous type of labor and it turns the other workers into machines. It produces intelligence – but for the worker, stupidity, cretinism.

The direct relationship of labor to its products is the relationship of the worker to the objects of his production. The relationship of the man of means to the objects of production and to production itself is only a *consequence* of this first relationship – and confirms it. We shall consider this other aspect later.

When we ask, then, what is the essential relationship of labor we are asking about the relationship of the *worker* to production.

Till now we have been considering the estrangement, the alienation of the worker only in one of its aspects, i.e. the worker's *relationship to the products of his labor*. But the estrangement is manifested not only in the result but in the *act of production*, within the *producing activity*, itself. How could the worker come to face the product of his activity as a stranger, were it not that in the very act of production he was estranging himself from himself? The product is after all but the summary of the activity, of production. If then the product of labor is alienation, production itself must be active alienation, the alienation of activity, the activity of alienation. In the estrangement of the object of labor is merely summarized the estrangement, the alienation, in the activity of labor itself.

What, then, constitutes the alienation of labor?

First, the fact that labor is *external* to the worker, i.e. it does not belong to his essential being; that in his work, therefore, he does not affirm himself but denies himself, does not feel content but unhappy, does not develop freely his physical and mental energy but mortifies his body and ruins his mind. The worker therefore only feels himself outside his work and in his work feels outside himself. He is at home when he is not working and when he is working he is not at home. His labor is therefore not voluntary, but coerced; it is *forced labor*. It is therefore not the satisfaction of a need; it is merely a *means* to satisfy needs external to it. Its alien character emerges clearly in the fact that as soon as no physical or other compulsion exists, labor is shunned like the plague. External labor, labor in which man alienates himself, is a labor of self-sacrifice, of mortification. Lastly, the external character of labor for the worker appears in the fact that it is not his own, but someone else's, that it does not belong to him, that in it he belongs, not to himself, but to another. Just as in religion the spontaneous activity of the human imagination, of the human brain and the human heart, operates independently of the individual – that is, operates on him as an alien, divine or diabolical activity – so is the worker's activity not his spontaneous activity. It belongs to another; it is the loss of his self.

As a result, therefore, man (the worker) only feels himself freely active in his animal functions – eating, drinking, procreating, or at most in his dwelling and in dressing-up, etc.; and in his human functions he no longer feels himself to be anything but an animal. What is animal becomes human and what is human becomes animal.

Certainly eating, drinking, procreating, etc. are also genuinely human functions. But abstractly taken, separated from the sphere of all other human activity and turned into sole and ultimate ends, they are animal functions.

We have considered the act of estranging practical human activity, labor, in two of its aspects.

1. The relation of the worker to the *product of labor* as an alien object exercising power over him. This relation is at the same time the relation to the sensuous external world, to the objects of nature, as an alien world inimically opposed to him.

2. The relation of labor to the *act of production* within the *labor* process. This relation is the relation of the worker to his own

activity as an alien activity not belonging to him; it is activity as suffering, strength as weakness, begetting as emasculating, the worker's *own* physical and mental energy, his personal life; indeed, what is life but activity? – as an activity which is turned against him, independent of him and not belonging to him. Here we have *self-estrangement*, as previously we had the estrangement of the *thing*.

We have still a third aspect of *estranged labor* to deduce from the two already considered.

Man is a species being,[6] not only because in practice and in theory he adopts the species as his object (his own as well as those of other things), but – and this only another way of expressing it – also because he treats himself as the actual, living species; because he treats himself as a *universal* and therefore a free being.

The life of the species, both in man and in animals, consists physically in the fact that man (like the animal) lives on inorganic nature; and the more universal man is compared with an animal, the more universal is the sphere of inorganic nature on which he lives. Just as plants, animals, stones, air, light, etc., constitute theoretically a part of human consciousness, partly as objects of

6. Species being, *Gattungswesen*, a term used by Feuerbach, who takes as the *Gattung*, mankind as a whole, hence the human species.

Species nature (just like species being), *Gattungswesen*: man's essential nature, *menschliches Wesen*; see *Wesen* in 'Note on terminology' [in *Economic and Philosophic Manuscripts of 1844*].

The following passages from Feuerbach's *Essence of Christianity* may help readers to understand the ideological background to this part of Marx's thought and, incidentally, to see how Marx accepted but infused with new content concepts made current by Feuerbach as well as by Hegel and the political economists:

'What is this essential difference between man and the brute? . . . Consciousness – but consciousness in the strict sense; for the consciousness implied in the feeling of self as an individual, in discrimination by the senses, in the perception and even judgement of outward things according to definite sensible signs, cannot be denied to the brutes. Consciousness in the strictest sense is present only in a being to whom his species, his essential nature, is an object of thought. The brute is indeed conscious of himself as an individual – and he has accordingly the feeling of self as the common center of successive sensations – but not as a species. . . . In practical life we have to do with individuals; in science, with species. . . . But only a being to whom his own species, his own nature, is an object of thought, can make the essential nature of other things or beings an object of thought. . . . The

natural science, partly as objects of art – his spiritual inorganic nature, spiritual nourishment which he must first prepare to make palatable and digestible – so also in the realm of practice they constitute a part of human life and human activity. Physically man lives only on these products of nature, whether they appear in the form of food, heating, clothes, a dwelling, etc. The universality of man appears in practice precisely in the universality which makes all nature his *inorganic* body – both inasmuch as nature is (a) his direct means of life and (b) the material, the object and the instrument of his life activity. Nature is man's *inorganic body* – nature, that is, in so far as it is not itself the human body. Man *lives* on nature – means that nature is his *body*, with which he must remain in continuous interchange if he is not to die. That man's physical and spiritual life is linked to nature means simply that nature is linked to itself, for man is a part of nature.

In estranging from man (a) nature and (b) himself, his own active functions, his life activity, estranged labor estranges the *species* from man. It changes for him the *life of the species* into a means of individual life. First, it estranges the life of the species and individual life and, secondly, it makes individual life in its abstract form the purpose of the life of the species, likewise in its abstract and estranged form.

---

brute has only a simple, man a twofold life; in the brute, the inner life is one with the outer. Man has both an inner and an outer life. The inner life of man is the life which has relation to his species – to his general, as distinguished from his individual nature. . . . The brute can exercise no function which has relation to its species without another individual external to itself; but man can perform the functions of thought and speech, which strictly imply such a relation, apart from another individual. . . . Man is in fact at once I and Thou; he can put himself in the place of another, for this reason, that to him his species, his essential nature, and not merely his individuality, is an object of thought. . . . An object to which a subject essentially, necessarily relates, is nothing else than this subject's own, but objective nature. . . .

'The relation of the sun to the earth is, therefore, at the same time a relation of the earth to itself, or to its own nature, for the measure of the size and of the intensity of light which the sun possesses as the object of the earth is the measure of the distance, which determines the peculiar nature of the earth. . . . In the object which he contemplates, therefore, man becomes acquainted with himself. . . . The power of the object over him is therefore the power of his own nature.'

(L. Feuerbach, *The Essence of Christianity*, trans. from 2nd German edn by M. Evans, Chapman, 1854, pp. 1–5.)

Indeed, labor, *life activity*, *productive life* itself, appears in the first place merely as a *means* of satisfying a need – the need to maintain physical existence. Yet the productive life is the life of the species. It is life-engendering life. The whole character of a species – its species character – is contained in the character of its life activity; and free, conscious activity is man's species character. Life itself appears only as a *means to life*.

The animal is immediately one with its life activity. It does not distinguish itself from it. It is *its life activity*. Man makes his life activity itself the object of his will and of his consciousness. He has conscious life activity. It is not a determination with which he directly merges. Conscious life activity distinguishes man immediately from animal life activity. It is just because of this that he is a species being. Or rather, it is only because he is a species being that he is a conscious being, i.e. that his own life is an object for him. Only because of that is his activity free activity. Estranged labor reverses this relationship, so that it is just because man is a conscious being that he makes his life activity, his *essential* being, a mere means to his *existence*.

In creating a *world of objects*[7] by his practical activity, in *his work upon* inorganic nature, man proves himself a conscious species being, i.e. as a being that treats the species as its own essential being or that treats itself as a species being. Admittedly animals also produce. They build themselves nests, dwellings, like the bees, beavers, ants, etc. But an animal only produces what it immediately needs for itself or its young. It produces one-sidedly, whilst man produces universally. It produces only under the dominion of immediate physical need, whilst man produces even when he is free from physical need and only truly produces in freedom therefrom. An animal produces only itself, whilst man reproduces the whole of nature. An animal's product belongs immediately to its physical body, whilst man freely confronts his product. An animal forms things in accordance with the standard and the need of the species to which it belongs, whilst man knows how to produce in accordance with the standard of every species and knows how to apply everywhere the inherent standard to the

7. Marx's term *gegenständlich* can be translated by 'objective', but what is meant is an adjective belonging to *Gegenständ*, object. We believe that *gegenständliche Welt* may be rendered best by 'world of objects'.

object. Man therefore also forms things in accordance with the laws of beauty.

It is just in his work upon the objective world, therefore, that man first really proves himself to be a *species being*. This production is his active species life. Through and because of this production, nature appears as *his* work and his reality. The object of labor is, therefore, the *objectification of man's species life*: for he duplicates himself not only, as in consciousness, intellectually, but also actively, in reality, and therefore he contemplates himself in a world that he has created. In tearing away from man the object of his production, therefore, estranged labor tears from him his *species life*, his real objectivity as a member of the species and transforms his advantage over animals into the disadvantage that his inorganic body, nature, is taken away from him.

Similarly, in degrading spontaneous, free, activity, to a means, estranged labor makes man's species life a means to his physical existence.

The consciousness which man has of his species is thus transformed by estrangement in such a way that species life becomes for him a means.

Estranged labor turns thus:

3. *Man's species being*, both nature and his spiritual species property, into a being *alien* to him, into a *means* to his *individual existence*. It estranges from man his own body, as well as external nature and his spiritual essence, his *human* being.

4. An immediate consequence of the fact that man is estranged from the product of his labor, from his life activity, from his species being is the *estrangement of man* from *man*. When man confronts himself, he confronts the *other* man. What applies to a man's relation to his work, to the product of his labor and to himself, also holds of a man's relation to the other man, and to the other man's labor and object of labor.

In fact, the proposition that man's species nature is estranged from him means that one man is estranged from the other, as each of them is from man's essential nature.

The estrangement of man, and in fact every relationship in which man stands to himself, is first realized and expressed in the relationship in which a man stands to other men.

Hence within the relationship of estranged labor each man views the other in accordance with the standard and the relationship in which he finds himself as a worker.

We took our departure from a fact of political economy – the estrangement of the worker and his production. We have formulated this fact in conceptual terms as *estranged*, *alienated* labor. We have analysed this concept – hence analysing merely a fact of political economy.

Let us now see, further, how the concept of estranged, alienated labor must express and present itself in real life.

If the product of labor is alien to me, if it confronts me as an alien power, to whom, then, does it belong?

If my own activity does not belong to me, if it is an alien, a coerced activity, to whom, then, does it belong?

To a being *other* than myself.

Who is this being?

The *gods*? To be sure, in the earliest times the principal production (for example, the building of temples, etc. in Egypt, India and Mexico) appears to be in the service of the gods and the product belongs to the gods. However, the gods on their own were never the lords of labor. No more was *nature*. And what a contradiction it would be if, the more man subjugated nature by his labor and the more the miracles of the gods were rendered superfluous by the miracles of industry, the more man were to renounce the joy of production and the enjoyment of the product in favor of these powers.

The *alien* being, to whom labor and the product of labor belongs, in whose service labor is done and for whose benefit the product of labor is provided, can only be *man* himself.

If the product of labor does not belong to the worker, if it confronts him as an alien power, then this can only be because it belongs to some *other man than the worker*. If the worker's activity is a torment to him, to another it must be *delight* and his life's joy. Not the gods, not nature, but only man himself can be this alien power over man.

We must bear in mind the previous proposition that man's relation to himself only becomes for him *objective* and *actual*[8]

8. *Gegenständlich*, *wirklich*, in Marx, see previous note. Just as *gegen-*

through his relation to the other man. Thus, if the product of his labor, his labor *objectified*, is for him an *alien*, hostile, powerful object independent of him, then his position towards it is such that someone else is master of this object, someone who is alien, hostile, powerful and independent of him. If his own activity is to him related as an unfree activity, then he is related to it as an activity performed in the service, under the dominion, the coercion and the yoke of another man.

Every self-estrangement of man, from himself and from nature, appears in the relation in which he places himself and nature to men other than and differentiated from himself. For this reason religious self-estrangement necessarily appears in the relationship of the layman to the priest, or again to a mediator, etc., since we are here dealing with the intellectual world. In the real practical world self-estrangement can only become manifest through the real practical relationship to other men. The medium through which estrangement takes place is itself *practical*. Thus through estranged labor man not only creates his relationship to the object and to the act of production as to men that are alien and hostile to him; he also creates the relationship in which other men stand to his production and to his product, and the relationship in which he stands to these other men. Just as he creates his own production as the loss of his reality, as his punishment; his own product as a loss, as a product not belonging to him; so he creates the domination of the person who does not produce over production and over the product. Just as he estranges his own activity from himself, so he confers to the stranger an activity which is not his own.

We have until now only considered this relationship from the standpoint of the worker and later we shall be considering it also from the standpoint of the non-worker.

Through *estranged, alienated labor*, then, the worker produces the relationship to this labor of a man alien to labor and standing outside it. The relationship of the worker to labor creates the relation to it of the capitalist (or whatever one chooses to call the

---

ständlich belongs to *Gegenständ*, so does *wirklich* belong to *Wirken*, to work. A better translation might be: 'man's relation to himself only becomes for him a relation of objects and of work'.

master of labor). *Private property* is thus the product, the result, the necessary consequence, of *alienated labor*, of the external relation of the worker to nature and to himself.

Private property thus results by analysis from the concept of *alienated labor*, i.e. of *alienated man*, of estranged labor, of estranged life, of *estranged* man.

True, it is as a result of the *movement of private property* that we have obtained the concept of *alienated labor* (*of alienated life*) from political economy. But on analysis of this concept it becomes clear that though private property appears to be the source, the cause of alienated labor, it is rather its consequence, just as the gods are *originally* not the cause but the effect of man's intellectual confusion. Later this relationship becomes reciprocal.

Only at the last culmination of the development of private property does this, its secret, appear again, namely, that on the one hand it is the *product* of alienated labor and that on the other it is the *means* by which labor alienates itself, the *realization of this alienation*.

This exposition immediately sheds light on various hitherto unsolved conflicts.

1. Political economy starts from labor as the real soul of production; yet to labor it gives nothing and to private property everything. Confronting this contradiction, Proudhon has decided in favor of labor against private property. We understand, however, that this apparent contradiction is the contradiction of *estranged labor* with itself and that political economy has merely formulated the laws of estranged labor.

We also understand, therefore, that *wages* and *private property* are identical: since the product, as the object of labor, pays for labor itself, therefore the wage is but a necessary consequence of labor's estrangement. After all, in the wage of labor, labor does not appear as an end in itself but as the servant of the wage. We shall develop this point later and meanwhile will only derive some conclusions.[9]

9. This obscure paragraph becomes somewhat more intelligible, if we remember that in Hegelian terminology 'identity' often stands for 'unity'. There is, Marx seems to say, a unity of opposites between wages and private property, since wages result in private property and private property is the

An enforced increase of wages (disregarding all other difficulties, including the fact that it would only be by force, too, that higher wages, being an anomaly, could be maintained) would therefore be nothing but *better payment for the slave* and would not win either for the worker or for labor their human status and dignity.

Indeed, even the *equality of wages* demanded by Proudhon only transforms the relationship of the present-day worker to his labor into the relationship of all men to labor. Society is then conceived as an abstract capitalist.

Wages are a direct consequence of estranged labor and estranged labor is the direct cause of private property. The downfall of the one must involve the downfall of the other.

2. From the relationship of estranged labor to private property it follows further that the emancipation of society from private property, etc. from servitude, is expressed in the *political* form of the *emancipation of the workers*; not that *their* emancipation alone is at stake, but because the emancipation of the workers contains universal human emancipation – and it contains this, because the whole of human servitude is involved in the relation of the worker to production, and every relation of servitude is but a modification and consequence of this relation.

Just as we have derived the concept of *private property* from the concept of *estranged*, *alienated labor* by *analysis*, so we can develop every *category* of political economy with the help of these two factors; and we shall find again in each category, e.g., trade, competition, capital, money, only a *definite* and *developed expression* of these first elements.

Before considering this aspect, however, let us try to solve two problems.

1. To define the general *nature of private property*, as it has arisen as a result of estranged labor, in its relation to *truly human* and *social property*.

2. We have accepted the *estrangement of labor*, its *alienation*, as a fact and we have analysed this fact. How, we now ask, does *man* come to *alienate*, to estrange, *his labor*? How is this estrangement

_____
result of the wage system. Labor, in this process, plays only a mediating role: wages and property are the real poles.

rooted in the nature of human development? We have already gone a long way to the solution of this problem by *transforming* the question of the *origin of private property* into the question of the relation of *alienated labor* to the course of humanity's development. For when one speaks of *private property*, one thinks of dealing with something external to man. When one speaks of labor, one is directly dealing with man himself. This new formulation of the question already contains its solution.

As to 1: the general nature of private property and its relation to truly human property.

Alienated labor has resolved itself for us into two elements which mutually condition one another or which are but different expressions of one and the same relationship. *Appropriation* appears as *estrangement*, as *alienation*; and *alienation* appears as *appropriation*, *estrangement* as true introduction into society.[10]

We have considered the one side – *alienated* labor in relation to the *worker* himself, i.e. the *relation of alienated labor to itself.* The *property relation of the non-worker to the worker and to labor* we have found as the product, the necessary outcome of this relationship. *Private property*, as the material, summary expression of alienated labor, embraces both relations – the *relation of the worker to work and to the product of his labor and to the non-worker*, and the relation of the *non-worker to the worker and to the product of his labor.*

Having seen that in relation to the worker who *appropriates* nature by means of his labor, this appropriation appears as estrangement, his own spontaneous activity as activity for another and as activity of another, vitality as a sacrifice of life, production of the object as loss of the object to an alien power, to an *alien* person – we shall now consider the relation to the worker, to labor and its object of this person who is *alien* to labor and the worker.

First, it has to be noted that everything which appears in the worker as an *activity of alienation, of estrangement*, appears in the non-worker as a *state of alienation, of estrangement.*

10. Marx calls estrangement, *die wahre Einbürgerung.* This means 'truly becoming a part of society'. The sentence seems to mean that alienation is the key to society.

Secondly, that the worker's *real, practical attitude* in production and to the product (as a state of mind) appears in the non-worker confronting him as a *theoretical* attitude.

Thirdly, the non-worker does everything against the worker which the worker does against himself; but he does not do against himself what he does against the worker.

Let us look more closely at these three relations.

[*At this point the first manuscript breaks off unfinished.*]

Antithesis of capital and labor. Landed property and capital

... forms the interest on his capital.[11] The worker is the subjective manifestation of the fact that capital is man wholly lost to himself, just as capital is the objective manifestation of the fact that labor is man lost to himself. But the *worker* has the misfortune to be a *living* capital and therefore a capital *with needs* – one which loses its interest, and hence its livelihood, every moment it is not working. The *value* of the worker as capital rises according to demand and supply, and even *physically* his *existence,* his *life,* was and is looked upon as a supply of a *commodity* like any other. The worker produces capital, capital produces him – hence he produces himself and man as *worker,* as a *commodity,* is the product of this entire cycle. To the man who is nothing more than a *worker* – and to him as a worker – his human qualities only exist in so far as they exist for capital *alien* to him. Because man and capital are foreign to each other, however, and thus stand in an indifferent, external and accidental relationship to each other, it is inevitable that this foreignness should also appear as something *real.* As soon, therefore, as it occurs to capital (whether from necessity or caprice) no longer to be for the worker, he himself is no longer for himself: he has *no* work, hence *no* wages, and as he has no existence as a *human being* but only as a *worker,* he can go and bury himself, starve to death, etc. The worker exists as a worker only when he exists *for himself* as capital; and he exists as capital only when some *capital* exists *for him.* The existence of capital is *his* existence, his *life*; as it determines the tenor of his life in a manner indifferent to him.

11. Page XL of Marx's second manuscript opens with these words. The beginning of the sentence is unknown, because the first thirty-nine pages of the manuscript are missing.

Political economy, therefore, does not recognize the unoccupied worker, the workingman, in so far as he happens to be outside this labor relationship. The cheat-thief, swindler, beggar and unemployed; the starving, wretched and criminal workingman – these are *figures* who do not exist for *political economy* but only for other eyes, those of the doctor, the judge, the grave digger and bumbailiff, etc.; such figures are specters outside its domain. For it, therefore, the worker's needs are but the one *need* – to maintain him *whilst he is working* in so far as may be necessary to *prevent the race of laborers from dying out*. The wages of labor have thus exactly the same significance as the *maintenance* and *servicing* of any other productive instrument, or as the *consumption of a capital*, in general, required for its reproduction with interest; or as the oil which is applied to wheels to keep them turning. Wages, therefore, belong to capital's and the capitalist's necessary *costs*, and must not exceed the bounds of this necessity. It was therefore quite logical for the English factory owners, before the Amendment Bill of 1834, to deduct from the wages of the worker the public charity which he was receiving out of the Poor Rate and to consider this to be an integral part of wage.

Production does not simply produce man as a *commodity*, the *human commodity*, man in the role of *commodity*; it produces him in keeping with this role as a *mentally* and physically *dehumanized* being. Immorality, deformity and dulling of the workers and the capitalists. Its product is the *self-conscious and self-acting commodity*. . . the human commodity. . . . Great advance of Ricardo, Mill, etc. on Smith and Say, to declare the *existence* of the human being – the greater or lesser human productivity of the commodity – to be *indifferent* and even *harmful*. Not how many workers are maintained by a given capital, but rather how much interest it brings in, the sum-total of the annual *savings*, is said to be the true purpose of production.

It was likewise a great and logical advance of the newer English political economy,[12] that, whilst elevating *labor* to the position of its *sole* principle, it should at the same time expound with complete clarity the *inverse* relation between wages and interest on capital, and the fact that the capitalist could normally *only* gain by pressing down wages, and vice versa. Not the defrauding of the

12. Ricardo, Mill, etc.

consumer, but the capitalist and the worker defrauding each other, is shown to be the *normal* relationship.

The relations of private property contain latent within them the relation of private property as *labor*, the relation of private property as *capital* and the *mutual* relation of these two to one another. There is the production of human activity as *labor* – that is, as an activity quite alien to itself, to man and to nature, and therefore to consciousness and the flow of life – the *abstract* existence of man as a mere *workman* who may therefore daily fall from his filled void into the absolute void – into his social, and therefore actual, non-existence. On the other hand, there is the production of the object of human activity as *capital* – in which all the natural and social characteristic of the object is *extinguished*; in which private property has lost its natural and social quality (and therefore every political and social illusion, and has lost even the *appearance* of human relationships); in which the *selfsame* capital remains the *same* in the most diverse social and natural manifestations, totally indifferent to its *real* content. This contradiction, driven to the limit, is of necessity the limit, the culmination and the downfall of the whole private-property relationship.

It is therefore another great achievement of the newer English political economy to have declared ground rent to be the difference in the interest yielded by the worst and the best land under cultivation; to have exposed the landowner's romantic illusions – his alleged social importance and identity of his interest with the interest of society, a view still maintained by *Adam Smith* after the physiocrats; and to have anticipated and prepared the movement of the real world which will transform the landowner into an ordinary, prosaic capitalist and thus simplify and sharpen the contradiction between labor and capital and hasten its resolution. *Land as land* and *ground rent as ground rent* have lost their *distinction of rank* and become dumb *capital* and *interest* – or rather, become *capital* and *interest* that only talk money.

The *distinction* between capital and land, between profit and ground rent, and between both and wages, and *industry*, and *agriculture*, and *immovable* and *movable* private property – this distinction is not rooted in the nature of things, but is a *historical* distinction, a *fixed* moment in the formation and development of the contradiction between capital and labor. In industry, etc., as opposed to immovable landed property, is only expressed the way in which industry came into being and the contradiction to agriculture in which industry developed. This distinction of industry only continues to exist as a *special* sort of work – as an *essential*, *important* and *life-embracing* distinction – so long as industry (town life) develops *over* and *against* landed property (aristocratic feudal life) and itself continues to bear the feudal character of its opposite in the form of monopoly, craft, guild, corporation, etc., within which labor still has a *seemingly social* significance, still the significance of *real community life*, and has not yet reached the stage of *indifference* to its content, of complete being-for-self,[13] i.e. of abstraction from all other being, and hence has not yet become *liberated* capital.

But liberated industry, *industry* constituted for itself as such, and *liberated capital* are the necessary *development* of labor. The power of industry over its opposite is at once revealed in the emergence of *agriculture* as a real industry, while previously it left most of the work to the soil and to the *slave* of the soil, through whom the land cultivated itself. With the transformation of the slave into a *free* worker – i.e. into a *hireling* – the landlord himself is transformed into a captain of industry, into a capitalist – a transformation which takes place at first through the intermediacy of the *tenant farmer*. The tenant *farmer*, however, is the landowner's representative – the landowner's revealed *secret*: it is only through him that the landowner has his *economic* existence – his existence as a private proprietor – for the rent of his land only exists due to the competition between the farmers. Thus, in the person of the *tenant farmer* the landlord has already become in essence a *common* capitalist. And thus must work itself out, too, in actual fact: the capitalist engaged in agriculture – the tenant – must become a landlord, or vice versa. The tenant's *industrial trade* is the *landowner's* industrial trade, for the being of the former postulates the being of the latter.

But mindful of their contrasting origin, of their line of descent – the landowner knows the capitalist as his insolent, liberated, enriched slave of yesterday and sees himself as a *capitalist* who is threatened by him. The capitalist knows the landowner as the

13. Being-of-self, *Sein für sich selbst*, another Hegelian expression. Here it stands for 'a fully self-contained being'.

idle, cruel and egotistical master of yesterday; he knows that he injures him as a capitalist and yet that it is to industry that he, the landowner, owes all his present social significance, his possessions and his pleasures; he sees in him a contradiction to *free* industry and to *free* capital – to capital independent of every natural limitation. This contradiction between landowner and capitalist is extremely bitter and each side tells the truth about the other. One need only read the attacks of immovable on movable property and vice versa to obtain a clear picture of their respective worthlessness. The landowner lays stress on the noble lineage of his property, on feudal mementoes, reminiscences, the poetry of recollection, on his romantic disposition, on his political importance, etc.; and when he talks economics, it is *only* agriculture that he holds to be productive. At the same time he depicts his adversary as a sly, haggling, deceitful, greedy, mercenary, rebellious, heart- and soulless cheapjack – extorting, pimping, servile, smooth, flattering, fleecing, dried-up rogue without honor, principles, poetry, substance or anything else – a person estranged from the community who freely trades it away and who breeds, nourishes and cherishes competition and with it pauperism, crime and the dissolution of all social bonds. (Amongst others see the physiocrat *Bergasse*, whom Camille Desmoulins flays in his journal, *Révolutions de France et de Brabant*[14]; see von Vincke, Lancizolle, Haller, Leo, Kosegarten[15] and also Sismondi.[16])*

* See the garrulous, old-Hegelian theologian Funke who tells, after Herr Leo, with tears in his eyes how a slave had refused, when serfdom was abolished, to cease being the *property of the gentry*. See also the *Patriotic Visions* of Justus Möser, which distinguish themselves by the fact that they never for a moment abandon the ingenuous, petty-bourgeois 'home-baked', *ordinary*, narrow, horizon of the philistine, and which nevertheless remain *pure* fancy. This contradiction has given him such an appeal to the German heart.[17]

14. C. Desmoulins, *Révolutions de France et de Brabant, second Trimestre, contenant Mars, Avril et Mai.* Paris, *l'an premier*, no. 16, pp. 139 ff, no. 23, pp. 425 ff, no. 26, pp. 580 ff. Desmoulins was the famous journalist among the Dantonists of the French Revolution; the year is 1793.

15. All German conservative writers of the early nineteenth century.

16. Jean-Charles Simonde de Sismondi (1773–1842), already mentioned before, French historian with socialist tendencies.

17. Justus Möser (1720–94), a lawyer in Osnabrück, wrote the *Patriotische Phantasien* (1774–6), in their day quite influential. The conservative professor in Halle, Heinrich Leo (1799–1878), wrote a history of the Middle Ages (1830).

Movable property for its part, points to the miracles of industry and progress. It is the child of modern times, its legitimate, native-born son. It pities its adversary as a simpleton, *unenlightened* about his own nature (and in this it is completely right), who wants to replace moral capital and free labor by brute, immoral force and serfdom. It depicts him as a Don Quixote, who under the guise of *bluntness, decency, the general interest and stability*, conceals incapacity for progress, greedy self-indulgence, selfishness, sectional interest and evil intent. It declares him an artful *monopolist*; it pours cold water on his reminiscences, his poetry and his romanticism by a historical and sarcastic enumeration of the baseness, cruelty, degradation, prostitution, infamy, anarchy and rebellion, of which romantic castles were the workshops.

It claims to have obtained political freedom for the people; to have loosed the chains which fettered civil society; to have linked together different worlds; to have created trade promoting friendship between the peoples; to have created pure morality and an agreeable degree of culture; to have given the people civilized needs in place of their crude wants and the means of satisfying them. Meanwhile, it claims, the landowner – this idle, troublesome, parasitic grain-jobber – raises the price of the people's basic necessities and so forces the capitalist to raise wages without being able to increase productivity, thus impeding the growth of the nation's annual income, the accumulation of capital and therefore the possibility of providing work for the people and wealth for the country, eventually canceling it, thus producing a general decline – whilst he parasitically exploits *every* advantage of modern civilization without doing the least thing for it and without even abating in the slightest his feudal prejudices. Finally, let him – for whom the cultivation of the land and the land itself exist only as a source of money, which comes to him as a present – let him just take a look at his *tenant farmer* and say whether he himself is not a '*naive*', *deluded, sly* scoundrel who in his heart and in actual fact has for a long time belonged to *free* industry and to *beloved* trade, however much he may protest and prattle about historical memories and ethical or political goals. Everything which he can really advance to justify himself is true only of the *cultivator of the land* (the capitalist and the laborers), of whom the *landowner* is rather the *enemy*. Thus he gives evidence against himself. *Without* capital, landed property is dead, worthless matter. It has been exactly movable property's civilized victory to have discovered and made human labor the source of wealth in place of the dead thing. (See Paul Louis Courier, Saint-Simon, Ganilh, Ricardo, Mill, McCulloch and Destutt de Tracy, and Michel Chevalier.)[18]

The *real* course of development (to be inserted at this point) results in the necessary victory of the *capitalist* over the *landowner* – that is to say, of developed over undeveloped immature private property – just as in general, movement must triumph over immobility – open, self-conscious baseness over hidden, unconscious baseness; *greed* over *self-indulgence*; the avowedly restless, adroit self-interest of *enlightenment* over the parochial, worldwise, naive, idle and deluded *self-interest of superstition*; and *money* over the other forms of private property.

Those states which divine something of the danger attaching to fully developed free industry, to fully developed pure morality and to fully developed philanthropic trade, try, but in vain, to hold in check the capitalization of landed property.

Landed property in its distinction from capital is private property – capital – still afflicted with *local* and political prejudices; it is capital which has not yet regained itself from its entanglement with the world – capital not yet *fully developed*. It must achieve its abstract, that is, its *pure*, expression in the course of its *worldwide development*.

The character of *private property* is expressed by labor, capital, and the relations between these two.

The movement through which these constituents have to pass is:

[*First*] *Unmediated* or *mediated unity of the two*.

Capital and labor, at first still united. Then, though separated and estranged, they reciprocally develop and promote each other as *positive* conditions.

[*Second*] *The two in opposition*, mutually excluding each other. The worker knows the capitalist as his own non-existence, and vice versa: each tries to rob the other of his existence.

[*Third*] *Opposition* of each *to* itself. Capital = stored-up labor

18. French and English economists of the early decades of the nineteenth century.

= labor. Capital as such — splitting into capital *itself* and into its *interest*, and this latter again into *interest* and *profit*. The capitalist completely sacrificed. He falls into the working class, whilst the worker (but only exceptionally) becomes a capitalist. Labor as a moment of capital – its *costs*. Thus the wages of labor – a sacrifice of capital.

Splitting of labor into *labor itself* and the *wages of labor*. The worker himself a capital, a commodity.

Clash of mutual contradictions.

[*The second manuscript ends here.*]

4 István Mészáros

Conceptual Structure of Marx's Theory of Alienation

Excerpts from István Mészáros, *Marx's Theory of Alienation*, Merlin Press, 1970, pp. 99–114 and 123–50.

Conceptual framework of Marx's theory of alienation

The difficulties of Marx's discourse in his *Manuscripts of 1844* are not due merely to the fact that this is a system *in statu nascendi* in which the same problems are taken up over and over again, at an increasingly higher level of complexity, in accordance with the emergence and growing concretization of Marx's vision as a whole – though of course this is one of the main reasons why people often find this work prohibitively complicated. Some of its major difficulties, however, are inherent in Marx's method in general and in the objective characteristics of his subject of analysis.

Marx investigates both the *historical* and the *systematic-structural* aspects of the problematics of alienation in relation to the dual complexities of 'real life' and its 'reflections' in the various forms of thought. Thus he analyses:

1. The manifestations of labour's self-alienation in reality, together with the various institutionalizations, reifications and mediations involved in such a practical self-alienation, i.e. Wage Labour, Private Property, Exchange, Money, Rent, Profit, Value, etc., etc.

2. The reflections of these alienations through religion, philosophy, law, political economy, art, 'abstractly material' science, etc.

3. The interchanges and reciprocities between 1 and 2; for 'the gods in the beginning are not the cause but the effect of man's intellectual confusion. Later this relationship becomes reciprocal' (p. 80).[1]

---

1. Page numbers in brackets throughout this Reading refer to Marx's *Economic and Philosophic Manuscripts of 1844*, trans. M. Milligan, Lawrence & Wishart, 1959. [*Eds.*]

4. The inner dynamism of any particular phenomenon, or field of inquiry, in its development from a lesser to a higher complexity.

5. The structural interrelations of the various social phenomena with each other (of which the reciprocity between 1 and 2 is only a specific type) as well as the historical genesis and renewed dialectical transformation of this whole system of manifold inter-relations.

6. A further complication is that Marx analyses the particular theories themselves in their concrete historical embeddedness, in addition to investigating their structural relations to each other at a particular time (e.g. Adam Smith the political economist compared to Adam Smith the moral philosopher; at the same time the types of answers given by Adam Smith – both as an economist and as a moralist – are situated historically, in relation to the development of capitalism in general).

As we can see, then, the main difficulties we experience in reading the *Economic and Philosophic Manuscripts of 1844*, with the exception of those due to their being a system *in statu nascendi*, are expressions of Marx's efforts directed at adequately dealing with the mystifying complexities of his subject of analysis on the basis of concrete empirical enquiry in place of mere philosophical abstraction.

In the course of his analysis of the various theoretical reflections of actual human self-alienation Marx makes the general point that:

It stems from the very nature of estrangement that each sphere applies to me a *different and opposite yardstick* – ethics one and political economy another; for each is a specific estrangement of man and focuses attention on a *particular round of estranged essential activity*, and each stands in an *estranged relation* to the other. Thus M. Michel Chevalier reproaches Ricardo with having abstracted from ethics. But Ricardo is allowing political economy to speak its own language, and if it does not speak ethically, this is not Ricardo's fault (121).

Thus he emphasizes that the contradictions we encounter in these fields are necessarily inherent in the structural relation of the various disciplines of thought to each other and to a common determinant which paradoxically makes them oppose each other. But how is such a paradoxical relationship possible? How does this double alienation come about?

Before we can make an attempt at elucidating Marx's enigmatic answers to these far from easy questions, we have to embark on a journey back to some fundamentals of Marx's discourse.

Marx's immediate problem is: why is there such a gulf between philosophy and the natural sciences? Why does philosophy remain as alien and hostile to them as they remain to philosophy? This opposition is absurd because

natural science has invaded and transformed human life all the more practically through the medium of industry; and has prepared human emancipation, however directly and much it had to consummate dehumanization. Industry is the actual historical relation of nature, and therefore of natural science, to man. If, therefore, industry is conceived as the exoteric revelation of man's essential powers, we also gain an understanding of the human essence of nature or the natural essence of man. In consequence, natural science will lose its *abstractly material* – or rather, its *idealistic* – tendency, and will become the *basis of human science*, as it has already become the basis of actual human life, albeit in an estranged form. One basis for life and another basis for science is *a priori* a lie. The nature which comes to be in human history – the genesis of human society – is man's real nature; hence *nature* as it comes to be *through industry*, even though in an *estranged form*, is true *anthropological nature* (110–11).

From this quotation it becomes clear that in his criticism of philosophy Marx is not led by some misconceived ideal of remodelling philosophy on *natural* science. Indeed he sharply criticizes both philosophy and the natural sciences. The first for being 'speculative' and the latter for being 'abstractly material' and 'idealistic'. In Marx's view both philosophy and the natural sciences are manifestations of the same estrangement. (The terms 'abstractly material' and 'idealistic' indicate that natural science is now 'in an estranged form' the basis of 'actual human life', because of the fact that it is necessarily interconnected with an alienated form of industry, corresponding to an alienated mode of production, to an alienated form of productive activity.) This is why Marx opposes to *both* 'speculative philosophy' and to 'abstractly material, idealistic natural science' his ideal of a '*human science*'.

What Marx means by 'human science' is a science of concrete synthesis, integrated with real life. Its standpoint is the ideal of non-alienated man whose *actual human* – as opposed to both 'speculatively invented' and to practically dehumanized, 'abstractly material' – needs determine the line of research in every particular field. The achievements of the particular fields – guided right from the beginning by the common frame of reference of a non-fragmented 'human science' – are then brought together into a higher synthesis which in its turn determines the subsequent lines of investigations in the various fields.

This conception of 'human science', in its opposition to 'abstractly material and idealistic' natural science, is obviously directed against the fragmentation and 'unconscious', alienated determination of science. Many instances of the history of science testify that the extent to which certain fundamental lines of research are carried out are greatly determined by factors which lie, strictly speaking, far beyond the boundaries of natural science itself. (To take a topical example: there can be no doubt whatever that *automation* is at least as fundamentally a *social* problem as a *scientific* one.) The lines of research actually followed through in any particular age are necessarily *finite* whereas the lines of *possible* research are always virtually *infinite*. The role of social needs and preferences in scaling down the infinite to the finite is extremely important. However – and this is the point Marx is making – in an alienated society the process of scaling down itself, since it is 'unconsciously' determined by a set of alienated needs, is bound to produce further alienation: the subjection of man to increasingly more powerful instruments of his own making.

The structure of scientific production is basically the same as that of fundamental productive activity in general (all the more because the two merge into one another to a considerable extent): a lack of control of the productive process as a whole; an 'unconscious' and fragmented mode of activity determined by the inertia of the institutionalized framework of the capitalistic mode of production; the functioning of 'abstractly material' science as a mere *means* to predetermined, external, alienated ends. Such an alienated natural science finds itself between the Scylla and Charybdis of its 'autonomy' (i.e. the idealization of its 'unconscious', fragmentary character) and its subordination as a mere *means* to external, alien ends (i.e. gigantic military and quasi-military programmes, such as lunar flights). Needless to say, the subjection of natural science as a mere means to alien ends is by no means accidental but necessarily connected with its fragmented, 'autonomous' character and, of course, with the structure of alienated productive activity in general. Since science develops in a fragmented, compartmentalized framework, it cannot conceivably have overall aims which, therefore, have to be imposed on it from outside.

Philosophy, on the other hand, expresses a twofold alienation of the sphere of speculative thinking (a) from all practice – including the, however alienated, practice of natural science – and (b) from other theoretical fields, like political economy, for instance. In its speculative 'universality' philosophy becomes an 'end in itself' and 'for itself', fictitiously opposed to the realm of means: an abstract reflection of the institutionalized alienation of means from ends. As a radical separation from all other modes of activity philosophy appears to its representatives as the only form of 'species-activity', i.e. as the only form of activity worthy of man as a 'universal being'. Thus instead of being a universal dimension of all activity, integrated in practice and in its various reflections, it functions as an independent (*verselbständigt*) 'alienated universality', displaying the absurdity of this whole system of alienations by the fact that all this fictitious 'universality' is realized as the most esoteric of all esoteric *specialities*, strictly reserved for the alienated 'high priests' (the *Eingeweihten*) of this intellectual trade.

If the 'abstractly material' character of the particular natural sciences is linked to a productive activity fragmented and devoid of perspectives, the 'abstractly contemplative' character of philosophy expresses the radical divorce of theory and practice in its alienated universality. They represent two sides of the same coin: labour's self-alienation manifest in a mode of production characterized by Marx and Engels as 'the unconscious condition of mankind'.

This takes us back to our original problem. Why is it that the different theoretical spheres apply 'a different and opposite yardstick' to man? How is it possible that though both philosophy and political economy express the same alienation, their 'language' is so different that they cannot communicate with each other?

In order to simplify these matters to some extent, let us try and illustrate, however schematically, the structural interrelationship of the principal concepts involved in Marx's theory of alienation. (Schematic illustrations of this kind are always problematical because they have to express in a fixed, 'two-dimensional' form the complexity of dynamic interchanges. It must be stressed, therefore, that they are not meant to be substitutes for an adequate conceptual understanding but merely a visual aid towards it.)

The fundamental terms of reference in Marx's theory of alienation are 'man' (M), 'nature' (N), and 'industry' or 'productive activity' (I). For an understanding of 'the human essence of nature or the natural essence of man' (110) the concept of 'productive activity' (or 'industry' – used from now on for the sake of brevity) is of a crucial importance. 'Industry' is both the *cause* of the growing complexity of human society [by creating new needs while satisfying old ones: 'the first historical act is the *production of new needs*' (Marx and Engels, 1846, p. 40 of 1965 edn)] and the *means* of asserting the supremacy of man – as 'universal being' who is at the same time a unique 'specific being' – over nature. In considering Marx's views we have to remember that when he applies the term 'actual' (*wirklich*) to man he either equates it with 'historical' (110), or simply implies historicity as a necessary condition of the human predicament. He wants to account for every aspect of the analysed phenomena in inherently historical terms, which means that nothing can be taken for granted and simply assumed as an ultimate datum. On the contrary, the whole theory hinges on the proof of the historical *genesis* of all its basic constituents. Accordingly, Marx pictures the relationship between 'man' (M), 'nature' (N), and 'industry' (I) in the form of a *threefold interaction* between its constituent parts. This is illustrated in Figure 1.

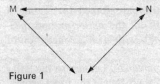

Figure 1

As we can see, here we have a dialectical *reciprocity* (indicated by the double-ended arrows) between all three members of this relationship which means that 'man' is not only the *creator* of industry but also its *product*. (Similarly, of course, he is both product and creator of 'truly anthropological nature' – above all in himself, but also outside him, in so far as he leaves his mark on nature. And since man's relation to nature is mediated through an alienated form of productive activity, 'anthropological nature' outside man bears the marks of this alienation in an ever-extending form, graphically demonstrated by the intensity of *pollution* that menaces the very existence of mankind.)

Talking about this process of reciprocal interaction, Marx calls it the 'genesis of human society'. At the same time he designates the two main aspects of industry's fundamental (first order) mediating function by the expressions 'natural essence of man' and 'human essence of nature' (110). His expression: 'man's real nature' – as opposed to man's biological or animal nature – is meant to embrace both aspects and thus to define *human nature* in terms of a necessarily *threefold* relationship of dialectical reciprocity. Man's biological or animal nature, by contrast, can only be defined in terms of a *twofold* relationship or, to put it the other way round, picturing the basic ontological situation merely in terms of a twofold relationship, between 'man' and 'nature', would only account for the characteristics of man's biological-animal nature. For human consciousness implies already a specific human relation to 'industry' (taken in its most general sense as 'productive activity'). One of the basic contradictions of theories which idealize the *unmediated* reciprocity between 'man' and 'nature' is that they get themselves into the impasse of this animal relationship from which not a single feature of the dynamism of human history can be derived. Then, in an attempt to get rid of this contradiction – in order to be able to account for the specifically human characteristics – they are forced to assume a 'ready-made human nature', with all the *apriorism* and *theological teleologism* that necessarily go with such a conception of philosophy.

Rousseau's conception, *mutatis mutandis*, belongs to the latter category, though in a paradoxical way. For in the most generic terms Rousseau is aware of the ludicrous character of idealizing nature. He stresses that

> he who wants to preserve, in civil society, the primacy of natural feelings, has no idea of what he wants. Always standing in contradiction to himself, always oscillating between his inclinations and his duties, he will be neither a man nor a *citoyen*; he will be good neither for himself nor for others. He will be one of those people of our age; a Frenchman, an Englishman, a *bourgeois*: a *nothing* (Rousseau, 1762, p. 40 of 1966 edn).

And yet, this insight never induces Rousseau to elaborate a genuinely historical account of man and his relationships. On the contrary, despite his insights he continues to operate with the fictitious notion of 'preserving man's original constitution'[2]. (It must be emphasized that his idealization of a – hierarchical – *family* as the *anthropological model* of 'natural' relations – opposed to the system which produces an 'artificial being' – proves to be a major drawback in his analyses.) Even if he recognizes the irrevocable remoteness of the 'original' direct unity – in Hegelian terms the inherently *past* character of Er-*innerung* as opposed to the *present* actuality of Ent-*äusserung* – he continues, unlike Hegel, to postulate it, often in a negative form, in his sentimental negation of 'civilization'. In Rousseau's conception, 'industry' (civilization) exercises an essentially *disruptive* function, by putting an end to a 'natural' relationship. Such an interpretation may enable the philosopher to grasp certain

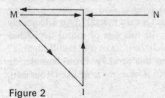

Figure 2

contradictions of a given stage of society, but it does not allow him to indicate a solution that could stand the test of actual historical development. 'Industry' (civilization) comes into the picture as something '*evil*', even if Rousseau recognizes, nostalgically, that

2. See, for instance, a few pages after this criticism of the 'bourgeois . . . a nothing' (Rousseau, 1762, p. 51 of 1966 edn).

it cannot be done away with. Thus his system, at its very foundations, is profoundly *ahistorical*. It is illustrated in contrast to
Marx's conception in Figure 2.

As we can see, there is a kind of 'short circuit' in this account,
and the one-sided interaction between man and industry results in
the tragic negativity of divorcing or alienating man from nature.
(It would be interesting to inquire into the relationship between
Rousseau's conception of man and nature and the Kantian notion
of *das Böse* – 'evil' – and in general the Kantian philosophy of
history, its tragic vision of man.) Since the fundamental ontological relations are pictured by Rousseau in these terms, his
educational ideal of preserving the 'original' substance of human-
ness by cultivating the 'naturally good' in man, is bound to
remain not only Utopian but also tragically hopeless. The 'short-
circuit' produces a 'vicious circle' which cannot be broken except
by the unwarranted assumption of a 'ready-made' educator.
Rousseau himself is conscious of the problematic character of
such a construction but, given his fundamental concepts, he cannot do anything against it.

The more we reflect the more we recognize the growing difficulties. For
the educator *ought to have been* educated for his pupil; the servants
ought to have been educated for their masters, so that all those who
are in the pupil's vicinity would communicate to him the right things;
one should go backwards from education to education up to I do not
know which point. Otherwise how could one expect the proper education of a child from someone who himself had not been properly
educated? Is it impossible to find such a rare mortal? [An adequately
educated educator.] I do not know. In this age of moral decadence
who knows the height of virtue of which the human soul is still capable?
But *let us assume* that we have found this prodigy. From considering
what he *ought* to do we can find out what he *ought to be* like (Rousseau,
1762, p. 53 of 1966 edn).

Being is thus derived from *ought* in order to serve as the pivotal
point of this whole system of postulates opposed to the actuality
of 'civilization'. Since the foundation of all historicity – which is
also the only possible ground of an 'education of the educator' –
is negated, the educator must be fictitiously assumed and assigned
the unreal function of protecting the 'natural being' from the
temptations of civilization, money, sophistication, etc., thus edu-

cationally rescuing him from the perspectives of becoming an 'artificial being'. The tragic Utopianism of this whole approach is manifest in the all-pervasive contradiction that while Rousseau *negates* the ontologically fundamental mediation of man and nature through 'industry' (not only in his explicit polemics against 'civilization' but primarily by postulating 'natural man') he positively *affirms* the alienated mediations of this mediation (a) by idealizing the alleged anthropological primacy of a rigidly hierarchical family; (b) by postulating an – equally hierarchical – system of education in which 'the servant is educated for the master', and 'everyone is educated for his own station' etc., and in which the educator is miraculously 'set above' the rest of society; and (c) by asserting the atemporal nature and ideal necessity of the capitalistically institutionalized second order mediations – 'fair and advantageous exchange', the eternal permanence of 'meum' and 'tuum', etc. – as we have seen already. No wonder, therefore, that the overall impression of Rousseau's conception is a *static* one, adequately expressed in the tragic pathos of a revolt condemned to inertia and impotence. A pathos expressing the unfavourable configuration of a set of contradictions, perceived and depicted from a specific socio-historical standpoint by this great philosopher and writer.

Marx's approach is radically different. He is not talking simply about man's alienation from 'nature' as such, but about man's alienation from *his own* nature, from 'anthropological nature' (both within and outside man). This very concept of 'man's own nature' *necessarily implies* the ontologically fundamental self-mediation of man with nature through his own productive (and self-producing) activity. Consequently 'industry' (or 'productive activity') as such, acquires an essentially *positive* connotation in the Marxian conception, rescuing man from the theological dilemma of 'the fall of man'.

If such an essentially positive role is assigned to 'industry' in the Marxian conception, how then can we explain 'alienation' as 'self-alienation', i.e. as the 'alienation of labour', as the 'alienation of human powers from man through his own productive activity'?

To anticipate, briefly, the central topic of the next chapter in so far as is necessary in this connection, let us draw up a comparative diagram. Let M stand for 'man', P for 'private property and its owner', L for 'wage labour and the worker', AN for 'alienated nature' (61–3), and AI for 'alienated industry' or 'alienated productive activity', then we can illustrate the changed relationships as in Figure 3.

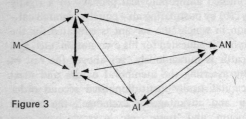

Figure 3

Here, as a result of 'labour's self-alienation' – the objectification of productive activity in the form of 'alienated labour' (or 'estranged essential activity', to use another of Marx's expressions) – we have a multiplicity of basic interrelations:

1. M is split into P and L.

2. P and L antagonistically oppose each other.

3. The original M ↔ I ↔ N reciprocity is transformed into the alienated interrelationships between:

(a) P ↔ AI ↔ AN and
(b) L ↔ AI ↔ AN.

Furthermore, since now everything is subordinated to the basic antagonism between P and L, we have the additional alienated interrelations of:

4. P ↔ L ↔ AI and

5. P ↔ L ↔ AN.

In these sets of relationships in which the second order mediations of P and L have taken the place of 'man' (M), the concepts of 'man' and 'mankind' may appear to be mere philosophical abstractions to all those who cannot see beyond the direct immediacy of the given alienated relations. (And they are indeed abstractions if they are not considered in terms of the socio-historically concrete forms of alienation which they assume.) The disappearance of 'man' from the picture, his practical suppression through the second order mediations of P and L – (we had to omit the other institutionalized second order mediations, e.g. Exchange, Money, etc., partly because they are already implied in P and L, and partly in order to simplify the basic interrelations as far as possible) – means not only that there is a *split* now at every link of these alienated relationships but also that Labour can be considered as a mere '*material fact*', instead of being appreciated as the *human* agency of production.

The problem of the reflection of this 'reification' in the various theoretical fields is inseparable from this double mediation, i.e. from the 'mediation of the mediation'. The political economist gives a 'reified', 'fetishistic' account of the actual social relations of production when, from the standpoint of idealized Private Property (P) he treats Labour (L) as a mere material fact of production and fails to relate both P and L to 'man' (M). (When Adam Smith, as Marx observes, starts to take 'man' into account, he leaves immediately the ground of political economy and shifts to the speculative viewpoint of ethics.)

Now we are in a better position for understanding Marx's assertion according to which each theoretical sphere applies a different, indeed opposite yardstick to man and 'each stands in an estranged relation to the other'. For if the foundation of theoretical generalizations is not the fundamental ontological relationship of $M \leftrightarrow I \leftrightarrow N$ but its *alienated form*: the reified 'mediation of the mediation' – i.e. $M \leftrightarrow P \leftrightarrow L \leftrightarrow AI \leftrightarrow AN$ – then political economy, for instance, which *directly* identifies itself with the standpoint of private property, is bound to formulate its discourse in terms of P and L, whereas ethics, in accordance with its own position which coincides only *indirectly* with 'the standpoint of political economy' (i.e. the standpoint of private property), will speculatively oppose the abstract concept of 'man' to P and L. The fact that both disciplines approach, from different – though only methodologically, not socially different – points of view, the same complex phenomenon, remains hidden from the representatives of both speculative, moralizing philosophy and empiricist political economy.

We could illustrate the respective positions of ethics, political economy and the 'abstractly material' natural sciences in relation to the alienated and reified social relations of production (Figure 4).

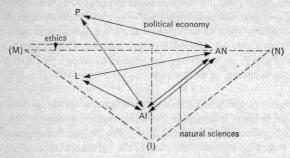

Figure 4

As we can see, the 'language' of political economy and ethics – not to mention the natural sciences – cannot be common because their central points of reference are far from being the same (118–19). Political economy's points of reference are P ↔ AN ↔ L and P ↔ AI ↔ AN, whereas ethics (and, *mutatis mutandis*, speculative philosophy in general) has for its centre of reference abstract 'man' (or its even more abstract versions, like 'world spirit' etc.), depicted in his relations with 'nature' and 'industry' or 'civilization' more often than not in a Rousseau-like fashion, with all the apriorism and transcendentalism involved in it. (The points of reference of the natural sciences are, of course, AN and AI, in their dual orientation towards nature, or 'basic research', on the one hand, and towards productive technology, or 'applied science', on the other. Intensified 'alienation of nature' – e.g. *pollution* – is unthinkable without the most active participation of the natural sciences in this process. They receive their tasks from 'alienated industry', in the form of capitalistic 'targets of production' – i.e. targets subordinated to the 'blind natural laws' of the market – irrespective of the ultimate human implications and repercussions of the realization of such tasks.)

Moreover, as Marx emphasizes, the idealization of abstract 'man' is nothing but an alienated, speculative expression of the $P \leftrightarrow L$ relationship. The nature of the actual relationships is such that to comprehend them adequately it is necessary to assume a radically critical attitude towards the system of alienations which 'externalizes' (or 'objectifies') man in the form of 'alienated labour' and 'reified private property'. 'Real man' – the 'real, human person' – does not actually exist in a capitalist society except in the alienated and reified form in which we encounter him as 'labour' and 'capital' (private property) antagonistically opposing each other. Consequently the 'affirmation' of 'man' must proceed via the *negation* of the alienated social relations of production. Speculative philosophy, however, does not *negate* the $P \leftrightarrow L \leftrightarrow AI \leftrightarrow AN$ relationship but merely *abstracts* from it. And through its abstract concept of 'man' which ignores the basic antagonism of society, the actuality of $P \leftrightarrow L$, speculative philosophy depicts the alienated social relations of production – in accordance with its own specific ideological function – in a 'sublimated' fashion, transforming the 'palpable reality' of actual social contradictions into a fictitious, and *a priori* insoluble, opposition between the 'realm of here and now' and its 'transcendental' counterpart.

It is clear from the Marxian account that the various theoretical spheres reflect – in a necessarily alienated form, corresponding to a set of specific alienated needs – the actual alienation and reification of the social relations of production. They all focus attention 'on a particular round of estranged essential activity' (i.e. political economy on the reproduction of the economic cycle of production; speculative philosophy on 'spiritual activity' and on the norms regulating human behaviour, in its most general terms; and the 'abstractly material' natural sciences on the conditions of a direct interchange between man and nature) and they stand 'in an estranged relation to each other'.

Since neither political economy nor speculative philosophy have a real awareness of the social dynamism inherent in the antagonism between private property and labour – and precisely because they cannot possibly recognize the objective character of this antagonism as one 'hastening to its annulment' – their systems must remain *static*, corresponding to the necessarily ahistorical

István Mészáros 137

standpoint of private property which they represent, directly or indirectly. Viewed from such a standpoint they can only perceive – at best – the *subjective* aspect of this basic contradiction: the direct clash of individuals over 'goods' or 'property', but they cannot grasp the *social necessity* of such clashes. Instead they either interpret them as manifestations of 'egoistic *human nature*' – which amounts to an actual defence of the position of private property under the semblance of a 'moral condemnation' of 'human egoism' – or, more recently, treat these clashes as problems of a 'lack of communication', as tasks for a 'human engineering', aiming at devising methods for a minimization of 'conflicts about property', in order to ensure the continued existence of the alienated social relations of production.

Marx, by contrast, grasps this whole complexity of interrelated concepts at their strategic centre: the *objective* social dynamism of the contradiction between Property and Labour. He recognizes that 'human life required private property for its realization' (134) because 'only through developed industry – i.e. through the *medium* of private property – does the *ontological essence* of human passion come to be both in its totality and in its humanity' (136). Alienation, reification and their alienated reflections are therefore socio-historically *necessary* forms of expression of a fundamental ontological relationship. This is the 'positive aspect' of labour's self-alienation.

At the same time Marx emphasizes the negative aspect as well. The latter is directly displayed in the social contradiction between Private Property and Labour: a contradiction which, however, cannot be perceived from the standpoint of private property, nor from that of a spontaneous identification with labour in its partiality, but only from the critically adopted standpoint of labour in its self-transcending universality. In Marx's eyes the increasing evidence of an irreconcilable social antagonism between private property and labour is a proof of the fact that the ontologically necessary phase of labour's self-alienation and reified self-mediation – 'through the medium of private property', etc. – is drawing to its close. The intensification of the social antagonism between private property and labour demonstrates the innermost contradiction of the given productive system and greatly contributes to its disintegration. Thus human self-objectification in the form of self-alienation loses its relative historical justification and becomes an indefensible social anachronism.

Ontological necessity cannot be realistically opposed except by another ontological necessity. Marx's line of reasoning – in stressing the *relative* (historical) necessity of self-alienation as well as the disruptive *social anachronism* of self-objectification as self-alienation at a later stage of development – establishes *Aufhebung* (the transcendence of alienation) as a concept denoting *ontological necessity*. Marx argues that what is at stake is the *necessity* of an *actual* supersession of the earlier indispensable but by now increasingly more paralysing (therefore historically untenable) reification of the social relations of production. In this respect, too, his theory brings a radical break with the views of his predecessors who could picture 'transcendence' either as a mere *moral postulate* (a *Sollen*) or as an abstract *logical requirement* of a speculative scheme devoid of practical relevance.

As to the transcendence of alienation in the theoretical fields, it must be clear from what has been said so far that Marx's ideal of a 'human science' is not meant to be a programme of remodelling philosophy and the humanities on the natural sciences. Not only because the latter are also specific forms of alienation but, above all, because we are concerned here with a practical, not with a theoretical issue. For whatever model we may have in mind as our ideal of philosophical activity, its applicability will depend on the totality of social practice which generates, in any particular sociohistorical situation, the practicable intellectual needs not less than the material ones. The realization of Marx's ideal of a 'human science' presupposes, therefore, the 'self-sustaining' ('*positive*') existence of such – non-alienated – needs in the social body as a whole. Marx's formulation of the ideal itself, by contrast, corresponds to the needs of *negating* – under their theoretical aspects – the totality of the existing social relations of production. 'Human science', therefore, becomes a reality to the extent to which alienation is *practically* superseded and thus the totality of social practice loses its fragmented character. (In this fragmentation, theory is opposed to practice and the particular fields of 'estranged essential activity' – both theoretical and practical – oppose each other.) In other words, in order to realize 'human science' philosophy, political economy, the 'abstractly material' natural sciences, etc. must be *reciprocally integrated* among themselves, as well as with the totality of a social practice no longer characterized by the alienation and reification of the social relations of production. For 'human science' is precisely this *dual integration* – in transcendence of the earlier seen *dual alienation* – of the particular theoretical fields (a) among themselves and (b) with the totality of a non-alienated social practice.

The *übergreifendes Moment* (overriding factor) of this complex is, of course, the supersession of alienation in social practice itself. Since, however, alienated social practice is already integrated, in an 'inverted' and alienated form, with 'abstractly material' science and speculative philosophy, the actual transcendence of alienation in social practice is inconceivable without superseding at the same time the alienations of the theoretical fields as well. Thus Marx conceives the actual process of *Aufhebung* as a *dialectical interchange* between these two poles – the theoretical and the practical – in the course of their *reciprocal reintegration*. [...]

Marx's critique of political economy

The general character of a work is determined by its writer's standpoint. It is important to ask, therefore, what is Marx's standpoint when he analyses the various aspects of alienation. It is relevant here, that Marx had reproached Proudhon with having criticized political economy from the standpoint of political economy, thus ending up with the contradiction of abolishing political-economic estrangement *within* political-economic estrangement.[3] Likewise Marx characterized Hegel as having the standpoint of modern political economy (154).

The problem of the philosopher's standpoint, as regards alienation, is identical, in the final analysis, to the problem of his attitude towards the *supersession* (*Aufhebung*) of alienation. To share 'the standpoint of political economy' means to be unable to work out in concrete terms the conditions of an actual supersession. And to supersede alienation 'within political-economic alienation' means not to supersede it at all.

When Marx writes about alienation, he is careful to distinguish

3. See in particular Marx and Engels, *Werke*, vol. 2, pp. 32, 34 and 44.

his position from the Utopian criticism of political economy. In fact he had criticized Proudhon as early as the 1840s for his inability to detach himself from the Utopian approach to the category of property of the French socialists like Saint-Simon and Fourier.[4] We shall soon see the concrete economic problems involved in Proudhon's Utopianism as criticized in Marx's *Manuscripts of 1844*. It was Proudhon's inability to solve these problems that made him adopt contradictorily, in spite of his explicit programmatic intentions, the standpoint of political economy 'in a roundabout way'.[5]

Why had Marx to oppose the standpoint of political economy?

Basically because it was in contradiction to the historical approach that could envisage the supersession of alienation.

Marx characterizes the position of political economy as one based on a 'fictitious primordial condition'. This fictitious primordial condition is a fallacious line of reasoning: in this case it exhibits the characteristic of a *petitio principii*. The political economist

assumes in the form of fact, of an event, what he is supposed to *deduce* – namely the necessary relationship between two things – between, for example, division of labour and exchange. Theology in the same way explains the origin of evil by the fall of man; that is, it *assumes as a fact*, in historical form, *what has to be explained* (68–9).

Fallacies of this kind pervade the history of thought. Their varieties are determined by the particular character of the disregarded concrete historical interconnections. (Some neglect or ignore the existing relations; others assert non-existing connections; others again reverse the order of the actual interrelations, etc.)

Here we see a good example of a basic characteristic of Marxian thought; namely that the historical approach to everything is at the same time a substantiation of the categories of logic in concrete historical terms. In this sense *petitio principii* is nothing but a

4. For a general evaluation of Marx's relation to Proudhon see his letter to J. B. von Schweitzer, 24 January 1865, Marx and Engels, *Werke*, vol. 16, p. 25.

5. See Marx and Engels, *Werke*, vol. 16, p. 28.

relational determination which excludes the question of the concrete historical *becoming* (*Werden*) by *assuming* an *a priori being* (*Sein*), in order to explain away the difficulties and contradictions of a *determinate being* (*bestimmtes Dasein*).

On this account no relation or social fact – which is, by definition, a relation – can be accepted as given. Everything specific, everything that has a form (since every particular form expresses a specific *relation* to its *content*) must be explained in terms of *becoming*, and so no primordial condition can be assumed. This is why Marx starts out by defining the historically primary relationship between man and nature as *nature's relation to itself*, on the grounds that man is a specific part of nature. Even as regards nature itself, without a concrete historical reference nothing more can be asserted than that it is identical with itself, whereas the assertion of the part–whole relationship (man as a specific part of the totality of nature) requires an inherently historical conception.

In order to define man as a specific part of nature, one must have not only a comprehensive historical conception of nature itself, which accounts for the possibility, indeed necessity, of differentiation within nature (a necessity dependent on the generation of conditions incompatible with the previous state of affairs), but also a particular factor which necessitates a *peculiar form of differentiation* that results in the intrinsic man–nature relationship.

The factor that involves this peculiar form of differentiation (that is the one which reformulates the part–whole relationship in this way: man, a specific part of nature) is 'industry', 'purposive activity', 'essential life-activity'. In this sense the concept of activity (labour) is logically (and historically) *prior* to the concept of man. But this priority is, of course, a *relative* one, for all three members of this dialectical relationship belong to the same complex whole and none of them can be abstracted from it without destroying this specific relationship as such.

Marx opposes to the approach of the political economist,[6] which has at its point of departure the logical structure of a *petitio principii*, a method of proceeding 'from an actual economic fact'. And this fact is that 'Labour produces not only commodities: *it produces itself and the worker as a commodity* – and does so in the

6. Marx often compares the political economists to the theologians. In

proportion in which it produces commodities generally' (69).

This point about labour producing itself and the worker as a commodity is of the utmost importance for the understanding of Marx's position on the question of supersession. Since the very foundation of human existence and of all human attributes is the purposive productive activity which has, as we have seen, a relative priority over the concept of man, if one cannot present labour in a historical framework, showing the actual process in which purposive productive activity *becomes* wage labour (or 'alienated labour'), one has no ground for envisaging a supersession.

Marx formulates this point very clearly in *Capital* when he writes:

It is clear that capital presupposes labour as wage labour. But it is just as clear that *if labour as wage labour is taken as the point of departure*, so that the identity of labour in general with wage labour appears to be self-evident, then capital and monopolized land must also appear as the *natural* form of the conditions of labour in relation to labour in general. To be capital, then, appears as the natural form of the means of labour and thereby as the purely real character arising from their function in the labour process in general. *Capital and produced means of production thus become identical terms.* . . . Labour as such, in its simple capacity as *purposive productive activity, relates to the means of production, not in their social determinate form,* but rather in their concrete substance, as material and means of labour (Marx, 1894, p. 804 of 1958 edn).

As we see, Marx's concept of 'alienated labour' (or wage labour) is inseparable from his idea that the *social determinate form* of the productive activity which obtains the 'increasing value of the world of things' at the price of the 'devaluation of the world of men' is one that can be superseded.

---

his *Capital*, for instance, he quotes the following passage from the original French edition of his work, *Misère de la philosophie* (1847): 'Les économistes ont une singulière manière de procéder. Il n'y a pour eux que deux sortes d'institutions, celles de l'art et celles de la nature. Les institutions de la féodalité sont des institutions artificielles, celles de la bourgeoisie sont des institutions naturelles. Ils ressemblent en ceci aux théologiens, qui eux aussi établissent deux sortes de réligions. Toute réligion qui n'est pas la leur, est une invention des hommes, tandis que leur propre réligion est une émanation de Dieu – ainsi il y a eu de l'histoire, mais il n'y en a plus' (Marx, 1867, p. 81 of 1958 edn).

Marx's interest in problems of political economy is directly related to this question of supersession. He emphasizes that 'the entire revolutionary movement necessarily finds both *its empirical and its theoretical basis* in the movement of private property – in that of *economy*, to be precise' (102), and most of the criticism the young Marx directs against his political comrades concerns their relation to the problem of a practical transcendence of human alienation.

One of the most important passages on this point, in the *Manuscripts of 1844*, reads as follows:

This material, immediately sensuous private property is the material sensuous expression of estranged human life. Its movement – production and consumption – is the sensuous revelation of the movement of all production hitherto – i.e. the realization or the reality of man. Religion, family, state, law, morality, science, art, etc., are only particular modes of production, and fall under its general law. The positive transcendence of private property as the appropriation of human life is, therefore, the positive transcendence of all estrangement – that is to say, the return of man from religion, family, state, etc., to his human, i.e. social mode of existence. Religious estrangement as such occurs only in the realm of consciousness, of man's inner life, but economic estrangement is that of real life; its transcendence therefore embraces both aspects (102–3).

It is self-evident that one cannot fight estrangement of real life – that is, economic estrangement – without mastering in theory the complex economico-social problems involved in it. But the kind of economic investigations that Marx envisages make no sense whatsoever unless one's attitude to the question of 'practice' is essentially the same as his. Thus Marx's criticism here is directed not only against the representatives of speculative philosophy, but also against those who, like Feuerbach, are only capable of conceiving practice in its 'dirty-judaical form of appearance'.[7]

On the other hand the attempts of the '*piecemeal reformers*' (30) at formulating their views in economico-institutional form is also condemned to futility, because the reformer aims at an improvement *within* the given structure, and by the means of the same

7. (109–10). Although Feuerbach's name is not mentioned here, the implicit criticism applies to his work as well.

structure, and is therefore subject to the very contradictions which he intends to counteract or neutralize.

To Marx, in contradistinction to the reformer, economic investigations do not serve as theoretical grounds of an *economic* action, but of a *political* one. He is interested in problems of economy only in so far as they reveal the complex hierarchy of the structure that he wants to see positively transcended. He wants to unveil not the '*weak*' points of the capitalist system (which were anyway quite obvious, because of their striking human repercussions, to many moralist critics well before Marx), but its *strong* ones. Those which converge into the outcome he calls '*movable property*'s *civilized victory*' (91) i.e. the victory of early capitalism over feudalism.

Marx's economic investigations helped him to discover the internal contradictions of the economic force that resulted in this 'civilized victory', and so to open up the field for action of a quite different kind. Different, because an *economic action* could only alleviate the contradictions of a dynamic force – the one behind movable property's civilized victory – which is itself *economic* in character.

This is why Marx objects so strongly, already in the *Manuscript of 1844*, to Proudhon's approach to the matter. He writes:

The diminution in the interest of money, which Proudhon regards as the annulling of capital and as the tendency to socialize capital, is really and immediately . . . only a symptom of the victory of working capital over extravagant wealth – i.e. the transformation of all private property into industrial capital. It is a total victory of private property over all those of its qualities which are still in appearance human, and the complete subjection of the owner of private property to the essence of private property – labour. . . . The decrease in the interest-rate is therefore a symptom of the annulment of capital only inasmuch as it is a symptom of the rule of capital in the process of perfecting itself – of the estrangement in the process of becoming fully developed and therefore of hastening to its annulment. This is indeed the only way in which that which exists affirms its opposite (127–8).

As we see, the standpoint of this economic analysis is not an economic but a *political* one, and everything culminates in the reference to the 'process of becoming fully developed', interpreted as a hastening of estrangement to the point at which it is annulled.

Indeed the question of a positive transcendence can only be put in *political* terms so long as the society which is thought of as an actual supersession of the one criticized is still to be born. It is a characteristic of politics (and, naturally, of aesthetics, ethics, etc.) to *anticipate* (and thus to further) future social and economic developments. Politics could be defined as the *mediation* (and, with its institutions, as a means of this mediation) between the *present and future* states of society. Its categories, accordingly, exhibit the character appropriate to this mediating function, and references to the future are therefore an integral part of its categories. (Conservative politics exhibits just as much as radical politics the characteristics of this mediating function. Only its categories are less explicit and the positive stress is, of course, on defining its relation to the present. The conservative kind of political mediation tries to maximize the element of continuity in its attempt at linking the present with the future whereas radical politics, of course, lays the emphasis on discontinuity.)

Economics, by contrast, has no such function of mediation and therefore cannot operate with categories of the future. If it does, it necessarily becomes *Utopian politics* (or Utopian social philosophy) disguised as political economy.

From this it follows that 'supersession' cannot be envisaged in purely economic terms but in *politically, morally, aesthetically,* etc. qualified categories. Marx's treatment of the subject is by no means an exception in this respect. He can only use economic categories when he analyses the existing social form of productive activity. When it comes to the question of 'positive transcendence', 'supersession' etc., he uses expressions like 'the complete emancipation of all human senses and attributes' (106). We can note not only that the point has very strong *moral* overtones, but also the fact that the key word – *emancipation* – underlined by Marx himself, is a specifically political term.

The term – applied by Marx to characterize 'supersession' – which comes the nearest to the categories of economics is 'association' (63–4). But precisely because of its comprehensive, all-embracing character, it cannot be other than a general political principle envisaged as the centre of reference of a future socialist economy. And to define its character as a *socialist* economic principle it must be related to specifically political and moral issues (such as 'equality', 'emancipation of all human senses and attributes', 'earth as personal property of man' etc.). 'Association' can be of various kinds and in its economic references, as used by Marx indicates only:

1. Something that already belongs to the existing economic structure (e.g. 'economic advantage of large-scale landed property').
2. A *negativity* (i.e. that 'association' is a guarantee against economic crises).

It is through the references to political and moral issues that the category of 'association' acquires its Marxian meaning – in sharp contrast to the possible corporative interpretation and application of the term – which makes it suitable to become the basic principle of socialist economics. (This is one of the main reasons behind the Marxian method of analysis which closely relates the economic issues to the political, moral, etc., ones. Even the aesthetic problems are analysed in a manner that puts into relief their interconnections with the most general economic and political issues, and thus help to substantiate the specifically socialist character of the solutions envisaged to these general formulations.) However if one disrupts the link between the political, moral and economical aspects of these issues then in view of the above-mentioned reasons they lose their Marxian socialist character, and their relevance to a positive transcendence of alienation becomes extremely doubtful.

Marx's procedure is, thus, to start out from an *economic analysis* conceived as the theoretical basis of an envisaged *political action*. This does not mean, however, that he identifies 'transcendence' with this political action. On the contrary, he often emphasizes that the alienation of productive activity can only be ultimately overcome in the *sphere of production*. Political action can only create the general conditions which are not identical with, but are a necessary *prerequisite to* the actual supersession of alienation. The concrete process of supersession itself lies in the future, well ahead of the period of political action that establishes the conditions which are necessary for the process of positive transcendence to get started. How far that process lies in the future, cannot be said, because it depends upon so many conditions, including that of scientific development. Anyway there can be little doubt about it that the old Marx located this process of positive transcendence in an even more distant future than the young one (Marx, 1894, pp. 799–800 of 1958 edn).

If we compare this conception to that of Proudhon, it becomes clear that what is missing from the latter is the *intermediary link* necessary to create the prerequisites of a positive transcendence. The *Utopian* character of Proudhon's philosophy is determined by the lack of this intermediary link, just as the theological character of Rousseau's concept of man is determined by his negative attitude to the necessary mediation (industry, or 'civilization') between man and nature, that is, by the lack of this mediating link in his concept of the 'natural state'.

Proudhon envisages a direct *economic measure* to tackle the negative aspects of the given situation and thus in the final analysis he dissolves politics into *Utopian* economics. Because of this identification of politics with economic action he must locate the process of supersession in the present or immediate future and also must operate with the categories of political economy.

This is what Marx calls 'abolishing political-economic estrangement within political-economic estrangement'. Since in the wages of labour 'labour does not appear as an end in itself but as the servant of the wage', Proudhon's idea of 'forcing-up of wages', Marx argues, solves nothing. For

even the equality of wages demanded by Proudhon only transforms the relationship of the present-day worker to his labour into the relationship of all men to labour. *Society is then conceived as an abstract capitalist*. Wages are a direct consequence of estranged labour and estranged labour is the direct cause of private property. The downfall of the one aspect must therefore mean the downfall of the other (81).

This whole criticism leads to the conclusion that the appropriation of capital by the community does not mean an end to alienation. For even if the community owns capital and the principle of equality of wages is carried through, in so far as the community is no more than a community of *labour* (that is, wage-labour), the whole relation of estrangement survives in a different form. In this new form, labour is raised to an 'imagined universality' (100), but does not conquer the human status and dignity, 'does not appear as an end in itself', because it is confronted by another imagined universality: 'the community as the universal capitalist'. Only if this relation of being confronted by a power outside oneself, which is the same thing as not being an end in oneself, is superseded, may one speak of a positive transcendence of alienation.

From partial to universal alienation

As we have already mentioned, the young Marx wants to find out the secret of 'movable property's civilized victory'. Political economy guides him in this enterprise. He often acknowledges and praises the merits of classical political economy, because he sees in it a successful attempt at investigating the actual relations of production in modern society. In *Capital*, Marx calls the categories of political economy 'forms of thought expressing with social validity the conditions and relations of a definite, historically determined mode of production, viz., the production of commodities' (Marx, 1867, p. 76 of 1958 edn), and this judgement is in complete agreement with his assessment of political economy in the *Economic and Philosophic Manuscripts of 1844*.

The point about movable property's civilized victory refers both to the actual socio-economic development and to political economy, as conceptualizing the laws of this development. According to Marx the important achievement was to treat *human labour* as 'the source of wealth' (91). He describes the development of political economy in terms of its degree of awareness of the fact that labour is the source of wealth. In this sense he distinguishes four stages in the development of political economy, the first two of which are very closely connected:

1. Monetary system.
2. Mercantile system.
3. Physiocracy.
4. Liberal political economy.

Following the young Engels, he calls Adam Smith the 'Luther of Political Economy' (93–4) and, in contradistinction, the adherents of the monetary and mercantile system are called 'idolators, fetishists, Catholics' (93) and elsewhere 'fetish-worshippers of metal-money' (123). Physiocracy provides a link between the first two and the fourth stage in the development of political economy, in so far as it achieves 'the dissolution of feudal property in political economy', while at the same time it accomplishes feudal property's 'metamorphosis and restoration in political economy, save that now its language is no longer feudal but economic' (95–6).

The fourth stage, identified in the first place with the work of Adam Smith, not only unveils the fetishism of the monetary and mercantile system, but also supersedes the inconsistencies and the one-sidedness of physiocracy, by extending to the entire field of economy the principle of labour as the universal source of wealth. To use Marx's words in characterizing the achievement of liberal political economy as contrasted with physiocracy, 'labour appears at first only as agricultural labour; but then asserts itself as labour in general' (97).

What does all this mean with respect to alienation?

The answer is given at once when we consider that one cannot even discuss alienation if one remains in the realm of fetishism. Fetishism, in Marx's use of the term, means in this connection simply to view wealth as something outside man and independent of him: as something that possesses the character of absolute objectivity.

If it does possess this character of absolute objectivity, then it is of course 'sacrosanct'. It is important to remember in this context that the first great controversial issues, connected with alienation, at the end of the Middle Ages, were 'alienability of land' and interest obtained through lending money without the 'alienation of capital'. If the source of wealth – in this case land – possesses such absolute objectivity, then obviously it cannot be alienated. And 'movable property's civilized victory' could not become real without defeating this view. On the other hand movable property also needed a kind of stability, although an entirely different one from the 'non-alienability of land'. This new kind of *dynamic* stability was asserted by pressing for the legitimacy of profit '*without* the alienation of capital': an essential condition of accumulation. As a consequence, many heretics were condemned, or even burned by the Catholic Church for maintaining that profit upon lending without alienation of capital was not a sin, let alone a capital sin. Significantly enough a representative of physiocracy, the French politician and economist Turgot, as late as the sixties of the eighteenth century, had to defend the adherents of this 'heretical' view.[8]

To consider wealth only as an external object, and not as a specific manifestation of human relations, means that the problem of alienation cannot even be raised beyond the generality – and at the same time the absoluteness – of 'the fall of man'. And it is only appropriate that once wealth (the product of human efforts) acquires this character of absolute objectivity, then the other side of the relationship – human nature as manifest in the various kinds of human activity – also appears under the aspect of absoluteness and metaphysical eternity. This is graphically expressed in the concept of the fall of man, often implicitly assumed as the foundation of theoretical explanations related to this matter.

Physiocracy represents a stage in the development of political economy when this appearance of absoluteness is questioned as regards both sides of the relationship. Human activity is considered as the source of wealth, for it is recognized that land has no value in and by itself but only in connection with human labour. [This is what is meant by the rather obscure Marxian expression that 'the subjective essence of wealth has already been transferred to labour' (96).] On the other hand, activity is defined in concrete terms, as *agriculture*, and only in this specific form is acknowledged as the source of value.

However, in a definition of wealth-producing activity in this *specific* form, as Marx says,

labour is not yet grasped in its generality and abstraction: it is still bound to a particular natural element as its matter, and it is therefore only recognized in a particular mode of existence determined by nature. It is therefore still *only a specific, particular alienation of man,* just as its product is conceived only as a specific form of wealth, due more to nature than to labour itself. The land is here still recognized as a phenomenon of nature independent of man – not yet as capital, i.e. as an aspect of labour itself. Labour appears, rather, as an aspect of the

8. 'C'est d'après ce point de vue que je hasarde d'entrer ici dans une discussion assez étendue, pour faire voir le peu de fondement des opinions de ceux qui ont *condemné l'intérêt du prêt fait sans aliénation du capital*, et la fixation de cet intérêt par la seule convention' (Turgot, 1844, p. 118).

land. But since the *fetishism* of the old external wealth, of wealth existing only as an object, has been reduced to a very simple natural element, and since – even if only partially and in a particular form – its essence has been recognized within its subjective existence, there is the necessary step forward in that *the general nature of wealth has been revealed* and that labour has therefore in its total absoluteness (i.e. its abstraction) been raised and established as the principle (96).

This revelation of the general nature of wealth and the establishing of labour 'in its total absoluteness and abstraction' (that is to say, irrespective of its specific forms within the given mode of production) as the universal principle of production and development, nevertheless, has not been accomplished by the representatives of physiocracy, but by those of the next stage: liberal political economy.

Physiocracy could not realize that *agriculture*, as the particular form, has to be subsumed under the universal one: *industry* (that is, productive activity in general), and its comprehensive manifestation at the given historical stage, *wage labour*. This is why physiocracy, unlike liberal political economy, could not completely detach itself from the old fetishism.

Obviously the fact that the major representatives of physiocracy are to be found in France, and not in England, is inseparable from the general state of French economy in the eighteenth century, characterized by the young Marx as the economy of a 'not yet fully developed money-nation'. And here we can see again a concrete instance of Marx's method of grasping in a unity the socio-historical and systematic-structural elements.

It is in the context of fetishism – taken as an example to illustrate a general point – that Marx emphasizes the intimate interrelation between theory and social practice. After contrasting a France 'still dazzled by the sensuous splendour of precious metals' with the fully developed money-nation, England, he writes that 'the extent to which the solution of theoretical riddles is the task of practice, just as true practice is the condition of a real and positive theory, is shown, for example, in fetishism' (123). And he analyses in the same spirit the previous stages of socio-economical and theoretical development.

Alienation, in his account, is already inherent in feudal relations, for landed property is the basis of the dominion of private property. Feudal landed property is considered as a particular manifestation of alienation because the fact that land is possessed by a few great lords means that earth is estranged from man in general and confronts him as an alien power.

Once land is monopolized then, from the point of view of developing industry, the great issue is obviously the alienability of land. But in this general sense in which earth is the first condition of man's existence, land is, of course, absolutely *inalienable* from *man*. In fact feudal ideology (contemporary to conditions in which land is already alienated by a *group* of men) could not assert its standpoint in terms of 'man', but only in terms of its own *partiality*. This partiality then had to be elevated above the rest of society, by the claim of *divine* ascendancy. The claimed divine ascendancy gave it a form of legitimacy, even if a fictitious one. Since, however, the claim of divine ascendancy directly justified the absolute rule of a *partial* position, there was no need for an appeal to the concept of 'man' in feudal ideology. Nor was there any room for it.

The concept of 'man' was popularized by those who fought feudal power and its ideology. What is paradoxical, however, is that in the writings of these anti-feudal thinkers the concept of man is not put forward to *negate* alienation, but to *affirm* and sustain it, although in a different form. They affirmed and sustained the principle of alienation and alienability in a *universal* form, extending its realm over every aspect of human life, including '*self-alienation*' and '*self-alienability*'. And this they did in the name of 'man'.

This universalization of the principle of alienation and alienability carries with it, naturally, the notion of *equality*, in the sense that follows.

We have to remember here that according to Marx the original tendency inherent in the division of land is equality (64). And elsewhere he says that 'The political economist reduces everything (just as does politics in its *Rights of Man*) to man, i.e. to the individual whom he strips of all determinateness so as to class him as capitalist or worker' (129). This concept of man, in its political or economic form, is, of course, not short of asserting, even if only abstractly, the principle of equality. Land is alienable because we all belong to the general class of 'man' and in this sense we are all equal. (If, however, possession of land were of divine ascendancy, nobody could advocate its alienability. Nor could they challenge the social hierarchy that goes with the dogma of non-alienability of land.)

Yet no sooner is this equality asserted, it is already denied, because the concept of alienation and alienability implies *exclusion*. In fact the form in which land can be alienated is necessarily one that transfers the *rights of possession* – though not in principle, as in feudal ideology, but *de facto* – to a limited number of people. At the same time – again not in principle, but in a practice necessarily implied in the notion of alienability – the rest of the population is *excluded* from the possession of land.

Thus the concrete form in which the principle of equality is realized is formal-legalistic: the possession of equal rights to have the Rights of Man. That is to say, if the idea of equality is related to the *right of possession* it is necessarily transformed into the abstract formal principle of *possession of rights*. In other words: it is deprived of its content.

The abstractness and formal-legalistic character of the Rights of Man is determined by the irreconcilable contradiction between content and form: the new *partiality* of motivating content and the formal *universality* of ideological appeal. This is not a conceptual abstractness that could be removed or improved upon. It is an objectively necessary abstractness, determined by the internal contradictions of a concrete historical situation. It is quite impossible to 'demystify' this abstract structure without exposing the contradiction between actual partial content and formally universal ideological appeal. But to do this one needs a socio-historical standpoint very different from that of the original champions of the Rights of Man.

This is why the assertion of equality as a content (that is, a theory that wants to go beyond the point marked by the abstract formalism of the Rights of Man) must set out from denying alienation and alienability. And for the same reason, this assertion of equality must also oppose all forms of individualistic possession that may imply exclusion.

From political to economic alienation

In feudal landed property the ties between land and its proprietor are not yet reduced to the status of mere material wealth. As Marx puts it:

The estate is *individualized* with its lord: it has his rank, is baronial or ducal with him, has his privileges, his jurisdiction, his political position, etc. It appears as the *inorganic body* of its lord. Hence the proverb *nulle terre sans maître*, which expresses the fusion of nobility and landed property. Similarly the rule of landed property does not appear directly as the rule of mere capital. For those belonging to it, the estate is more like their fatherland. It is *a constricted sort of nationality* (61).

This kind of individualization and personification also means that the relation between the owner of land and those working on the estate – his serfs – is predominantly *political*. Consequently its negation must also first take an essentially political form. Accordingly, at the beginning of its development, modern economic thought is still an integral part of politics. Only later, when feudal landed property is defeated and the new mode of production well established, does economic thought acquire the form of an independent science. Then it finds a *specifically economic* equivalent to what was *politically* formulated in the manifestoes of the Rights of Man.

The development of political economy, in its reference to the concept of man, takes the course of negating this 'constricted sort of nationality'. It becomes increasingly clear that political economy aims at a universality, first on a national scale and then on a cosmopolitan one. Mercantilism has still a predominantly national character. Liberal political economy, however, makes amply clear that its most general laws know no frontiers and are subject to no limitations.

In this development from partiality to universality, from personification to impersonalization, from political limitations and mediations to economic freedom and immediateness, political economy gradually supersedes the old fetishism and clearly formulates the conditions of unhampered alienation. Thus the development from political partiality to economic universality means that particular or 'specific' alienation is turned into one that is universal.

At the beginning of this development we find feudal property, which conceals the fact that the original unity: man (M) had split in the course of historical development into property (P) and labour (L). Feudal property relations conceal this split by means of a *political* mediation. This political mediation creates the false appearance of a unity that historically disappeared ages ago.

Marx, after analysing feudal individualization and personi- fication, as opposed to the later state when 'a man is bound to his land, not by his character, but only by his purse-strings', says that it is necessary that the false appearance of unity be abolished,

that landed property, the root of private property, be dragged com- pletely into the movement of private property and that it become a *commodity*; that the rule of the proprietor appear as the *undisguised* rule of private property, of *capital, freed of all political tincture* (62).

When this is accomplished, the medieval proverb *nulle terre sans maître* automatically loses its validity and thus the basic relations become characterized, as Marx says, by the newly adopted pro- verb: *l'argent n'a pas de maître*. It is quite obvious that the proverb *nulle terre sans maître* expresses a directly political relationship, in contradistinction to the later stage when the relationship between P and L is an essentially *economic* one. It is freed not only of all *political tincture*, but also of all remnants of *personification*.

However, at the beginning of these developments the facts, on one hand, that land is *individualized* and, on the other, that the serf (L) *belongs* to the feudal lord (P), make it appear as if there existed a *unity* of the two. But this 'unity' is only an external one. It is not kept alive by an internal cohesive force of a positive economic nature, but by the strength of a political institution and by the absence (or weakness) of an economic force that could effectively challenge it.

Later, when this economic force becomes stronger within the feudal system, the split appears more and more marked, and the relatively short distance of P and L from the 'political axis' that originally created the impression of a real unity, increases con- siderably. This is illustrated in Figure 5.

The more this distance increases, the more the old politics loses its mediating power and leaves this function to *money*. Or, to put it in another way: the more money overtakes the mediating function of politics, the more evident becomes the split between property and labour, and the more the power and range of direct politics decreases. (Of course we are talking about a *trend* and therefore it must be emphasized that direct politics *never* loses completely its mediating power and function.)

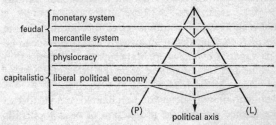

Figure 5

In this process of transferring the mediating power of politics to an economic factor, landed property is opposed by movable private property and the liberation of the labourer from his political bonds is accomplished by an alliance between labour and industrial capital. When Marx makes this point, he also points out that the opposition between landed and movable property is not a basic opposition, because they belong to the same category. Landed property in its continuing opposition to capital is nothing but '*private property – capital* – still afflicted with local and political prejudices; it is capital which has not yet regained itself from its entanglement with the world – *capital not yet fully developed*. It must in the course of its world-wide development achieve its abstract, that is, its *pure expression*' (91).

As we see, Marx's analysis sets out from defining private property as capital and from this standpoint contrasts one form of private property (landed property) to another (movable property or industrial capital). Only if industrial capital is grasped as the 'pure expression' of capital can private property be defined as capital, and landed property – in its contrast to industrial capital – as 'capital not yet fully developed'. Here, again, we can note that the degrees of *logical* complexity and abstraction (from the limited validity of the locally affected form to the universal validity of the 'pure expression') correspond to degrees of *historical* maturity.

But why does the development of capital (private property) follow this course, characterized by the well-known contradiction between movable and landed property that eventually leads to movable property's civilized victory? What makes necessary the development of labour as alienated labour in this form?

We would seek in vain for an answer to this question in the *Manuscripts of 1844*. The key to an answer, nevertheless, can be found in a passage of *Capital*, where Marx says that all production of surplus-value has for its *natural basis* the productiveness of *agricultural labour* (Marx, 1894, p. 766 of 1958 edn).

It is self-evident, that no society of even limited complexity can come into existence without the production of basic foodstuffs that exceed the individual requirements of the labourers. But it is equally self-evident that the existence of agricultural surplus-product does not contain any *economic* determination as to the manner of its appropriation. It can be appropriated by a limited group of people, but it can also be distributed on the basis of the strictest equality. Now the point is that the most elementary requirements of the capitalistic mode of production (competition, growth, accumulation, etc.) prescribe by *economic* necessity a *fixed* relation between production and appropriation (i.e. private ownership).

To render stable the relation between production and appropriation when agricultural surplus-product first becomes available and to secure in this way the accumulation of wealth as well as to increase the power of the given society, one must have a *political* determination as the fundamental regulative principle of the society in question. What brings this political determination into existence may be, of course, enormously varied, from an outside challenge menacing the life of the community to a favourable geographical location furthering a speedier accumulation of wealth, and its discussion does not belong here. What matters in this connection is:

1. That the first stage in the development of the alienation of labour must have a *political* form.

2. That an absolute prerequisite of the genesis of a capitalistic society based on an inherent *economic* principle is the previous existence of a *politically fixed relation* between property and labour, regulating the distribution or allocation of all surplus product and making accumulation possible. (Without the existence of such a relation – as in the case of egalitarian natural societies – there can be no accumulation and the society is bound to remain a stagnating one.) In other words: an essential prerequisite of *universal* (economic) alienation is the realization of *specific* (politically affected) alienation. Universal alienation logically implies partial alienation and, as we see, also historically alienation first must be political-partial before becoming economic-universal.

Division and alienation of labour, competition and reification

The question of alienation is directly related to the issue of surplus-product and surplus-value, and the various phases in the development of political economy are characterized by Marx according to their positions as regards the origin and nature of surplus-value. Table 1 is a comparative table to illustrate their interrelations and development. Thus the development of political economy from the monetary system to liberal political economy corresponds to the historical development from feudal landed property to industrial capital and from labour's complete political dependence (serfdom) to politically emancipated industrial labour.

As we can see, liberal political economy is the culmination of this development. Its superiority is recognized by Marx on the ground of the following considerations:

1. It defines capital as 'stored-up labour' (38).

2. It points out that the accumulation of capital mounts with the division of labour and that the division of labour increases with the accumulation of capital (131).

3. It develops sharply and consistently – however one-sidedly – the idea that labour is the sole essence of wealth (95).

Table 1

Dominant form of property	Dominant form of labour	Corresponding stage of political economy	Its sphere of reference and its view on surplus-value
Landed property that has reached a relatively high degree of accumulation of wealth	Serfdom	*Monetary* system	*Circulation*; has no definite view on surplus-value
Commercially interested and *colonially* expanding – therefore *nation-conscious* – *landed property*	*Feudally bound labour*, making the first steps towards a political emancipation	*Mercantile* system	*Circulation*; surplus-value is identified with surplus-money, *the balance of trade surplus*
By the advancement of commercial capital and by the accomplishments of the manufacture system deeply affected, *modernized landed property*	*Agricultural labour*, still submitted to political determinations	*Physiocracy*	*Agricultural production*; surplus-value is grasped as the product of *agricultural labour*, set in motion by *rent-yielding* property
Industrial capital, freed of all political and natural determinations	Politically emancipated *industrial labour* (day labour, wage labour)	*Liberal political economy*	*Production* in general; surplus-value is defined as being produced by *labour in general*, set in motion by *capital*

4. It demolishes the mysticism attached to rent.[9]

5. It proves that the governing power of modern society is not political, but economic: the purchasing power of capital (37–8).

6. It establishes itself as the sole politics and sole universality, making plain its own cosmopolitan character (94–5).

Needless to say that in all the above characteristics the problem of the alienation of labour, directly or indirectly, is involved.

But now we come to a turning-point in the analysis.

We have already seen that liberal political economy detaches itself from the old fetishism. However, according to Marx, it becomes powerless when facing fetishism in a new form, called the fetishism of commodities. This is the point where the historical limitations of liberal political economy come to light.

The main problems we have to consider in this context concern the division of labour and its relation to private property, money-system and the form of value, competition and monopoly.

Marx's principal objection to liberal political economy is that it is unable to prove the assertion that the essence of private property is labour (134). And this question is inseparably connected with the assessment of the nature of the division of labour. The correct assessment is vital to the whole issue of alienation. This is why Marx dedicates so much time to the analysis of the division of labour.

According to Marx the political economists are all in agreement not only in asserting the mutual interrelation between division of labour and accumulation of capital, but also in pointing out that only liberated private property could accomplish a really comprehensive and economically rewarding division of labour. The weakness, however, lies in their attempts at founding the division of labour in *human nature* ('propensity to exchange and barter', Adam Smith). At this point they contradict each other (133) although in the final analysis all of them maintain that division

9. Political economy deals 'the deathblow to rent – the last, individual, natural mode of private property and source of wealth existing independently of the movement of labour, that expression of feudal property, an expression which has already become wholly economic in character and therefore incapable of resisting political economy (the Ricardo school)' (95).

of labour, based on exchange, is absolutely indispensable to a civilized society.

Marx cannot accept this kind of assessment of the relationship of private property – exchange – division of labour, for an acceptance would amount to admitting that alienation cannot be superseded in reality. He defines division of labour as an economic expression that only applies to the conditions of alienation. In Marx's view the political economists confuse 'the social character of labour' (129) – an absolute condition of society – with the division of labour. One can think of superseding alienation precisely because it is possible to oppose the social character of labour to the alienating historical condition of the division of labour. According to Marx, once life-activity ceases to be regulated on the basis of private property and exchange, it will acquire the character of activity of man as a species-being. In other words: the social character of labour will manifest itself directly, without the alienating mediation of the division of labour. As things stand, however, division of labour makes the conditions and powers of life become independent of man and rule over him.[10]

The genesis of the division of labour, as conceived by the political economists, is illustrated in Figure 6.

Figure 6

In this view egoism is an absolute condition, not a historical product. It is also identified with private property (133–4). At the

10. 'Die Individuen sind immer von sich ausgegangen, gehen immer von sich aus. Ihre Verhältnisse sind Verhältnisse ihres wirklichen Lebensprozesses. Woher kömmt es, dass *ihre Verhältnisse sich gegen sie verselbständigen*? dass *die Mächte ihres eignen Lebens übermächtig gegen sie werden*? Mit einem Wort: die Teilung der Arbeit, deren Stufe von der jedesmal entwickelten Produktivkraft abhängt' (Marx and Engels, *Werke*, vol. 3, p. 540; from a notebook of the young Marx).

same time, the mutual interplay is confined to the sphere of exchange and the division of labour. It is recognized that value is produced in the sphere of this mutual interaction, but egoism (private property) is conceived as the absolute condition, indispensable to set in motion the other two.

By contrast, Marx's conception could be schematized as in Figure 7.

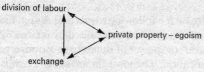

division of labour

private property – egoism

exchange

Figure 7

Here we have a three-way interaction and egoism is rather the outcome of the interplay than the cause of it.

One of the most important categories of liberal political economy is *competition*, in its radical opposition to monopoly. The young Marx and Engels, however, point out that this opposition is hollow. It is hollow because competition presupposes monopoly: the basic monopoly of private property. On the other hand, they also show that only one side of the coin is that competition presupposes monopoly. The other is that monopoly breeds competition and competition turns into monopoly. They distinguish two kinds of competition. *Subjective* competition is between workers and workers on one hand, and capitalists and capitalists on the other. *Objective* or fundamental competition is between workers and property owners.

Competition based on the monopoly of private property[11] goes

11. In opposition to such a system the young Engels writes about a future socialist society: 'The truth of the relationship of competition is *the relationship of the power of consumption to the power of production*. In a world worthy of mankind there will be no other competition than this. The community will have to calculate what it can produce with the means at its disposal; and in the light of the relationship of this productive power to the mass of consumers it will determine how far it has to raise or lower production, how far it has to give way to or curtail, luxury' (197). Only some elements of this conception are tenable. The influence of the English and French Utopian socialists can be detected in this assessment of com-

with a mode of production that appears to be governed by a *natural law*, not the will of the people involved. In this characteristic can one recognize the new type of *fetishism*. (The term 'fetishism' is used in the sense as before, meaning that the phenomenon in question appears as something outside man, confronting him as an alien power.)

The most important aspects of this mode of production directly relevant to our problem are 'reification', 'abstract labour' and 'imaginary appetites'.

Marx quotes with approval the following words of E. Buret, the French economist: 'Poverty is not so much caused by men as by the *power of things*' (49). But the power of things to cause poverty is only one aspect of reification. The most important of them is that the worker is made into a *commodity* (69). Marx also points out that the law of supply and demand governs the production of men just as much as of every other commodity (22), and that the worker as a 'living capital' is a special sort of commodity that has the misfortune to be 'a capital with needs'. But, as a result of the law of supply and demand, the worker's 'human qualities only exist in so far as they exist for capital alien to him' (84). This means that human needs can only be gratified to the extent to which they contribute to the accumulation of wealth. The labourer is a commodity because he is reproduced only as a *worker* and it is in accordance with the needs of private property – needs asserted in the form of the above-mentioned 'natural law' – that this reproduction takes place.

Abstract labour is one-sided, machine-like labour and, of course, it is the result of the division of labour under conditions of competition. Marx defines the factory-system as 'the essence of industry – of labour – brought to its maturity' (97). But the price of this maturity is the 'reduction of the greater part of mankind to abstract labour' (30), because the conditions of competition under which this maturity is accomplished are alienating. Competition carries with it a rationalization of the production process

---

petition and Engels himself invites the reader, on the same page, to 'consult the writings of the English Socialists, and partly also those of Fourier', in order to see how great an increase in productivity can be expected 'from a rational state of affairs within the community.'

– in the sense of breaking up complex processes into their simplest elements so that they can be easily executed through competitively advantageous large-scale production – irrespective of its human consequences. The outcome is the diffusion of industrial machinery and the mechanization of human labour (132). For the worker this means not only that he finds no human satisfaction in his labour because he is 'depressed spiritually and physically to the condition of a machine and from being a man becomes an *abstract activity and a stomach*' (25), but also that since he has 'sunk to the level of the machine he can be *confronted by the machine as a competitor*' (26). Paradoxically, the greater the bargaining power of labour and the higher its price is, the more deeply is it affected by the competitive power of the machine. In the diffusion of automation this is just as important as the technological virtues of the scientific discoveries that made automation possible. Although this last point is not made by Marx, clearly it offers a topical support to his idea that it is impossible to supersede 'political-economic alienation within political-economic alienation', i.e. by simply improving the competitive power of labour, by 'forcing-up wages', etc.

The question of '*imaginary appetites*' is, of course, very closely connected with the previous two. For, if everything is subordinated to the need of the accumulation of wealth, it is irrelevant whether the needs thus created are properly human, or indifferent or even dehumanizing needs. Marx writes that 'every person speculates on creating a *new need* in another, so as to drive him to a fresh sacrifice, to place him in a *new dependence*' and that 'the extension of products and needs falls into contriving and ever-calculating subservience to inhuman, refined, unnatural and *imaginary appetites*' (115–16).

So, division of labour turns into the opposite of its original sense and function. Instead of liberating man from his dependence on nature, it continues to create new and artificial, unnecessary limitations. Thus, paradoxically, because of the 'natural law based on the unconsciousness of the participants', the more private property – obeying the law of competition – extends its power and realm, supplying commodity-man with a great abundance of commodities, the more everything becomes subjected to a power outside man. And, to make the contradiction even sharper, this applies not only to the worker but also to the owner of private property (126).

Alienated labour and 'human nature'

The whole economic argument culminates in a new concept of man. For, in discussing the crucial problems of the division of labour, Marx radically challenges the account of *human nature* given by the political economists.

We may remember that he praised liberal political economy for having abstracted from the individual appearances of human interrelations, for having developed sharply and consistently, though one-sidedly, the idea of labour as the sole essence of wealth and for having incorporated private property in man himself. He praised them because in these achievements they have effectively overcome the limitations of 'idolators, fetishists, Catholics'. However, these achievements have another side too. Abstracting consistently from the individual appearances carried with it a further estrangement from man. And incorporating private property in man himself amounted to bringing man within the orbit of private property and alienation (94).

Marx is passionately opposed to the attitude of political economy which does not consider the worker 'when he is not working, as a *human being*; but leaves such consideration to criminal law, to doctors, to religion, to the statistical tables, to politics and to the workhouse beadle' (30). He objects to the acceptance of reification by political economy under the form of considering labour 'in the abstract *as a thing*' (34). He objects to the practice of carrying to the extremes a virtue which first resulted in the supersession of the old fetishism, but then necessarily implied a submission to a new type of fetishism: to fetishism brought to its maturity in its highest, most abstract and universal form (95).

The political economists often emphasize that there is a mutual interaction between the division of labour and the accumulation of capital. However, since they are not interested in the worker as a human being, they are unable to grasp this interrelation in its complexity. Instead of considering all of its main aspects (Figure 8) they confine their attention to the division of labour-accumulation of capital relationship. Similarly, they do not consider that labour does not simply produce commodities and value, but also produces itself as a commodity (84–5), as well as the devaluation of the world of men (69).

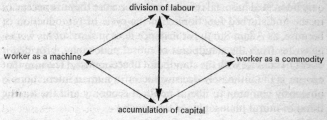

division of labour

worker as a machine

worker as a commodity

accumulation of capital

Figure 8

This abstraction from the human side of these interrelations follows from the basic conception of political economy that *assumes* private property as an essential attribute of human nature. Consequently, political economy cannot 'grasp the essential connection between private property, avarice, and the separation of labour, capital and landed property; between exchange and competition, value and the devaluation of men, monopoly and competition, etc.; the connection between this whole estrangement and the money-system' (68).

Marx indicates *alienated labour* as the essential connection between the whole estrangement and the money-system. Private property is considered only as the *product*, the necessary consequence of alienated labour, that is, 'of the external relation of the worker to nature and to himself' (80).

This conclusion is reached on the ground that the worker could not come to face the product of his own activity as a stranger if he were not alienating himself from himself in the very *act of production*. Activity cannot be unalienated activity if its product is alienation; for the product is nothing but the sum of activity, of production (72).

Political economy cannot reach this conclusion. From the standpoint of economics as a special science, what matters is, of course, not the assessment of the *human* implications of an objective economic process, but the analysis of the necessary conditions of an undisturbed functioning and reproduction of the given process.

This is why the political economist is interested in the conditions of the worker only in so far as these conditions are necessary to production in general, that is to say, in so far as they are the conditions of the *worker*. The political economist, therefore, is only interested in social reforms either because they are necessary to the undisturbed functioning of the cycle of reproduction or because, as Adam Smith for instance does in some of his works, he writes from the standpoint of moral philosophy, provided it does not conflict with the standpoint of economics. (The idea that egoism is the ultimately decisive factor in human interactions is obviously common to liberal political economy and the leading trend of moral philosophy of the epoch.)

Marx's whole approach is characterized by a constant reference to man as opposed to wage labourer. This is made possible only because his approach is based on a conception of human nature radically opposed to that of political economy. He denies that man is an essentially *egoistic* being, for he does not accept such a thing as a *fixed* human nature (or, indeed, a fixed anything). In Marx's view man is by nature neither egoistic nor altruistic. He is *made*, by his own activity, into what he is at any given time. And so, if this activity is transformed, today's egoistic human nature will change in due course.

And here we can see how crucially important is the fact that in Marx's theory there is no static element. The complex manifestations of human life, including their objectified and institutional forms, are explained in an ultimate reference to a dynamic principle: *activity* itself. This is in sharp contrast to the conceptions that tried to *deduce* the various characteristics of the given form of society, including private property, from an arbitrarily *assumed* static conception of a fixed human nature. In Marx's view private property and its human consequences have to be historically explained, not assumed or deduced from an assumption. According to Marx private property is called into existence by alienated activity and then in its turn it does, of course, profoundly affect human aspirations. As Marx writes: 'Private property made us so stupid and one-sided that an object is only ours when we have it – when it exists for us as capital, or when it is *directly possessed*, eaten, drunk, worn, inhabited, etc. – in short, when it is utilized by us' (106).

This condemnation of 'having', as opposed to 'being', was not, of course, first voiced by Marx. His approach was directly influenced by the Utopian Socialists and by Proudhon and Moses Hess. But with him what is new is a coherent insistence on the ultimate foundations of human interrelations, developing in detail the implications of an approach first attempted by the young Engels in his *Outlines of a Critique of Political Economy*.[12]

This approach – whose centre of reference is productive activity or *praxis* – carries with it that what emerges as the 'essence of human nature' is not *egoism*, but *sociality* (i.e. 'the *ensemble* of social relations', as Marx puts it in his sixth thesis on Feuerbach). 'Sociality' as the defining characteristic of human nature is radically different from those criticized by Marx. Unlike 'egoism', it cannot be an abstract quality inherent in the single individual. It can only exist in the relations of individuals with each other.

By implication, the adequate fulfilment of human nature cannot

---

12. One of the most important passages of this work reads as follows: 'The immediate consequence of private property was *the split of production into two opposing sides – the natural and the human sides*, the soil which without fertilization by man is dead and sterile, and human activity, whose first condition is that very soil. Furthermore we have seen how human activity in its turn was dissolved into labour and capital, and how these two sides antagonistically confronted each other. Thus already we had the struggle of the three elements against one another, instead of their mutual support; and to make matters worse, private property brings in its wake the splintering of each of these elements. One *estate* stands confronted by another, one piece of *capital* by another, one unit of *labour-power* by another. In other words, because *private property isolates everyone in his own crude solitariness*, and because, nevertheless, everyone has the same interest as his neighbour, one landowner stands antagonistically confronted by another, one capitalist by another, one worker by another. In this discord of identical interests resulting precisely from this identity, is consummated the immorality of mankind's condition hitherto; and this consummation is competition. The opposite of competition is monopoly. Monopoly was the war-cry of the mercantilists; competition the battle-cry of the liberal economists. It is easy to see that this antithesis is again a quite *hollow antithesis*. . . . Competition is based on self-interest, and self-interest in turn breeds monopoly. In short, competition passes over into monopoly. . . . Moreover, competition already presupposes monopoly – namely, *the monopoly of property* (and here the *hypocrisy of the liberals* comes once more to light)' (193–4).

be *competition* – this 'unconscious condition of mankind' that corresponds to egoism and to the Hobbesian *bellum omnium contra omnes* – but *conscious association*. 'Activity and consumption' – writes Marx,

both in their content and in their mode of existence, are social: social activity and social consumption; the human essence of nature first exists only for social man; for only here does nature exist for him as a bond with man – as his existence for the other and the other's existence for him – as the life-element of the human world; only here does nature exist as the foundation of his own human existence. Only here has what is to him *his natural existence become his human existence*, and nature become man for him. Thus society is the consummated oneness in substance of man and nature – the true resurrection of nature – the naturalism of man and the humanism of nature both brought to fulfilment (103–4).

Thus it is expected that human nature ('sociality') liberated from institutionalized egoism (the negation of sociality) will supersede 'reification', 'abstract labour' and 'imaginary appetites'. It is not difficult to see that so long as competition is the governing power of production, or in other words, so long as 'cost-effectiveness' is the overriding principle of productive activity, it is quite impossible to consider the worker *as a man* at the various stages and phases of the cycle of production. Human activity under the conditions of competition is bound to remain wage labour, a commodity submitted to the 'natural law' of the objective, independent needs of competition. Similarly, it is easy to see the relevance of the supersession of competition to the achievement of the human requirements of self-fulfilling activity (as opposed to 'abstract labour', the negation of sociality) and to the elimination of 'imaginary appetites'.

At this point several problems could be raised as regards the nature of the developments envisaged by Marx. Since, however, the moral and political as well as the aesthetic aspects of Marx's theory of alienation have to be systematically explored before we can tackle such problems, their analysis must be left to later chapters.

References

MARX, K. (1867), *Capital*, vol. 1, Progress Publishers, 1958.

MARX, K. (1894), *Capital*, vol. 3, Progress Publishers, 1958.

MARX, K., and ENGELS, F. (1846), *The German Ideology*, Lawrence & Wishart, 1965.

ROUSSEAU, J.-J. (1762), *Émile ou de l'education*, Garnier-Flammarion, Paris, 1966.

TURGOT, A. R. J. (1844), *Oeuvres*, vol. 1, Guillaumin, Paris.

5 Thorstein Veblen

Professor Clark's Economics

Excerpts from Thorstein Veblen, 'Professor Clark's economics',
Quarterly Journal of Economics, vol. 22, 1908, pp. 147–95 Reprinted in
The Place of Science in Modern Civilization, 1919, reissued 1961, Russell
& Russell, pp. 180–230.

For some time past economists have been looking with lively
anticipation for such a comprehensive statement of Mr Clark's
doctrines as is now offered. The leading purpose of the volume
(Clark, 1907) is 'to offer a brief and provisional statement of the
more general laws of progress'; although it also comprises a
more abridged restatement of the laws of 'economic statics'
already set forth in fuller form in his *Distribution of Wealth*.
Though brief, this treatise is to be taken as systematically complete, as including in due correlation all the 'essentials' of Mr
Clark's theoretical system. As such, its publication is an event of
unusual interest and consequence. [. . .]

Since hedonism came to rule economic science, the science
has been in the main a theory of distribution – distribution of
ownership and of income. This is true both of the classical school
and of those theorists who have taken an attitude of ostensible
antagonism to the classical school. The exceptions to the rule are
late and comparatively few, and they are not found among the
economists who accept the hedonistic postulate as their point of
departure. And, consistently with the spirit of hedonism, this
theory of distribution has centered about a doctrine of exchange
value (or price) and has worked out its scheme of (normal)
distribution in terms of (normal) price. The normal economic
community, upon which theoretical interest has converged, is a
business community, which centers about the market and whose
scheme of life is a scheme of profit and loss. Even when some
considerable attention is ostensibly devoted to theories of consumption and production, in these systems of doctrine the
theories are constructed in terms of ownership, price and
acquisition and so reduce themselves in substance to doctrines of

distributive acquisition (see e.g. Marshall, 1890, vol. 1, books 2–5; Mill, 1848, book 1). In this respect Mr Clark's work is true to the received canons. The 'essentials of economic theory' are the essentials of the hedonistic theory of distribution, with sundry reflections on related topics. The scope of Mr Clark's economics, indeed, is even more closely limited by concepts of distribution than many others, since he persistently analyses production in terms of value, and value is a concept of distribution.

As Mr Clark justly observes (p. 4), 'The primitive and general facts concerning industry . . . need to be known before the social facts can profitably be studied.' In these early pages of the treatise, as in other works of its class, there is repeated reference to that more primitive and simple scheme of economic life out of which the modern complex scheme has developed and it is repeatedly indicated that in order to obtain an understanding of the play of forces in the more advanced stages of economic development and complication, it is necessary to apprehend these forces in their unsophisticated form as they work out in the simple scheme prevalent on the plane of primitive life. Indeed, to a reader not well acquainted with Mr Clark's scope and method of economic theorizing, these early pages would suggest that he is preparing for something in the way of a genetic study – a study of economic institutions approached from the side of their origins. It looks as if the intended line of approach to the modern situation might be such as an evolutionist would choose, who would set out with showing what forces are at work in the primitive economic community and then trace the cumulative growth and complication of these factors as they presently take form in the institutions of a later phase of the development. Such, however, is not Mr Clark's intention. The effect of his recourse to 'primitive life' is simply to throw into the foreground, in a highly unreal perspective, those features which lend themselves to interpretation in terms of the normalized competitive system. The best excuse that can be offered for these excursions into 'primitive life' is that they have substantially nothing to do with the main argument of the book, being of the nature of harmless and graceful misinformation.

In the primitive economic situation – that is to say, in savagery and the lower barbarism – there is, of course, no 'solitary hunter', living either in a cave or otherwise and there is no man who 'makes by his own labor all the goods that he uses', etc. It is, in effect, a highly meretricious misrepresentation to speak in this connection of 'the economy of a man who works only for himself' and say that 'the inherent productive power of labor and capital is of vital concern to him', because such a presentation of the matter overlooks the main facts in the case in order to put the emphasis on a feature which is of negligible consequence. There is no reasonable doubt but that, at least since mankind reached the human plane, the economic unit has been not a 'solitary hunter', but a community of some kind; in which, by the way, women seem in the early stages to have been the most consequential factor instead of the man who works for himself. The 'capital' possessed by such a community – as, for example, a band of California 'Digger' Indians – was a negligible quantity, more valuable to a collector of curios than to anyone else and the loss of which to the 'Digger' squaws would mean very little. What was of 'vital concern' to them, indeed, what the life of the group depended on absolutely, was the accumulated wisdom of the squaws, the technology of their economic situation.[1] The loss of the basket, digging-stick and mortar, simply as physical objects, would have signified little, but the conceivable loss of the squaw's knowledge of the soil and seasons, of food and fiber plants, and of mechanical expedients would have meant the present dispersal and starvation of the community.

This may seem like taking Mr Clark to task for an inconsequential gap in his general information on Digger Indians, Eskimos and palaeolithic society at large. But the point raised is not of negligible consequence for economic theory, particularly not for any theory of 'economic dynamics' that turns in great part about questions of capital and its uses at different stages of economic development. In the primitive culture the quantity and the value of mechanical appliances is relatively slight; and whether the group is actually possessed of more or less of such appliances at a given time is not a question of first-rate importance. The loss of these objects – tangible assets – would entail a transient inconvenience. But the accumulated, habitual knowledge of the ways and means involved in the production and use

1. Cf., for example, such an account as Barrows (1900).

of these appliances is the outcome of long experience and experimentation; and, given this body of commonplace technological information, the acquisition and employment of the suitable apparatus is easily arranged. The great body of commonplace knowledge made use of in industry is the product and heritage of the group. In its essentials it is known by common notoriety, and the 'capital goods' needed for putting this commonplace technological knowledge to use are a slight matter – practically within the reach of everyone. Under these circumstances the ownership of 'capital goods' has no great significance and, as a practical fact, interest and wages are unknown and the 'earning power of capital' is not seen to be 'governed by a specific power of productivity which resides in capital goods'. But the situation changes, presently, by what is called an advance 'in the industrial arts'. The 'capital' required to put the commonplace knowledge to effect grows larger and so its acquisition becomes an increasingly difficult matter. Through 'difficulty of attainment' in adequate quantities, the apparatus and its ownership become a matter of consequence; increasingly so, until presently the equipment required for an effective pursuit of industry comes to be greater than the common man can hope to acquire in a lifetime. The commonplace knowledge of ways and means, the accumulated experience of mankind, is still transmitted in and by the body of the community at large; but, for practical purposes, the advanced 'state of the industrial arts' has enabled the owners of goods to corner the wisdom of the ancients and the accumulated experience of the race. Hence 'capital', as it stands at that phase of the institution's growth contemplated by Mr Clark.

The 'natural' system of free competition, or, as it was once called, 'the obvious and simple system of natural liberty', is accordingly a phase of the development of the institution of capital; and its claim to immutable dominion is evidently as good as the like claim of any other phase of cultural growth. The equity, or 'natural justice', claimed for it is evidently just and equitable only in so far as the conventions of ownership on which it rests continue to be a secure integral part of the institutional furniture of the community; that is to say, so long as these conventions are part and parcel of the habits of thought of the community; that is to say, so long as these things are currently held to be just and equitable. This normalized present, or 'natural', state of Mr Clark, is, as near as may be, Senior's 'natural state of man' – the hypothetically perfect competitive system; and economic theory consists in the definition and classification of the phenomena of economic life in terms of this hypothetical competitive system.

Taken by itself, Mr Clark's dealing with the past development might be passed over with slight comment, except for its negative significance, since it has no theoretical connection with the present, or even with the 'natural' state in which the phenomena of economic life are assumed to arrange themselves in a stable, normal scheme. But his dealings with the future, and with the present in so far as the present situation is conceived to comprise 'dynamic' factors, is of substantially the same kind. With Senior's 'natural state of man' as the baseline of normality in things economic, questions of present and future development are treated as questions of departure from the normal, aberrations and excesses which the theory does not aim even to account for. What is offered in place of theoretical inquiry when these 'positive perversions of the natural forces themselves' are taken up (e.g. in chapters 22–9) is an exposition of the corrections that must be made to bring the situation back to the normal static state, and solicitous advice as to what measures are to be taken with a view to this beneficent end. The problem presented to Mr Clark by the current phenomena of economic development is: how can it be stopped? or, failing that, how can it be guided and minimized? Nowhere is there a sustained inquiry into the dynamic character of the changes that have brought the present (deplorable) situation to pass, nor into the nature and trend of the forces at work in the development that is going forward in this situation. None of this is covered by Mr Clark's use of the word 'dynamic'. All that it covers in the way of theory (chapters 12–21) is a speculative inquiry as to how the equilibrium reestablishes itself when one or more of the quantities involved increases or decreases. Other than quantitive changes are not noticed, except as provocations to homiletic discourse. Not even the causes and the scope of the quantitive changes that may take place in the variables are allowed to fall within the scope of the theory of economic dynamics.

So much of the volume, then, and of the system of doctrines of which the volume is an exposition, as is comprised in the later eight chapters (pp. 372–554), is an exposition of grievances and remedies, with only sporadic intrusions of theoretical matter, and does not properly constitute a part of the theory, whether static or dynamic. There is no intention here to take exception to Mr Clark's outspoken attitude of disapproval toward certain features of the current business situation or to quarrel with the remedial measures which he thinks proper and necessary. This phase of his work is spoken of here rather to call attention to the temperate but uncompromising tone of Mr Clark's writings as a spokesman for the competitive system, considered as an element in the Order of Nature, and to note the fact that this is not economic theory.[2] [. . .]

The classical school, including Mr Clark and his contemporary associates in the science, is hedonistic and utilitarian – hedonistic in its theory and utilitarian in its pragmatic ideals and endeavors. The hedonistic postulates on which this line of economic theory is built up are of a statical scope and character, and nothing but statical theory (taxonomy) comes out of their development.[3] These postulates, and the theorems drawn from them, take

2. What would be the scientific rating of the work of a botanist who should spend his energy in devising ways and means to neutralize the ecological variability of plants, or of a physiologist who conceived it the end of his scientific endeavors to rehabilitate the vermiform appendix or the pineal eye, or to denounce and penalize the imitative coloring of the Viceroy butterfly? What scientific interest would attach to the matter if Mr Loeb, e.g., should devote a few score pages to canvassing the moral responsibilities incurred by him in his parental relation to his parthenogenetically developed sea-urchin eggs?

Those phenomena which Mr Clark characterizes as 'positive perversions' may be distasteful and troublesome, perhaps, but 'the economic necessity of doing what is legally difficult' is not of the 'essentials of theory'.

3. It is a notable fact that even the genius of Herbert Spencer could extract nothing but taxonomy from his hedonistic postulates; e.g., his *Social Statics*. Spencer is both evolutionist and hedonist, but it is only by recourse to other factors, alien to the rational hedonistic scheme, such as habit, delusions, use and disuse, sporadic variation, environmental forces, that he is able to achieve anything in the way of genetic science, since it is only by this recourse that he is enabled to enter the field of cumulative change within which the modern post-Darwinian sciences live and move and have their being.

account of none but quantitive variations, and quantitive variation alone does not give rise to cumulative change, which proceeds on changes in kind.

Economics of the line represented at its best by Mr Clark has never entered this field of cumulative change. It does not approach questions of the class which occupy the modern sciences – that is to say, questions of genesis, growth, variation, process (in short, questions of a dynamic import) – but confines its interest to the definition and classification of a mechanically limited range of phenomena. Like other taxonomic sciences, hedonistic economics does not, and cannot, deal with phenomena of growth except so far as growth is taken in the quantitative sense of a variation in magnitude, bulk, mass, number, frequency. In its work of taxonomy this economics has consistently bound itself, as Mr Clark does, by distinctions of a mechanical, statistical nature and has drawn its categories of classification on those grounds. Concretely, it is confined, in substance, to the determination of and refinements upon the concepts of land, labor and capital, as handed down by the great economists of the classical era, and the correlate concepts of rent, wages, interest and profits. Solicitously, with a painfully meticulous circumspection, the normal, mechanical metes and bounds of these several concepts are worked out, the touchstone of the absolute truth aimed at being the hedonistic calculus. The facts of use and wont are not of the essence of this mechanical refinement. These several categories are mutually exclusive categories, mechanically speaking. The circumstance that the phenomena covered by them are not mechanical facts is not allowed to disturb the pursuit of mechanical distinctions among them. They nowhere overlap and at the same time between them they cover all the facts with which this economic taxonomy is concerned. Indeed, they are in logical consistency, required to cover them. They are hedonistically 'natural' categories of such taxonomic force that their elemental lines of cleavage run through the facts of any given economic situation, regardless of use and wont, even where the situation does not permit these lines of cleavage to be seen by men and recognized by use and wont; so that, for example, a gang of Aleutian Islanders slushing about in the wrack and surf with rakes and magical incantations for the capture of shell-fish are held, in point of taxonomic reality, to be engaged on a feat of hedonistic equilibration in rent, wages and interest. And that is all there is to it. Indeed, for economic theory of this kind, that is all there is to any economic situation. The hedonistic magnitudes vary from one situation to another, but, except for variations in the arithmetical details of the hedonistic balance, all situations are, in point of economic theory, substantially alike.[4]

Taking this unfaltering taxonomy on its own recognisances, let us follow the trail somewhat more into the arithmetical details, as it leads along the narrow ridge of rational calculation, above the tree-tops, on the levels of clear sunlight and moonshine. For the purpose in hand – to bring out the character of this current economic science as a working theory of current facts and more particularly 'as applied to modern problems of industry and public policy' (title page) – the sequence to be observed in questioning the several sections into which the theoretical structure falls is not essential. The structure of classical theory is familiar to all students and Mr Clark's redaction offers no serious departure from the conventional lines. Such divergence from conventional lines as may occur is a matter of details, commonly of improvements in detail; and the revisions of detail do not stand in such an organic relation to one another, nor do they support and strengthen one another in such a manner, as to suggest anything like a revolutionary trend or a breaking away from the conventional lines.

So as regards Mr Clark's doctrine of capital. It does not differ substantially from the doctrines which are gaining currency at the hands of such writers as Mr Fisher or Mr Fetter; although there are certain formal distinctions peculiar to Mr Clark's exposition of the 'capital concept'. But these peculiarities are peculiarities of the method of arriving at the concept rather than peculiarities

4. 'The capital goods have to be taken unit by unit if their value for productive purposes is to be rightly gauged. A part of a supply of potatoes is traceable to the hoes that dig them. . . . We endeavor simply to ascertain how badly the loss of one hoe would affect us or how much good the restoration of it would do us. This truth, like the foregoing ones, has a universal application in economics; for primitive men as well as civilized ones must estimate the specific productivity of the tools that they use' (p. 43).

substantial to the concept itself. The main discussion of the nature of capital is contained in chapter 2, 'Varieties of economic goods'. The conception of capital here set forth is of fundamental consequence to the system, partly because of the important place assigned capital in this system of theory, partly because of the importance which the conception of capital must have in any theory that is to deal with problems of the current (capitalistic) situation. Several classes of capital goods are enumerated, but it appears that in Mr Clark's apprehension – at variance with Mr Fisher's view – persons are not to be included among the items of capital. It is also clear from the run of the argument, though not explicitly stated, that only material, tangible, mechanically definable articles of wealth go to make up capital. In current usage, in the business community, 'capital' is a pecuniary concept, of course, and is not definable in mechanical terms; but Mr Clark, true to the hedonistic taxonomy, sticks by the test of mechanical demarcation and draws the lines of his category on physical grounds; whereby it happens that any pecuniary conception of capital is out of the question. Intangible assets, or immaterial wealth, have no place in the theory; and Mr Clark is exceptionally subtle and consistent in avoiding such modern notions. One gets the impression that such a notion as intangible assets is conceived to be too chimerical to merit attention, even by way of protest or refutation.

Here, as elsewhere in Mr Clark's writings, much is made of the doctrine that the two facts of 'capital' and 'capital goods' are conceptually distinct, though substantially identical. The two terms cover virtually the same facts as would be covered by the terms 'pecuniary capital' and 'industrial equipment'. They are for all ordinary purposes coincident with Mr Fisher's terms, 'capital value' and 'capital', although Mr Clark might enter a technical protest against identifying his categories with those employed by Mr Fisher.[5] 'Capital is this permanent fund of productive goods, the identity of whose component elements is forever changing. Capital goods are the shifting component parts of this permanent aggregate' (p. 29). Mr Clark admits (pp. 29–33) that capital is colloquially spoken and thought of in terms of

5. Cf. a criticism of Mr Fisher's conception in the *Political Science Quarterly* for February 1908.

value, but he insists that in point of substantial fact the working concept of capital is (should be) that of 'a fund of productive goods', considered as an 'abiding entity'. The phrase itself, 'a fund of productive goods', is a curiously confusing mixture of pecuniary and mechanical terms, though the pecuniary expression, 'a fund', is probably to be taken in this connection as a permissible metaphor.

This conception of capital, as a physically 'abiding entity' constituted by the succession of productive goods that make up the industrial equipment, breaks down in Mr Clark's own use of it when he comes (pp. 37–8) to speak of the mobility of capital; that is to say, so soon as he makes use of it. A single illustration of this will have to suffice, though there are several points in his argument where the frailty of the conception is patent enough.

The transfer of capital from one industry to another is a dynamic phenomenon which is later to be considered. What is here important is the fact that it is in the main accomplished without entailing transfers of capital goods. An instrument wears itself out in one industry and instead of being succeeded by a like instrument in the same industry, it is succeeded by one of a different kind which is used in a different branch of production (p. 38)

– illustrated on the preceding page by a shifting of investment from a whaling-ship to a cotton-mill. In all this it is plain that the 'transfer of capital' contemplated is a shifting of investment and that it is, as indeed Mr Clark indicates, not a matter of the mechanical shifting of physical bodies from one industry to the other. To speak of a transfer of 'capital' which does not involve a transfer of 'capital goods' is a contradiction of the main position, that 'capital' is made up of 'capital goods'. The continuum in which the 'abiding entity' of capital resides is a continuity of ownership, not a physical fact. The continuity, in fact, is of an immaterial nature, a matter of legal rights, of contract, of purchase and sale. Just why this patent state of the case is overlooked, as it somewhat elaborately is, is not easily seen. But it is plain that, if the concept of capital were elaborated from observation of current business practice, it would be found that 'capital' is a pecuniary fact, not a mechanical one; that it is an outcome of a valuation, depending immediately on the state of mind of the valuers; and that the specific marks of capital, by which it is distinguishable from other facts, are of an immaterial character. This would, of course, lead directly to the admission of intangible assets; and this, in turn, would upset the law of the 'natural' remuneration of labor and capital to which Mr Clark's argument looks forward from the start. It would also bring in the 'unnatural' phenomena of monopoly as a normal outgrowth of business enterprise.

There is a further logical discrepancy, avoided by resorting to the alleged facts of primitive industry, when there was no capital, for the elements out of which to construct a capital concept, instead of going to the current business situation. In a hedonistic-utilitarian scheme of economic doctrine, such as Mr Clark's, only physically productive agencies can be admitted as efficient factors in production or as legitimate claimants to a share in distribution. Hence capital, one of the prime factors in production and the central claimant in the current scheme of distribution, must be defined in physical terms and delimited by mechanical distinctions. This is necessary for reasons which appear in the succeeding chapter, on 'The measure of consumers' wealth'.

On the same page (38), and elsewhere, it is remarked that 'business disasters' destroy capital in part. The destruction in question is a matter of values; that is to say, a lowering of valuation, not in any appreciable degree a destruction of material goods. Taken as a physical aggregate, capital does not appreciably decrease through business disasters, but, taken as a fact of ownership and counted in standard units of value, it decreases; there is a destruction of values and a shifting of ownership, a loss of ownership perhaps; but these are pecuniary phenomena, of an immaterial character, and so do not directly affect the material aggregate of the industrial equipment. Similarly, the discussion (pp. 301–14) of how changes of method, as, for example, labor-saving devices, 'liberate capital' and at times 'destroy' capital is intelligible only on the admission that 'capital' here is a matter of values owned by investors and is not employed as a synonym for industrial appliances. The appliances in question are neither liberated nor destroyed in the changes contemplated. And it will not do to say that the aggregate of 'productive goods' suffers a diminution by a substitution of devices which increases its aggregate productiveness, as is implied, for example, by the passage on p. 307,[6] if Mr Clark's definition of capital is strictly adhered to. This very singular passage (pp. 306–11, under the captions, 'Hardships entailed on capitalists by progress' and the 'Offset for capital destroyed by changes of method') implies that the aggregate of appliances of production is decreased by a change which increases the aggregate of these articles in that respect (productivity) by virtue of which they are counted in the aggregate. The argument will hold good if 'productive goods' are rated by bulk, weight, number or some such irrelevant test, instead of by their productivity or by their consequent capitalized value. On such a showing it should be proper to say that the polishing of plowshares before they are sent out from the factory diminishes the amount of capital embodied in plowshares by as much as the weight or bulk of the waste material removed from the shares in polishing them.

Several things may be said of the facts discussed in this passage. There is, presumably, a decrease, in bulk, weight or number, of the appliances that make up the industrial equipment at the time when such a technological change as is contemplated takes place. This change, presumably, increases the productive efficiency of the equipment as a whole and so may be said without hesitation to increase the equipment as a factor of production, while it may decrease it, considered as a mechanical magnitude. The owners of the obsolete or obsolescent appliances presumably suffer a diminution of their capital, whether they discard the obsolete appliances or not. The owners of the new appliances, or rather those who own and are able to capitalize the new technological expedients, presumably gain a corresponding advantage, which may take the form of an increase of the effective capitalization of their outfit, as would then be shown by an increased market value of their plant. The largest theoretical outcome of the supposed changes, for an economist not bound by Mr Clark's conception

6. 'The machine itself is often a hopeless specialist. It can do one minute thing and that only, and when a new and better device appears for doing that one thing, the machine has to go, and not to some new employment, but to the junk heap. There is thus taking place a considerable waste of capital in consequence of mechanical and other progress.' 'Indeed, a quick throwing away of instruments which have barely begun to do their work is often the secret of the success of an enterprising manager, but it entails a destruction of capital.'

of capital, should be the generalization that industrial capital – capital considered as a productive agent – is substantially a capitalization of technological expedients and that a given capital invested in industrial equipment is measured by the portion of technological expedients whose usufruct the investment appropriates. It would accordingly appear that the substantial core of all capital is immaterial wealth and that the material objects which are formally the subject of the capitalist's ownership are, by comparison, a transient and adventitious matter. But if such a view were accepted, even with extreme reservations, Mr Clark's scheme of the 'natural' distribution of incomes between capital and labor would 'go up in the air', as the colloquial phrase has it. It would be extremely difficult to determine what share of the value of the joint product of capital and labor should, under a rule of 'natural' equity, go to the capitalist as an equitable return for his monopolization of a given portion of the intangible assets of the community at large.[7] The returns actually accruing to him under competitive conditions would be a measure of the differential advantage held by him by virtue of his having become legally seized of the material contrivances by which the technological achievements of the community are put into effect.

Yet, if in this way capital were apprehended as 'an historical category', as Rodbertus would say, there is at least the comfort in it all that it should leave a free field for Mr Clark's measures of repression as applied to the discretionary management of capital by the makers of trusts. And yet, again, this comforting reflection is coupled with the ugly accompaniment that by the same move the field would be left equally free of moral obstructions to the extreme proposals of the socialists. A safe and sane course for the quietist in these premises should apparently be to discard the equivocal doctrines of the passage (pp. 306–11) from which this train of questions arises and hold fast to the received dogma, however unworkable, that 'capital' is a congeries of physical objects with no ramifications or complications of an immaterial kind,

7. The position of the laborer and his wages, in this light, would not be substantially different from that of the capitalist and his interest. Labor is no more possible, as a fact of industry, without the community's accumulated technological knowledge than is the use of 'productive goods'.

and to avoid all recourse to the concept of value, or price, in discussing matters of modern business.

References

BARROWS, D. P. (1900), *Ethno-Botany of the Coahuilla Indians*, University of Chicago Press.

CLARK, J. B. (1907), *The Essentials of Economic Theory, as Applied to Modern Problems of Industry and Public Policy*, Macmillan.

MARSHALL, A. (1890), *Principles of Economics*, Macmillan Co.

MILL, J. S. (1848), *Principles of Political Economy*, John W. Parker.

6 E. K. Hunt

Economic Scholasticism and Capitalist Ideology

E. K. Hunt, 'Orthodox economic theory and capitalist ideology', *Monthly Review*, vol. 19, 1968, pp. 50–55. Specially revised and enlarged for this volume.

The intellectual achievements of the medieval scholastics consisted primarily of intricate and esoteric deductive elaborations of the religious first-principles which were nearly universally accepted without question. Within their static and rigidly fixed cosmology, the basis of their social and moral philosophy was the search for ways in which men could best understand the immutable laws of God's creation and bring their lives into complete harmony with these laws.

In the eighteenth century there was what superficially appears to be a major intellectual revolution. The cosmology implicit in Newtonian physics rapidly became the dominant intellectual framework for both the 'natural sciences' and the 'social sciences'. The Newtonian concept was basically that of an atomistic world governed by eternal and immutable mechanical laws of motion. All change was absolutely governed by these immutable laws. Change and movement could be understood as series of equilibria of atomistic elements, each self-contained and deterministically 'programmed' by the totality of forces buffeting it about in accordance with the laws of mechanics.

This point of view rapidly came to dominate social inquiry in the eighteenth century. The 'method of the new physical science became all important, for men proceeded to apply it in every field of investigation' (Randall, 1926, p. 261). The social sciences very rapidly came 'almost completely under the domination of the physio-mathematical method' (Randall, 1926, p. 261).

But the new world view was, in many essential respects, very similar to the older, medieval cosmology. A scholarly study of these similarities asserts that one can 'furnish an explanation of eighteenth-century thought, from a historical view, by showing that it was related to something that came before' (Becker, 1932, p. 29). This something was medieval cosmology. The eighteenth-century philosophers merely substituted nature and natural laws for God and God's laws.

[The] disciples of the Newtonian philosophy had not ceased to worship. They had only given another form and a new name to the object of worship: having denatured God, they deified nature. They could therefore, without self-consciousness and with only a slight emendation in the sacred text, repeat the cry of the psalmist: 'I will lift up mine eyes to Nature from whence cometh my help' (Becker, 1932, p. 63).

David Hamilton (1970, pp. 19–20) has shown the result of Newtonianism in the social sciences:

The eighteenth century viewed social forms as fixed in nature and what change took place was at most a quantitative one within fixed limits set by a natural order of things. The universe was a mechanical piece often likened to a clock whose moving parts, when once wound up by a divine Creator, would run eternally in the same pre-established mechanical arrangement. The best interest of man could be attained by an objective scrutiny of the workings of this mechanical universe. This inquiry was to be guided by reason, which would uncover the great principles by which the social universe was guided in its rhythmical pattern of movement. By laying bare these principles man would be able to conform to them and thus would enhance his contentment and happiness on earth. Misery and despair, the product of man's ignorance, which was also the source of his folly in flaunting these immutable natural principles, could be banished from the world.

Adam Smith's *The Wealth of Nations* was the denouement of the eighteenth-century philosophy. In place of Newton's law of gravitation Smith substituted 'self-interest'. A society which operated in accordance with natural law would be a private-property, capitalist, market system in which each atomistic individual exercised his 'natural right' to seek his own self-interest. Each selfish, acquisitive individual would simultaneously promote the social good while he sought only his own welfare.

Smith's assertion that the 'invisible hand' of the capitalist, market system would harmonize all individual egoistic actions and lead to an 'optimal' allocation of productive resources has remained the most consistent basis for an ideological defence of capitalism down to the present time. 'The whole basis of modern price theory is to be found in Adam Smith without "modern refinement" ' (Hamilton, 1970, p. 22).

Orthodox economists of the last 150 years, like the medieval scholastics, accepted the basic axioms of their system almost without question. They worked endlessly to create a brilliant deductive edifice on these axioms. By introducing complicated models of mathematical reasoning they have made it difficult, if not impossible, for all but the professional economist to follow the tortuous paths by which they arrive at their conclusions. Their conclusions are the same as Smith's: inherent in the capitalist economic system are forces which, if nurtured properly, will tend to create an ideal society.

The 'common core' or ideological and cosmological framework of economics has been only infrequently challenged. Rather, with scholastic zeal economists have endlessly produced esoteric trivia to embellish the decorative trim of their magnificent edifice. Milton Friedman (1970, p. 80) has succinctly described modern economics and modern economists:

Economics is a scientific discipline that has a core that is common to almost all professional economists. *Naturally*, economists devote little professional research and writing – except in textbooks – to this common core. They concentrate on the issues that are on the frontier where economics is being made rather than taught or applied (italics added).

What is the common 'core' accepted by all and propagated in textbooks? How does it relate to the deductive esoteria at the 'frontier' to which the modern scholastic economists are devoted?

Most college textbooks in microeconomic theory begin by describing an economic system in which: (a) market choices by consumers are determined by a coherent subjective preference ordering; (b) the decisions concerning what commodity mix to produce and how to produce it are governed solely by the desire of producers to maximize profits; and (c) buyers and sellers are pitted against each other in a market which is so large that no individual buyer or seller can, through his own purchases or sales, affect the market price.

Then, from certain axioms about the nature of consumer preference orderings and the technical relationships between inputs and outputs, a consistent line of deductive reasoning leads to the conclusion that an economic system of this description will allocate its resources in such a way that any possible change in production, distribution or consumption that could possibly make one person better off (leave him in a preferred position) could only be brought about by making someone else worse off (leave him in a less preferred position). In short, resources would be efficiently allocated so that, given existing tastes and the existing income distribution, it would be impossible to augment the aggregate value of production through a reallocation.

It is then argued that scientific objectivity prohibits the economist from making a normative choice between two situations which involve the bettering of one person or class of persons at the expense of another person or class of persons. Hence, the conclusion is reached that the criterion of 'economic efficiency' is scientific, whereas the criterion of 'equity' is not. The competitive capitalist economy is shown most perfectly to satisfy the criterion of 'economic efficiency'.[1] Therefore, no other system can, on 'objective and scientific' grounds alone, be shown to represent an improvement over this capitalist price-market system. By extension, this doctrine becomes a claim that *laissez-faire* capitalism represents the best of all possible worlds.

To be sure, some flaws in the system are acknowledged. The principal admitted weaknesses are:

1. Some buyers and sellers *are* large enough to affect prices and, moreover, the economies of large-scale production seem to render this inevitable.

2. Some commodities are 'consumed socially' and their production and sale would never be profitable in a *laissez-faire* capitalist economy even though they may be deemed highly desirable by most citizens within the economy (e.g., roads, schools, armies, etc.).

3. The costs to the producer of a commodity may differ significantly from the social costs of producing that commodity, so

---

1. Although Lange and Taylor (1964) have shown that an economy in which the means of production are collectively owned and for which the same assumptions are made will also result in a state of 'optimal economic efficiency'.

that it is possible that for society as a whole the costs of production exceed the benefits of production for the commodity even though the producer still profits from making and selling it (e.g., the poisoning of the water and air by producers making profits but doing little or nothing about this evil side effect which could eventually endanger human life itself).

4. An unrestrained price-market system appears to be inherently unstable and is subject to recurring depressions that incur enormous social costs.

The principal differences separating 'liberal' economists from 'conservative' economists stem from an inability to agree on the extent and significance of these flaws. It is generally agreed that to the degree that the flaws do exist and do disrupt the otherwise beneficial workings of the capitalist system, they can only be corrected by government intervention into the market system.

It is argued that government anti-trust actions can force firms to act *as if* they were competitive, and something called 'workable competition' can be achieved. Roads, schools, armies and other socially 'consumed' commodities can be provided by the government. Extensive systems of taxes and subsidies can be used to equate private and social costs where they differ. Finally, through the wise use of fiscal and monetary policy the government can eliminate the instability of the system.

The flaws are thus seen as minor and ephemeral. An enlightened government can correct them and free the 'invisible hand' once again to create the best of all possible worlds.

This, as I view it, represents a fair précis of orthodox economic ideology. I do not propose to argue here with either its assumptions or the reasoning by which the conclusions are reached. Rather, I wish to show how the rigorous working out of all the implications of this theory has led to a fruitless dead-end. One can argue that the ideology, when pushed to the logical extremes inherent in it, contains the seeds of its own intellectual destruction.

One of the most devastating intellectual attacks came from J. de V. Graaff's tightly reasoned book, *Theoretical Welfare Economics*. Graaff showed that economists had not really appreciated the long and restrictive list of assumptions necessary for the optimally efficient allocation of resources envisioned in the model of a competitive, free-market capitalism to be realized. He lists seventeen such assumptions which he has shown to be necessary (Graaff, 1957, pp. 142–54). Many of them are so restrictive that one must agree with Graaff that 'the measure of acceptance . . . [this theory] has won among professional economists would be astonishing were not its pedigree so long and respectable' (Graaff, 1957, p. 142). A few of Graaff's seventeen conditions will suffice to illustrate the point. The theory requires (a) that any individual's welfare is identical with his preference ordering, i.e. that children, drug addicts, fiends, criminals and lunatics, as well as all other persons, always prefer that which is best for them; (b) that neither risk nor uncertainty is ever present; (c) that productivity is totally unaffected by the existing distribution of wealth; and (d) that all capital goods as well as consumer goods are infinitely divisible. These represent but four of Graaff's seventeen restrictive conditions which must obtain before the price-market system can achieve 'optimal economic efficiency'.

In the light of this, it is obvious that perfect competition could never be anything more than a normative model toward which government policies might attempt to move a capitalist economy. The goal could not possibly ever be achieved.

The next important piece of iconoclastic literature, well known to professional economists, is 'the general theory of the second best'.[2] In the words of the eminent economist, William J. Baumol (1965, p. 138):

In brief, this theorem [of the second best] states, on the basis of a mathematical argument, that in a concrete situation characterized by *any* deviation from 'perfect' optimality, partial policy measures which eliminate only some of the departures from the optimal arrangement may well result in a net decrease in social welfare.

This important argument shows that, judged by the criterion furnished by the economic ideologists themselves, anti-trust actions or any other attempts by the government to bring about 'workable competition' may result in effects diametrically opposed to those envisioned by the authors of these policies.

2. For a definitive formulation of this theory see Lipsey and Lancaster (1956–7).

Further work by Buchanan and Kafoglis (1963) and Baumol (1964) has shown that the rather naïve faith held by many economists that a system of taxes and subsidies could nullify the adverse effects encountered when private costs differ from social costs was based on an oversimplified view. Baumol showed that once again policies based on traditional arguments may actually diminish rather than augment social welfare (again using the orthodox economist's criterion of welfare).

In addition, concerning the stability of the system, Friedman (1953) and Baumol (1961) have shown that even if it were practically possible for monetary and fiscal authorities to use their powers in the manner prescribed in textbooks (and this is a big 'if') and if they were helped by a system of 'automatic stabilizers', the problem of instability would probably still be insuperable.

Finally, Arrow (1963) has shown that if we adopt consumer sovereignty as a fundamental normative criterion and simultaneously deny interpersonal comparisons of relative well-being (two of the basic tenets of orthodox economic ideology), then any coherent programme of government action must be imposed from above. No type of democratic voting under these two basic assumptions can be shown to yield a consistently ordered set of alternatives with which to guide government policies.

The significance of these recent developments in economic theory lies in the fact that each of these theoreticians has been in the mainstream of orthodox economics. Economic ideology as refined and systematized in the rarefied atmosphere of the professional academic economist has ended by destroying its own foundations.

Significantly, if one can judge by the best-selling textbooks in economics, at both the beginning and advanced undergraduate levels, a student who graduates from a North American or European university with a bachelor's degree in economics has probably never encountered these iconoclastic exercises which rigorously work out the full implications of orthodox economic theory.

References

ARROW, K. J. (1963), *Social Choice and Individual Values*, Wiley.
BAUMOL, W. J. (1961), 'Pitfalls in counter-cyclical policies: some tools and results', *Rev. Econ. Stat.*, vol. 43, pp. 21–6.

BAUMOL, W. J. (1964), 'External economies and second-order optimality conditions', *Amer. econ. Rev.*, vol. 54, pp. 358–72.

BAUMOL, W. J. (1965), 'Informed judgment, rigorous theory and public policy', *S. econ. J.*, vol. 32, pp. 137–45.

BECKER, C. (1932), *The Heavenly City of Eighteenth Century Philosophers*, Yale University Press.

BUCHANAN, J. M., and KAFOGLIS, M. Z. (1963), 'A note on public goods supply', *Amer. econ. Rev.* vol. 53, pp. 403–14.

FRIEDMAN, M. (1953), 'The effects of a full employment policy on economic stability: a formal analysis', in *Essays in Positive Economics*, University of Chicago Press.

FRIEDMAN, M. (1970), 'On Paul Samuelson', *Newsweek*, 9 November, p. 80.

GRAAFF, J. DE V. (1957), *Theoretical Welfare Economics*, Cambridge University Press.

HAMILTON, D. (1970), *Evolutionary Economics*, University of New Mexico Press.

LANGE, O., and TAYLOR, F. M. (1964), *On the Economic Theory of Socialism*, McGraw-Hill.

LIPSEY, R. G., and LANCASTER, K. (1956–7), 'The general theory of second best', *Rev. econ. Stud.*, vol. 24, pp. 11–32.

RANDALL, J. H., Jr (1926), *The Making of the Modern Mind*, Houghton Mifflin.

Part Three
The Capital Controversy and Income Distribution

The five Readings in this Part deal with the discovery of anomalies associated with the neo-classical concept of capital. At first these were regarded as 'exceptions' but the publication of Piero Sraffa's *Production of Commodities by Means of Commodities* led to a deeper inquiry. Joan Robinson (Reading 7), in her review paper, was the first to recognize the full significance of Sraffa's critique, that the structure of conventional economics itself was being called into question. Maurice Dobb (Reading 8) and D. M. Nuti (Reading 9) discuss the untenability of the whole notion, dating back to Jevons, Walras and the Austrian School, of a production function and the explanation of the distribution of income between capital and labour on the basis of 'marginal productivity'. In Reading 10 Joan Robinson outlines the ensuing controversy in which the neo-classicals attempted unsuccessfully a direct refutation – 'the reswitching debate' – and resorted to reducing the whole argument to the implausibilities of a 'one-commodity world'. Another defence, equally unsuccessful, was put forward by Paul Samuelson in terms of his 'surrogate production function'. This is discussed by P. Garegnani in Reading 11.

7 Joan Robinson

Prelude to a Critique of Economic Theory

Joan Robinson, 'Prelude to a critique of economic theory', *Oxford Economic Papers*, vol. 13, 1961, pp. 7–14. Reprinted in Joan Robinson, *Collected Economic Papers*, vol. 3, Blackwell, 1965, pp. 7–14.

It is no wonder that this book [Sraffa, *Production of Commodities by Means of Commodities*] took a long time to write. It will not be read quickly. Addicts of pure economic logic who find their craving ill-satisfied by the wishy-washy products peddled in contemporary journals have here a double-distilled elixir that they can enjoy, drop by drop, for many a day.

For some, indeed, the logic may be too pure. We plunge immediately into the argument without any preliminary discussion of assumptions and delimitation of topics. Evidently we are in a capitalist economy, but to avoid the ambiguities which have clustered around the word, capital is never mentioned. There is profit, but no enterprises; wages, but no pay-packets; prices, but no markets. Nothing is mentioned but the equations of production and the necessary conditions of exchange.

There is a great deal to be said for this method of exposition (over and above its lapidary style), for every attempt by an author to explain himself in terms of the preconceptions of one reader confuses another. Best leave each to work it out for himself.

To find a clue, let us go back a stage and pick up the argument from Sraffa's Preface to Ricardo's *Principles*. Postulate that corn is the only commodity consumed by workers and that the corn-wage rate is fixed. Corn is required also as seed and there is no other commodity or equipment necessary for the production of corn. Then a stock of corn in existence at the beginning of a year has reproduced itself with a surplus at the end of the year. The ratio of the surplus to the stock is the rate of profit. The workers are, so to speak, intermediate goods, like machines, necessary for the process by which corn produces corn.

The corn-profit may be used to employ more workers either to produce luxuries or to carry out investment; or it may rot in the barns. The way it is used cannot affect the rate of profit, which is fixed by technical conditions, and the equilibrium prices of all other products are determined in terms of corn (and so in terms of each other) by their costs of production, including profit at the corn-rate upon the capital (valued in corn) required to produce them.

Can the propositions derived from this model survive the removal of the postulate that only corn is required to produce corn?

The first step – here the present argument begins – is to introduce a variety of wage goods. Let there be a number of distinct commodities each of which is required, in a particular quantity, to be consumed by a worker, just as particular quantities of oil and fuel are required to operate a machine. The commodities are also required to produce each other and themselves. (To set us off on the right tack, wheat, iron and pigs are mentioned. But they soon become commodities a, b, . . . , k.) The same argument applies as before. The commodities reproduce themselves with a physical surplus. The condition that the rate of profit is uniform throughout the economy settles their relative prices. The value of the stock of commodities at the beginning of the year and of the surplus after they have been replaced can be expressed in terms of any one of the commodities. The value of the real wage (which is fixed in physical composition by technical necessity) is also determined and the cost of production of any commodities that do not enter into the real wage (subject to the condition that they yield the ruling rate of profit) settles their prices. This merely elaborates the corn-wage model without altering its essence.

The next step takes us much further. Instead of the real wage being fixed by physical necessity, the workers receive a share of the surplus. The author toys with the idea of separating the wage into a part which is necessary and the rest; he rejects it in deference to ordinary usage. He makes this concession with evident reluctance, but readers may welcome it, not only to avoid verbal clumsiness but also because we could hardly imagine that, when the workers had a surplus to spend on beef, their physical need for wheat was unchanged. Wage goods thus cease to be necessary for production in technically fixed proportions. There remain, however, commodities which are necessary as means of production for themselves and each other. (The pigs and wheat presumably drop out, but the iron remains.) They reproduce themselves with the aid of labour and yield a surplus out of which the labour is paid.

We are now launched on the main problem – the effect upon prices of changes in the division of the surplus between wages and profits.

Nothing is said about what determines the division. We are to consider the consequences, not the causes, of changes in the real wage.

It is this, not the austere style, that makes the book difficult. We are concerned with equilibrium prices and a rate of profit uniform throughout the economy, but we are given only half of an equilibrium system to stand on. We need a fence to prevent us plunging off into the abyss. The author suggests as a helpful (but not necessary) provisional assumption that constant returns prevail. I, for one, found that this only made me all the more dizzy. It seems better to assume that changes in the share of wages do not affect the composition of output.

There is a further difficulty. The wage 'changes' only in the sense that the value of x changes as we run our eye up and down a curve. In the year that we are examining, each change has already happened. So long as all commodities reproduce themselves within a year, this is easy to accept; but when long-lived machines come into the picture (in a later chapter) it causes discomfort. Can the equalization of the rate of profit throughout the economy come about except through the equalization of expected profits on new investment in various lines? If the rate of profit has changed during the lifetime of machines in existence this year, there is no equality between expected and realized profits in any one line – why should there be equality between realized profits in different lines? Let us add to the protective fence of provisional assumptions that we need not take the word 'change' literally. We are only to compare the effects of having differing rates of profit, with the same technical conditions and the same composition of output. Thus reassured, we can remain on the narrow ledge without vertigo.

When the wage is not given by technical conditions, what do prices mean? A change in the division of the surplus between wages and profits alters relative prices. But we need to know the prices to value the surplus that is to be divided. This was the problem that flummoxed Ricardo.

Sraffa's solution is ingenious and satisfying. He isolates those *basic* commodities which enter directly or indirectly into the production of all commodities and, from the technical equations which show how each enters into the production of the others, he constructs a standard of value in the form of a composite commodity into which each particular item enters, as means of production, in the same proportion as it appears as output.

The beauty of this is that, as the wage reckoned in terms of this standard rises, the prices of some of the commodities composing it (in which wages are a high proportion of cost) rise, and others (in which profits are a high proportion of cost) fall, to just such an extent as to balance each other and leave the ratio of the value of the surplus to the value of the means of production unchanged. This provides a technically determined ratio of surplus to means of production which is independent of the division of the surplus between wages and profits.

Now, given the n technical equations for n commodities and the wage rate in terms of the standard, the $n - 1$ prices and the rate of profit are determined. Or, given the n equations and the rate of profit, the wage is determined.

Assuming that wages are paid at the end of the year (no capital is required to finance a wage fund) there is a linear relationship between the share of wages in the surplus and the rate of profit.

This having been established, the standard commodity can be left to look after itself and the argument is conducted in terms of the rate of profit corresponding to zero wages (that is, the ratio of surplus to means of production), and the actual rate of profit, with the wage rate that it entails.

In order to construct the standard commodity it must be possible to find a quorum of basics – commodities that enter directly or indirectly into the production of all commodities. So long as there are necessary wage goods there are bound to be basics, for, via labour, the wage goods enter into all production. But when wages are part of the surplus, we have to fall back on an assumption that there is at least one basic commodity. Certainly that is plausible enough, but it is natural to ask what would happen if there were none. Does the whole method stand or fall on this assumption? I think not.

Suppose that technical equations could be divided into two systems without any overlap, in one of which iron enters directly or indirectly into the production of all commodities, and in the other, wood. The two systems of equations belong to the same economy in the sense that the rate of profit and the wage rate are the same in both. Now, when the rate of profit is given, the wage rate in terms of the iron-standard is determined for the iron system and the wage rate in terms of the wood-standard is determined for the wood system. The fact that the wage is uniform determines the price of iron in the wood-standard. The assumption of at least one basic commodity thus appears to be a mere simplification, not a crucial step in the argument.

After exploring the properties of a system in which each productive process takes one year and produces one commodity, we are shown the application of the method to joint products, fixed capital and land, and to the choice of technique when alternative methods are available for producing a single commodity. The argument then ceases as suddenly as it began.

In elaborating the method to deal with complexities such as long-lived machines, many points of great interest are turned up (including a version of the formula for the relation of the value of a machine to its cost which was worked out, presumably, much later, though published earlier, by Kahn and Champernowne), but the main point of dealing with these problems is just to show that it can be done. The essence of the argument remains that which is exhibited with circulating capital only.

The sub-title gives a hint of the purpose for which it has been established – *Prelude to a Critique of Economic Theory*. In the preface, after referring to a draft of the book which he discussed with Keynes in 1928, Sraffa writes:

As was only natural during such a long period, others have from time to time independently taken up points of view which are similar to one or other of those adopted in this paper and have developed them further or in different directions from those pursued here. It is, however, a peculiar feature of the set of propositions now published that, although they do not enter into any discussion of the marginal theory of value and distribution, they have nevertheless been designed to serve as the basis for a critique of that theory.

The significant word is 'however'. Others have developed input–output systems and process analysis to higher degrees of elaboration than are shown here, but they have not brought them to bear on the foundations of orthodox doctrine.

Can we divine what the critique will be? There are three main propositions which can be derived from the corn-wage model and which have been shown to survive all the necessary modifications that follow from elaborating its assumptions.

The first is that, when we are provided with a set of technical equations for production and a real wage rate which is uniform throughout the economy, there is no room for demand equations in the determination of equilibrium prices. (When we take down our protective fence and allow that changes in distribution affect the composition of output, we shall need a fresh set of equations relating them, but that is quite another matter.)

Some might complain that this is only flogging a dead Marshallian horse (which Sraffa himself helped to kill, even before 1928). But to my mind it emphasizes a point which, both in its scholastic and in its political aspect, is of great importance; in a market economy, either there may be a tendency towards uniformity of wages and the rate of profit in different lines of production, or prices may be governed by supply and demand, but not both. Where supply and demand rule, there is no room for uniform levels of wages and the rate of profit. The Walrasian system makes sense if we interpret it in terms of an artisan economy, where each producer is committed to a particular product, so that his income depends on his output and its price. Each can have a prospective rate of return on investment in his own line, but there is no mechanism to equalize profits between one line and another. In real life, no one expects to see an equalization of the rates of profit obtainable from sugar in Cuba and cocoa in Ghana or can even say what an equal rate of profit would mean.

The intrusion of demand equations into the theory of the wage economy, and the attempt to foist a rate of profit onto the exchange economy, have led to endless confusion; a critique to clear it up is long overdue.

The second proposition is mentioned by Sraffa in his *References to the Literature*. It is the rejection of the claim 'that the price of every commodity, either immediately or ultimately, resolves itself entirely (that is to say, without leaving any commodity residue) into wage, profit, and rent'.

In the corn-wage economy, the production of corn this year requires that there should be a stock of corn already in existence, to provide seed and the subsistence of the workers until the next harvest. Sraffa has removed the assumption of a technically determined physical real wage. This throws great weight upon commodities regarded as means of production, a weight made all the greater by the assumption that capital is not required for a wage fund. *Production of Commodities by Means of Commodities* is his central theme.

It leads to the very striking proposition that there is a technically determined maximum notionally possible rate of profit, which would obtain at zero wages. (It is only notionally possible, for even when the postulate of a precise physically necessary wage has been abandoned, there is still a vague but tough lower limit to possible real wages and so an upper limit to the possible rate of profit.)

The third proposition, if we may indulge in a loose mode of expression that the author carefully avoids, is that the marginal productivity theory of distribution is all bosh.

Sraffa does not deny any sensible arguments that can be expressed in marginal terms. His treatment of diminishing returns from land and of the choice of technique makes room for legitimate uses of the concept of a production function. What he demonstrates decisively (though doubtless the deaf adders will take no notice) is that there is no such thing as a 'quantity of capital' which exists independently of the rate of profit.

It is important to realize that the third proposition does not depend upon the second.

Certainly the proposition that no production, by the methods known today, could take place without some pre-existing commodities, is highly plausible, but it is a matter of fact, not of logic. It does not mean that if prices could be reduced without residue, to wage, profit and rent, then the marginal productivity theory of distribution would be cogent.

Flint mines were dug with antlers picked up in the forest. If this economy was run on capitalist lines, it must have been necessary to advance wages to the men collecting antlers (otherwise they would be self-employed traders). Men dug the pits and shaped the flints. All processes could be reduced to terms of dated inputs of labour. To find the capital required for production (in the sense in which capital is the principal on which profit is the interest) we must know either the wage in terms of axes or the rate of profit.

Certainly, Sraffa is right that in Ricardo's time, or our own, commodities are necessary to produce commodities. But even the neolithic rate of profit was not determined by the 'marginal product of capital'.

Presumably, it will be a little time before the critique to which this is the prelude will be published. We might have some self-criticism meanwhile.

Postscript

The comment upon Sraffa's second proposition is evidently incorrect. When wages are advanced to the workers searching for antlers, there must be a stock of wage-goods already in existence or productive capacity to supply them. If these are purchased from an independent peasantry, outside the capitalist economy, the peasants, in turn, must be able to support themselves while the production is going on. Either way, commodities are required to produce commodities, and Sraffa's proposition holds.

The reference to deaf adders has turned out to be sadly correct, as the following papers in this section show [not included here; see section I of *Collected Economic Papers*, vol. 3].

8 Maurice Dobb

The Sraffa System and Critique of the Neo-Classical Theory of Distribution

Maurice Dobb, 'The Sraffa system and critique of the neo-classical theory of distribution', *De Economist*, vol. 118, 1970, pp. 347–62.

I should, perhaps, start by explaining that the intention of this paper is to assess, in very general terms, some of the implications of the method and approach represented by Mr Sraffa's (1960) system, especially in relation to the discussion of recent years about the so-called 'neo-classical' theory of distribution. This discussion, I think, is of special interest and importance for anyone who is at all attracted to the Ricardo–Marx tradition in economic thought (and should not be dismissed by him on the ground of its abstract character as mere formalism); and for this reason I shall try to sketch the historical relation of this modern debate to the earlier (truly 'classical') tradition.

It may be remembered that the sub-title of Sraffa's book is *Prelude to a Critique of Economic Theory*. It is to such a critique that this work has so largely contributed (if not originating it) over the last decade. What is at stake here is the logical tenability of the whole line of theoretical doctrine dating back to Jevons and the Austrians – to what has been called the Jevonian Revolution (itself a conscious counter-revolution against the classical school and against Ricardo and Marx in particular). This has usually been discussed in terms of a difference between two rival theories of value, one emphasizing conditions of production (in particular, expenditures of labour) and the other conditions of demand as represented by utility to consumers. What I am concerned to emphasize here is the crucial contrast between them as *theories of distribution*. What the 'modern' theory (as I shall call it) in its several variants since Jevons and the Austrians essentially does is to locate a theory of distribution entirely within the circle of market relations or the sphere of exchange: to derive the prices of what Walras called the productive services of factors (and hence income distribution) as part of the general pricing process of commodities; and this without introducing any sociological *datum* and quite independently of what Marx called the social relations of production. Upon this its whole claim to universality and independence of institutional conditions depends: for example the corollary often drawn from it to the effect that the long-run level of wages is not capable of substantial modification by collective bargaining and trade union action. With the Austrians this determination of distribution within the general pricing process is particularly clear: as exemplified in Menger's derivation of the prices of goods of so-called 'higher order', and hence prices of factors by a process of 'imputation', from the prices of goods of 'first order' (products sold to final consumers). But it is true also of the Walrasian system, as is brought out by Walras himself when he says: 'Though it is true that productive services are bought and sold in their own special markets, nevertheless the prices of these services are determined in the market for products' (Walras, 1874, p. 422 of 1954 edn).

The linch-pin of this whole conception is of course the notion of marginal productivity of a factor (as governing the pricing of the latter); and this is why the calling in question of the notion of determination by marginal productivity, especially as regards capital and the rate of profit (or interest), by the modern critique is of more than ordinary importance.

It must be remembered that the use of marginal productivity as a concept necessarily involves two things. Firstly it involves the notion of varying the quantity of one factor, in use in combination with a fixed quantity of others. This requires that factors should be reasonably homogeneous (like labour) or else reducible (in the long-run view, at least) to some homogeneous quantity (as capital has been traditionally regarded). Secondly, and as an extension of the first, it involves the notion of a 'production function' – or a curve representing all the diverse factor-combinations possible in a given state of technical knowledge; each point on this curve representing a distinct method of production or 'technique'. At each of these points the ratio of factor-substitution (or its inverse the ratio of marginal productivities) must in competitive equilibrium of course be equal to the ratio of factor-prices. It follows that as relative factor-prices change the least-cost technique will change; and in any well-ordered production function as wages rise and profits fall, technique shifts in a more capital-intensive direction (i.e. more capital using and less labour using).

It is precisely the logical validity of these two notions that the recent debate has challenged; and this is why the critique is fundamental to the whole modern post-Jevons approach. For some time most economists have been aware, mainly from the writings of Professor Joan Robinson, that there is a crucial problem of measurement of capital as a factor of production. If capital is not reducible to a single quantity, then how can one even conceptually calculate the effect on output of varying it by a unit amount? (Of course, when valued at current prices, heterogeneous capital goods acquire a common monetary expression; but this process of pricing or valuation presupposes a rate of return on the plant and equipment in question of which the latter value is the capitalization, and one is here involved in circular reasoning – one has to *assume* a rate of interest in order to demonstrate how this equilibrium rate of return is determined. In other words, if capital is treated simply as a sum of values, these values are *not* independent of the profit–wage ratio to be determined.)

One way out is not to talk of capital as a *genus* at all, but to treat each different capital good as a separate factor. There then remains the difficulty as to how and what uniform rate of return is then established on all these heterogeneous capital goods (uniform it may well tend to be if their relative supplies are allowed to vary, but at what level?).[1] The other way out is to identify a common substance to which heterogeneous capital goods are reducible. To do so without introducing a metaphysical entity such as Joan Robinson has ridiculed with her reference to 'ectoplasm' is not easy, to say the least. Böhm-Bawerk tried to do so with his notion of a 'period of production', compounded of labour and time, of which more will be said later. In the modern literature one quite commonly meets the explicit assumption of some primary substance variously called meccano sets, malleable clay, putty, jelly, even butter, which can be supposedly converted at will into this or that kind of capital good. Needless to say, this assumption is quite arbitrary. Some defenders of orthodox

1. See Garegnani's (1960, pp. 91 ff.) critique of Walras.

doctrine seek to salvage certain propositions which they claim to be independent of any measurement of capital (such as Solow's recent attempt to give an unambiguous meaning to a 'social rate of return' on investment in a socialist system and to show that this must equal the rate of interest). But as Bhaduri (1969) and Pasinetti (1969) show, to invent a particular definition and to make what is defined equal to something else is to say nothing about how profit or 'rate of return' is *determined*. Again, Professor Samuelson has introduced the parable of a 'surrogate production function', of which again more later on.

What in the past few years had added weight and point to this whole critique is the possibility, effectively demonstrated for the first time in Sraffa's slender book of ten years ago, of the so-called 'switching of techniques'. This could summarily be said, indeed, to give the *coup de grâce* to the whole notion of a production function and hence to the very idea of marginal productivity as determinant of profit. Let me emphasize that what we are confronted with here is not just some technical difficulty within the specialized field of capital theory, but with the much more general problem of the relativity of all price relations to income distribution: i.e. to the wage–profit relation. The latter can*not*, therefore, be determined within the sphere of price relations (what Marx called the sphere of circulation): for its determination one has to look beyond and outside it (or, if you like, beneath it). This is 'back to Marx' with a vengeance.

In case the implication of this 'switching of techniques' and how it can happen is still unclear, perhaps a summary word of explanation should be added. The occurrence should not, I believe, seem at all surprising or obscure to anyone at all familiar with Marx, since it amounts simply to the changing relative deviations of prices (Marx's 'prices of production', i.e.) from values – in particular, prices of inputs and of inputs into those inputs – as the rate of surplus value (or the profit–wage ratio) changes. But to those reared in the modern tradition it may seem so paradoxical as to be hard to comprehend.

Let me put it as summarily as I can in this way. To this end I must anticipate by asking you to think of the cost and final price of a commodity as being arrived at as the summation of a vertical series of stages of production spread out backwards in time, each consisting of a labour input plus commodity inputs (machines, raw materials) that are products of some earlier stage; each stage with its labour input having its attached date in the vertical series. Manifestly everything will depend on how these labour terms are distributed in time. Suppose two commodities, one with larger total labour inputs but these bunched at recent dates and the other with much smaller total labour inputs bunched at distant dates. With low wages and high interest the first may come out cheaper despite its larger wage bill. As wages rise and interest falls, the second will at some stage have the advantage because of its lower wage bill: an advantage that one would expect it to retain however high wages rose and interest fell. This is the orthodox case to which an ordinary production function can be fitted. But suppose a case where one commodity has all or most of its labour inputs applied at some *intermediate* date, the other one having some labour at a very distant date but the bulk of it at a quite recent date. It is perfectly possible for the second of the pair to have the price advantage at intermediate levels of interest and wages, but the first one to be preferred (because cheaper) *both* at very high levels of interest (with low wages) *and* at very low levels of interest (with equivalently high wages). The reason is the possibility of differences in the compounding effect of interest-rate changes on the comparative cost of inputs of very distant and of intermediate dates. Of this Sraffa (1960, p. 37) gives an example, which he calls that of wine and the old oak chest.

Another way of expressing it would be to say that it depends on widely different proportions of labour and other inputs at successive 'layers' of production. To quote Mr Sraffa (1960, p. 15):

The relative price movements of two products come to depend, not only on the 'proportions' of labour to means of production by which they are respectively produced, but also on the 'proportions' by which those means have themselves been produced, and also on the 'proportions' by which the means of production of those means of production have been produced, and so on. The result is that the relative price of two products may move with the fall in wages in the opposite direction to what we might have expected on the basis of their respective 'proportions'; besides, the prices of their respective means of production may move in such a way as to reverse the order of the two products as to higher and lower proportions.

He proceeds immediately to underline the relevance of this to 'the attempts that have been made to find in the "period of production" an independent measure of the quantity of capital which could be used, without arguing in a circle, for the determination of prices and of the shares in distribution'. 'The reversals in the direction of the movement of relative prices [as wages change], in the face of unchanged methods of production' are not only 'conclusive in showing the impossibility of aggregating the "periods" belonging to the several quantities of labour into a single magnitude which could be regarded as representing the quantity of capital', but 'cannot be reconciled with *any* notion of capital as a measurable quantity independent of distribution and prices' (Sraffa, 1960, p. 38).

With regard to Samuelson's 'surrogate production function', it turns out[2] that it is viable only on the very assumption of uniform proportions (or uniform compositions of capital) which has always been considered insufficiently realistic when used as a basis for exchange according to values in Marx's volume 1: an assumption that would *ipso facto*, of course, exclude the possibility of multiple switching of techniques.

Someone may wish to say at this point: granted that the modern school of theory has run into a blind alley and that some reconsideration is necessary. But why should this mean that we should do any better if we were to return to Ricardo or Marx? Even if the Sraffa system be held to offer a more promising approach, it may not be at all clear what, if any, relation this bears to the older classical tradition. Before making further comments about the positive aspects of the Sraffa system, it may therefore be advisable to go back, historically speaking, and say a few words about the way in which with Ricardo and Marx distribution was connected with their value theory.

What I want to suggest is that the crucial link – it could be called an organic connection – between the Ricardo–Marx theories of value and distribution is that the former immediately provides a theory of profit once the level of real wages is given (i.e. given together with the conditions of production and comparative labour expenditures involved in producing wage goods

2. See a to-be-published article by Professor Garegnani [Garegnani, 1970] cited in Harcourt (1969, pp. 393 and 401).

and producing output in general[3]). So far as price formation is concerned, since the *rate* of profits is here involved (and not only their ratio to wages), 'conditions of production', as we shall see, must be interpreted so as to include other immediate inputs than labour and/or the time over which the labour embodied in those inputs (and in the inputs into those inputs) have to be advanced, i.e. the time intervening between the labour expenditures in question and the emergence of the final product.

Thus Ricardo in his earliest formulation of a theory of profit, when he was still expressing things in simple product terms, spoke of profit being determined by 'the proportion of production to the consumption necessary to such production'. So long as a single wage good, corn, was taken as appearing both as input (workers' subsistence) and as output in the wage-goods industry, this was, of course, a proportion expressible in purely product terms, without the introduction of any theory of relative values. Having 'got rid of rent' by operating at the margin of corn production, he adopted the position that the *general* rate of profit, in manufacture generally as well as in agriculture, must conform to this ratio of corn-produced to corn-consumed at the margin of agriculture. A theory of value was, of course, necessary to demonstrate how and why prices of manufactures were brought into appropriate relationship with the price of corn as wage good *par excellence*. By the time of his *Essay on Profit* of 1815 he was putting the matter in this way: when as a result of diminishing returns productivity of labour at the agricultural margin falls, this must bring about a fall in the *general* rate of profit, because if 'more labour [is] necessary in the production of corn, whilst no more labour is required to produce gold, silver, cloth, linen, etc. the exchangeable value of corn will necessarily rise as compared with those things'. By the time of his *Principles* of two years later he was quite aware that different prices would be *differently* affected by a rise of wages (according to the proportions of fixed capital to current (or 'living') labour employed in their production); and for this additional reason a theory of value and of price was necessary to establish the main proposition about profits and wages.

3. See Ricardo's statement that profits depend upon the 'proportion of the annual labour of the country [which] is devoted to the support of the labourers' (in Sraffa, 1951, p. 49).

But was this theory of profit determination valid, especially when the latter consideration is taken into account? Leading figures in the reaction against Ricardo have argued that it was not, including von Thünen, Walras and Böhm-Bawerk. Walras accused him of trying to make 'one equation determine two unknowns' by suggesting that price is determined by cost of production, consisting of profit plus wages (once rent is eliminated) and profit determined as the difference between aggregate prices and wages. The Russian writer Dmitriev at the turn of the century (now regarded as the father of Russian mathematical economics) was the first, I believe, to provide a rigorous demonstration that Ricardo's theory was immune to Walras's criticism and was perfectly sound.

Referring to this criticism, Dmitriev (1898, pp. 46 and 45n. of 1968 edn) says:

A single equation cannot serve to determine two unknowns. Thus we are apparently enclosed in a vicious circle: to define value one must know the size of profit, and profit itself depends upon the size of value. . . . The immortal merit of Ricardo consists precisely in his brilliant resolution of this problem which had seemed insoluble: . . . the principal merit of Ricardo in his theory of profit lies in establishing the laws which determine the *absolute* level of profit.

He then goes on to show that this merit of Ricardo consists in having been

the first to show that, among the equations of production there exists one which affords the possibility of determining *r* [profit] *directly* (that is to say without resort to other equations). This equation is provided for us by the conditions of production of *a* [the wage good], to which in the final analysis expenditures in all productions *A*, *B*, *C* . . . are reducible (Dmitriev, 1898, p. 47 of 1968 edn).

The simple two-product case (where one product is input in the production both of itself and of the other) he represents in the equation:

$$Y_{AB} = \frac{N_A\, ax_a(1+r)^{t_A}}{N_B\, ax_a(1+r)^{t_B}},$$

where *Y* is the price ratio of *A* to *B*; the real wage per unit of labour time is *a* units of wage good *A*; price per unit of *A* is x_a;

N_A is the number of units of labour (say, days) required to produce a unit of product A (and similarly for N_B); r is the rate of profit and t is the time over which labour is advanced (or the production period). If (but only if) $t_A = t_B$ will

$$Y_{AB} = \frac{N_A}{N_B}.$$

He then proceeds to show that r can be directly derived from N and t in the wage-good industry once a (the real wage) is known. N, t and a are part of the data in the aforementioned equation, depending on the technical conditions of production in A; and it is *not* necessary for the *price* of the wage good A *first* to be determined before r can be derived. Accordingly the equation for the two-product case suffices to determine the price ratio, given the Ns and the ts and a. [In Marxian terminology this is equivalent to saying: given the rate of surplus value and the turnover periods of variable capital (there is of course no constant capital in the two-product case), or the time over which wages are advanced.]

Having established this in the two-product case, Dmitriev then demonstrates that no difference is made in principle if instead of one wage good there are several; also that to express cost in terms of labour does not lead one into infinite regress when labour always works with other inputs (Marx's constant capital), since this can always be expressed in terms of simultaneous production by means of a set of input–output equations. In conclusion, he generalizes his result to the statement that, if there is any input (or groups of inputs) a which when fed into a productive process turns out more of itself (or themselves) as well as turning out other products, the rate of surplus product or profit will be perfectly determinate and independent of the price of a; a generalization that will be true independently of whether this input is human labour power or some inanimate object or automaton (Dmitriev, 1898, pp. 43 and 51–2 of 1968 edn). One can say, therefore, that the first problem for a theory of distribution of the classical type is the problem of production: why is there a surplus product at all, in the sense of some input (or inputs) yielding more of itself as output than is used-up in the process? This was of course Marx's starting point.

Those of you who happen to have followed the discussion of

the 'transformation problem' (i.e. transformation of Marx's values into his prices of production) may recall one of von Bortkievicz's arithmetical examples which perfectly illustrates the 'pure' Ricardian case. This is where there is no constant capital in the wage-goods industry (the second of von Bortkievicz's three departments), wage goods being produced by direct labour alone, and where the rate of profit in the price situation is equal to the rate of surplus value (S/V) in the value situation. I have included this as a curiosity in the Appendix to this article. In all *other* cases the rate of profit will be different *both* from the rate of surplus value and from the ratio of surplus to the sum of constant and variable capital expressed in *value* terms. None the less this rate of profit will be dependent on the conditions of production of the input-producing industries (whether wage goods or constituents of constant capital) and *on these alone*: i.e. on the first two out of von Bortkievicz's three departments or sectors.

To come to the Sraffa system: this shows certain differences from Dmitriev's method of determining profit and prices; but in essentials it can be said, I think, to be the same. If in the Dmitriev equation we have cited one were to substitute for the labour terms (the Ns) the quantities of A, the wage good needed to produce a unit of A and B respectively, one would have the nucleus of the Sraffa system. Sraffa's equational system (his price equations in chapter 2) provides for a series of products that are also inputs, some of them in the form of subsistence for workers; and the price equation for each product consists of the sum of the various input quantities times their several prices, with the addition of the rate of profit times that sum, as shown in the Appendix. There are k equations for the k products, all of which appear both as inputs in some or all other products and as outputs. These k independent equations 'determine the $k-1$ prices and the rate of profits'. Thus in his system both prices and rate of profits are simultaneously determined by the conditions of production of all the products that figure both as inputs and as outputs. These products he calls 'basics'; and it is emphasized that it is *only* the conditions of production of 'basics' that play a part in determining prices and the rate of profit. If there are products that do *not* play a productive role as inputs (he calls them 'non-basics' or 'luxuries'), then these products have no part in the determination of the system. Their role is purely passive. If an invention were to reduce by half the quantity of the means of production which are required to produce a unit of a luxury commodity of this type, the commodity itself would be halved in price, but there would be no further consequences; the price relations of the other products and the rate of profit would remain unaffected.

In a later chapter he shows how each of the price equations of which we have spoken could be replaced by a series of labour terms each with its appropriate date. This is what he calls 'reduction to dated quantities of labour'. The reduction equation for each commodity would then consist of a series of labour terms each multiplied by the wage, with the addition to this of the rate of profit for the period intervening between the date of the labour input in question and the emergence of the final product (Sraffa, 1960, pp. 4–5, 7–8 and 34–5).

The upshot, accordingly, is that there are two main ways in which prices can be derived from production conditions: (a) by describing the latter in terms of the labour expenditures per unit of output, with a time period attached to these expenditures, seeing that the *rate* of profit is involved in price determination; (b) by describing the situation in terms of total commodity inputs per unit of output, in which case *both* the rate of profits *and* the prices are simultaneously determined as resultants. In the first case the level of real wages has to be explicitly postulated, in terms either of labour cost or of product, and in the second case included as one of the commodity inputs. It should be added that with durable fixed capital in the picture the first alternative cannot be used without some *ex cathedra* postulation of a depreciation principle, since outputs of different time periods or dates are *joint products* of the durable equipment in question.

What, then, is special about this approach *qua* theory of distribution, giving it the claim to rank as substitute for the much-battered-by-criticism neo-classical theory? Ricardo's notion of profits as 'the proportion of production to the consumption necessary to such production' afforded at least the framework for a theory of profit as a surplus value, product of surplus labour over necessary consumption ('productive consumption'), and came closer to such a conception than Adam Smith's hint (it was scarcely more) of a 'deduction theory' of profit and rent. Ricardo's treatment also stressed the antagonism between real wages and profit, at any rate in his special sense of real wages as the cost in labour of producing wage goods – even if this was subordinated to the antagonism between rent and profit as rival shares in net revenue. Moreover von Bortkievicz rubbed in very aptly the corollary of Ricardian determination of profit by the conditions of production of wage goods: namely that 'the origin of profit [lies] in surplus labour', in the sense of 'profit as a deduction of some of the produce of labour'. 'If it is indeed true', he wrote,

that the level of the rate of profit in no way depends on the conditions of production of those goods which do not enter into real wages, then the origin of profit must clearly be sought in the wage relationship and not in the ability of capital to increase production. For if this ability were relevant here, then it would be inconceivable why certain spheres of production should become irrelevant for the question of the level of profit (von Bortkievicz, 1906–7).

Most explicitly, of course, this fuller significance comes out in Marx's presentation. This not only had as its central core the explicit treatment of property income as a surplus value, fruit of exploitation of human labour, but – what is indeed more fundamental – treated income distribution as basically determined by what he called the 'social relations of production', or prevailing property institutions and the socio-class relations consequent thereon. These he regarded as constituting the essence of bourgeois society, or the capitalist mode of production – an essence that is hidden by superficial appearance in a theoretical approach that treats value and distribution at the level of the market, or of exchange pure and simple, in terms of certain abstractly disembodied 'factors of production'.

Someone may, perhaps, feel like objecting at this point: did not Marx say that the existence of profit as surplus value has to be explained in terms of the law of value or it cannot be explained at all; and did this not mean that he determined distribution within the framework of a theory of value, just as much as did Jevons and the Austrians? There are, I think, two answers to this. Firstly, his value theory was itself written in terms of (and prices derived from) conditions of production and not from conditions of demand and individual consumption. Secondly, what he meant was that existence of surplus value must be explained *consistently* with the rules and requirements of a competitive market: he did *not* mean that the determination of surplus value and the rules of the exchange process must be *identified*; or the former derived esoterically from the latter. The important point is that as determinant of wages, and hence of the rate of exploitation, he introduced a crucial socio-historical datum: the historical process whereby property ownership had been concentrated and a proletariat created, with labour power converted into a marketable commodity and sold at its 'value'. It was in this context that he attached such importance to his distinction between labour and labour power, the latter being the human energy used up in work (or labour as an activity) and needing current replacement in the form of subsistence. Without this socio-historical postulate there would have been no warrant for his assertion that what labour could produce in a day exceeded what the replacement of the labour power used up in a day itself cost. This was the unique characteristic of the capitalist mode of production and of the role of labour in it. Reverting to Dmitriev's way of generalizing the problem of surplus, one might say that if in the future mechanical automata were to be invented such that these could reproduce more of themselves than were needed for their own periodic replacement (*plus* such current repair and maintenance as they needed), there would come into existence an analogous productive system (if with a very different social significance). If these automata were in private ownership, whether by capitalists or by workers who initially made them, there would be an analogous source of profit and enrichment (as Dmitriev remarked). The substantial point here is that what is crucial to the result, *qua* theory of distribution, is the relation of individuals or classes to the productive process and hence in a socio-economic sense to one another.

As a brief footnote to what has been said about the Sraffa system, I would add that some people, apparently, are puzzled by the fact that he initially treats labour on a par with a material input, valued *qua* input at a subsistence wage 'on the same footing as the fuel for engines or feed for cattle'. Surplus then has the same significance as Marx's surplus value or Ricardian net revenue. To allow for the possibility that wages 'may include a share of the surplus product', he then shifts to 'treating the whole wage as variable', which means excluding it from among the inputs and treating wage goods not as 'basics' but as 'non-basics', with net income conforming to the conventional definition of national income as including *both* wages *and* profits. But the wage is still explicitly stated, of course, in the equations of price determination, having to be introduced there along with the quantities of labour used in the various industries (instead of appearing in the guise of necessary subsistence inputs). This change is made merely as a matter of convenience in defining maximum profit for purpose of the standard commodity and for demonstrating the effect of a changing wage–profit ratio upon relative prices. Nothing in principle is involved in the change. Indeed, as he himself says, translation of things into 'the more appropriate, if unconventional, interpretation of the wage' can easily be made at the cost of some additional circumlocution. If one seeks an analogy in Marx's presentation, I suggest it would be this. Marx's concept of the value of labour power is within the context of what might be called 'pure' capitalism, with labour power of individuals sold competitively like everything else. The introduction of collective bargaining into the picture is itself an element of 'impurity': the price of labour power may no longer correspond with its value and may rise at the expense of the rate of surplus value. From a theoretical point of view one will then have to postulate how much surplus value is included in the wage as a result of the existing balance of social forces (or alternatively postulate simply what the real wage is).

As a second footnote: some explanation may be sought by some about the so-called standard commodity (or set of commodities) and the reason for the prominence given to it in the Sraffa system. I will be as brief as possible about this. This is devised to deal with Ricardo's problem of finding an 'invariable standard', or measure of value, that will be invariant to changes in the profit–wage ratio: in other words a measure of commodity magnitudes and of relations between them that is independent of distribution and of relative prices. Ricardo sought this in labour as his absolute value; but found that this ran into difficulties unless the composition of capital was uniform in all industries (or at least in the production of the things being compared). Sraffa does it by selecting (hypothetically) a commodity, or set of commodities, having the required properties, so that if this were to be used as money (or as *numéraire*) measurement in terms of it would be invariant to distribution shifts in two crucial respects. Firstly, if wages are defined in terms of it, there is a linear relationship between changes in wages and resulting (and inverse) changes in profit (and this irrespective of whether profit be expressed in terms of the standard system or the actual system). Secondly, and consequentially, 'the ratio of the net product to the means of production would remain the same whatever variations occurred in the division of the net product between wages and profits'.

If one were to look for a single commodity, the qualities it would have to possess for the purpose can be described as follows. In Sraffa's own words:

The key to the movement of relative prices consequent upon a change in the wage lies in the inequality of the proportions in which labour and means of production are employed in the various industries. It is clear that if the proportion were the same in all industries no price changes could ensue, however great was the diversity of the commodity composition of the means of production in different industries. For in each industry an equal deduction from the wage would yield just as much as was required for paying the profits on its means of production at a uniform rate without need to disturb the existing prices (Sraffa, 1960, pp. 12–13).

He then goes on to postulate a 'critical proportion' of labour to means of production; such that, if a commodity could be found that was produced with this proportion, its price would be invariant to a change in wages (since such a change yielded just that addition to, or subtraction from, profit as was needed to yield the new uniform rate of profit on its means of production). This 'critical proportion', incidentally, would have to apply to each 'layer' in its vertical chain of production: to the production of the means of production themselves *and* to the means of production in turn used to produce the first set, and so on.

Definition of this proportion is then reduced to two alternative '"pure" ratios between homogeneous quantities . . . namely the quantity ratio of direct to indirect labour employed, and the value ratio of net product to means of production'. A standard 'composite commodity' is then defined as a set so chosen that 'the various commodities are represented among its aggregate means of production *in the same proportions* as they are among its products'; or alternatively a set of commodities arranged 'in such proportions that the commodity composition of the aggregate means of production and that of the aggregate product are identical'. Reflection will show, I think, that the ratio of net product (or surplus) to means of production (or inputs) of this system has a unique meaning, expressible in product terms as much as Ricardo's simple product case of corn as both output and input.

Appendix

Von Bortkievicz's special case:
transformation of values into prices
in a three-sector model

(a) Value calculation:

Depts	C	V	S	Values
I	180	90	60	330
II	0	180	120	300
III	150	30	20	200
	330	300	200	830

(b) Price calculation:

Depts	C	V	Profit	Prices	Rate of profit
I	$138\frac{6}{13}$	$13\frac{11}{13}$	$101\frac{7}{13}$	$253\frac{11}{13}$	$66\frac{2}{3}\%$
II	0	$27\frac{9}{13}$	$18\frac{6}{13}$	$46\frac{2}{13}$	$66\frac{2}{3}\%$
III	$115\frac{5}{13}$	$4\frac{8}{13}$	80	200	$66\frac{2}{3}\%$
	$253\frac{11}{13}$	$46\frac{2}{13}$	200	500	

[N.B. The three departments produce respectively: capital goods (elements of constant capital); wage goods (elements of variable capital); 'luxury' goods, meeting capitalists' expenditure out of surplus value. Zero net investment is assumed. Gold, as the money commodity or standard of prices, is produced in Dept III.]

Sraffa's equations

$$(A_a p_a + B_a p_b + \ldots K_a p_k)(1+r) = A p_a$$
$$(A_b p_a + B_b p_b + \ldots K_b p_k)(1+r) = B p_b$$
$$\cdots \cdots \cdots \cdots \cdots \cdots \cdots \cdots \cdots$$
$$(A_k p_a + B_k p_b + \ldots K_k p_k)(1+r) = K p_k.$$

In the case of his 'reduction to dated labour' these would have the form of:

$$L_a w + L_{a_1} w(1+r) + \ldots L_{a_n} w(1+r)^n + \ldots = A p_a, \text{ etc.}$$

References

BHADURI, A. (1969), 'On the significance of recent controversies on capital theory: a Marxian view', *Econ. J.*, vol. 79, pp. 532–9.

DMITRIEV, V. K. (1898), *Essais économiques*, Editions du Centre National de la Recherche Scientifique, Paris 1968.

GAREGNANI, P. (1960), *Il capitale nelle teorie della distribuzione*, Giuffrè, Milan.

GAREGNANI, P. (1970), 'Heterogeneous capital, the production function and the theory of distribution', *Rev. econ. Stud.*, vol. 37, pp. 407–36.

HARCOURT, G. C. (1969), 'Some Cambridge controversies in the theory of capital', *J. econ. Lit.*, vol. 7, pp. 369–405.

PASINETTI, L. L. (1969), 'Switches of technique and the "rate of return" in capital theory', *Econ. J.*, vol. 79, pp. 508–25.

SRAFFA, P. (ed.) (1951), *The Works and Correspondence of David Ricardo*, vol. 1, Cambridge University Press.

SRAFFA, P. (1960), *Production of Commodities by Means of Commodities*, Cambridge University Press.

VON BORTKIEVICZ, L. (1906–7), 'Wertrechnung und Preisrechnung im Marxschen System', *Archiv für Sozialwissenschaft und Sozialpolitik*, trans. in *Int. econ. Pap.*, no. 2, 1952.

WALRAS, L. (1874), *Elements of Pure Economics*, trans. W. Jaffé, Allen & Unwin, 1954.

9 D.M.Nuti

'Vulgar Economy' in the Theory of Income Distribution

D. M. Nuti, '"Vulgar economy" in the theory of income distribution', *De Economist*, vol. 118, 1970, pp. 363–9.

The inadequacy of the so-called 'neo-classical'[1] theory as a macroeconomic theory of production and distribution has been widely discussed in recent economic literature[2] and reaffirmed in a lucid and learned paper by Maurice Dobb (1970).

Maurice Dobb rightly disputes the connection of this theory – as represented for instance by the writings of Samuelson and Solow and their British epigones – with the 'classical' economic thought. Joan Robinson calls it 'neo-neo-classical' to stress the remoteness of the connection with both the classical thought of Ricardo and Marx and the 'neo-classic' – mainly microeconomic – tradition of Marshall and Wicksell (Robinson, 1966). Following Marx, we could label the 'so-called neo-classical theory' as a species of 'vulgar economy'. By 'classical political economy' Marx meant the investigation of

the relations of production in bourgeois society, in contradistinction to vulgar economy, which deals with appearances only, ruminates without ceasing on the materials long since provided by scientific economy, and there seeks plausible explanations of the most obtrusive phenomena, for bourgeois daily use, but for the rest, confines itself to systematizing in a pedantic way, and proclaiming for everlasting truths, the trite

1. By 'neo-classical' theory I mean a macroeconomic theory of production and distribution stating that in the economy (a) there is a relation between output per man and the relative quantities of production factors (capital, labour, land, technical knowledge mostly represented by time) and in particular the value of capital per man; and (b) this relation is such that the higher the value of capital per man, the higher is output per man and the lower the marginal product of capital. In these conditions, perfect competition and profit maximization ensure that profit rates are inversely related to the value of capital per man and the capital–output ratio.

2. For an excellent survey of this discussion, see Harcourt (1969).

ideas held by the self-complacent bourgeoisie with regard to their own world, to them the best of all possible worlds (Marx, 1867, see part 1, ch. 1, p. 81n. of 1961 edn).

This is a definition that fits well a theory which gives an impersonal and politically neutral solution to what was for Ricardo 'the principal problem in political economy'. The state of technology and relative factor supplies determine relative income shares. There are classes but there is no room for, nor point in class struggle in a world where everybody, by implication, is getting his 'fair' share according to his individual contribution to the production process. For the sake of simplicity we shall go on calling it neo-classical theory.

What makes the neo-classical theory vulnerable is the extension of microeconomic concepts to the field of macroeconomics. From the viewpoint of the investing *firm* operating in competitive markets, at a given set of actual and expected prices of commodities (including capital goods) and labour, capital as finance can take any physical form; the conditions necessary for the validity of neo-classical theory could hold (although difficulties arise in the case of increasing returns to scale). But from the viewpoint of the *economy* as a whole, an additional condition is required; the profit rate postulated in the pricing of commodities and capital goods should be equal to that prevailing in the economy as the outcome of the choice of individual economic agents. The fulfilment of this condition requires either perfect foresight, which simply rules out all problems of macroeconomic equilibrium, or the malleability of capital, i.e. the reversibility of choices by their nature irreversible. This is true also of the Walrasian approach to capital and distribution. The equilibrium position of a Walrasian system with net capital formation requires the equality of the net rates of return on all kinds of capital goods, with the price of capital goods equal to their cost of production. As Piero Garegnani (1960, part 2, chs. 2 and 3) has shown, a Walrasian system cannot obtain simultaneously the equalization of net rates of return under these conditions *and* the quantities of new capital goods currently produced. The simultaneous determination of these unknowns depends on the possibility of treating 'capital' as a single object which can indifferently take the form of any particular type of capital good 'as if it were a fluid which can be freely transferred from one container to another' (Garegnani, 1960, p. 115).

Failing these conditions, neo-classical theory runs against the critique raised in the debate summarized by Dobb and Harcourt. It is true that the first severe blow was given by Sraffa, Robinson and others who have shown the possibility of reswitching of techniques;[3] when this occurs it becomes impossible to order production techniques according to the profit or wage rate associated with them; even the approach based on index numbers – ingenious but operationally meaningless – ceases to hold. It seems to me, however, that the *coup de grâce* has been given not so much by the reswitching phenomenon, as Maurice Dobb puts it, but by the more recent work of Pasinetti, Garegnani and Spaventa. Pasinetti (1969, p. 529) has shown that another pillar of neo-classical theory, the notion of 'rate of return' cannot be defined independently of the rate of profit and 'is devoid of any autonomous theoretical content'. Garegnani and Spaventa have shown that *even in the absence of reswitching*, the same *value* of capital per man can occur at more than a single level or range of the interest rate; furthermore, that both the value of output per man and capital per man are affected by the growth rate of the economy, so that even for a given interest rate the same value of capital per man can occur at more than a single level or range of the growth rate.[4]

The acceptance of the neo-classical theory of production and distribution therefore requires *faith* that neither reswitching of techniques nor any of the other awkward cases pointed out in recent literature occur in reality. This is openly admitted in the latest neo-classical literature. C. E. Ferguson, the author of a book entitled *The Neoclassical Theory of Production and Distribution* (1969) writes in the introduction:

My point of view is uncompromisingly neo-classical. . . . [The validity

3. This is the eligibility of a production technique at more than one level or range of the profit rate, with other techniques being eligible at intermediate levels or ranges.

4. This proposition has been stated by Spaventa for a two-sector model, by Garegnani for a multisector model and by myself for a model of production of the Austrian type. (See Garegnani, 1970; Nuti, 1970; Spaventa, 1968; 1970.)

of the Cambridge criticism of neo-classical theory] is unquestionable, but its importance is an empirical or an econometric matter that depends upon the amount of substitutability there is in the system. Until the econometricians have the answer for us, placing reliance upon neo-classical economic theory is a matter of faith. I personally have faith; but at present the best I can do to convince others is to invoke the weight of Samuelson's authority.

The validity of any kind of econometric work based on the notion of an aggregate production function is undermined by the critique mentioned above, so that econometricians have no way of settling the dispute. The answer might perhaps come from engineers, i.e. from a detailed analysis of the specific aspects of the state of technology, but this is not yet in sight. Until then, reliance upon the neo-classical theory of macroeconomic production and distribution will remain a matter of faith.

Although the notion of 'value of capital' is neither useful nor necessary to determine technical choice, in a capitalist (nor, for that matter, in a socialist) economy, the concept of 'value of capital' – as I have said elsewhere – is indispensable to the political economy of capitalism because it performs two fundamental roles, one practical and one ideological:

At a practical level the evaluation of machines of different kinds and ages in terms of output is needed to settle transactions among capitalist firms, to determine the value of the legal exclusive right to use machinery and the value of the pieces of paper embodying such rights. It is necessary to determine distribution of income not between the haves and the have-nots but among the haves.

The ideological role of 'the value of capital' is that of breaking the direct actual link between the *time pattern* of labour inputs and the *time pattern* of output in which any technology can be resolved, and establishing instead a relation between *current* output and *current* labour. To this purpose the *current* 'value of the capital stock' is needed; a mythical conceptual construction in which the past and the future of the economy are telescoped into the present. Attention is focused not on past labour but on the present value of the embodiment of past labour and its current productiveness can be taken to provide a justification for the attribution of the surplus of current output over the wage bill to those who have appropriated the embodiment of past labour, thereby providing the current basis of future appropriation (Nuti, 1970).

A political element in the theory of distribution was introduced by Kalecki (1938; 1939; 1964) in his theory based on the 'degree of monopoly'. Kalecki assumed a reverse L-shaped cost curve, prime costs being constant up to full capacity output and marginal costs equal to average prime costs. The degree of monopoly defined as the excess of price over marginal cost, divided by price, was hence equal to the share of profits in the output of each firm, and the share of profits in the national income was a weighted average of the degree of monopoly in all the firms of the economy. Unfortunately this way of introducing monopolistic production relations in the theory of distribution is not satisfactory because, as Kaldor (1955) wrote, either the degree of monopoly is simply defined as the excess of actual price over actual marginal cost, and in the circumstances considered (i.e. marginal equal to average cost) the statement is tautological, or the degree of monopoly is obtained from the demand curve of each firm and found equal to the inverse of the demand elasticity given the hypothesis of profit maximization; the theory runs against the same problems as neo-classical theory, namely the reliance upon microeconomic concepts (here, the elasticity of demand) to explain a macroeconomic problem.

The relation between the real wage rate and the profit rate uncovered by Sraffa and before him by the Russian economist Dmitriev (1898, p. 47 of 1968 edn), restates the conflict between capitalists and workers in the problem of income distribution and provides scope for the concept of class struggle in the determination of relative shares. Unfortunately, however, there is no simple way of closing his system, i.e. of determining which point of the wage–profit relation is actually reached and how in any economy.

The real wage rate cannot be taken as exogenously determined, as in classical thought, fixed at a subsistence level in conditions of elastic labour supply. Nor can it be determined *directly* by the class struggle, as it is postulated in French literature by Marchal and others (Marchal, 1951; 1952; Marchal and Lecaillon, 1958), because after Keynes we have to recognize that wage bargaining determines *money* wages, whilst the real wage rate is determined by the behaviour of the price level. Sraffa (1960, ch. 5, p. 33) provides a suggestion that the profit ratio 'is susceptible of being determined from outside the system of production, in particular by the level of the money rates of interest'. It seems to me, however, that – apart from the imperfections of the financial market – the level of the money rates of interest can determine technical choice only in a world of constant price level. If prices are expected to rise or fall in future, the real wage rate that firms can afford to pay will depend not on the money rates of interest, but on the *real* cost of borrowing, i.e. the interest rate *minus* the expected rate of price change. An alternative way of closing the system has been suggested by the post-Keynesian Cambridge theory of distribution, stating the dependence of the profit rate and relative shares upon the growth rate of the economy and the saving propensities of capitalists (Kaldor, 1955; Pasinetti, 1962). This, however, is a *necessary* relation that must *always* hold for macroeconomic equilibrium among *ex-post* magnitudes. As such it cannot be disproved and therefore it does not provide a *theory* of the determination of the profit rate and income shares, especially in the short run. There is no reason to assume that at full employment the *ex-ante* propensity to save of capitalists should be equal to the *ex-ante* ratio of investment to profits. If there is *ex-ante* macroeconomic disequilibrium between saving and investment decisions, the economy in the real world will somehow accommodate the disequilibrium through changes in inventories and waiting lists, price changes and revisions of expenditure plans; this has a feedback on prices and the whole process will continue until supply equates with demand. *Ex post*, we observe a level of investment but this need not be the same, as a share of profits, as the proportion which capitalists would have wished to save at the level of profits actually obtained. It may be higher, or lower, depending on the effects of price changes on the different categories of expenditure plans in real terms, the relative speed of response of different categories of income to price increases and their relative propensities to spend, the relative liquidity strength of different categories of spenders, and the state and change of their expectations.

The most appropriate way of approaching the theory of distribution, reintroducing the reality of class struggle into this important branch of political economy, seems therefore that of combining the Sraffian relation between wage and profit rates with the little we know – not least from Marx (1894, part 5; 1898) – about the interaction of real and monetary phenomena.

References

DMITRIEV, V. K. (1898), *Ekonomicheskie ocherki*, French trans. of 1904 edn, Editions du Centre National de la Recherche Scientifique, Paris, 1968.

DOBB, M. (1970), 'The Sraffa system and critique of the neo-classical theory of distribution', *De Economist*, vol. 118, pp. 347–62.

FERGUSON, C. E. (1969), *The Neoclassical Theory of Production and Distribution*, Cambridge University Press.

GAREGNANI, P. (1960), *Il capitale nelle teorie della distribuzione*, Giuffrè, Milan.

GAREGNANI, P. (1970), 'Heterogeneous capital, the production function and the theory of distribution', *Rev. econ. Stud.*, vol. 37, pp. 407–36.

HARCOURT, G. C. (1969), 'Some Cambridge controversies in the theory of capital', *J. econ. Lit.*, vol. 7, pp. 369–405.

KALDOR, N. (1955), 'Alternative theories of distribution', *Rev. econ. Stud.*, vol. 23, pp. 83–100.

KALECKI, M. (1938), 'The determinants of distribution', *Econometrica*, vol. 6, pp. 97–112.

KALECKI, M. (1939), *Essays in the Theory of Economic Fluctuations*, Allen & Unwin.

KALECKI, M. (1964), *Theory of Economic Dynamics*, Unwin.

MARCHAL, J. (1951), 'The construction of a new theory of profit', *Amer. econ. Rev.*, vol. 41, pp. 549–65.

MARCHAL, J. (1952), 'Contribution à une étude réaliste de la répartition', *Revue économique*, pp. 147–82.

MARCHAL, J., and LECAILLON, J. (1958), *La répartition du revenu national*, Génin, Paris.

MARX, K. (1867), *Capital*, vol. 1, Foreign Languages Publishing House, Moscow, 1961.

MARX, K. (1894), *Capital*, vol. 3, Foreign Languages Publishing House, Moscow, 1959.

MARX, K. (1898), *Value, Price and Profit*, Sonnenschein.

NUTI, D. M. (1970), 'Capitalism, socialism and steady growth', *Econ. J.*, vol. 80, pp. 32–54.

PASINETTI, L. L. (1962), 'Rate of profit and income distribution in relation to the rate of economic growth', *Rev. econ. Stud.*, vol. 29, pp. 267–79.

PASINETTI, L. L. (1969), 'Switches of technique and the "rate of return" in capital theory', *Econ. J.*, vol. 79, pp. 508–25.

ROBINSON, J. (1956), *The Accumulation of Capital*, Macmillan.

ROBINSON, J. (1966). 'Let the hundred schools contend, but let them state their assumptions', mimeo., Cambridge.

SPAVENTA, L. (1968), 'Realism without parables in capital theory', in CERUNA, *Recherches récentes sur la fonction de production*, Universitaire de Namur, pp. 15–45.

SPAVENTA, L. (1970), 'Rate of profit, rate of growth, and capital intensity in a simple production model', *Oxf. econ. Pap.*, vol. 22, 129–47.

SRAFFA, P. (1960), *Production of Commodities by Means of Commodities*, Cambridge University Press.

Postscript

The essence of the neo-classical theory of income distribution – which, I recently argued, deserves the Marxian label of 'vulgar economy' (Nuti, 1970) – is summarized in the following quotation from a leading textbook:

The traditional theory of distribution states that distribution is simply a special case of price theory. The income of any factor of production (and hence the amount of the national product that it is able to command) depends on the price that is paid for the factor and the amount that is used. If we wish to build up a theory of distribution we thus need a theory of factor prices and quantities. Such a theory is a special case of the theory of price (Lipsey, 1963, p. 407 of 1966 edn).

The most common version of this theory is the approach to distribution as the theory of supply of and demand for productive *factors* conceived in *aggregate* terms:

To understand what determines labor and property's share in national product, and to understand forces acting on the degree of equality of income, distribution theory studies the problem of how the different factors of production – land, labor, capital, entrepreneurship and risk taking – are priced in the market or how supply and demand interact to determine all kinds of wages, rents, interest yields, profits and so forth (Samuelson, 1948, p. 637 of 1964 edn).

It is this version of the theory that was discussed in my paper. There is, however, another version of income distribution theory as a special case of price theory, which is not dealt with there. This is the view that distribution is a by-product of general equilibrium theory: in its simplest version, which we could call 'neo-Fisherian',[5] income distribution is a special case of the theory of price of *dated commodities*.

5. From Fisher's work (1907, 1912, 1930), and in its modern presentation as, for instance, in Hirshleifer (1970).

Within this approach, the *wage rate* (of dated labour) is a price like any other; investment is regarded as exchange – with nature or with other individuals – of dated commodities, *interest* an element in the price ratio between dated commodities and *capital* the present embodiment of future-dated consumption goods. The essence of the approach is that

The equilibrium between supplies and demands that sets the pattern of market rates of interest will also simultaneously establish the aggregate levels of dated consumptions for the community as a whole – just as, in ordinary price theory, the equilibrium of supply and demand that fixes prices also determines the corresponding quantities produced and exchanged (Hirshleifer, 1970, p. 99).

The problem is first considered under no uncertainty. The individual has an initial *endowment*, i.e. 'a combination of goods that provides a starting point for optimizing choice' (Hirshleifer, 1970, p. 2). He has a system of intertemporal preferences for dated consumption goods, and access to exchange in perfect current and forward markets. The firm 'is a grouping of one or more individuals specialized to productive activities (transformations of commodity combinations effected through dealing with nature rather than through exchange with other economic agents' (Hirshleifer, 1970, p. 12). 'The possibilities of production are summarized by an opportunity set – a range of alternative combinations of *consumptive* commodities attainable by physical transformations' (Hirshleifer, 1970, p. 27), where an investment project is a trade-off between dated commodities. Optimization of both consumption and production behaviour leads to a price system for dated commodities (including labour) that contains an implicit income distribution.

The limitation of this approach can be summed up in one sentence: 'Production is "exchange" with nature' (Hirshleifer, 1970, p. 12), productive investment being treated as forward exchange with nature. This restricts the validity of the analysis to the following cases: a technology where production is the growth in time of a seed effortlessly dropped on earth and equally effortlessly harvested; a slave economy where workers are like horses; an economy of working and self-breeding robots; an economy of individual or cooperative producers. Outside these cases workers are hired and no labour other than one's own can be part of the initial endowment; hence the production possibility set corresponding to a given initial 'endowment' (whether this is a bundle of goods or 'finance') will itself change with the wage rate of dated labour. If, on the other hand, one's own labour is part of the initial endowment, it should be remembered that of all commodities *labour power is the one for which in a capitalist system there are no conceivable forward markets*. This is due to the special feature of labour as an input: workers – unlike bondsmen, slaves, horses and robots – can leave their job whenever they like. No forward commitment expressed in labour time can be enforced; this is not a market imperfection; on the contrary, it is a necessary condition for a perfect labour market in each period. The symmetry between production and exchange might be intellectually pleasing, but the price to be paid for this generalization is tremendous, namely, the inability to understand present-day economy where labour power is a commodity and production is a relation among men as well as with nature.

This type of approach is also to be found in various versions of general equilibrium theory, such as those by Arrow and Debreu (1954; Debreu, 1959), who have also incorporated uncertainty about the environment in a general equilibrium model. Within their framework, commodities are distinguished not only by their physical characteristics (including where and when they are available) but also by the 'environmental event' which is associated with their availability. In this way the number of 'commodities' is greatly increased, but it is envisaged that perfect markets determine a complete price system for all commodities and for all possible states of the world, and the standard results of the theory of competitive equilibrium are obtained. This approach however is designed to handle uncertainty about events independent of the action of economic agents (e.g. the weather) and not uncertainty about events resulting from the combined action of economic agents (e.g. the willingness of workers to supply labour in the future at a given wage rate). Again *labour is different from all other inputs* and this difference, that should be the starting point of a satisfactory theory of production and distribution, is completely ignored in this version of neo-classical theory. By ignoring the implications deriving from specific modes of production and the fundamental distinction between labour and labour power, these versions of neo-classical theory seem to deserve the Marxian label of 'vulgar economy' just as much as the version based on the notions of aggregate productive factors.

References

ARROW, K. J. and DEBREU, G. (1954), 'Existence of an equilibrium for a competitive economy', *Econometrica*, vol. 22, pp. 265-90.

DEBREU, G. (1959), *Theory of Value*, Wiley.

FISHER, I. (1907), *The Rate of Interest*, Macmillan.

FISHER, I. (1912), *The Nature of Capital and Income*, Macmillan.

FISHER, I. (1930), *The Theory of Interest*, Macmillan.

HIRSHLEIFER, J. (1970), *Investment, Interest and Capital*, Prentice-Hall.

LIPSEY, R. G. (1963), *An Introduction to Positive Economics*, Weidenfeld & Nicolson, 2nd edn, 1966.

NUTI, D. M. (1970), ' "Vulgar economy" in the theory of distribution', *De Economist*, vol. 118, pp. 363–9.

SAMUELSON, P. A. (1948), *Economics: An Introductory Analysis*, McGraw-Hill, 6th edn, 1964.

10 Joan Robinson

Capital Theory Up to Date

Joan Robinson, 'Capital theory up to date', *Canadian Journal of Economics*, vol. 3, 1970, pp. 309–17.

The lectures which Professor Solow (1963) gave in Holland opened with the remark: 'Everybody except Joan Robinson agrees about capital theory.' He did not say what it was that they agreed and a few years later the 'reswitching' controversy brought some important differences of opinion to light. Now, fortunately, we have a clear exposition of what Professor Solow must have meant. Professor Ferguson (1969) asserts that belief in neo-classical theory is a matter of faith. 'I personally have the faith', he declares, so that we can learn from him what it is that the neo-classicals believe neo-classical theory to be. But first let us trace the history of the 'reswitching' affair.

Reswitching

In the course of investigating the meaning of a production function for output as a whole, I set up what Professor Solow later correctly described as a pseudo-production function, showing the possible positions of equilibrium, corresponding to various values of the rate of profit, in an imagined 'given state of technical knowledge'. The analysis showed that there is no meaning to be given to a 'quantity of capital' apart from the rate of profit, so that the contention that the 'marginal product of capital' determines the rate of profit is meaningless. (In the present argument 'land' as a separate factor of production is not taken into account.) Incidentally, I found that over certain ranges of the pseudo-production function the technique that becomes eligible at a higher rate of profit (with a correspondingly lower real wage rate) may be less labour-intensive (that is, may have a higher output per man employed) than that chosen at a higher wage rate, contrary to the rule of a 'well-behaved production function' in which a lower wage rate is always associated with a more labour-intensive technique. (I attributed this discovery to Ruth Cohen – a private joke.)

I had picked up the clue from Piero Sraffa's Preface to Ricardo's *Principles* and my analysis (errors and omissions excepted) was a preview of his. When his own treatment of the subject was finally published (Sraffa, 1960), the 'Ruth Cohen case' (which I had treated as a *curiosum*) was seen to have great prominence; the striking proposition was established that it is perfectly normal (within the accepted assumptions) for the same technique to be eligible at several discrete rates of profit. It was from this that the sobriquet 'reswitching of techniques' was derived. (The difference between my treatment and Sraffa's was accidental. I put the main emphasis on differences in the amounts of 'labour embodied' in the equipment appropriate to different techniques while Sraffa illustrates his point with a case in which two commodities require the same labour applied in different time patterns. The backward switch, from a lower to a higher output per head with lower wages, is connected with the interrelations of the time patterns of the techniques; his examples gave more scope for it than mine.)

The neo-neo-classicals took no notice; they went on as usual drawing production functions in terms of 'capital' and labour and disseminating the marginal productivity theory of distribution. In 1961 I encountered Professor Samuelson on his home ground; in the course of an argument I happened to ask him: 'When you define the marginal product of labour, what do you keep constant?' He seemed disconcerted, as though none of his pupils had ever asked that question, but next day he gave a clear answer. Either the physical inputs other than labour are kept constant, or the rate of profit on capital is kept constant.

I found this satisfactory, for it destroys the doctrine that wages are regulated by marginal productivity. In a short-period case, where equipment is given, at full-capacity operation the marginal physical product of labour is indeterminate. When nine men with nine spades are digging a hole, to add a tenth man could increase output only to the extent that nine dig better if they have a rest from time to time (see Robertson, 1930). On the other hand, to subtract the ninth man would reduce output by more or less the average amount. The wage must lie somewhere between the average value of output per head and zero, so that marginal product is much greater or much less than the wage according as equipment is being worked below or above its designed capacity.

In conditions of imperfect competition, under-capacity operation of plant is normal (except in an acute seller's market) and, in industry as a whole, it seems that, on average, wages are usually about half of value added. The marginal product of labour, in the short-period sense, is therefore generally about twice the wage (cf. Okun, 1962).

In long-period equilibrium, with a constant rate of profit, the stock of equipment and the amount of employment have been adjusted to each other. When competition prevails in the long-period sense of free entry to all markets, so that a uniform rate of profit tends to be established throughout the economy, the wage is equivalent to what Marshall called the marginal *net* product of labour – that is, the value of average output per head *minus* a gross profit sufficient to pay for replacement and net profit at the going rate on the value of capital per man employed, when all inputs are reckoned at the prices appropriate to the given rate of profit. The wage is determined by technical conditions and the rate of profit, as at a particular point on a pseudo-production function. The question then comes up, what determines the rate of profit?

But this was going too far. Professor Samuelson retreated behind what he called a surrogate production function (Samuelson, 1962). It was a special case [as Piero Garegnani (see Samuelson, 1962, p. 202 n.) promptly pointed out] of a pseudo-production function with labour-value prices. When, for any one technique, the capital–labour ratio and the time pattern of inputs are uniform throughout all the processes of production, prices are proportional to labour time. The value of capital in terms of product, for that technique, is then independent of the rate of profit. When each technique in the 'given state of knowledge' has this character and the time patterns are all alike, the order of techniques in terms of output per head is the same as the order in terms of value of capital per man for each technique at the rate of profit that makes that technique eligible; a higher output per man is associated with a higher wage and lower rate of profit. When a pseudo-production function of this type is set out as a relationship between 'capital' and output it looks just like a well-behaved production function.

Professor Samuelson believed that in this he had provided for the 'neo-classical parables' of J. B. Clark 'which pretend there is a single thing called "capital" that can be put into a single production function and along with labour will produce total output' (Samuelson, 1962, p. 194).

At first the neo-neo-classicals were happy to accept his parable. (This was the period of Professor Solow's lectures and of the first draft of Professor Ferguson's book in which, he tells us, he relied upon the surrogate production function to protect him from what he calls Cambridge Criticism.) For some years they remained cooped up in this position, repelling all attacks with blank misunderstanding. Then, growing bold, they descended to the plains and tried to prove Sraffa wrong.

This rash enterprise was not successful; Professor Samuelson (1966) very handsomely admitted that he had been mistaken. But he mistook his mistake. The trouble was not merely that he had ignored Garegnani's warning and treated labour-value prices as the general case. The real mistake was to suppose that a pseudo-production function, which relates the rate of profit to the value of capital at the prices corresponding to that rate of profit, provides the 'neo-classical parable'. Neo-classical 'capital' is a physical quantity which is independent of prices.

Capital

The neo-neo-classicals' concept of capital is derived from Walras, but they have transformed it into something quite different. In a Walrasian market, when dealing begins, there are particular supplies of factors already in existence, each measured in physical terms – man-hours, acres, tons, pints and yards. In the neo-neo-classical concept of capital all the man-made factors are boiled into one, which we may call *leets* in honour of Professor Meade's *steel* (Meade, 1961). But leets, though all made of one physical substance, is endowed with the capacity to embody various techniques of production – different ratios of leets to labour – and a change of technique can be made simply by squeezing up or spreading out leets, instantaneously and without cost. A higher output per man requires a larger amount of leets per man employed. In Walrasian competitive equilibrium there can never be increasing returns from one factor applied to a given quantity of another. This rule is observed by leets. There is a well-behaved production function in leets and labour for each kind of output, including leets. Moreover, leets can absorb technical progress, without losing its physical identity, again instantaneously and without cost. Then to simplify still further, output is also taken to be made of leets; the whole Walrasian system is reduced to a 'one-commodity world'.

This is the conception in which Professor Ferguson has reaffirmed his faith.

Many economists, nowadays, who are interested in practical questions are impatient of doctrinal disputes. 'What does it matter?' they are inclined to say. 'Let him have his leets; what harm does it do?' But the harm that the neo-neo-classicals have done is, precisely, to block off economic theory from any discussion of practical questions.

When equipment is made of leets, there is no distinction between long- and short-period problems. The answer to Dennis Robertson's question is simply fudged. Nine spades are a lump of leets; when the tenth man turns up it is squeezed out to provide him with a share of equipment nine-tenths of what each man had before.

There is no such thing as a degree of utilization of given equipment rising or falling with the level of effective demand. (Professor Solow pretends that his production functions are drawn in terms of concrete capital goods, but the fact that the short-period utilization function is identical with the long-period pseudo-production function gives him away.)

There is no room for imperfect competition. There is no possibility of disappointed expectations – indeed, there is no difference between the past and the future, for the past can always be undone and readjusted to a change in the present situation.

There is no problem of unemployment. The wage bargain is made in terms of product and there is perfect competition both between workers for jobs and between employers for hands. Unemployed workers would bid down wages and the pre-existing quantity of leets would be spread out to accommodate them. The neo-neo-classicals have reconstructed the vague doctrines of the neo-classicals from which was derived the dogma which Keynes had to attack in the great slump of the thirties, that unemployment can be caused only by wages being too high.

In long-period analysis, the neo-neo-classics are prone to confuse a comparison of positions of equilibrium (as in a pseudo-production function) with a 'Wicksell process' of accumulation without technical progress. 'A given state of technical knowledge' consists simply of a production function in terms of leets and labour. Accumulation consists of adding some leets to the pre-existing stock and squeezing it into a new quantity per man employed. This entails raising the wage rate and reducing the return per ton of leets. Thus a process of raising the capital–labour ratio means creeping along the production function, moving step by step from lower to higher ratios of leets to labour. (It is notable that when Professor Samuelson conceded defeat in the 'reswitching' controversy, he did so in this form. He seemed to suppose that if the process of accumulation hit a backward switch, where a lower rate of profit is associated with a lower value of capital per man, the economy would suddenly find itself able to consume part of its capital without reducing its productive capacity.)

This brings into play the other aspect of pre-Keynesian theory. Saving consists in a decision not to consume a part of the current output and this causes investment to make a corresponding addition to the stock of 'capital'. The neo-neo-classicals have succeeded in tying themselves up again in habits of thought from which Keynes had had 'a long struggle to escape'. [. . .]

Wages and profits

The main function of the concept of leets is to provide a theory of the distribution of the product of industry between wages and profits.

At any moment, with a given quantity in existence of leets regarded as capital equipment, the wage in terms of leets regarded as product is at the level compatible with full employment of the available labour force. Then, with a few extra assumptions, such as that there is no charge for interest on the part of working capital which represents the wage fund, it is shown that the wage is equal to the marginal product of the available labour force, that is, the amount of product per week that would be lost if one less man were employed and the stock of leets squeezed up appropriately. If the wage were less than this, competition for hands would drive it up. If it was greater, less men would be employed and competition for jobs would drive it down. The wage being equal to the marginal product of labour, it is shown by Euler's theorem that the product minus the wage is the marginal product of a ton of leets multiplied by the quantity of leets in existence.

Now, capital in the world we live in has two aspects. It consists of the stocks of equipment and materials which (with education and training) permit workers to produce marketable goods and it consists of the command over finance which permits employers to organize the production of goods which they can sell at a profit. In the 'one-commodity world' the price of a ton of leets capital in terms of leets output is unity. The two aspects of capital are fused. A ton of leets is both a piece of equipment and a sum of purchasing power. Then the return to a unit of leets, leets over leets, is the rate of profit on capital. Thus labour and capital each receive a 'reward' equal to their marginal productivity. As J. B. Clark (1891, p. 313) himself put it: 'What a social class gets is, under natural law, what it contributes to the general output of industry.'

Here, indeed, we find the origin of the concept of leets. First came the dogma that the rate of profit that the owners of capital enjoy is equal to the productivity of capital equipment, and that saving continues to cause capital to accumulate so long as its marginal product exceeds the rate of interest which represents the 'discount of the future' in the minds of its owners. Then the question is asked, 'What is this "capital" that has a marginal product?' Leets had to be invented to give an answer to that question.

Of course, all this is not intended to be taken literally. Even Professor Ferguson admits that capital equipment actually consists of a variety of hard objects that cannot be squeezed up or pressed out, without cost, to accommodate less or more workers. Leets is only a parable, as Professor Samuelson claimed. But as soon as they give it up, their argument comes unstuck.

Professor Ferguson, for instance, incorporates a 'vintage model' in his system. The vintage model is taken over from Harrod's conception of an economy realizing the 'natural' rate of growth given by technical progress.

Gross investment, in each period, is embodied in equipment for the latest, most superior technique. The conditions for equilibrium growth are that technical progress should be raising output per head at a steady rate and that it should be neutral in Harrod's sense, so that a constant rate of profit on capital is compatible with a constant capital–output ratio and constant relative shares of wages and profits in net output. A constant share of gross investment in total output then produces growth of output per head at a steady rate.

On any one equilibrium path, the rate of profit on capital is constant through time, but there may be different paths (with the same sequence of technical innovations) with different rates of profit. Thus there is a kind of pseudo-production function relating the rate of profit to the value of capital in terms of product and the share of gross investment in output.

The level of wages in terms of product rises in step with output per head (this follows from the condition that the rate of profit and the share of wages in output are constant) and the equipment for each technique is scrapped when the wage absorbs its whole output so that its quasi-rent is reduced to zero. A higher share of profit entails a wider gap between the wage rate and output per head with the latest, best, technique. Thus it entails a longer service life of equipment, therefore a higher proportion of older, more inferior, techniques in use at any moment and lower average output per head. There is then a presumption that the pseudo-production function relating the rate of profit to the capital–output ratio will be well behaved (a lower output per man being associated with a lower value of capital per man) though there still might be some 'Cambridge' tricks in it. But what determines the rate of profit?

Professor Ferguson follows Professor Solow's argument that a very small *extra* investment over and above that required by the equilibrium path yields a return equal to the rate of profit. That is true, whatever the rate of profit may be. And he shows that the marginal product of labour in the short-period sense is equal to the wage; the 'last man' is employed in the equipment that is just about to be scrapped. This is true because, for a given pseudo-production function, both the wage relative to output per head with the latest technique and the age of the least productive equipment are determined together by the rate of profit. Evidently they are so used to thinking in terms of leets (for whatever he may say, Professor Solow's capital is made of leets) that they forget that, when capital is embodied in specific equipment, the short-period marginal physical product of labour is not the same thing as the value of the net product allowing for profit at a particular rate. They describe the competitive equilibrium position corresponding to a given rate of profit without offering any explanation of what the rate of profit is.

There have been three types of theory of the distribution of the product of industry between wages and profits. In classical theory (of which von Neumann provides the most systematic account) the real wage per man is a technical datum; the rate of profit on capital emerges as a residual. In Marx, the rate of exploitation (the ratio of net profit to wages) is the result of the balance of forces in the class struggle. For Marshall, there is a normal rate of profit and the real wage emerges as a residual; an extension of Keynes's General Theory into the long period finds a clue to the level of profits in the rate of accumulation and the excess of consumption out of profits over saving out of wages.

When the neo-neo-classicals reconstituted orthodoxy after the Keynesian revolution they eschewed all these and went to Walras, who does not have a theory of profits at all.

Econometrics

The strangest part of the whole affair is that many neo-neo-classicals seek to identify leets-capital with the dollar value of capital as it appears in statistics. Professor Ferguson (1969, p. 266) concludes his account of 'reswitching' thus: 'The question that confronts us is not whether the Cambridge Criticism is theoretically valid. It is. Rather the question is an empirical or econometric one: is there sufficient substitutability within the system to establish neo-classical results?' And he states in the Preface: 'Until the econometricians have the answer for us, placing reliance upon neo-classical economic theory is a matter of faith.' Statisticians, though with a very coarse mesh, can catch evidence of the capital–output ratio in terms of dollar values, and the shares of wages and profits in value added, over a particular period in a particular economy, and so they can offer an estimate of the *ex-post*, overall rate of profit being realized. They cannot say what expectations of profit were in the minds of the managers of firms, or whether alternative schemes were on the drawing boards of engineers, when the investment decisions were taken that brought a particular stock of capital equipment into existence. Still less can they say what decisions would have been taken if present and expected prices and wage rates had been different from what they were. Professor Ferguson expects too much.

Consider a run of figures for a prosperous period of development in a modern industrial economy which conform more or less (as they often seem to do) to what Kaldor calls the 'stylized facts'. The capital–output ratio and the wage and profit shares are fairly constant over time, while the dollar value of output per man employed and the dollar value of capital per man have a strong upward trend. This would lend itself to interpretation as an approximation to the story of accumulation on a Harrod path, as in the vintage model, with neutral technical progress and a fairly steady overall average rate of profit (fluctuations in effective demand being smoothed out).

This will not do for the neo-neo-classicals. They want to separate out increases in the quantity of 'capital' from the effects of technical progress. To find this distinction, they puzzle themselves with their leets. Leets can absorb technical progress without any investment being required. An 'invention' raises the output per head of a set of workers equipped with a given quantity of leets. But output also consists of leets, so that if the share of saving in income is constant, leets per man employed begins to rise as a result of the invention. Is this to be attributed to accumulation or to the invention? To attribute the growth of leets per man to saving, it would be necessary to define as saving, refraining from consuming so much of additional leets as to keep leets per man constant (cf. Rymes, 1968).

In any case, the statistics are in dollars, not in tons of leets. Whether technical progress is embodied in new types of equipment or affected by a rearrangement of existing equipment or comes from 'learning by doing' by workers without any change in equipment at all, the figures would be the same. The difference would appear only in the amount of gross investment required to keep the economy going.

Output of capital equipment must be reckoned not in tons of any metal or in lists of items (a bus is a bus and a lathe is a lathe) but in terms of productive capacity. Over all, wages in terms of product are rising in step with output per head, and the rate of profit is constant. The capital–output ratio, over all, does not change much, either way. For embodied technical progress, therefore, the cost per unit of productive capacity is rising at the same rate as output per head.

Equally, the value of equipment absorbing disembodied progress (if there is such a thing) would rise at the same rate. Profit per man employed rises with output per head (since the real wage rises at the same rate) and no depreciation is required. Capitalize the profits at a rate of interest equal to the overall rate of profit and the value of the equipment rises at the same rate as output per head.

Professor Jorgenson uses just this procedure to account for the rise in the value of capital shown in his statistics but then he attributes its growth entirely to accumulation and maintains that no technical progress has occurred in US industry since 1945 (Jorgenson and Griliches, 1967). More often a set of statistics is used to draw up a production function in terms of 'capital' and labour, and to separate the growth of the value of output per head into the part due to the increase in the quantity of 'capital' and the 'residual' due to technical progress. This requires the statisticians to find out from the record of what actually happened, what the growth of output *would have been* if the value of capital had grown as much as it did without any technical progress having taken place. [It must have needed an even tougher hide to survive Phelps-Brown's (1957) article on 'The meaning of the fitted Cobb–Douglas function' than to ward off Cambridge Criticism of the marginal productivity theory of distribution.]

No doubt Professor Ferguson's restatement of 'capital' theory will be used to train new generations of students to erect elegant-seeming arguments in terms which they cannot define and will confirm econometricians in the search for answers to unaskable questions. Criticism can have no effect. As he himself says, it is a matter of faith.

References

CLARK, J. B. (1891), 'Distribution as determined by a law of rent', *Q. J. Econ.*, vol. 5, pp. 289–318.

FERGUSON, C. E. (1969), *The Neoclassical Theory of Production and Distribution*, Cambridge University Press.

JORGENSON, D. W., and GRILICHES, Z. (1967), 'The explanation of productivity change', *Rev. econ. Stud.*, vol. 34, pp. 249–83.

MEADE, J. (1961), *A Neoclassical Theory of Economic Growth*, Allen & Unwin.

OKUN, A. M. (1962), 'Potential GNP: its measurement and significance', *Cowles Found. Pap.*, no. 189.

PHELPS-BROWN, E. H. (1957), 'The meaning of the fitted Cobb–Douglas function', *Q. J. Econ.*, vol. 71, 546–60.

ROBERTSON, D. H. (1930), 'Wage grumbles', *Economic Fragments*, King.

RYMES, T. K. (1968), 'Professor Read and the measurement of total factor productivity', *Canad. J. Econ.*, vol. 1, pp. 359–67.

SAMUELSON, P. A. (1962), 'Parable and realism in capital theory: the surrogate production function', *Rev. econ. Stud.*, vol. 29, pp. 193–206.

SAMUELSON, P. A. (1966), 'A summing up', in 'Paradoxes of capital theory: a symposium', *Q. J. Econ.*, vol. 80, pp. 568–83.

SOLOW, R. M. (1963), *Capital Theory and the Rate of Return*, North-Holland Publishing Co.

SRAFFA, P. (1960), *Production of Commodities by Means of Commodities*, Cambridge University Press.

11 P. Garegnani

Heterogeneous Capital, the Production Function and the Theory of Distribution [1,2]

P. Garegnani, 'Heterogeneous capital, the production function and the theory of distribution', *Review of Economic Studies*, vol. 37, 1970, pp. 407–36.

The notion of capital as a 'factor of production', on which the theories of production and distribution dominant since the latter part of the last century ultimately rely, has been the object of considerable discussion in recent years. As is well known, these theories had their origin in a reformulation in terms of homogeneous land and 'intensive' margins, of the Malthusian theory of rent. It was shown that the rent of land – which had appeared as the residuum left after deducting the share of wages and profits calculated at the rate given by the marginal product of a dose of 'labour with capital' – could also be viewed as the marginal product of land, with the sum of wages and profits as the residuum. The two factors, land and 'labour with capital', could then be put on the same footing and the theory extended to any number of factors.

The way was thus open, it was thought, to explaining in terms of marginal productivity the division of the product between labour and capital, which the classical economists had analysed by altogether different principles. But in order to explain the rate of profit along these new lines, capital had to be conceived,

1. A paper containing the material now included in sections I to III of the present paper was submitted for publication in April 1963 and accepted for publication subject to revision shortly afterwards. The present paper is a revised version of the extended paper, including three new sections, which reached the editors in October 1968 (*Eds.* of *Review of Economic Studies*).

2. I wish to thank Mr Sraffa for his comments and criticisms. I am also grateful for the help derived from discussion of this paper in seminars at the Faculty of Economics in Cambridge, and at the Consiglio Nazionale delle Ricerche in Rome. Professor Gandolfo of the University of Siena has been of considerable help with the mathematics underlying some propositions of section IV.

ultimately, as a single magnitude: and had accordingly to be measured as a value quantity, unlike labour or land which were physical quantities. The extension of the 'law of rent' to distribution between labour and capital therefore raised the danger of circular reasoning: the value of a capital good, like that of any product, changes with those very rates of wages and interest which are to be explained by means of 'quantities' of capital. Some of the originators of these theories were conscious of the difficulty, but their attempts to deal with it were limited to very special hypotheses. It is therefore not surprising that in recent literature instances should have cropped up showing that the basic propositions of the theory are in fact controvertible. Up to now, however, little or no attempt seems to have been made to see the implications of the failure of these propositions for the problem of value and distribution. An attempt to do this is the main aim of the present article.

We shall begin by discussing a defence of traditional theory put forward by Samuelson (1962) and claiming that in some cases heterogeneous capital goods can be reduced to quantities of a homogeneous 'capital', the marginal product of which equals the rate of interest: this, Samuelson thought, would display the corresponding version of traditional theory as a useful 'parable' giving 'insights into the fundamentals of interest theory' (Samuelson, 1962, p. 193).

Sections I and II of this paper will therefore examine the relations between the wage, the rate of interest and the product per worker in the two-commodity economy – with only a consumption good and a capital good – which Samuelson used for his argument.

Section III will then show that a production function giving the interest rate as the marginal product of capital is compatible with these relations *if, and only if*, the conditions of production of the capital good are always identical with those of the consumption good: an hypothesis which turns the original 'heterogeneous capital model' into one where capital, besides being homogeneous and hence measurable in physical terms, is also homogeneous with the consumption good.

In section IV, the results reached that far will be generalized from Samuelson's two-commodity economy to one where any number of commodities are produced.

In that more general setting, sections V and VI will consider how the discussion in the earlier sections bears on various formulations of traditional theory. Attention will be focused on the idea that in a competitive economy, wages and interest are governed by the demand and supply for 'capital' and labour, the core of traditional theory in all its versions. The fact that 'capital intensity' in the economy need not increase as the rate of interest falls (the wage rises) undermines, it will be argued, the explanation of distribution in those terms. In the Appendix, these negative conclusions will be illustrated by numerical examples showing how far the relations between the rate of interest, the wage, the value of capital and the physical product per worker may differ from what received theory claims.

The final pages of section VI will then consider some of the problems which arise when that explanation of value and distribution is abandoned. In this connection, we shall refer to the different approach used by the classical economists up to Ricardo.

I. Production with a single 'system'

The economy Samuelson assumes in his article is one where production takes place in yearly cycles and where a single consumption good A exists, obtainable by a number of alternative 'systems of production', a, β, γ, etc. Each 'system', e.g. a, consists of two 'methods of production': a method for the direct production of A by means of fixed quantities $l_a^{(a)}$ of labour, and $c_a^{(a)}$ of a capital good $C^{(a)}$ specific to the method; and the method for producing $C^{(a)}$ by $l_c^{(a)}$ of labour and $c_c^{(a)}$ of itself. The capital good $C^{(a)}$ is assumed to decay according to a yearly 'rate of mortality' $d^{(a)}$, independent of age.[3] Constant returns to scale are assumed in both industries and, hence, for the 'system of production' as a whole.

3. Samuelson (1962, p. 197). This way of dealing with fixed capital evades the problems specific to *fixed* capital, which are problems of joint production (cf. below, page 262). In these sections, however, we shall retain the assumption of a 'rate of mortality' d, since $d = 1$ gives the correct treatment of *circulating* capital.

Further, the system is such that: (a) a surplus can be obtained over the pure replacement of machines (i.e. $1-d^{(a)}c_c^{(a)} > 0$); (b) the capital good enters the production of both commodities (i.e. both $c_c^{(a)}$ and $c_a^{(a)}$ differ from zero); (c) some labour is required directly or indirectly to produce each of the two commodities (i.e. $l_c^{(a)}$ differs from zero, as do either $l_a^{(a)}$, or $d^{(a)}$ or both).

To begin with, suppose that only one system is known. The hypotheses of a uniform rate of interest or of profits r, and of a uniform wage w, enable us to write the two price equations

$$1 = l_a w + c_a p_c(r+d),$$
$$p_c = l_c w + c_c p_c(r+d),$$
1

where we assume w to be paid at the *end* of the production cycle, and where p_c is the price of the capital good C expressed, like w, in terms of A. In system **1**, l_a, c_a, d, l_c, c_c are all known quantities, while r, w and p_c are the three unknowns. The two equations are then sufficient to define the relation between r and w in the economy, given by

$$w = \frac{1-c_c(r+d)}{l_a+(l_c c_a - l_a c_c)(r+d)}.$$
2

Assumptions (a), (b) and (c) we made about the system of production ensure that for $r = 0$ there is a positive 'maximum wage' which we shall indicate by W. On the same assumptions, as r rises from zero, w falls as a continuous differentiable function of r, reaching zero for a finite 'maximum rate of interest' R. It can also be shown that for $0 \leqslant r \leqslant R$ the price p_c of the capital good is positive.[4] The curve representing function **2** in the relevant

4. For $r = 0$, function **2** gives
$$W = \frac{1-dc_c}{l_a(1-d_c)+dl_c c_a}$$
where W must be positive by assumption (a) above, and finite by assumption (b). Similarly for $w = 0$ we have $R = (1 - dc_c)/c_c$, with R as the net 'rate of reproduction' of the capital good, positive by assumption (a) and finite by assumptions (b) and (c). We now note that function **2** defines a straight line in the special case $l_c c_a - l_a c_c = 0$, and a rectangular hyperbola with asymptotes parallel to the r and w axes in the general case where $l_c c_a - l_a c_c \neq 0$. In the first case we have the *decreasing* straight line:
$$w = \frac{1-dc_c}{l_a} - \frac{c_c}{l_a} r.$$

interval $0 \leqslant r \leqslant R$ (Figure 1) is Samuelson's 'factor-price frontier': we shall call it the *wage-curve* of the given system of production.

It is now convenient to introduce the notion of 'integrated consumption-good industry'. By that we shall mean the composite industry where the proportion I of the C industry to the A industry is the one which just ensures the replacement of the capital goods consumed in the composite industry. The proportion I can be easily calculated. To a unit of the A industry, there must correspond a size of the C industry sufficient to replace the quantity $c_a d$ of C consumed in the A industry *plus* the quantity $c_a Id$ of it consumed in the C industry at its size I. The proportion I is therefore given by $I = c_a d + c_c Id$, i.e.

$$I = \frac{c_a d}{1 - c_c d}.$$

(In what follows we shall, for short, refer to the 'integrated consumption-good industry' as the *integrated industry*.)

Recourse to the integrated industry is necessary if the *net* product – the product to be divided between wages and interest – is to consist of a *physical quantity* of the consumption good. An economy with zero net accumulation merely consists of the integrated industry.

In the case of the hyperbola, the product of the distances of each point of the curve from the asymptotes is the *positive* quantity

$$\frac{l_c c_a}{(l_c c_a - l_a c_c)^2},$$

and consequently we have a *decreasing* hyperbola. The positive intercepts, W and R, then imply that the segment of the curve for $0 \leqslant r \leqslant R$ lies on a single portion of the hyperbola, and is therefore continuous and differentiable.

Turning now to the positivity of p_c, we note that system 1 in the text gives p_c as the following function of r:

$$p_c = \frac{l_c}{l_a + (l_c c_a - l_a c_c)(r+d)}.$$

It follows that if $l_c c_a - l_a c_c \geqslant 0$, then p_c is positive for any non-negative value of r. In the remaining case, where $l_c c_a - l_a c_c < 0$, we have $p_c > 0$ for $r < l_a/(l_a c_c - l_c c_a) - d$; but $l_a/(l_a c_c - l_c c_a) - d > R$ because $R = (1/c_c) - d$, and we can conclude $p_c > 0$ for $0 \leqslant r \leqslant R$.

A few important quantities and relations can now be read from the wage-curve WR of Figure 1.

1. The segment OW – measuring the wage when interest is zero – also measures the net *physical* product per labourer obtainable from the 'integrated industry' with the given system of production.

2. As a result, given a wage Ow_1, the segment $w_1 W$ measures the amount of the consumption good received as interest for each worker employed in the integrated industry.

3. The tangent of the angle $w_1 PW$ measures the value, relative to the consumption good, of physical capital per worker in the integrated industry at the wage Ow_1. This is so because:

$$\tan w_1 PW = w_1 W/w_1 P = w_1 W/Or_1 = \frac{\text{interest per worker}}{\text{rate of interest}}$$
$$= \text{value of capital per worker.}$$

(For brevity we shall refer to the tangent of the angle $w_1 PW$ as the *slope* of WP.)

4. Since physical capital per worker in the integrated industry is a fixed physical quantity of capital good C, the change in the slope of WP, as we move along the wage-curve WR, indicates how p_c changes with changes in the division of the product between wages and interest.

It follows from 4 that p_c is constant only when the wage-curve is a straight line. This will be the case if the proportion between physical capital and labour is the same in the two industries (i.e. $c_c/l_c = c_a/l_a$). Then, as r varies, the change in interest costs relative to wage costs must affect the two products equally, leaving their relative value p_c unchanged.

In general, however, the wage-curve will be either concave or convex to the origin. A concave curve, like WR in Figure 1, shows that p_c rises with r. That will happen when, with the given system, the proportion between physical capital and labour is higher in the C industry (i.e. $c_c/l_c > c_a/l_a$), so that the rise in interest costs affects the capital good more than the consumption good. Similar reasoning shows that the wage-curve will be convex in the remaining case, where the ratio of physical capital to labour is lower in the C industry.

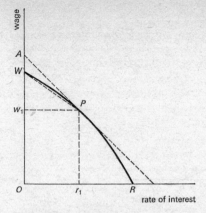

Figure 1 The 'wage-curve': OW is the net physical product per worker; $\tan w_1 PW$ is the value of capital per worker when the wage is Ow_1

II. Production with many 'systems'

We may now return to the hypothesis that several systems are available for the production of A. We shall have as many wage-curves as there are alternative systems. Since w is always measured in terms of the same commodity A, all the wage-curves can be drawn in the same diagram, as illustrated in Figure 2 for the case of two systems.

At any level of the rate of interest, producers will choose the cheaper way of producing A. But, clearly, the costs of A produced with different systems will depend on the system which happens to be in use. We may take the example of Figure 2. If a is in use at r_2, the wage is $w_2^{(a)}$ and the prices of $C^{(a)}$ and $C^{(\beta)}$ are calculated for r_2 and $w_2^{(a)}$. If however β and not a is in use at r_2, the wage is $w_2^{(\beta)}$: the prices of $C^{(a)}$ and $C^{(\beta)}$ are different and thus the costs of A produced with the two alternative systems will also differ from what they are when a is in use. The question is then whether the order of the two systems as to cheapness might not itself change according as system a or β is in use. If the order should so change we would have endless switching back and forth between a and β or, alternatively, no tendency to change whichever system happens to be in use.

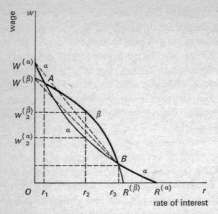

Figure 2 Production with two systems and the 'wage-frontier'

These possibilities, however, can be ruled out: the cheaper system will be the same at both wage rates and price systems. Moreover, the tendency of producers to switch to whichever system is cheaper in the existing price situation will bring them to the system giving the highest w; while systems giving the same w for the same r will be indifferent and can co-exist.[5] It follows

5. Let us suppose that, at a given level r^* or r, *a system a is in use*, and a second system β is considered in order to know the price $p_{c\beta}^{(a)}$ of $C^{(\beta)}$ and have the price (cost) $p_{a\beta}^{(a)}$ of A produced with β. We shall assume that r^* is smaller than $R^{(a)}$ and $R^{(\beta)}$, so that neither $w^{(a)}$ nor $w^{(\beta)}$ is zero. To determine $p_{c\beta}^{(a)}$ and $p_{a\beta}^{(a)}$, we must add to the price equations of $C^{(a)}$ and A produced with a, those of $C^{(\beta)}$ and A produced with β:

$$1 = l_a^{(a)} w^{(a)} + c_a^{(a)} p_c^{(a)}(r^* + d^{(a)}), \quad p_c^{(a)} = l_c^{(a)} w^{(a)} + c_c^{(a)} p_c^{(a)}(r^* + d^{(a)}),$$
$$p_{a\beta}^{(a)} = l_a^{(\beta)} w^{(a)} + c_a^{(\beta)} p_{c\beta}^{(a)}(r^* + d^{(\beta)}), \quad p_{c\beta}^{(a)} = l_c^{(\beta)} w^{(a)} + c_c^{(\beta)} p_{c\beta}^{(a)}(r^* + d^{(\beta)}). \quad \text{(i)}$$

Using the value of $w^{(a)}$ resulting from the first two equations, we can determine $p_{c\beta}^{(a)}$ and hence $p_{a\beta}^{(a)}$; system β will be cheaper or dearer than a (in the price situation corresponding to a) according as $p_{a\beta}^{(a)}$ is less or more than 1. If β, and not a, had been in use we would have had:

$$p_{aa}^{(\beta)} = l_c^{(a)} w^{(\beta)} + c_a^{(a)} p_{ca}^{(\beta)}(r^* + d^{(a)}), \quad p_{ca}^{(\beta)} = l_c^{(a)} w^{(\beta)} + c_c^{(a)} p_{ca}^{(\beta)}(r^* + d^{(a)}),$$
$$1 = l_c^{(\beta)} w^{(\beta)} + c_c^{(\beta)} p_c^{(\beta)}(r^* + d^{(\beta)}), \quad p_c^{(\beta)} = l_c^{(\beta)} w^{(\beta)} + c_c^{(\beta)} p_c^{(\beta)}(r^* + d^{(\beta)}). \quad \text{(ii)}$$

Now, w and the prices of the four commodities (A produced with a appearing as different from A produced with β) which result from equations (ii) will generally differ from those obtained from equations (i). But the difference can be seen to arise here purely from a change of the value unit, which was

that the relation between r and w will be represented by the 'outside' broken line generated by the intersecting wage-curves: the line which Samuelson named 'north-east frontier' and which we shall call *wage-frontier*. Where the 'wage-frontier' has a 'corner' a switch of systems occurs, while at the 'corner' itself the two systems, which we may call 'adjacent', can co-exist. Thus, in the example of Figure 2, the 'wage-frontier' is $W^{(a)}ABR^{(a)}$, with switches from a to β, and back from β to a occurring as r rises from zero to its maximum $R^{(a)}$.

We could now examine how net physical product and value of capital per worker in the integrated industry change as r varies and producers switch from system to system. So, for example, Figure 2 shows that, at r_3 – with r rising – producers switch to system a, having a *higher* product per labourer (measured by $OW^{(a)}$, larger than $OW^{(\beta)}$) and having, at r_3, a *higher* value of capital per worker (measured by the slope of $W^{(a)}B$, steeper than that of $W^{(\beta)}B$). These results are both in striking contrast with received theory, as is the fact that in the highest range of r producers 'switch back' to a system which had already been in use for low levels of r. It is convenient however to postpone these matters and make some further assumptions which – while necessary for a discussion of Samuelson's surrogate production function – will allow us to meet traditional theory on the more familiar ground where systems of production 'change continuously' with r.

A produced with a in (i), and is A produced with β in (ii). (It should be noted that this result is due purely to the fact that the two systems have no common commodity input and does not hold for more complex systems of production.) The ratios between the prices and the wage are therefore the same in both systems of equations, and we have

$$\frac{w^{(\beta)}}{w^{(a)}} = \frac{1}{p^{(a)}_{a\beta}} = p^{(\beta)}_{aa}.$$

Since when $p^{(a)}_{a\beta} \lesseqgtr 1$, then $p^{(\beta)}_{aa} \gtreqless 1$, the order of the two systems as to cheapness is the same at both systems of prices. Moreover, $p^{(a)}_{a\beta} < 1$ if, and only if, $w^{(\beta)} > w^{(a)}$: thus the systems giving a w higher than $w^{(a)}$ are cheaper than a at the prices corresponding to a. Accordingly, whichever the system initially in use, the switch to cheaper methods will finally bring us to the system giving the highest wage. On the other hand, when $w^{(a)} = w^{(\beta)}$, $p^{(a)}_{a\beta} = 1$: systems giving the same w are therefore equally profitable at the given level of r and can co-exist.

We shall assume, accordingly, that the four coefficients l_a, d, c_c and $(l_c\,c_a)$[6] can change as given continuous functions of a parameter u: i.e. to each value of u included in a certain range, there will correspond a unique set of values of the coefficients and, hence, a system for the production of A. (As an example, we might imagine 'wine' being produced with a continuously variable quantity of direct labour, where the 'wine' produced with a given quantity of labour requires a specific *quality* of grapes, in turn produced by themselves and labour in fixed quantities.)[7]

We shall also suppose that the 'family' of systems thereby defined is such that: (a) the wage-curve of each system cannot contribute segments, but only points, to the 'wage frontier'; (b) that the 'wage frontier' no longer shows any 'corner'. The 'wage frontier' then becomes a smooth 'envelope' which is tangent at each point to one wage-curve and encloses the whole family of them from above. An illustration is given in Figure 3, where we have drawn some members of one such family of wage-curves having E as their 'envelope'.[8]

6. Function **2** (see page 248 above) depends on $l_c\,c_a$ and not on l_c and c_a taken separately. This is as we should expect, since the arbitrary choice of the physical unit of C (which affects l_c and c_a, but not $l_c\,c_a$) cannot alter the relation between r and w.

7. The assumption of continuity in the text is made *only* in order to show that the criticisms of traditional theory raised in this paper are independent of whether or not we assume systems of production which change by indefinitely small steps. In fact this assumption would be justified if the qualitative differences in the means of production used in different systems could be reduced to quantitative differences of the *single input* 'capital'. But when differences in the kinds of input have to be taken into account, the only acceptable hypothesis is that of a *finite* number of alternative systems.

8. In mathematical terms the position is as follows. The four coefficients are given by the functions $l_a = v_1(u)$, $l_c\,c_a = v_2(u)$, $c_c = v_3(u)$ and $d = v_4(u)$, defined for an interval of u in which all four functions are positive. Substituting these functions in function **2**, we obtain

$$w = \frac{1 - v_3(u)\{r + v_4(u)\}}{v_1(u) + \{v_2(u) - v_1(u)v_3(u)\}\{r + v_4(u)\}}, \qquad \textbf{2.1}$$

where **2.1** is the 'parametric equation' of the family of wage-curves. When the functions giving the four coefficients are appropriate, the family of curves defined by **2.1** admits a 'smooth' envelope enclosing them from above. The equation of the envelope, or its points, can then be found by well-known procedures (see e.g. Courant, 1962, pp. 171–4).

On these assumptions, the system of production – i.e. the level of u defining the system in use – 'changes continuously' with r. By this expression we mean that: (a) any change of r, however small, brings about a change of system; (b) one system only is in use at each possible level of r.

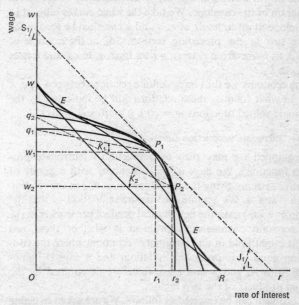

Figure 3 E is the 'envelope' of the wage-curves

Let us now consider the properties of an economy meeting these hypotheses. As the rate of interest rises, the wage must fall because the 'envelope' is tangent to a decreasing curve at each point. Little however can be said about its curvature. Where the envelope is tangent to wage-curves which are either convex to the origin or straight lines, the envelope must be convex: but where the wage-curves are concave, the envelope may well be concave or a straight line. The envelope may therefore have any curvature, with convex and concave segments alternating.

As we have just seen, at any possible level of r, a single system is in use in the economy.[9] We shall therefore find in the 'integrated industry' (page 249) a determinate physical product and a definite physical capital per worker. We shall indicate this net product by q, using k for the value of the physical capital per worker, expressed in terms of A and calculated at the given level of r. The way in which q and k vary with r can easily be seen from the diagram of the envelope. We take the wage-curves tangent to the envelope at given levels of r: q and k can then be read in the way we saw in the preceding section. So, in the example of Figure 3, as r rises from r_1 to r_2, q rises from q_1 to q_2, and k rises from k_1 to k_2.

In the economy we thus have definite relations between w, q, k and r. In what follows, these relations will be indicated by the three single-valued functions $w = e(r)$, $q = q(r)$, $k = k(r)$.

III. The 'surrogate production function'

Thus equipped we may turn to Samuelson's 'surrogate production function'. We have a 'real' economy with a family of alternative systems giving the 'envelope' $w = e(r)$ as the relation between r and w. We assume zero net accumulation so that the function $q = q(r)$ gives the net physical product per worker in the 'real' economy. Samuelson's problem is whether these two relations might hold in an 'imaginary' economy where the consumption good A is produced by labour and a capital homogeneous with A, and w and r are therefore determined by the marginal products of the two factors.

The problem can be restated as follows. We are asked to define a function $S = S(J, L)$ homogeneous of the first degree – with S as the quantity of (net) product, J that of capital and L that of labour – satisfying the following two conditions:

1. $\partial S/\partial L = e(\partial S/\partial J)$, where $w = e(r)$ is the relation between w and r in the 'real' economy.

9. The hypothesis of a 'smooth' envelope has ruled out the co-existence of 'adjacent' systems, shown by 'corners' of the wage-frontier. A second kind of co-existence is however conceivable: that in which two or more wage-curves are *tangent* to each other. Indeed, we might conceive families of wage-curves where two or more of them are tangent to each point of the 'envelope'. These possibilities have been ignored in the text. (Cf., however, footnote 40, page 287, in the Appendix.)

2. $S/L = q(\partial S/\partial J)$, where $q = q(r)$ is the relation between net product per worker and r in the same 'real' economy.

The function $S(J, L)$, if it existed, would be a 'surrogate production function' for the 'real' economy in the sense that it would determine the relations between r, w and q once J – the quantity of 'surrogate capital' – has been appropriately defined. This would in fact show that heterogeneous capital goods can be expressed as quantities of an appropriately defined homogeneous capital, in accordance with what Samuelson calls the 'Clark–Ramsey parable'.

To see whether the 'surrogate function' can be defined, we begin by using Euler's theorem to write $S(J, L)$ in the form

$$\frac{S}{L} = \frac{\partial S}{\partial L} + \left(\frac{\partial S}{\partial J}\frac{J}{L}\right). \qquad \qquad 3$$

In the 'imaginary' economy, the equilibrium rate of interest would always be equal to $\partial S/\partial J$. Condition 1 then permits us to write function 3 in the form

$$\frac{S}{L} = e(r) + r\left(\frac{J}{L}\right). \qquad \qquad 3.1$$

Differentiation of function 3 with respect to $\partial S/\partial J$ gives[10]

$$\frac{J}{L} = -\frac{d(\partial S/\partial L)}{d(\partial S/\partial J)}, \qquad \qquad 4$$

and, using condition 1 again,

$$\frac{J}{L} = -e'(r), \qquad \qquad 4.1$$

where $e'(r)$ is the derivative of the envelope-equation for the 'real' economy.

Result 4.1 is of some interest and, by itself, sufficient to rule out the 'surrogate function' in a first class of cases. It shows that, *if*

10. We first obtain:

$$\frac{d(S/L)}{d(J/L)}\frac{d(J/L)}{d(\partial S/\partial J)} = \frac{d(\partial S/\partial L)}{d(\partial S/\partial J)} + \frac{J}{L} + \frac{\partial S}{\partial J}\frac{d(J/L)}{d(\partial S/\partial L)},$$

and then, since $d(S/L)/d(J/L) = \partial S/\partial J$, we have

$$\frac{J}{L} = -\frac{d(\partial S/\partial L)}{d(\partial S/\partial J)}.$$

$S(J, L)$ is to give the relation between r and w in the 'real' economy, *then* to each level of $\partial S/\partial J$ there must correspond a ratio J/L equal to the 'slope' of the envelope at the point where $r = \partial S/\partial J$. We saw, however, that the 'real' economy may give an 'envelope' which – in parts or throughout – is *concave* to the origin. Then J/L would *rise* with $\partial S/\partial J$, and the function $S(J, L)$ could not be a production function: equilibrium in the 'imaginary' economy of the 'Clark–Ramsey parable' requires that the marginal product of 'capital' should *not* rise when the ratio of 'capital' to labour J/L rises. A straight-line envelope, which we saw was also conceivable, would be in even more striking contrast with the 'parable': we should then have to admit that the 'marginal products' change, when the ratio of capital to labour does not.[11] But even the convexity of the relation between r and w does not ensure the existence of the 'surrogate function': the conditions for that are stricter.

To find them, let us return to function **3.1** and, using result **4.1**, rewrite it in the form

$$\frac{S}{L} = e(r) + r\{-e'(r)\}. \qquad \textbf{3.2}$$

It is now clear that condition 1 above is *sufficient* to define the function $S(J, L)$. No freedom is left for adapting $S(J, L)$ so as to satisfy condition 2: we can only ascertain whether S/L as defined by **3.2** is identical with $q = q(r)$. That this is in general *not* so can be easily seen from the graph of the envelope (see Figure 3). Function **3.2** gives S/L as the intercept on the w axis of the *straight-line* tangent to the 'envelope' at the corresponding level of r. On the other hand, q is the intercept on the w axis of the *wage-curve* touching the envelope at the same point. Function **3.2** therefore overestimates q at all levels of r where the system in use gives a wage-curve concave to the origin (see Figure 3 at the point where $r = r_1$). It underestimates q when the wage-curve is convex. It only gives the correct q when the wage-curve is a straight line. Consequently, function **3.2** satisfies condition 2 as well as condition 1 and a 'surrogate production function' exists, *if and only if* all wage-curves are straight lines (see Figure 4).

11. In fact, in the case of a straight-line envelope, no differentiable homogeneous function can satisfy condition 1 above.

The implications of this condition must now be traced. We know from section I that the wage-curve is a straight line when, in a given system, the proportion of capital goods to labour is the same in the A and C industries, so that the relative value of the two commodities is constant as the division of the product between wages and interest changes. We may now go further and note that, but for the arbitrary choice of the capital-good unit, the input coefficients of the two industries are identical. The system is therefore *indistinguishable* from one where A is produced by itself and labour.[12] Indeed, since 'heterogeneity' of commodities can here be properly defined only as a difference in their conditions of production, a straight-line wage-curve *means* that A is produced by itself and labour.

When this is true for the whole family of systems, we have that A is produced with varying proportions of itself to labour: the proportions indicated by the 'slopes' of the wage-curves. It is then no surprise that the relations between r, w and q are compatible with the 'Clark–Ramsey parable'. The assumption of equal proportions of inputs has turned the 'real' economy with 'heterogeneous capital goods' into the 'imaginary' economy of the 'Clark–Ramsey parable', where, in Samuelson's own words,

labour and homogeneous capital . . . produce a flow of *homogeneous net national product* which can consist of consumption goods or of net capital . . . formation *the two being infinitely substitutable* (in the long run, or, possibly even in the short run) *on a one-for-one basis.*[13]

---

12. Samuelson writes: 'under our postulations, one can rigorously estimate (surrogate capital) by

$$J = V = P_\alpha K_\alpha + P_\beta K_\beta + \cdots$$

where the equilibrium market *numéraire*) prices of the heterogeneous physical capitals are weights which *most definitely do change* as the real wage and interest rate are higher along the factor price frontier' (Samuelson, 1962, p. 201, Garegnani's italics). But in fact, under Samuelson's hypothesis of 'equal proportions of inputs', the prices of the 'heterogeneous' physical capitals are 'weights' which do *not* change as r and w change.

13. Samuelson (1962, p. 200, Garegnani's italics). It should be noted how Samuelson himself emphasizes that when the price of 'consumption' is constant relative to 'net capital formation' (i.e. in his words: 'the two [are] infinitely substitutable . . . on a one-for-one basis'), the two commodities are *homogeneous* (i.e. they constitute 'a flow of homogeneous net national product').

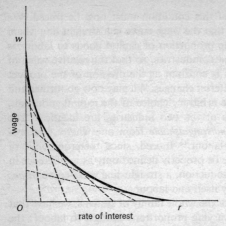

Figure 4 The 'envelope' when the consumption good is homogeneous with the capital good

In fact 'surrogate capital' and 'capital' are one and the same thing: at any given level of r, J/L, the 'slope' of the envelope, is also the 'slope' of the wage-curve tangent to the envelope at that rate of interest, and measures the proportion of A to labour required to produce A with the system in use at that level of r. Samuelson's 'surrogate production function' is thus nothing more than the production function, whose existence in such an economy no critic has ever doubted.[14]

14. We have supposed a stationary economy (above, page 256). This is in fact the assumption we must make in order to discuss the 'surrogate function' in the case where A and C are heterogeneous (if A and C are homogeneous, the level of accumulation is irrelevant). For, with some net accumulation, the net product would consist of A and of capital goods different at different levels of r. Then, as r changes, the net product per worker (a product measurable only in value terms) reflects also the changes in the *composition* of output – a circumstance quite distinct from the changes in the system of production, which alone the production function is meant to express. So, for example, should the economy grow in scale year by year, at a proportional rate equal to the rate of interest, the value relative to A of net product per worker would be equal to the S/L of equation 3.2 [cf. Bhaduri (1966, p. 288) and, for a more general discussion of the ratio of capital to labour in conditions of accumulation, Spaventa (1968)]: but it would be incorrect to describe this case as one where the traditional production function is valid. By doing so we would have to admit, whenever the

260 The Capital Controversy and Income Distribution

IV. A generalization

Suppose now, for a moment, that a second consumption good was produced in the economy besides A, and let it be a 'luxury good', a good not consumed by workers. The introduction of this good would not have affected the relation between r and w. Each 'system' for the production of A – i.e. a 'method of production' of A, and the 'method of production' of the corresponding capital good – would still give the two equations 1; and these would determine the relation between r and w *independently* of the new price equations for the 'luxury good' and any means of production specific to it. The part these additional equations would play is only that of determining the prices of the 'luxury good' and its means of production (once r, w and p_c are known).

What we have here is the application of a principle which Ricardo first perceived:[15] in any economy, the relation between the wage and the rate of interest depends exclusively on the methods of production of the commodities that are either wage goods *or* means for their direct or indirect production. The way

---

envelope is concave, equilibrium with rising 'marginal products': or even, should the envelope be a straight line, 'marginal products' changing without any change in the proportions of the factors (page 258 above).

The problem of the 'surrogate function' has been associated by Samuelson with the measurement of relative shares of labour and capital by means of the elasticity of the wage-curve (cf. 1962, pp. 199–200). Now, if in Figure 1 (page 251) we draw the tangent AP to the wage-curve at the point P, the elasticity of the curve a that point is Ow_1/w_1A. On the other hand, relative shares in the stationary economy are Ow_1/w_1W at P (cf. proposition 2 on page 250). Consequently, the elasticity of the wage-curve does *not* measure relative shares in the stationary economy unless the wage-curve is a straight line. (In the latter case, A and C being homogeneous, the elasticity of the wage-curve measures relative shares, whatever the level of accumulation.) When A and C are heterogeneous, the elasticity measures relative shares only when the proportional rate of accumulation equals r.

15. Both in letters of 1814 and in his *Essay on the Effect of the Low Price of Corn on the Profits of Stock* (1815), Ricardo maintained that 'it is the profits of the farmer that regulate the profits of all other trades' (see Sraffa, 1950–55, vol. 6, p. 104; cf. also vol. 4, p. 23). As Mr Sraffa pointed out, that principle is founded on the assumption that 'corn' is the only constituent of the wage, and requires only labour and itself to be produced (1950–55, vol. 1, p. xxxi): 'corn' is then the only commodity 'entering the wage' and the conditions of its production determine the rate of profits in the economy, once the wage is given. The principle was then taken up in a more general

is now open for extending the inquiry of the preceding sections to an economy with any number of commodities.

Let us consider an economy where commodities A_1, A_2,..., are produced in yearly cycles, each in a distinct industry. By assuming an industry for each commodity we rule out joint production and thus the possibility of a satisfactory treatment of fixed capital. We shall therefore complete the step and assume that the means of production are entirely consumed in each yearly cycle of production. As before, we suppose that no scarce natural resources exist and that each industry has constant returns to scale. To begin with, we shall also assume that only one 'method of production' is known for each industry. Thus, the production of a unit of commodity A_1 requires fixed quantities l_1 of labour and a_{11}, a_{21},..., of commodities A_1, A_2, etc.: these quantities define the 'method of production' of A_1. Similarly the 'methods of production' of A_2, A_3, etc., are defined, respectively, by the sets of input coefficients l_2, a_{12}, a_{22},...; l_3, a_{13}, a_{23},...; etc.

The wage w is paid at the end of the yearly production cycle and is a quantity of the *wage commodity G* consisting of the h *wage goods* A_1, A_2,..., A_h taken in the quantities λ_1, λ_2,..., λ_h, respectively.[16] We can now sort out from among all the commodities those which are means of production for the h wage goods, or means of production for those means of production, etc. We shall indicate by $m(m \geqslant h)$, the number of commodities which either are wage goods or enter (directly or indirectly) the production of the wage goods. For short, we shall call these m

form by von Bortkievicz (1906–7, p. 21 of English trans.; 1907, p. 206 of English trans.); cf. also Pasinetti (1960, p. 85). For the principle and comments on its formulation in von Bortkievicz, see Garegnani (1960, pp. 31–3, 54n., 202).

16. Changes in the wage level are generally associated with changes in the kinds and proportions of the commodities consumed by workers. It may then appear that a changing wage, measured in terms of an unchanging set of 'wage goods', becomes an abstract value quantity on the same footing as the wage in terms of any other commodity. However, certain commodities always play a primary role in workers' consumption and therefore provide a more significant measure of the wage. In addition, when, as in most concrete problems, the concern is for non-drastic changes in distribution around a given situation, the goods consumed by workers in that situation can be legitimately singled out as 'wage goods'.

commodities, 'commodities entering directly or indirectly the wage', or simply *commodities entering the wage*. We shall indicate them by $A_1, A_2,..., A_m$. The methods of the m 'commodities entering the wage' constitute the *system of production* of the 'wage commodity' G.

The assumption of a uniform wage and rate of interest allows us to write the following $m+1$ equations, the last of which defines G as the value unit:

$$p_1 = l_1 w + (a_{11} p_1 + a_{21} p_2 + ...a_{m1} p_m)(1+r),$$
$$p_2 = l_2 w + (a_{12} p_1 + a_{22} p_2 + ...a_{m2} p_m)(1+r),$$
$$...$$
$$p_m = l_m w + (a_{1m} p + a_{2m} p_m + ... + a_{mm} p_m)(1+r),$$
$$1 = \lambda_1 p_1 + \lambda_2 p_2 + ...\lambda_h p_h, \qquad \qquad 5$$

where $l_1, a_{11},..., a_{m1}$; $l_2, a_{12},..., a_{m2}$;...; $l_m, a_{1m},..., a_{mm}$; are all known quantities, as are $\lambda_1, \lambda_2,..., \lambda_h$. There are $m+2$ unknowns: r, w and the prices $p_1, p_2,..., p_m$.

Having $m+1$ independent equations for $m+2$ unknowns, system 5 has one degree of freedom, which we may use to obtain w and the prices as functions of r.

To analyse the relation between r and w, it is first necessary to distinguish those commodities, if any, which are used either directly or indirectly as means of production of *all* the m commodities. These commodities we shall call commodities (or products) *basic to the system*[17] (e.g., in the systems discussed in the preceding sections, C, the capital good, was 'basic' while A, the consumption good, was not). We shall now make the following assumptions about the 'system' for producing the wage commodity G:

1. The system is viable, i.e. is capable of yielding a surplus over the pure replacement of the means of production.

2. At least one of the m commodities is basic to the system.

3. The direct production of at least one of its basic products

17. Cf. Sraffa (1960, pp. 7–8). Mr Sraffa defines as basic commodities those which enter directly or indirectly the production of *all commodities in the economy*. This stricter definition seems inconvenient here since the relation between r and w depends only on the conditions of production of the commodities 'entering the wage'.

requires some labour (so that labour enters directly or indirectly into the production of all m commodities).

4. Where a group of non-basics exists such that each of them enters directly or indirectly the production of all commodities in the group, the group's 'own net rate of reproduction' is greater than the 'net rate of reproduction' of the basic products.[18]

Assumptions 1, 2 and 3 are the generalization of the parallel assumptions (on page 248) for our earlier two-commodity systems. (There, assumption 4 was unnecessary because consumption good A, the non-basic product, did not enter its own production.)

We can now return to the relation between r and w as determined by system **5**. Assumptions 1, 2, 3 and 4 ensure that, for $r = 0$, we shall have a positive 'maximum' wage W and that, as r rises from zero, w falls as a continuous differentiable function of r, reaching zero for a finite 'maximum' rate of interest R. The same assumptions imply that, for $0 \leqslant r \leqslant R$, the prices of the m commodities are positive and finite.[19] The system for the production of G therefore defines a 'wage-curve' (Figure 5) as with Samuelson's two-commodity systems, except that, under the present more general assumptions, concave and convex segments may alternate along the wage-curve.[20]

Let us now take the m industries in the unique set of proportions which ensures a net physical product consisting entirely of G,[21] and call the resulting composite industry the 'integrated wage-commodity industry' or, for short, the *integrated industry*.

18. The 'net rate of reproduction' of the basic products is Mr Sraffa's 'standard ratio' (1960, p. 21). The 'own net rate of reproduction' of a group of connected non-basics is the analogous concept obtained by considering those non-basics as if their production did not require as means of production any commodity outside the group.

19. It should be noted that assumptions 1, 2, 3 and 4 do not ensure, for $0 \leqslant r \leqslant R$, positive prices for the 'luxury goods' or their specific means of production: zero or negative prices for some of these goods would mean that they cannot be produced at the given rate of interest.

20. The wage-curve is a ratio between a polynomial of the mth degree and one of the $(m-1)$th degree in r. By a known property such rational functions admit up to $(3m-6)$ points of inflexion. (Cf., e.g., Enriques, 1915). Further inquiry would be needed to find whether that maximum number can be reached in the relevant interval $0 < r < R$.

21. Cf. the notion of a 'subsystem' in Sraffa (1960, p. 89).

Then, for the reasons we saw in section I (page 250), the vertical intercept OW of the wage-curve (Figure 5) measures the net physical product per worker in the 'integrated industry'; while the 'slope' of the straight line WP measures the value – relative to the wage commodity – of physical capital per worker in the same industry, at point P.

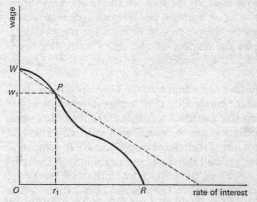

Figure 5 The wage-curve for systems with many commodities

A straight-line wage-curve therefore indicates that the value of the physical capital used in the integrated industry does not change relative to the wage commodity G as the division of the product between wages and interest changes. In that case, the equations of system 5 can be reduced to the following single price-equation for the wage commodity:

$$1 = lw + a(1+r)$$

where l (given by $l_1 \lambda_1 + l_2 \lambda_2 + \dots l_h \lambda_h$) is the quantity of labour necessary for the direct production of a unit of G, and a, a constant, results from the commodity input coefficients of the m industries. This single price equation shows that the conditions of production of G are identical to those of its means of production: G and its means of production are therefore homogeneous (page 259 above).

In all other cases, the value (in terms of G) of the capital employed in the integrated industry changes with r and – as is shown by the alternation of convex and concave segments along the curve – the direction of change will itself change as r rises from zero to R.

So far, we have assumed that only one method is known for producing each of the commodities 'entering the wage'. Let us now assume alternative methods for some or all the m commodities. Each *combination of m methods, one for each commodity*, constitutes a system for the production of the wage commodity G. (If $i_1, i_2, \ldots, i_m$ are the number of alternative methods of production of $A_1, A_2, \ldots, A_m$ respectively, we have $i_1 \times i_2 \times \ldots i_m$ alternative systems.)[22]

We can go further and admit that the alternative methods of production of some commodity may require different means of production. Changing a method may then entail discarding some commodities and introducing new ones, each with its own method of production (or one of their alternative methods). In comparing any two systems, we shall therefore have to distinguish the commodities into two classes: those which 'enter the wage' with *both* systems and are 'common' to them (among these commodities we shall always find the h wage goods), and those which are 'specific' to one of the systems (e.g. the two-commodity systems of the earlier sections had 'in common' only commodity A, the wage good).

After combining the alternative methods in order to form all possible systems of production of G, we may draw the corresponding wage-curves in one diagram. The problem now is to find which system will be in use at any specified level of r, given the tendency, in each industry, to switch to whichever method is cheaper in the existing price situation.

Here, as in section II (page 251), the question is complicated by the fact that the price situation, on the basis of which the methods are chosen, itself depends on the system which happens to be in use. It can be proved however that, whichever the system initially

22. It should be noted that a change in the method of production of a commodity may entail a change in the list of basic products. It is also conceivable that certain sets of available methods may give rise to systems having no basic products. This last possibility will be ignored here, in accordance with assumption 2 of page 263 above.

in use, the switch to cheaper methods will eventually bring into use the system giving the highest w. When two (or more) systems give the same w for the given r, and that w is higher than those of all other possible systems, the two (or more) systems give the same prices for all commodities they have in common and can therefore co-exist.

The more general hypotheses of this section do not therefore affect the main conclusion in section II about the relation between r and w in an economy with many systems for producing the wage commodity. That relation is represented by the 'wage frontier' generated by the intersecting 'wage-curves': methods, and hence systems of production, change at the 'corners' of the frontier, at which points two 'adjacent' systems (page 253) can co-exist. The same wage-curve however may now contribute more than two separate segments to the wage frontier since any two wage-curves may intersect more than twice.

If we were prepared to make the necessary assumptions,[23] we could imagine the 'wage frontier' becoming a 'smooth' envelope enclosing the family of wage-curves from above. The problem of a 'surrogate production function' could then be approached in the same way as in section III.

Let $w = e(r)$ be the equation of the envelope and $q = q(r)$ be the relation between r and the net product per worker in the integrated wage-commodity industry. The problem is whether there is a function $S = S(J, L)$, homogeneous of the first degree, such that $\partial S/\partial L = e(\partial S/\partial J)$ and $S/L = q(\partial S/\partial J)$. For the reasons given above (page 258), the function exists if, and only if, all the wage-curves are straight lines. We have already noted that a system giving a straight-line wage-curve implies that G is produced by itself and labour. It follows that $S(J, L)$ exists only when G is produced by variable proportions of itself and labour. Then J is the capital used *in the production of* G, and $S(J, L)$ is the production function of G.

But, in contrast to what we saw in section III, the condition that all wage-curves are straight lines is now insufficient to ensure

23. The number of commodities 'entering the wage' should not change from system to system, and the $m(m+1)$ input coefficients should be appropriate functions of a single parameter u (cf. footnote 8).

the existence of a 'surrogate production function', i.e. a function giving not only the relation between r and w, but also the relation between r and the net product *in the economy as a whole*. This is so because 'luxury goods' can be produced in addition to G. The value relative to G of the net product per worker in the economy will then depend on the relative size of the various industries and will differ from $S/L = q$.[24] This, however, only confirms the conclusion we reached in section III: a 'surrogate production function' exists only for an economy where a single commodity is produced by itself and labour.

V. Heterogeneous capital and the premises of the traditional theory of distribution

Our inquiry into the properties of economies with heterogeneous capital goods now offers a convenient basis for examining the validity of traditional theory from an angle less special than that of Samuelson's 'surrogate production function'. This we shall do by discussing three questions which, as we shall see, correspond to three different versions of the theory. The discussion will be conducted on the basis of the economy considered in the last section, with constant returns to scale, no joint production and no scarcity of natural resources.

The first question is whether there exists an *aggregate* production function in which quantities of labour and 'capital' explain both the level of the national product and, by means of the 'marginal products' of the two factors, its distribution (cf. Samuelson, 1962, pp. 193–4). A second question is whether a similar production function can be conceived for any *single* commodity. The third and most important question concerns the basic premise of the traditional theory of distribution in all its formulations: the notion that a fall of r will cheapen the more capital-intensive processes of production.

Our discussion of Samuelson's 'surrogate function' makes it

24. A similar difference between S/L and the value of the net product per worker in the economy could arise if the wage goods were produced in proportions other than those in G. However, the assumption of a multiplicity of wage goods can hardly be maintained where all wage-curves are straight lines: it would indeed be a fluke if G, consisting of different commodities in given proportion, required as means of production *those* commodities in *those* proportions in *all* alternative systems.

easy to dismiss the first question. Either a single commodity is produced in the economy and no problem of aggregation arises, or different commodities are produced and no 'aggregate production function' exists. But, despite the fashion for 'aggregate production functions' in recent economic literature, they are only of secondary interest. In traditional theory, distinct production functions were generally attributed to each consumption good, and consumer demand was brought in to determine the proportions in which these goods are produced.

We therefore get nearer to the core of traditional theory when we turn to the notion that the technical conditions of production for any commodity A_i can be represented by a production function with 'capital' and labour as the factors. In these versions of traditional theory it is claimed that, in any equilibrium situation, the ratio of 'capital' to labour in the production of A_i would be that for which the marginal product of 'capital' is equal to the ruling rate of interest. To that ratio, there would correspond a 'marginal product' of labour, giving the wage in terms of A_i, and a determinate physical product to be divided between wages and interest.

To discuss this view of production we must refer to the notions of 'system of production' and 'integrated industry', applying them to the commodity A_i.[25] In parallel with the assumptions of continuity inherent in the notion of 'marginal products', we must assume that the system for the production of A_i 'changes continuously' with r. What we saw about the relations between r, w and q, and their representation by means of the 'envelope' of wage-curves, can then be applied to the relations between r, the wage in terms of A_i and the net physical product per worker in the production of A_i. The question we must now ask is whether these relations could result from a production function, with labour and an appropriately defined 'capital' as the two factors.

25. So far, we have used these notions only for the wage commodity G, but they can be applied to any commodity A_i. A 'system of production' for A_i is a set of methods of production; one method for A_i and one for each of the commodities which enter directly or indirectly the production of A_i. Appropriate proportions of these industries will give the 'integrated industry' of A_i.

This is simply Samuelson's problem of the existence of a 'surrogate production function', restated for the production of a single commodity A_i and not for aggregate production. And, for exactly the reasons we saw above (page 258), the function exists if, and only if, A_i is produced with varying proportions of itself and labour.[26]

But expressing the conditions of production of a commodity in terms of a production function with 'capital' as a factor is a feature of only *some* versions of the traditional theory of distribution. They are the versions stemming from authors like Marshall or J. B. Clark, who thought that the principle of substitution, drawn from the reformulation of the Malthusian theory of rent in terms of homogeneous land and 'intensive' margins, could be applied *without modification* to labour and 'capital'. In production with unassisted labour and land, variable proportions of the factors can be shown to imply equality between the marginal products of the two factors and the rates of wages and rents in terms of the product. It was therefore thought that, in production with 'capital' and labour, a similar equality would hold between the rates of interest and wages and the marginal products of these factors.

But this analogy between 'capital' and labour or land was misleading. To give a marginal product equal to the *rate of interest*, 'capital' must be conceived as a magnitude homogeneous with the product and must therefore be measured as the *value* of the means of production and not in physical units as is the case with labour or land. This value, however, like that of the other products, changes as r and w change. Consequently, the 'quantities' of capital per worker corresponding to each system – and

26. The hypothesis that each commodity in the economy is produced by itself and labour would involve logical difficulties, unless we supposed that G, the wage commodity, consisted of a single wage good. This is so because each wage good would have a distinct net 'rate of reproduction'. Consequently, as r reaches the minimum of those 'rates', say that for A_1, the price of all wage goods other than A_1 would be zero in terms of A_1. Thus, at that level of r, where the wage is zero in terms of G (but still positive in terms of wage goods other than A_1), the economic system would become unworkable. (This difficulty is due to the fact that the systems of production of G would have no 'basic' product.)

with it, the 'production function' where those quantities appear – cannot be known independently of distribution. Every conclusion reached by postulating the contrary cannot be defended on *that* ground. And we have just seen that *one* of those conclusions is invalid: no definition of 'capital' allows us to say that its marginal product is equal to the rate of interest.

The trap of drawing such a close analogy between capital and labour or land has been avoided in other versions of traditional theory. As we shall see, traditional theory – reduced to its core as the explanation of distribution in terms of demand and supply – rests in fact on a single premise. This premise is that any change of system brought about by a fall of r must increase the ratio of 'capital' to labour in the production of the commodity: 'capital' being the value of physical capital in terms of some unit of consumption goods, a value which is thought to measure the consumption given up or postponed in order to bring that physical capital into existence. Now, this proposition about 'capital intensity' was one of the conclusions reached by postulating a production function in which 'capital' is included as a factor: the principle of decreasing marginal products would ensure that, as r falls, the ratio of capital to labour rises, causing the marginal product of capital to fall in step with r. Some authors however thought that the proposition could be defended on other, more consistent grounds.

This was the position assumed by Böhm-Bawerk and Wicksell in what are, perhaps, the most careful formulations of the traditional theory. In their production functions, the capital goods appear in the form of a magnitude or set of magnitudes (Böhm-Bawerk's 'average period of production' or Wicksell's 'dated quantities of labour') which are independent of distribution: it is to these magnitudes that the marginal productivity conditions are applied. 'Capital', the value magnitude, comes in at a second stage; when, to lay the basis for explaining interest and wages in terms of supply and demand, it is argued that a fall of r will result in a relative cheapening of the systems of production requiring capital goods of a smaller value per worker.[27]

27. On the theories of Böhm-Bawerk and Wicksell, and the reasons for the failure of their arguments supporting the principle about 'capital intensity', cf. Garegnani (1960, pp. 563-4) and the references given there.

We must therefore turn our attention to the proposition that systems with a higher 'capital intensity' become profitable at lower levels of r and thus to the third of the questions outlined above (page 268). That proposition is strictly associated with a second one, which claims that a fall of r lowers the relative price of the consumption goods whose production requires a higher proportion of capital to labour. Both propositions are in fact expressions of a single principle, according to which a fall of r cheapens the more capital-intensive processes of production. Granted this principle, the way is open for explaining distribution in terms of demand and supply. As r fell, both the change in the system of production for each consumption good, and consumer substitution in favour of the more capital-intensive goods, would raise the ratio of 'capital' to labour in the economy. If we then assume that the quantity of labour employed remains equal to its supply (and the supply rises or, in any case, shows no drastic fall as w rises with the fall of r), it will follow that the amount of capital employed in the economy *increases* as r falls. This relation between r and the amount of capital employed could then be viewed as a demand function for capital; and competition in the capital market could be thought of as ensuring the absorption of 'net saving' through appropriate falls of r.

On the other hand, the assumption of a persisting equality between the employment of labour and its supply would be justified by a parallel mechanism at work in the labour market. A regular demand function for labour would exist for any given amount of capital employed in production, and competition could be thought of as bringing the wage to the level where all labour finds employment.

[After Keynes, this alluring picture of a tidy interplay between demand and supply in the labour- and capital-markets would of course be qualified as applying 'in the absence of risk and uncertainty' (cf., e.g., Solow, 1956, p. 81) or where monetary authorities offer a visible beneficent hand should the invisible one fail.]

This elaborate theory of distribution therefore rests on the principle that a fall of r cheapens the more capital-intensive processes of production relative to the others. But this principle is no more valid than that of the equality between the rate of interest and the marginal product of capital: in just the same way, it is invalidated by the dependence of the value of capital goods on distribution.[28]

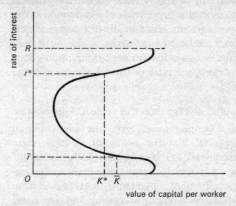

Figure 6 The relation between rate of interest and value of capital per worker with the family of systems of Figure 3

That a fall of r may cheapen the *less* capital-intensive systems of a commodity A_i can be seen from the examples given for the consumption good in Samuelson's two-commodity systems. So, at point B of Figure 2 (page 252), the switch with falling r is in favour of system β, whose capital goods have, at switch-point prices, the lower value per worker. And the position would not be altered if we assumed that the system of production of the commodity 'changes continuously' with r. So, in the family of systems of Figure 3 (page 255), a fall of r can lower, as well as raise, the value of physical capital per worker in terms of the product (a value which we shall here indicate by k_i). Figure 6 shows the relation between r and k for that family of systems. Other examples of that relation are shown in Figure 9 of the Appendix,

28. If the relative value of the two sets of capital goods required by any two systems of production remained constant as r changes, a fall of r could not fail to cheapen the more 'capital intensive' of the two systems. But the fall of r can *reduce* the relative value of the set of capital goods used in the *less* capital-intensive system: and this reduction may well make that system cheaper than the more capital-intensive one.

relating to families of systems which we shall examine there: as some of these examples show, k_i and r may fall together even in the lowest range of r.[29]

We have seen that a fall of r may cheapen the less 'capital intensive' of two systems for the production of a commodity. The same applies if the two systems relate to distinct commodities. Then by the traditional analysis of consumer choice we should conclude that, as r falls, substitution among consumption goods may lower, as well as raise, the ratio of capital to labour in the economy.

VI. Heterogeneous capital and the theory of value and distribution

Particular theoretical examples have forced the admission, in recent economic literature, that the switch of systems might operate in a direction contrary to the one traditionally assumed.[30] The tendency however has been to label those cases as 'exceptions': as if the principle about capital intensity had resulted from observed regularities, always liable to exception, and was not a pure deduction from postulates (like Böhm-Bawerk's 'average period of production') now generally admitted to be invalid.

Instead, it must be recognized that the traditional principle, drawn from incorrect premises, is itself incorrect. Moreover, the examples of the Appendix do not seem to indicate that the conditions in which a fall of r results in a relative cheapening of the less capital-intensive productive processes are any less plausible than those in which the opposite would be true. This appears to undermine the ground on which rests the explanation of distribution in terms of demand and supply for capital and labour.

To see why that is so, we may begin from the relation between r and the value, in the chosen unit, of the physical capital employed

29. In the examples referred to in the text, k_i is measured in terms of the commodity whose production we are considering. But the conclusion that k_i and r may fall together over any range of r is not affected if any other commodity is chosen as value unit. It should be noted however that the direction in which k_i changes with r may be different with different value units since the relative value of such units will itself change with r.

30. Cf. Champernowne (1953–4, pp. 118–19, 128–9), Hicks (1965, p. 154), Morishima (1964, p. 126), Robinson (1953–4, p. 106; also 1956, pp. 109–10 and 418). Cf. also Levhari (1965) and the ensuing Symposium (1966).

in the economy. This value we shall indicate by K. The relation between r and K – the traditional 'demand function' for capital (saving) – was based on two assumptions: (a) that in the situation defined by each level of r, the labour employed is equal to the supply of it at the corresponding level of w; (b) that the composition of consumption output is that dictated by consumer demand at the prices and incomes[31] defined by the level of r. We shall now grant these assumptions, but we shall restrict the choice of the consumers by supposing, at first, zero net savings (i.e. in each situation, the capital goods are consumed and reproduced in unchanging quantities year by year). From these assumptions, and from what we saw about changes in the systems of production and the relative prices of consumption goods, it follows that K may fall or rise, as r falls.

To clear the ground, we must now grant traditional theory two further assumptions in addition to (a) and (b): namely (c) that a tendency to net saving (i.e. a fall in consumption) appearing in the situation defined by a given level of r, brings about a fall of r; (d) as r and w change, with systems of production and relative outputs changing accordingly, net savings realized in the economy can still be meaningfully defined and can be measured – however broadly – by the difference between the K of the final and that of the initial situation.[32]

31. In order to determine, simultaneously with the wage and prices, the incomes of consumers and hence the quantities of goods demanded and produced, some hypothesis is necessary regarding the distribution of the ownership of the capital goods in the situation defined by each level of r.

32. These assumptions are themselves highly questionable. It is beyond the scope of this article to discuss fully assumption (d). It should however be noted that, in order to justify this traditional assumption, we should once more refer to the economy of Samuelson's 'parable', where a single commodity is produced by itself and labour. In that economy, physical capital and K would be one and the same thing. No change of relative outputs could arise there and changes in the systems of production would not require any qualitative change of the existing physical capital. Then, once we admit, with traditional theory, a tendency to the full utilization of resources, any change of K could be seen as resulting from an equal opposite change in consumption. But in an economy with heterogeneous capital goods, none of the conditions listed above is verified. The changes in systems of production or in relative outputs will affect the capital stock by changing the *kind* of capital goods or by increasing the quantity of some capital goods and decreasing that of others. The possibility of referring to

Let us now imagine that the economy is initially in the situation defined by the level r^* of the rate of interest, with K^* as the amount of capital.[33] Then a tendency to positive net savings appears (i.e. consumption is reduced). We assume that, after a time, the tendency to net saving disappears so that, if a new equilibrium is ever reached, the level of consumption will become that of the situation which corresponds to the new lower equilibrium value of r.

We must now ask whether – as r falls from r^* to some level $\bar{r}$ because of the initial tendency to net saving – a new situation can always be found with an additional quantity of capital ΔK representing the net savings which the community intended to make during the period. The form of the relation between r and K implies that such a new situation cannot always be found: however high r^* is, and however small ΔK, there may well not exist any lower rate of interest $\bar{r}$ at which $\bar{K} = K^* + \Delta K$. Or, to find a situation with an amount $\bar{K}$ of capital just larger than K^*, we may need a fall of r so drastic (cf. Figure 6 above) as to make it clear that, in this case too, it is impossible to determine r by the supply and demand of 'capital' (saving).[34]

---

physical increments of the capital stock will fail and with that will fail the possibility of any meaningful notion of 'net saving', not to mention 'net saving' in terms of K. Then, even if we could grant traditional theory the existence of a tendency to the full utilization of resources, we would have to admit that the changes in total consumption imposed by given changes in the physical capital stock would depend on the *kind* of changes in the stock and on the speed with which they have been accomplished – more than upon the difference between the K of the final and that of the initial situation.

As for assumption (c), we may note that Keynes's negative conclusions about the flexibility of r can only be strengthened if, as we shall argue in the text, changes in r provide no mechanism for equalizing 'demand' and 'supply' of capital (saving).

33. Unless we suppose that the system for the production of each commodity changes 'continuously' with r, K can assume, at any level of r where two systems co-exist, any value between the extremes set by the two systems.

34. This conclusion would not be affected if we chose to measure capital in the economy by means of the chain-index method proposed by Champernowne (1953–4) and supported by Swan (1956, pp. 348 ff.). It is beyond our scope to discuss this measure of capital or the claim that it permits us to consider as the increase of capital brought about by net saving 'not the change in the value of the stock [in terms of consumption goods], but rather the

This is not all. We saw (page 275) that, in traditional theory, our assumption (a) – of a persisting equality between the quantity of labour employed and the supply of it – found its justification in the idea of a demand function for labour. But the fact that, given the quantity of labour employed, K may rise as r rises, implies that the labour employed with a constant K must *fall* with the corresponding fall of w. Thus – even if, by assumption (d), we grant that, in the face of changes in systems of production and relative outputs, we can speak of a constancy of capital and take that to mean constancy of K – there is no reason to suppose a tendency to equality between the demand and supply for labour. Assumption (a) is then unwarranted: the failure of a demand and supply analysis, which we first saw from the viewpoint of the capital market, has its mirror-image in the labour market.

Analogous results would have been reached had we imagined an initial rise in consumption (i.e. a tendency to negative net saving); or an initial change in the 'demand' conditions for capital and labour (i.e. a change in the relation between r and K due to changes in consumer tastes or in the methods of production available).

Thus, after following in the footsteps of traditional theory and attempting an analysis of distribution in terms of 'demand' and 'supply', we are forced to the conclusion that a change, however small, in the 'supply' or 'demand' conditions of labour or capital (saving) may result in drastic changes of r and w. That analysis would even force us to admit that r may fall to zero or rise to its maximum, and hence w rise to its maximum or to fall to zero, without bringing to equality the quantities supplied and demanded of the two factors.

Now, no such instability of an economy's wage and interest rates has ever been observed. The natural conclusion is that, in

value of the change' (Swan, 1956, pp. 349 and 356) (cf. however page 275 above on 'physical increments' of the capital stock). It is sufficient to remark here that when measured in these terms the amount of capital per worker may fall together with r (though it cannot do so in the immediate proximity of $r = 0$). In similar cases, Champernowne (1953–4, p. 118) asserts 'the only way that investment could remain positive . . . would be for food wages to leap up and the rate of interest to leap down to levels where capital ·quipment . . . [giving a higher ratio of capital to labour] became competitive'.

order to explain distribution, we must rely on forces other than 'supply' and 'demand'. The traditional theory of distribution was built, and accepted, in the belief that a fall of r – an increase in w – would always raise the proportion of 'capital' to labour in the economy: the theory becomes implausible once it is admitted that this principle is not always valid.[35]

The idea that demand and supply for factors of production determine distribution has become so deeply ingrained in economic thought that it is almost viewed as an immediate reflection of facts and not as the result of an elaborate theory. For the same reason, it is easily forgotten how comparatively recent that theory is. In the first systematic analysis of value and distribution by the English classical economists up to Ricardo, we would look in vain for the conception that demand and supply for labour and 'capital' achieve 'equilibrium' as the proportions in which those 'factors' are employed in the economy change with the wage and rate of profits. Thus, Ricardo saw no inconsistency between free competition and unemployment of labour. In his view lower wages could eliminate unemployment only by decreasing the growth of population or by favouring accumulation.[36]

35. According to Professor Hicks (1965, p. 154), the failure of the principle about capital intensity leaves us in a position which, though not satisfactory, 'has parallels in other parts of economic theory'. He thus seems to suggest that the possible fall, as r falls, in the value of capital per worker does not affect traditional theory any more than do the well-known anomalies of the demand for inferior goods. This seems to ignore that the case of inferior goods did not call into question the general supply-and-demand analysis of prices only because it could be plausibly argued that (a) should those anomalies give rise to a multiplicity of equilibria, the equilibrium position with the highest price would be stable, while that with the lowest price would, in all likelihood be stable too; and (b) if the latter equilibrium were unstable, the rest of the economic system would not be affected since all we would have is that once the price has fallen below the level of that equilibrium the commodity would not be produced due to a lack of demand willing to pay the supply price. No analogous arguments have been advanced by Professor Hicks with respect to the fall of capital intensity as r falls.

36. For example, in his chapter 'On machinery' in the *Principles*, Ricardo wrote: 'the discovery and use of machinery may be attended with a diminution of gross produce; and whenever that is the case, it will be injurious to the labouring class, as some of their number will be thrown out

What we find in the classical economists is the idea that the wage is ruled by the 'necessaries of the labourer and his family'. Since they regarded these 'necessaries' as determined by social as much as physiological conditions, we may see them as recognizing that distribution is governed by social forces, the investigation of which falls largely outside the domain of the pure theory of value. The proper object of value theory was seen to be the study of the *relations* between the wage, the rate of profits and the system of relative prices. These relations would then provide the basis for studying the circumstances on which depends the distribution of the product between classes.

The distinction thus made by the classical economists between the study of value and the study of the forces governing distribution goes together with a separation between the study of value and that of levels of output. Since the inception of the marginal method this separation has been thought no more tenable than that between value and distribution. But the weakness of the marginalist position should now be apparent.

The outputs of commodities and, hence, consumer choice, can influence relative prices, *either* by modifying the technical conditions of production (i.e. the set of methods available for producing each commodity) *or* by affecting the rates of wages and profits.

The first possibility arises because increases in the output of a commodity may, on the one hand, bring about an increase of the division of labour in any of its possible forms and, on the other hand, where scarce natural resources are used, may force the adoption of methods which increase the output obtained from those resources. But with regard to the changes in the division of labour due to increases in output, the traditional analysis of the

of employment, and population will become redundant, compared with the funds that are to employ it' (see Sraffa, 1950–55, vol. 1, p. 390).

An interesting expression of the contrast between Ricardo and later theorists can be found in Wicksell's criticism of this position of Ricardo. Wicksell (1901, p. 137 of 1934–5 edn) holds that the decrease of 'gross produce' of which Ricardo speaks is not possible because 'as soon as a number of labourers have been made superfluous by these changes, and wages have accordingly fallen, then, as Ricardo failed to see [other] methods of production . . . will become more profitable . . . and absorb the surplus of idle labourers'.

firm has in fact restricted the theory of a competitive economy to those technical improvements that are 'external' to the firm. At the same time, the approach in terms of outputs of single commodities has ruled out the technical improvements deriving from the economy's general growth. Consequently, the only 'economies of scale' considered were those 'external to the firm', but 'internal to the industry' – the class which, it has been noted, 'is most seldom to be met with' (Sraffa, 1926, p. 186 of 1953 edn). There remains the case of scarce natural resources. This – as Ricardo showed – can be conveniently treated by first assuming the outputs of the commodities to be given, *then* moving on to inquire about the technical changes associated with changes in outputs, and the consequent changes in the relations between r, w and the prices (including the prices for the use of natural resources). This method would also allow a less restricted treatment of the 'economies of scale'.[37]

The second way in which consumer choice and, hence, outputs can influence relative prices is by affecting the relative scarcity of labour and capital, and thus the wage and rate of interest, given the supply of the two factors and the state of technical knowledge. This link between prices and outputs is one and the same thing as the explanation of distribution by demand and supply of factors of production: and it becomes untenable once that explanation is abandoned.

Thus, the separation of the pure theory of value from the study of the circumstances governing changes in the outputs of commodities does not seem to meet any essential difficulty. On the contrary, it may open the way for a more satisfactory treatment of the relations between outputs and the technical conditions of production. Moreover, by freeing the theory of value from the assumption of consumers' tastes given from outside the economic system, this separation may favour a better understanding of consumption and its dependence on the rest of the system.

37. This method is apparently the one Mr Sraffa points to, when in the Preface to *Production of Commodities by Means of Commodities* he writes 'no changes in output . . . are considered, so that no question arises as to the variation or constancy of returns' and adds: 'this standpoint, which is that of the old classical economists from Adam Smith to Ricardo, has been submerged and forgotten since the advent of the marginal method' (Sraffa, 1960, p. v).

With this, the theory of value will lose the all-embracing quality it assumed with the marginal method. But what will be lost in scope will certainly be gained in consistency and, we may hope, in fruitfulness.

Postscript

A mathematical appendix has been omitted for reasons of space. In sections 1–6 of that appendix a demonstration is given of the propositions set out at page 248 of the text on the positivity of prices and the properties of the relation between r and w. Then in sections 7 and 8 a proof is given of the statements on page 266 on the relative profitability of alternative systems of production. A copy of this appendix is available to students in the Marshall Library at Cambridge.

Appendix

The purpose of this Appendix is to show by a selection of numerical examples how far the relation between the rate of interest and the value of capital per worker in the production of a commodity can differ from what traditional theory postulates. For simplicity of calculation, we shall refer to the two-commodity systems of production discussed in sections I and II of the paper. We shall indicate by k_i the value, expressed in terms of the product, of capital per worker in the integrated production of a commodity A_i (cf. page 250 in the text); by w_i, the wage expressed in the same terms; and by q_i, the level of the net physical product per worker.

We shall begin by considering the family of systems giving the wage-curves and 'envelope' of Figure 3 (page 255). To give a more complete idea of the freedom with which k_i may vary as r changes, we shall then show how families of systems may be found giving *any* relation between r and k_i within an area defined purely by the shape of the envelope (cf. the area $STQO$ in Figure 9 on page 288).

We assume circulating capital, i.e. $d = 1$; and choose as the unit of any capital good C the quantity of it requiring a labour year for its direct production, so that $l_c = 1$ in each system. Let the remaining three coefficients be defined by the following functions

$$l_a = \frac{30 + 11u^{1.5} + u^{3.3} - 27e^{-2u}}{6 + u^{1.5}},$$

$$c_a = \frac{27e^{-2u}}{(6 + u^{1.5})^2},$$

$$c_c = \frac{5 + u^{1.5}}{6 + u^{1.5}}, \tag{i}$$

where $u \geqslant 0$ is the variable parameter and e is the base of natural logarithms. The family of systems defined by the functions (i) is such that, as l_a increases (i.e. u increases), c_a decreases and c_c increases (cf. Table 1).

Table 1

Parameter u	Production of a unit of the consumer good		Production of a unit of the capital good	
	Labour l_a	Physical capital c_a	Labour l_c	Physical capital c_c
0·000	0·500	0·750	1	0·833
0·250	2·584	0·424	1	0·839
0·500	3·930	0·237	1	0·845
0·750	4·834	0·133	1	0·851
1·000	5·478	0·075	1	0·857
1·250	5·974	0·042	1	0·863
1·505	6·391	0·023	1	0·868

Substituting the expressions for the five coefficients in function 2 of the text (page 248), we obtain the equation of the family of wage-curves,

$$w = \frac{1 - (5 + u^{1.5})r}{(5 + u^{1.5}) + \{27e^{-2u} - (5 + u^{1.5})^2\}r}.$$

The system defined by $u = 0$ gives a wage-curve convex to the origin and having $W = R = 0.20$, shown in Figure 7(a). As u increases, both W and R, given by $1/(5 + u^{1.5})$, decrease. At the same time, the ratio of C to labour decreases in the A industry and increases in the C industry; as a result the wage-curves become progressively less convex to the origin. Thus, the system for $u \cong 0.034$ gives a straight line wage-curve, while the wage-curves corresponding to still higher values of u are concave.

Table 2

Rate of interest % r	System in use u	Wage w_i	Net phys. prod. per worker q_i	Value of capital per worker k_i
00·0	0·000	0·200	0·200	1·080
2·6	0·250	0·175	0·192	0·635
4·1	0·500	0·169	0·183	0·393
6·1	0·750	0·159	0·175	0·257
8·3	1·000	0·151	0·167	0·184
10·5	1·250	0·144	0·159	0·148
12·9	1·505	0·129	0·152	0·179
14·4	1·250	0·105	0·159	0·379
15·1	1·000	0·083	0·167	0·552
15·9	0·750	0·061	0·175	0·715
16·9	0·500	0·041	0·183	0·850
17·5	0·250	0·026	0·192	0·947
20·0	0·000	0·000	0·200	1·000

The fall of W and R on the one hand, and the increasingly concave shape of the wage-curves on the other, are such that each cuts the wage-curves corresponding to any lower u twice and shows a middle section above all of them. See Figure 7(a). This is so up to the point where $u = 1·505$. As u rises further, the wage-curves recede towards the origin and the corresponding systems are less profitable than others at *all* possible levels of r.

As is clear from Figure 7(a), the family of wage-curves for $0 \leqslant u \leqslant 1·505$ admits an envelope E. Each wage-curve touches E twice (with the exception of that for $u = 1·505$ which touches E only once) and each system will be in use at *two* levels of r. Thus, as r rises from zero to the maximum of 20 per cent admissible in the economy, we shall run through the whole series of systems twice: first (up to $r = 13$ per cent) in the order of increasing u and then in the opposite order (Table 2). Accordingly q_i, the net physical product per worker in the integrated industry will first fall as r rises, and then rise, as shown by Figure 7(b) (cf. also Table 2). The same is true for k_i. See Figure 7(c).

The relation between k_i and q_i is shown by the curve of Figure 7(d), whose loop-like shape requires some explanation. As r rises

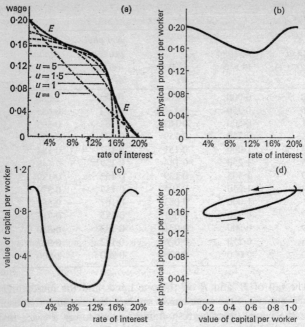

Figure 7 Relations between r, w, q_i, k, with the family of systems whose input coefficients are defined by functions (i)

from zero, we enter the diagram from the right and move in the direction of the arrows: q_i and k_i decrease together. But, as we reach $r \cong 12$ per cent, while q_i continues to decrease, k_i starts rising and we move down and to the right. Then, as r increases beyond 13 per cent, q_i also begins to rise and we move along the lower part of the loop. Thus, for the same q_i – indicating that the same system is in use – we have two levels of k_i due to the *two* levels of r at which the same physical capital is evaluated. So long as the systems are those in use for the middle range of r (i.e. the systems having a proportion of C to labour higher in the C than in the A industry), k_i is higher at the second (higher) rate of interest. The contrary is true for the systems in use in the two extreme ranges of r. We have the same q_i for the same k_i only when the system in use is that corresponding to $u \cong 0.034$, giving

$q_i \cong 1 \cdot 99$: the system in which the ratio of C to labour is the same in the A and in the C industries. In correspondence to that system the two parts of the loop intersect.

Suppose a decreasing rectangular hyperbola with asymptotes parallel to the r and w axes, which intersects both positive semi-axes: for short, we shall call *segment* the part of this hyperbola included between the two intersections. It can be shown that when the 'segment' is *concave* to the origin, it can always be interpreted as the wage-curve for a two-commodity system of the kind used for our numerical examples: i.e. the equation of the curve is always compatible with positive values of all the four coefficients l_a, $(c_a \, l_c)$, c_c, d.[38]

Let us now take the parabola defined by the equation

$$w = -20r^2 - r + 1$$

and call E the part of that curve included between the points of intersection $(0, 1)$ and $(0 \cdot 2, 0)$ with the positive semi-axes (Figure 8).

Consider the possible families of 'segments' having E as the envelope enclosing the family from above: an infinite number of such families can be conceived. Since E is concave to the origin, any family must include only concave 'segments' and is therefore a possible family of wage-curves. Accordingly, E can be con-

---

38. The equation of the hyperbola assumed in the text is

$$w = \frac{1 - xr}{y - zr},$$

where x, y, z are positive and such that $(xy - z) > 0$. On the other hand, the equation of a wage-curve (see function **2**, page 248) can be written as

$$w = \frac{1 - (c_c/1 - dc_c)r}{[\{l_a + (l_c \, c_a - l_a \, c_c)\}/1 - dc_c] + \{(l_c c_a - l_a c_c)/1 - dc_c\}r}.$$

Equating one by one the coefficients of the two functions we obtain the following three equations

$$\frac{c_c}{1 - dc_c} = x; \qquad \frac{l_a + (c_a - l_a \, c_c)}{1 - dc_c} = y; \qquad \frac{c_a - l_a \, c_c}{1 - dc_c} = z;$$

which give

$$l_a = \frac{y + dz}{1 + dx}; \qquad c_c = \frac{x}{1 + dx}; \qquad l_c c_a = \frac{xy - z}{1 + dx};$$

where l_a, c_c and $(l_c \, c_a)$ are positive because $x, y, z, (xy - z)$ and d are positive.

ceived as the relation between r and w for any among an infinite number of possible families of systems of production.

We may now define each family j of such systems in terms of the function $k_i^{(j)} = k_i^{(j)}(r)$, relating the rate of interest and the value of capital per worker in the family. To see the conditions which $k_i^{(j)}$ must satisfy, let us consider in Figure 8 the wage-curve QPS of the family j, tangent to E at the point P for $r = r^*$, where $0 < r^* \leqslant 0.2$: the 'slope' of the straight line QP measures $k_i^{(j)}(r^*)$ (see proposition 3 of page 250 in the text). If E is to enclose all wage-curves of the family j from above, that 'slope' must be lower than the 'slope' of the straight line drawn to P from T, a slope given by $(1-w^*)/r^* = 1+20r^*$. Further, $k_i^{(j)}(0)$ – the slope for $r = 0$ of the wage-curve tangent to E at point T – must equal the 'slope' of E at T, which is 1. Thus, the function $k_i^{(j)}(r)$, defining a possible family of systems having E as the envelope, must satisfy the conditions:

$$k_i^{(j)}(0) = 1; \qquad \text{and} \quad k_i^{(j)}(r) < 1+20r, \quad \text{for } 0 < r \leqslant 0.2. \qquad \text{(ii)}$$

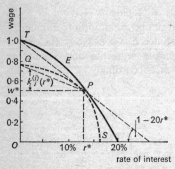

Figure 8 E is the envelope of the family of systems j defined by the function $k_i^{(j)}(r)$

To any function $k_i(r)$ satisfying these conditions there corresponds a family of wage-curves having E as its envelope.[39] It follows that families of systems can be conceived giving as the relation between r and k_i any curve which, in Figure 9, has Q as

39. Conditions (ii) above are sufficient to exclude that a wage-curve tangent to E would also intersect it. By equating the function of the hyper-

its point for $r = 0$, and then keeps within the area $STQO$ – an area depending upon the curve E of our example.[40]

We have chosen to illustrate this freedom of the relation between r and k_i by considering the families of systems defined by the following three functions, represented in Figure 9:

$$k_i^{(1)} = 1,$$

$$k_i^{(2)} = 1 + 10r,$$

$$k_i^{(3)} = 1 + 18r - 90r^2.$$

As in the preceding example we suppose $d = 1$ and $l_c = 1$. The coefficients l_a, c_a, c_c are functions of the parameter u, chosen so that the system defined by any value u^* of u is adopted at the level $r = u^*$ of r.

In what follows, we give for the three families of systems: (a) tables with the numerical values of the coefficients for some of the systems; and with the values of r, w, q_i and k_i in the situation where those systems are in use; (b) diagrams of the relation between net production and value of capital per worker (it should be noted how the curves differ from those rising and concave from below generally assumed).

---

bola giving the wage-curve with that of the parabola giving E, we obtain an equation of the third degree in r. Of its three possible roots, two are accounted for by the point of tangency, while the third root can be shown to be negative.

40. If we considered the possibility that *two* systems be in use at the same level of r (cf. footnote 9, page 256) the relation between r and k_i would be given by an area. An example is provided by the shaded area in Figure a:

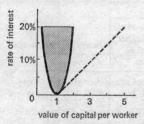

Figure a The shaded area is a possible relation between k_i and r

as r falls from its maximum of 20 per cent down to zero, the possible values of k_i narrow down to a single intermediate value OB.

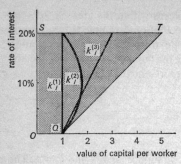

Figure 9 Any curve $k_i^{(j)}$ which starts from Q and stays within the area $STQO$ is a possible relation between the value of capital per worker k_i and the rate of interest

Table 3 The Case $k_i^{(1)} = 1$

Systems of production								Value of capital per worker
Param.	Input coefficients (*)				Net phys. prod. per worker	In use at		
u	l_a	c_a	l_c	c_c	q_i	r	w	k_i
0	0·976	0·0006	1	0·976	1	0	1	1
0·05	1·027	0·0017	1	0·932	0·95	0·05	0·9	1
0·10	1·216	0·0037	1	0·892	0·80	0·10	0·7	1
0·15	1·750	0·0097	1	0·857	0·55	0·15	0·4	1
0·20	4·537	0·0772	1	0·833	0·20	0·20	0	1

Table 4 The Case $k_i^{(2)} = 1+10r$

Systems of production								Value of capital per worker
Param.	Input coefficients (*)				Net phys. prod. per worker	In use at		
u	l_a	c_a	l_c	c_c	q_i	r	w	k_i
0	0·968	0·0010	1	0·969	1	0	1	1
0·05	0·959	0·0006	1	0·915	0·975	0·05	0·9	1·5
0·10	0·986	0·0159	1	0·873	0·9	0·10	0·7	2
0·15	2·978	0·0359	1	0·845	0·775	0·15	0·4	2·5
0·20	1·204	0·0772	1	0·834	0·6	0·20	0	3

Table 5 The Case for $k_i^{(3)} = 1 + 18r - 90r^2$

	Input coefficients (*)				Net phys. prod. per worker	In use at		Value of capital per worker
Param.								
u	l_a	c_a	l_c	c_c	q_i	r	w	k_i
0	0·958	0·0017	1	0·958	1	0	1	1
0·05	0·928	0·0083	1	0·907	0·984	0·05	0·9	1·675
0·10	1·010	0·0142	1	0·875	0·890	0·10	0·7	1·900
0·15	1·394	0·0211	1	0·850	0·651	0·15	0·4	1·675
0·20	4·537	0·0772	1	0·833	0·200	0·20	0	1

Systems of production

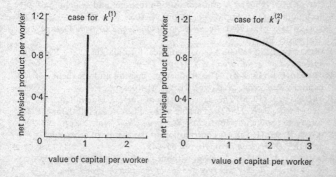

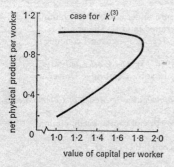

Figure 10 Relations between q_i and k_i for the three families of systems of the example

References

BHADURI, A. (1966), 'The concept of the marginal productivity of capital and the Wicksell effect', *Oxf. econ. Pap.*, vol. 18, pp. 284–8.

CHAMPERNOWNE, D. G. (1953–4), 'The production function and the theory of capital: a comment', *Rev. econ. Stud.*, vol. 21, pp. 112–35.

COURANT, R. (1962), *Differential and Integral Calculus*, vol. 2,

ENRIQUES, F. (1915), *Teoria geometrica delle equazioni e delle funzioni algebriche*, vol. 1, Zanichella, Bologna.

GAREGNANI, P. (1960), *Il capitale nelle teorie della distribuzione*, Giuffrè, Milan.

GAREGNANI, P. (1966), 'Switching of techniques', *Q. J. Econ.*, vol. 80, pp. 555–67.

HICKS, J. R. (1965), *Capital and Growth*, Clarendon Press.

LEVHARI, D. (1965), 'A non-substitution theorem and switching of techniques', *Q. J. Econ.*, vol. 79, pp. 98–105.

MORISHIMA, M. (1964), *Equilibrium, Stability and Growth*, Oxford University Press.

PASINETTI, L. L. (1960), 'A mathematical formulation of the Ricardian system', *Rev. econ. Stud.*, vol. 27, pp. 78–98.

ROBINSON, J. (1953–4), 'The production function and the theory of capital', *Rev. econ. Stud.*, vol. 21, pp. 81–106.

ROBINSON, J. (1956), *The Accumulation of Capital*, Macmillan.

SAMUELSON, P. A. (1962), 'Parable and realism in capital theory: the surrogate production function', *Rev. econ. Stud.*, vol. 29, pp. 193–206.

SOLOW, R. M. (1956), 'A contribution to the theory of economic growth', *Q. J. Econ.*, vol. 70, pp. 65–94.

SPAVENTA, L. (1968), 'Realism without parable in capital theory', in CERUNA, *Recherches récentes sur la fonction de production*, Universitaire de Namur, pp. 15–45.

SRAFFA, P. (1926), 'The laws of return under competitive conditions', *Econ. J.*, vol. 36, pp. 535–50. Reprinted in G. J. Stigler and K. E. Boulding (eds.), *Readings in Price Theory*, American Economic Association, 1953.

SRAFFA, P. (ed.) with DOBB, M. (1950–55), *The Works and Correspondence of David Ricardo*, 10 vols., Cambridge University Press.

SRAFFA, P. (1960), *Production of Commodities by Means of Commodities*, Cambridge University Press.

SWAN, T. W. (1956), 'Economic growth and capital accumulation', *Econ. Rec.*, vol. 32, pp. 343–61.

SYMPOSIUM (1966), 'Paradoxes in capital theory', *Q. J. Econ.*, vol. 80, pp. 503–83.

VON BORTKIEVICZ, L. (1906–7), 'Wertrechnung und Preisrechnung im Marxschen System', *Archiv für Sozialwissenschaft und Sozialpolitik*. Trans. in *Int. econ. Pap.*, no. 2, 1952.

VON BORTKIEVICZ, L. (1907), 'Zur Berichtigung der Grundlegenden Theoretischen Konstruktion von Marx in Dritten Bande des "Kapitals"', *Jahrbücher für Nationalökonomie*. Trans. in E. Böhm-Bawerk, *Karl Marx and the Close of his System*, ed. P. M. Sweezy, Kelley, 1949.

WICKSELL, J. G. K. (1901), *Lectures on Political Economy*, vol. 1, trans. from 3rd edn by E. Classen, Routledge & Kegan Paul, 1934–5.

Part Four
Values, Prices and Profits in Commodity Society

The utility theory of value and the labour theory of value are often treated as though they were merely alternative explanations of why a thing has some particular price rather than a different price. The difference lies deeper. The theories involve fundamentally different ways of viewing the economic processes of society.

The academic critique of Marx's theory of value is largely a recitation of Böhm-Bawerk's argument that Marx did not show properly how prices will deviate from values in certain circumstances and therefore Marx's entire system must be scrapped. The 'transformation problem' of values into prices has in fact long since been solved and there is an extensive literature on this. Both Leif Johansen (Reading 12) and Alfredo Medio (Reading 13) discuss the formal logic of several propositions associated with Marx's theory. Medio also outlines the differences between the Marxian and the Ricardian concepts of value. He argues that while Marx's theory is *not* an exception to the 'principle of the historical specificity of scientific inquiry', the Marxian method remains a powerful and vital point of departure for constructing a science of society.

Howard J. Sherman (Reading 14) argues that, from the standpoint of a simple theory of price determination, the Marxian theory is not logically incompatible with the Marshallian theory of value. It is only when one wishes to consider broader social, political and economic issues that Sherman believes the Marxian theory becomes clearly superior to the Marshallian theory.

12 Leif Johansen

Labour Theory of Value and Marginal Utilities[1]

Leif Johansen, 'Labour theory of value and marginal utilities', *Economics of Planning*, vol. 3, 1963, pp. 89–103.

I. Introduction

In a recent article (Johansen, 1963) I commented briefly on the relationship between the Marxist labour theory of value and the theory of marginal utilities. I quote from the article:

The Marxist labor theory of value has been the object of attacks particularly from the point of view of 'marginal utility theory' or 'subjective theory of value', which has been a main component of non-Marxist mathematical economics. Marxists have usually rejected this whole theory and all concepts and mathematical arguments introduced in connection with it, as if acceptance of it, or elements of it, would necessarily imply a rejection of the labor theory of value. However, this is not so. For goods which can be reproduced on any scale (i.e. such goods as have been the center of interest of Marxian value theory) it is very easy to demonstrate that a complete model still leaves prices determined by the labor theory of value even if one accepts the marginal utility theory of consumers' behavior. In my opinion, such a combination may give a very precise meaning to the Marxian thesis that the value of a product is determined by its labor content, *provided it has a use value*.

Since then I have received several letters asking me to substantiate the contention contained in the paragraph quoted above. The following is an attempt to do so.

A suitable starting point for such an attempt is the by now familiar input–output analysis. The similarities and connections between the price theory of input–output models and the labour

1. The present article does not deal explicitly with problems of economic planning. Nevertheless, we think the article will be of special interest to economists studying and working with the theory of centrally planned economies (*Ed.* of *Economics of Planning*).

theory of value have been pointed out, e.g., in Cameron (1952), Morishima and Seton (1961; see also Johansen, 1961), Schwartz (1961) and by the present writer (Johansen, 1955). On some points the presentation which is to be given here is influenced by Schwartz's analysis.

We shall in the following restrict ourselves to considering static models describing what is called in Marxian theory simple reproduction. I think this suffices for an elucidation of *some* of the basic problems of price and value theory.

II. The partial price model

Let us first consider a bare input–output model where no utilities and demand functions enter. Production is considered as a flow, i.e. we consider output volume per unit of time. There are n commodities denoted by $A_1, A_2, \ldots, A_n$. Other notations are as follows:

a_{ji} = the amount of A_j used up in the production of one unit of A_i. It includes wear and tear on equipment.

β_{ji} = the physical *stock* of A_j which is 'tied up' in the production of A_i, per unit of A_i per unit of time.

γ_i = the amount of (homogeneous) labour used up in the production of one unit of A_i.

We assume that a_{ji}, β_{ji} and γ_i for $i, j = 1, \ldots, n$ are technologically fixed coefficients. This is a standard assumption in input–output theory and it also conforms with the assumptions underlying the simpler expositions of the Marxian labour theory of value. In particular the coefficients are independent of the scale of production. (Cf. the expression 'goods which can be reproduced on any scale' in the above quotation.)

P_i = the price of A_i;

w = the wage rate (in money terms);

ρ = the rate of profit.

Assuming homogeneous labour, we have only one wage rate. Furthermore, assuming competition to prevail, and studying only equilibrium conditions and not fluctuations, the rate of profit will be the same in all branches. The price of A_i will then consist of three components: first, expenses on material inputs per unit of A_i which are $\Sigma_j P_j a_{ji}$; second, wage expenses which are $w\gamma_i$;

and third, normal profits on the capital stock. The value of the physical capital stock tied up in the production of A_i per unit of product (per unit of time), is in terms of prices, $\Sigma_j P_j \beta_{ji}$; the amount of profit on this per unit of output of A_i is accordingly $\rho \Sigma_j P_j \beta_{ji}$. Furthermore we shall assume that the producers must also hold an additional capital, as advances to labour, which is proportional to the wage sum per period. For simplicity we shall assume that the factor of proportionality equals unity.[2] Then an additional profit component equal to $\rho w \gamma_i$ must also be included in the price.

From this we obtain the following system of equations for the price formation:

$$P_i = \sum_{j=1}^{n} P_j a_{ji} + w\gamma_i + \rho\left(w\gamma_i + \sum_{j=1}^{n} P_j \beta_{ji}\right) \quad (i = 1,\ldots, n). \qquad 1$$

This is a system of n linear equations in the unknown prices $P_1,\ldots, P_n$, if we, for the moment, consider w and ρ as given magnitudes. Under plausible assumptions about the coefficients which enter the formula, this will determine the prices. (Compare, e.g., Schwartz, 1961, lecture 3.) We may therefore draw the following conclusion: if the wage rate and the profit rate are given, prices are determined completely by the coefficients a_{ji}, β_{ji} and γ_i which reflect the technology of production. If marginal utilities should affect the prices, it must therefore be through the wage rate and profit rate in an extended model where these magnitudes are no longer considered as determined by factors 'outside the model'.

The role of the wage rate is, however, a restricted one. The wage rate (in monetary terms) does not influence the relative prices. In fact, we could divide through the equations in **1** to get

$$\frac{P_i}{w} = \sum_{j=1}^{n} \frac{P_j}{w} a_{ji} + \gamma_i + \rho\left(\gamma_i + \sum_{j=1}^{n} \frac{P_j}{w} \beta_{ji}\right). \qquad 1*$$

Once the rate of profit ρ is given, this would determine all magnitudes $(P_1/w),\ldots, (P_n/w)$, i.e. all prices relative to the wage rate. Any change in w would cause only a proportional change in

2. If the factor is the same for all sectors, this is only a matter of choosing the length of the time unit.

$P_1, \ldots, P_n$, and the relative prices P_i/P_j would remain independent of w.[3] Therefore the interesting factor through which prices could depend on marginal utilities is the rate of profit. This possible dependence of prices upon marginal utilities is a rather weak and indirect one. If we consider the space of all relative prices, shifts in marginal utility curves can at most generate a one-dimensional variation in this space and the price of a commodity will not change in any obvious and simple way as a result of a shift in the marginal utility curve of that particular commodity (see Schwartz, 1961, pp. 188 and 196–7).

In a special case the relative prices would be independent of the rate of profit ρ. This is the case of 'equal organic composition of capital'. This assumption can be interpreted and expressed in different ways. Let us first express it by requiring that the value in money terms of physical capital in proportion to the total capital held should be the same in all sectors:

$$\sum_{j=1}^{n} P_j \beta_{ji} = \lambda \left(w\gamma_i + \sum_{j=1}^{n} P_j \beta_{ji} \right) \quad (i = 1, \ldots, n) \qquad 2$$

in which λ is independent of i. In this case 1 reduces to

$$P_i = \sum_{j=1}^{n} P_j a_{ji} + \left(1 + \frac{\rho}{1-\lambda} \right) w\gamma_i \quad (i = 1, \ldots, n). \qquad 3$$

It is well known from Marxian economics that prices should in the case of equal organic composition of capital be proportional to the labour values of the commodities. Let us now check this.

The labour values (expressed in units of labour) will be denoted by $Q_1, Q_2, \ldots, Q_n$.

The amount of labour used up directly in producing one unit of A_i is γ_i. The amount of labour used up indirectly through the inputs from other sectors is $\Sigma_j Q_j a_{ji}$. (Remember that wear and tear are included in a_{ji}.) The total amount of labour contained in

3. Instead of assuming w to be given in monetary terms, one could introduce a commodity, say no. 1, which serves as money. Then we should have $P_1 = 1$, and w would be one of the 'prices' to be determined by the equations in 1. This would correspond to some of Marx's considerations on money. The problem of how to determine the nominal level of those variables $P_1, \ldots, P_n$ and w which are expressed in monetary terms, is however not important for the following analysis.

one unit of A_i, i.e. the labour value of A_i expressed in units of labour, is therefore

$$Q_i = \gamma_i + \sum_{j=1}^{n} Q_j a_{ji} \quad (i = 1,..., n). \qquad 4$$

On the usual assumptions about the input–output coefficients, this system has a unique (positive) solution.[4]

It is now easy to demonstrate that the prices $P_1,..., P_n$ which solve the system **3** will be proportional to the labour values $Q_1,..., Q_n$ which are determined by **4**. For this purpose, let us write

$$P_i = \varphi Q_i \quad (i = 1,..., n) \qquad 5$$

where φ is a factor of proportionality. Let us insert this in **3**, to yield

$$\varphi Q_i = \varphi \sum_{j=1}^{n} Q_j a_{ji} + \left(1 + \frac{\rho}{1-\lambda}\right) w \gamma_i \quad (i = 1,..., n),$$

or

$$\varphi \left(Q_i - \sum_{j=1}^{n} Q_j a_{ji} \right) = \left(1 + \frac{\rho}{1-\lambda}\right) w \gamma_i \quad (i = 1,..., n).$$

Since we have, from **4**, $Q_i - \Sigma_j Q_j a_{ji} = \gamma_i$, we see that $P_1,..., P_n$ in **5** satisfy **3** if the factor of proportionality φ is

$$\varphi = \left(1 + \frac{\rho}{1-\lambda}\right) w. \qquad 6$$

By **2** we expressed the assumption of equal organic composition of capital in money terms by means of the prices $P_1,..., P_n$. We might also express the assumption by

$$\sum_{j=1}^{n} Q_j \beta_{ji} = \lambda' \left(\sum_{j=1}^{n} Q_j \beta_{ji} + \gamma_i \right) \quad (i = 1,..., n). \qquad 7$$

The condition **7** is equivalent to **2**, both being necessary and sufficient for the prices as obtained from **1** to be proportional to the labour values as obtained from **4**. The measures for the com-

---

4. For interpreting the concept of labour values it may be of some interest to observe that the equation system **4** is the same as **1*** [with $(P_1/w),..., (P_n/w)$ as variables], if $\rho = 0$, i.e. if there is no profit on capital included in price.

position of capital in **2** and **7** are, however, not necessarily equal, i.e. λ' is generally not equal to λ.[5]

By means of the concept of organic composition of capital, we can develop a simple correspondence between the rate of surplus value and the profit rate. In monetary units the profit in branch i per unit of output is

$$\pi_i = P_i - \sum_{j=1}^{n} P_j a_{ji} - w\gamma_i \quad (i = 1,...,n). \qquad \textbf{8}$$

Denoting now by λ_i the organic composition of capital in branch i, we have corresponding to **2**

$$\sum_{j=1}^{n} P_j \beta_{ji} = \lambda_i \left(w\gamma_i + \sum_{j=1}^{n} P_j \beta_{ji} \right). \quad (i = 1,...,n). \qquad \textbf{9}$$

Using **1**, **8** and **9**, we obtain the following relationship between profits as a proportion of the wage sum, the rate of profit and the organic composition of capital:[6]

$$\mu_i = \frac{\pi_i}{w\gamma_i} = \frac{\rho}{1-\lambda_i} \quad (i = 1,...,n). \qquad \textbf{10}$$

It may finally be of some interest to consider another case. Let us assume that $\beta_{ji} = a_{ji}$, i.e. that the physical capital tied up in a sector is equal to the consumption in one period of each input. I think some assumptions occasionally made by Marx in *Capital* can be expressed in this way. Then **1** can be written as

$$P_i = (1+\rho)\left(\sum_{j=1}^{n} P_j \beta_{ji} + w\gamma_i \right) \quad (i = 1,...,n). \qquad \textbf{11}$$

We now let the organic composition of capital vary as between sectors, as in **9**. Then

$$P_i = (1+\rho) \frac{w\gamma_i}{1-\lambda_i} \quad (i = 1,...,n). \qquad \textbf{12}$$

5. In section IV we shall introduce the concept of value of labour power, denoted by Q_L. Using that, we could instead of **7** write:

$$\sum_{j=1}^{n} Q_j \beta_{ji} = \lambda'' \left(\sum_{j=1}^{n} Q_j \beta_{ji} + Q_L \gamma_i \right) \quad (i = 1,...,n).$$

With the formula for Q_L given in section IV, this would again be equivalent to **2**, and we would have $\lambda'' = \lambda$.

6. Formula **10** corresponds to the formula given in Sweezy (1946, p. 68).

It is seen that there is in this case a simple relationship between the price of a commodity and the organic composition of capital in the branch, the price being (for a given γ_i) higher, the higher the organic composition of capital. This may be of interest in interpreting some propositions in Marx's *Capital*. However, it should be remembered that λ_i is itself calculated by using the price structure and is therefore not a purely technical characteristic.

III. A remark on macroeconomic relationships

Before we extend the model presented so far, let us consider briefly some implied macro relationships. We must then first introduce a symbol for the output of each branch: let it be X_i for branch no. i.

Total wage income will then be

$$W = w \sum_{i=1}^{n} \gamma_i X_i = wN, \tag{13}$$

where N is now total labour input.

Total profits will be

$$\Pi = \sum_{i=1}^{n} \left(P_i - \sum_{j=1}^{n} P_j a_{ji} - w\gamma_i \right) X_i. \tag{14}$$

From equation **1** it appears that this can be written as

$$\Pi = \rho \sum_{i=1}^{n} \left(w\gamma_i + \sum_{j=1}^{n} P_j \beta_{ji} \right) X_i = \rho K, \tag{15}$$

in which K now is total capital held in monetary terms. Using **9** we can further write this as

$$\Pi = \rho \sum_{i=1}^{n} \frac{w\gamma_i X_i}{1 - \lambda_i}. \tag{16}$$

If we define a certain average organic composition of capital $\bar{\lambda}$, **16** can be written as

$$\Pi = \rho \frac{wN}{1 - \bar{\lambda}} = \rho \frac{W}{1 - \bar{\lambda}}. \tag{17}$$

The precise nature of $\bar{\lambda}$ is given by the relation

$$\frac{1}{1 - \bar{\lambda}} = \frac{\sum_{i=1}^{n} (1/1 - \lambda_i)\gamma_i X_i}{\sum_{i=1}^{n} \gamma_i X_i}, \tag{18}$$

i.e. the complement of $\bar{\lambda}$ is a weighted harmonic mean of the complements of the organic composition of capital in the different branches.

From **17** we have

$$\mu = \frac{\Pi}{W} = \frac{\rho}{1 - \bar{\lambda}}. \qquad\qquad 19$$

This corresponds completely with equation **10** for the individual branches. Comparing **19** and **10**, we see that the ratio between profits and wages in a branch is higher than the same ratio for the economy as a whole when the organic composition of capital in that branch is higher than the average, and lower when the organic composition of capital is lower than the average. If the organic composition of capital is the same in all branches, the ratios between profits and wages in the different branches ($\mu_1, \ldots, \mu_n$) will all be equal and then, of course, also equal to the same ratio for the economy as a whole. From this it appears that the special case of equal organic composition of capital is both convenient and relevant when one wants to study problems of a macroeconomic type, and in particular the distribution between profits and wages which is at the centre of Marx's analysis. As is well known, many students of Marx interpret volume 1 of *Capital*, in which this special assumption is often made, as an attempt mainly at clarifying problems which in our present terminology could be classified as being of a macroeconomic type.

If the organic composition of capital is equal in all branches, we have seen that prices are proportional to values. The μ introduced above, which is then $\mu = \mu_1 = , \ldots, = \mu_n$, can then be interpreted as the rate of surplus value. This will be further clarified in the next section.

IV. An extended model with marginal utility functions for the capitalists and fixed consumption requirements for the workers

We have now satisfied ourselves that the price equations **1** embed the main assumptions of Marxian price theory and also bring out many of its conclusions. We shall next see how these equations can be combined with other equations so as to form more complete models. In particular we shall see how they can be combined with marginal utility functions without running into logical contradictions.

We shall first consider a model in which there are defined some minimum quantities of the different commodities which are necessary to 'reproduce the labour power' and assume that wages are just sufficient to buy these quantities.[7] In this sense the workers receive wages corresponding to the value of the labour power. Capitalists, however, enjoy a higher consumption per head than the necessary minimum. They are therefore in a position to weigh against each other marginal quantities of the different commodities and we shall now assume that they do this so as to maximize a utility function.

Let the quantity of the jth commodity which is necessary per unit of labour, be η_j. The wage rate must then be

$$w = \sum_{j=1}^{n} P_j \, \eta_j. \qquad 20$$

The consumption of each commodity by the workers is

$$C_i^w = \eta_i \, N = \eta_i \sum_{j=1}^{n} \gamma_j \, X_j \quad (i = 1,\ldots, n). \qquad 21$$

For the capitalists we shall for convenience proceed as if there be only one representative capitalist who consumes the quantities $C_1^c,\ldots, C_n^c$.[8] These quantities are determined by the maximization of a utility function

$$U^c(C_1^c,\ldots, C_n^c) \qquad 22$$

subject to a budget constraint

$$\sum_{i=1}^{n} P_i \, C_i^c = \Pi. \qquad 23$$

7. In Marx's analysis this 'necessary consumption' is, of course, not determined simply by physical or biological necessity. It is changing in response to changing technical conditions, social conditions, class struggle on the distribution of incomes, etc. But these are slow and gradual changes and cannot be subjected to analysis in such comparatively simple terms as other aspects of the mechanism which determine the prices.

8. It would only require some heavier notational equipment, but no change in reasoning, to develop the model with a number of capitalists who gain profits in proportion to their shares in the total capital in formula 15.

Defining the marginal utilities by

$$u_i^c(C_1^c,\ldots,C_n^c) = \frac{\partial U^c(C_1^c,\ldots,C_n^c)}{\partial C_i^c} \quad (i = 1,\ldots,n), \tag{24}$$

we have the following maximizing conditions:

$$\frac{u_1^c(C_1^c,\ldots,C_n^c)}{P_1} = \ldots = \frac{u_n^c(C_1^c,\ldots,C_n^c)}{P_n}. \tag{25}$$

These together with the budget equation 23 determine the consumption demand of the capitalist as functions of the profit sum and the prices.

We are now in a position to collect all equations of the model:

$$P_i = \sum_{j=1}^{n} P_j a_{ji} + w\gamma_i + \rho\left(w\gamma_i \sum_{j=1}^{n} P_j \beta_{ji}\right) \qquad (i = 1,\ldots,n) \quad \text{(a)}$$

$$w = \sum_{j=1}^{n} P_j \eta_j \tag{b}$$

$$C_i^w = \eta_i \sum_{j=1}^{n} \gamma_j X_j \quad (i = 1,\ldots,n) \tag{c}$$

$$\frac{u_1^c(C_1^c,\ldots,C_n^c)}{P_1} = \ldots = \frac{u_n^c(C_1^c,\ldots,C_n^c)}{P_n} \tag{d}$$

$$\Pi = \sum_{i=1}^{n}\left(P_i - \sum_{j=1}^{n} P_j a_{ji} - w\gamma_i\right)X_i\left[= \sum_{i=1}^{n} P_i C_i^c\right] \tag{e}$$

$$X_i = \sum_{j=1}^{n} a_{ij} X_j + C_i^w + C_i^c \quad (i = 1,\ldots,n). \tag{f}$$

All these equations are introduced previously, except for the last set (f). These are the usual input–output equations with $C_i^w + C_i^c$ as the 'final demand column', which is, however, endogenous in the present model.

One might ask whether the budget equation 23 for the capitalists should be introduced in the model as an independent equation. This equation is however already implied by the equations in (a to f). This can be seen by multiplying first (f) by P_i and summing over i. This yields

$$\sum_{i=1}^{n} P_i X_i - \sum_{i=1}^{n}\sum_{j=1}^{n} P_i a_{ij} X_j - \sum_{i=1}^{n} P_i C_i^w = \sum_{i=1}^{n} P_i C_i^c.$$

Interchanging here i and j in the double sum and using (b) and (c), we get

$$\sum_{i=1}^{n} \left(P_i - \sum_{j=1}^{n} P_j\, a_{ji} - w\gamma_i \right) X_i = \sum_{i=1}^{n} P_i\, C_i^c.$$

By the first equality in (e) this is now seen to imply **23**. We have, therefore, only indicated this equation in a bracket after (e).

In the model (a to f) there are then $4n+1$ equations and $4n+3$ variables: $P_1,\dots, P_n$, $X_1,\dots, X_n$, $C_1^w,\dots, C_n^w$, $C_1^c,\dots, C_n^c$, ρ, Π and w. Apparently there are then two degrees of freedom in the model. However, as explained earlier, the variable w does not play any interesting role in the model. We could divide through all equations (a), (b) and (e) by w and multiply by w in (d), thereby obtaining a system with only $4n+2$ variables $(P_1/w),\dots, (P_n/w)$, $X_1,\dots, X_n$, $C_1^w,\dots, C_n^w$, $C_1^c,\dots, C_n^c$, ρ, Π/w. Then there would be one degree of freedom left.[9] The reason for this is that we have not introduced *any* condition which determines so to speak the scale of operation of the economy – the level at which the 'constant reproduction' is taking place. This degree of freedom could be eliminated for instance by assuming a given total amount of physical capital somehow measured. The point is not important for our main problem and we shall not go deeper into it.

The most important property of the system (a to f) in the present context is that the set of equations (a) and (b) form a determinate subset of equations except for the fact already pointed out that there is an arbitrary factor of proportionality in the set of variables $P_1,\dots, P_n$, w. This means that also the rate of profit ρ is determined by this subset of equations.

The way in which ρ is determined may be clarified by inserting for w in (a) from (b). This yields the following set of equations in $P_1,\dots, P_n$ and ρ:

$$P_i - \sum_{j=1}^{n} P_j \{ a_{ji} + \eta_j\, \gamma_i + \rho(\eta_j\, \gamma_i + \beta_{ji}) \} = 0. \qquad \textbf{26}$$

This system is linear and homogeneous in the variables $P_1,\dots, P_n$. It has a solution with non-zero prices if and only if its determinant equals zero:

9. The same thing could, of course, be obtained by dividing by any of the variables $P_1,\dots, P_n$ and Π instead of w.

$$\begin{vmatrix} 1-g_{11}-\rho h_{11}, \ldots, & -g_{n1}-\rho h_{n1} \\ \cdot \quad \cdot \quad \cdot \quad \cdot \quad \cdot \quad \cdot \quad \cdot \quad \cdot \quad \cdot \quad \cdot \quad \cdot \\ -g_{1n}-\rho h_{1n}, \ldots, & 1-g_{nn}-\rho h_{nn} \end{vmatrix} = 0 \qquad \textbf{27}$$

in which

$$g_{ji} = a_{ji} + \eta_j \, \gamma_i \qquad \text{and} \qquad h_{ji} = \eta_j \, \gamma_i + \beta_{ji}. \qquad \textbf{28}$$

This condition is an equation in the unknown ρ. Mathematically it will in general be satisfied by a set of different solutions for ρ, but one may reasonably conjecture that only one of these will be economically meaningful.[10]

With the assumptions introduced by **20** to **21** it is possible to define the value of the labour power which is used in production. Per unit of labour expended the 'inputs for reproducing the labour power' are $\eta_1, \ldots, \eta_n$ units of the different commodities. The total value used to 'reproduce' one unit of labour, which is the definition of the labour value of the labour power, is accordingly

$$Q_L = \sum_{j=1}^{n} Q_j \, \eta_j \qquad \textbf{29}$$

in which $Q_1, \ldots, Q_n$ are determined by **4**.

In order to compare our presentation with Marx's, it is of some interest to consider the definition **29** more closely in the case of equal organic composition of capital, which is, as we have already observed, a particularly convenient case for macroeconomic interpretations of the model. In that case there is a simple correspondence **5** with φ determined by **6** between labour values and

10. Compare Morishima and Seton (1961, p. 207) where a mathematically rather similar system is investigated.

The condition **27** can be rewritten in another form which allows a formal interpretation. First write **27** in obvious matrix notations as

$$|(I-g')-\rho h'| = 0. \qquad \textbf{27*}$$

Assuming that $(I-g')$ is non-singular, we can write this condition as

$$\left|(I-g')^{-1}h' - \frac{1}{\rho}\right| = 0. \qquad \textbf{27**}$$

From this form it appears that $1/\rho$ is a latent root of the matrix $(I-g')^{-1}h'$

prices. Expressing the values $Q_1,\ldots,Q_n$ in terms of prices and the wage rate by means of **5** and inserting in **29**, we obtain

$$Q_L = \frac{\sum\limits_{j=1}^{n} P_j\, \eta_j}{(1+\rho/1-\lambda)w}.$$

However, using **20** or (b), this reduces to

$$Q_L = \frac{1}{1+\rho/1-\lambda}. \tag{30}$$

Using furthermore the relationship **19** between the rate of surplus value and the profit rate, and using λ instead of $\bar{\lambda}$ since the organic composition of capital is assumed to be the same in all branches, we have

$$Q_L = \frac{1}{1+\mu}. \tag{31}$$

It may perhaps be more interesting to solve this equation for μ to yield

$$\mu = \frac{1-Q_L}{Q_L}. \tag{32}$$

In this form the equation says that the rate of surplus value is the ratio between the value created by one unit of labour, i.e. unity, in excess of the value of the labour power itself, and this latter value; or, in Marxian terms, the rate of surplus value is equal to the ratio of surplus labour to necessary labour.

After this digression, we return to the study of the whole model (a to f). We have seen that the profit rate ρ and all proportions

$$P_1 : P_2 :\ldots: P_n : w$$

are determined by the subset (a to b) of equations in the model. This means that the marginal utilities which enter the model through (d) do not at all influence prices. What then is their role? Their role is to determine the *quantities* of the various commodities consumed by the capitalists. Thereby they influence the extent and composition of production. They will furthermore, through (c), influence the total labour input $\Sigma_j \gamma_j X_j$ and the scale of production for the consumption of the workers.

Briefly stated: prices (including the wage rate) are – except for an arbitrary factor of proportionality – determined by technological conditions as expressed by $a_{ji}, \gamma_i, \beta_{ji}$ and the consumption requirements for the 'reproduction of the labour power' (η_i). The marginal utility functions interact with the prices thus given only in determining the *quantities* to be produced and consumed of the different commodities.

The above is of course only a description of an equilibrium situation. As such I think our results conform very well with some statements by Karl Marx in volume 3, chapter 10 of *Capital*, where he first discusses the price formation and then adds that 'for a commodity to be sold at its market value, i.e. proportionally to the necessary social labour contained in it, the total quantity of social labour used in producing the total mass of this commodity must correspond to the quantity of the social want for it, i.e. the effective social want'. Other quotations from Marx in the same direction could be given (see Sweezy, 1946, pp. 47–52).

For a commodity to be produced at all ($X_i > 0$) and obtain a price as determined by (a to b), it is necessary: (1) either that it is a necessity for the workers ($\eta_i > 0$), or (2) that it for some quantity C_i^c consumed by the capitalists has a sufficiently high marginal utility u_i^c to allow the fulfilment of (d), or (3) that it directly or indirectly through the a-coefficients enters into the production of one or more commodities which satisfy (1) or (2) or both. In this sense we can say that the price of a commodity in the model (a to f) is determined as said by the equations (a to b) *provided that it has a use value.*[11]

V. Remarks on a model with marginal utility functions both for capitalists and workers

In the model in section IV we employed the assumption of fixed consumption requirements for the workers. We might, however, construct a model in which also the consumption of the workers is determined by marginal utilities. The model of section IV may in fact be considered as a limiting case of such a model.

Since the full exposition of such a generalized model will entail

11. If (2) is not satisfied for a certain commodity, which, however, satisfies (1) or (3), the corresponding ratio should be deleted from (d) and replaced by the condition $C_i^c = 0$.

many repetitions of what is already explained in previous sections of this article, we shall here only give some brief suggestions.

For the construction of the generalized model we could interpret N (see section III) simply as the number of workers employed. We must then introduce a utility function for each of the workers; for simplicity they could be assumed to be equal.

Per period of time each worker would receive a wage w and he would determine his consumption pattern so as to maximize his utility function subject to the budget constraint. Instead of being determined by such coefficients as $\eta_1, \ldots, \eta_n$ in (c), the variables $C_1^w, \ldots, C_n^w$ would then be determined by equations formally similar to (d).

The main problem which would occur in such a model is that we would have no obvious way of replacing equation (b) in the model (a to f), which together with (a) determined the distribution of income between workers and capitalists as reflected in the rate of profit ρ. Several ways are open to solve the problem:

1. One may simply consider the rate of profit ρ as determined by conditions outside our model, by struggle between labour and capital over distribution shares.

2. One could introduce the supply of labour in the model and use that in one way or other to determine the distribution between labour and capital, and thereby ρ.

3. The solution which would be nearest to the model in section IV would be to prescribe a certain 'necessary' utility level for the workers. Then the introduction of utility functions for the workers would simply change the model from assuming a minimum requirement for each commodity separately to assuming the existence of some necessary minimum satisfaction of wants which could, however, be achieved by different *compositions* of consumption.

Whichever of these solutions is chosen, all our conclusions from the partial price model in section II would hold. If (1) is chosen, also all conclusions of section IV would hold. If (2) or (3) is chosen, prices would no longer be determined quite independently of marginal utilities. However, as explained already in section II, the influence of marginal utilities upon prices would be the very indirect one through the rate of profit ρ. If the marginal utility function (workers' or capitalists') for a commodity should shift, the main effect would be that the quantity consumed would change. The price would only change to the extent that ρ would change; and if so, prices of other goods would also change.

As explained in section II, the relative prices would remain constant even if ρ changes, if the organic composition of capital is the same in all branches.

The conclusions of this section and section IV as regards the effects of utilities upon prices and quantities, may, in terms of demand and supply, be considered as a multi-commodity generalization of the case of a horizontal supply curve and a downward sloping demand curve.

VI. Concluding remarks

The present article has only been concerned with the logical question whether marginal utility theory and the labour theory of value do necessarily contradict each other or not. I shall not attempt to discuss and evaluate the realism of the models. Nor shall I discuss the usefulness of going via value theory to price theory as is done by Marx rather than restricting oneself to talking only about prices. Some arguments on this point are, however, given by Sweezy (1946, pp. 128–30).

In considering the conclusions reached in the previous sections, one should remember that we have studied only equilibrium positions. In a dynamic study of the movements of prices, demand functions would play a more important role. Also in the case of monopoly price formation the demand side would be important. Both the points mentioned here were clearly recognized by Marx (cf. Sweezy, 1946, pp. 47–52 and 54–5).

References

CAMERON, B. (1952), 'The labour theory of value in Leontief models', *Econ. J.*, vol. 62, pp. 191–7.
JOHANSEN, L. (1955), 'Forenklet Velferdsteoretisk Modell for en Sosialistisk Økonomi', *Nationaløkonomisk Tidsskrift*, vol. 93, pp. 149–69.
JOHANSEN, L. (1961), 'A note on "Aggregation in Leontief matrices and the labour theory of value"', *Econometrica*, vol. 29, pp. 221–9.

JOHANSEN, L. (1963), 'Marxism and mathematical economics', *Month. Rev.*, vol. 14, pp. 505–14.

MORISHIMA, M., and SETON, F. (1961), 'Aggregation in Leontief matrices and the labour theory of value', *Econometrica*, vol. 29, pp. 203–20.

SCHWARTZ, J. T. (1961), *Lectures on the Mathematical Method in Analytical Economics*, Gordon & Breach.

SWEEZY, P. M. (1946), *The Theory of Capitalist Development*, Dobson.

13 Alfredo Medio

Profits and Surplus-Value: Appearance and Reality in Capitalist Production [1]

First published in this volume.

Introduction: some warnings

The main subject of this paper is the Marxian theory of *value* [2] and its place in the history of economic thought. Economic theory is in a state of transition. The orthodox, neo-classical theories which have reigned supreme for six or seven decades are being subjected to a radical critique by a growing number of economists. This criticism has been based mainly on the inability of neo-classical economics to provide proper tools for the analysis of the structure and of the development of capitalism as a whole.

The 'revolution' in economic theory in the thirties did not challenge so much the internal coherence of the orthodox theory as the inadequacy of its fundamental assumptions. In particular, its 'methodological individualism' was re-examined critically, that is, the view that it is possible to reduce all statements about social phenomena to a special class of statements about *individual* behaviour, i.e. individual consumer's maximization of utility, individual firm's maximization of profits. Mainly under the influence of Keynes's *General Theory*, economics 'went macro' bringing into the analysis different premises concerning relations between aggregates – national income; total employment; total savings and investments.

More recently, a deeper critique has been developed which shows the logical inconsistency of the neo-classical theory of

1. I am indebted to Krishna Bharadwaj, Maurice Dobb, Piero Garegnani, Jerzy Osiatynski, Joan Robinson and Piero Sraffa for many helpful discussions and comments. I am especially grateful to my friend Jesse G. Schwartz without whose contribution this article would not have been written.

2. Every time '*value*' appears in italics, this refers to the Marxian meaning of the word, which will be made clear later.

value and distribution even on the basis of its assumptions when it is applied to the investigation of the economic system as a whole.[3]

Finally, the neo-classical 'vision' of the economic system as an efficient servant of the public's wants has gone under attack even by established economists like Galbraith as an ideological veil which prevents people from understanding what is really going on.

Basic failures of the neo-classical model in explaining most of the important problems have brought about a revival of interest in classical theory. This is due to two main reasons. In the first place the overall working of the capitalist economy which interests us now was the central object of classical analysis. Secondly, the theories of value that have been recently developed as alternatives to those of the neo-classicals take points of view and assumptions which come down from classical writers and especially from Ricardo – they may be indeed defined as 'neo-Ricardian'.

The relation between Marxian and 'neo-Ricardian' theories of value is not so clear. No doubt Marx's influence has played an important role in impelling economic thought in this neo-Ricardian direction and, to a certain extent, therefore the movement 'back to Ricardo' is 'back to Marx' as well. But, as Maurice Dobb (1970, p. 1) has recently reminded us, the relation between Marx and the classical economist is a dialectical one. I should like to go further than Mr Dobb would probably do, saying that most of the Marxian theory of *value* ought to be understood as a *critique* rather than a development of Ricardo's theory. It is worthwhile to stress this point, since an interpretation of Marx has gained currency which depicts him as a sort of left-wing Ricardian, with a strong inclination for philosophy and politics. According to this view a proper analysis of Marx's thought should sharply separate the 'economic', 'scientific', 'intellectually respectable' from the 'speculative', 'political', and other 'non-scientific' aspects of his doctrines. This opinion, which I have expressed here in rather stark form, is at the back of the minds of many friendly or unfriendly students of Marx. Whether they call him 'the last of great classical economists' or 'a minor post-

3. The best survey on this subject, with an extensive bibliography is Harcourt (1969).

Ricardian', all of them seem to agree in denying Marx's theory of *value* a role significantly different from the classical economists.

The point at issue is indeed crucial and I shall deliberately take the risk of coming under C. Wright Mills's (1962, p. 95) classification of 'sophisticated' Marxist in discussing this subject once again.

Some warnings should be given in advance. I am concerned here to emphasize the contrast between the Ricardian and the Marxian concept of value and therefore the current debate between the 'classical tradition' and the neo-classical school will enter into the picture only marginally.

I shall try to present my argument avoiding, as far as possible, the 'hegelese' form of reasoning – even if I am sure that the understanding of an author's own 'dialect' would help in properly interpreting him. This implies, to a certain extent, treating Marx's economic theories out of the wider context of his theory of society and of history.

Moreover, I do *not* think that the theory of *value*, or Marx's social theory as a whole, is an exception to the principle of the historical specificity of scientific inquiry. Thus the emergence of new conditions requires new tools of analysis.[4] However, I am convinced that a correct understanding of the Marxian method will be helpful in overcoming the present 'awkward corner' of social science and will increase also our ability of properly confronting *our* problems. Some people will maintain that the points in the present article are rather old fashioned and well known. To this I reply that, since the *dernier cris* on both sides of the barricade are, after all, Ricardo and Walras, I might just as well claim some room for Marx, also.

My article will be divided into two sections. In the first part I shall discuss the scientific status and the meaningfulness of the concept of *value* within Marx's theory of capitalist society.[5] In the

4. To what extent Marx himself was aware of the historical specificity of *his* theory of *value* can be seen in a famous passage of the *Grundrisse* (see Marx, 1939–41, pp. 220 ff. of 1967 edn).

5. I must emphasize at this point that much of the argument developed in the first part has been stimulated by reading Joan Robinson's numerous writings on the subject (see Robinson, 1942, 1953, 1954, 1956, 1965, 1968, 1969).

second part I shall make use of some recent results in formal economic analysis to test the logical soundness of Marx's argument.

Theory of *value*: social science or metaphysics?
Some misinterpretations of Marx's theory

In order to facilitate understanding I shall start from discussing what Marx did *not* mean by *value*.

Some economists still think that Marx's theory of *value* is based on the arbitrary assumption that labour – human purposive activity – is the only 'factor of production' and therefore the only source of material wealth (see, e.g., Fellner, 1960, p. 130; Rogin, 1956, p. 338). Now, an important feature of the Marxian theory is a sharp distinction between the relation of man with nature – the physical environment – and the relations of men with other men. When Marx speaks of labour as the only source of *value* he is dealing with social relations and *not* with the technical processes of production. He is simply saying that the human contribution to production is labour. He never overlooked the role of natural resources, tools, machines, etc. in improving the productivity of labour and thus increasing *material wealth*.[6]

Confusing the concepts of *value* and *wealth* is a classic example of what Marx would call 'fetishism of commodities'. This is by no means a simple verbal point. After all, capitalists get a profit because of their peculiar *social power* (ownership or some other form of control of means of production) and not because of the *technical power* of means of production themselves.[7]

A second, quite common, misinterpretation of Marxian *value* is closely related to the first one. It attributes to Marx the idea that commodities *ought to* exchange according to the amounts of labour embodied in them. That is this state of affairs will be eventually reached in a future, collectivistic, society, when exploitation and profits have been eliminated and all the social

6. See, for example, Marx's very explicit statement (1867, p. 43 of 1961 edn).

7. In Marx's approach, '. . . capital in its role of aid to labour – a role common to all societies, capitalist or socialist – can be separated from capital in its role of investible funds, belonging to those who own – have property in – the means of production and who obtain a share in the distribution of income because of their property rights' (Harcourt, 1969, p. 395).

product accrues to labourers. In other words, the theory of *value* would be something like a theory of *just price* whose forerunners were the medieval doctors, the doctrine of natural law and, of course, Adam Smith.

Now, this view simply rules out the contrast between Marx and the Utopian scholars. Marx makes it clear that his theory of *value* – and indeed his theory *tout court* – should not be interpreted as a *moral claim* or a normative proposition referring to the new post-capitalist society, but he emphasized that it was intended to be a tool of analysis of the *present* society.

Furthermore, he argued against Proudhon that, in order to revolutionize society, relations of production and not exchange ratios of commodities or the distribution of income were crucial. Whatever form a new society takes, it would be built not upon 'fairer' terms of exchange but on abolition of individual exchange. Indeed any form of distribution of the social product corresponds to a certain mode of production. In particular, distribution through the private exchange of commodities corresponds to the private form of production – private ownership of means of production and exploitation of labour power. Any attempt to get rid of the exploitative character of the capitalist system without changing relations of production is – in Marx's opinion – a very petty-bourgeois illusion (Marx, 1847, pp. 47 ff. of Foreign Languages Publishing House edition).

The third, and certainly most enduring, misinterpretation of the Marxian theory of *value* has gained currency since Böhm-Bawerk's criticism of Marx and is still widely shared by academic economists in spite of many refutations carried out by Marxian and non-Marxian authors. According to this view Marx's theory of *value*, as it stands in *Capital*, book 1, states that commodities tend to exchange at prices which correspond to their *values*, i.e. to the amounts of labour embodied in them. Deviations of prices from *values* would depend upon imperfections of market, changes in demand and so on, and could be therefore neglected in a theory of 'normal prices' which, by its very nature, deals with long-run situations. But – so the story runs – Marx soon realized that prices are not proportional to *values* even in the long-run period and that divergencies between prices and *values* are *permanent* and quite independent of temporary disturbances. The analysis of

Capital, book 3, is thus seen as a late, and unsuccessful attempt to cope with this problem and to build up a theory of 'prices of production' consistent with the general premises of *Capital*, book 1.[8]

Now, it is true that Marx thought that changes in the amount of labour embodied were the most important elements which accounted for changes in prices – and, in my opinion, he was perfectly correct. However, a careful investigation shows that, in *Capital*, book 1, Marx *never* tried to provide a theory of relative prices of commodities.

It should be well known – unfortunately it is not – that Marx was fully aware of the existence of permanent divergencies between prices of production and *values* and of the main reasons for this long *before* publishing *Capital*, book 1. Moreover, he explicitly criticized Smith and Ricardo who – in Marx's opinion – had confused prices and *values*. In a letter to Engels dated 2 August 1862 (see Torr, 1934, pp 129 ff. of 1936 edn) he sketched the theory of 'prices of production' which he expected to develop at a later stage and explicitly noticed that

with *equal* exploitation of the worker in *different* trades, different capitals [i.e. capitals with different organic compositions] of *the same size* will yield very *different* amounts of surplus value in different spheres of production and therefore *very different rates of profit* (Marx's italics).

He went on to observe that in order to yield a uniform rate of profit in the different sectors, commodities must be sold at prices higher or lower than their *values*.

[Price] = the expenses of capital + the average profit . . . is what Smith calls the *natural price*, *cost price*, etc. Competition does *not* therefore reduce commodities to their *value*, but to their *cost price*, which is *above*, *below* or *equal* to their *value*, according to the organic composition of the respective capitals. . . . [Ricardo's] identification of the *value* of commodities with their *cost price* is fundamentally false and traditionally accepted from A. Smith (Marx's italics).

The same argument is dealt with further in *Theories of Surplus Value* (and in a number of Marx's other writings) which –

8. See Böhm-Bawerk (1896, see 1949 edn). More recently see, for example, Fellner (1960, pp. 130–33) and Robinson (1942, p. 14 of 1966 edn).

as Engels told us – were published after but written *before* *Capital*, book 1.[9]

But even *in Capital*, book 1, there are unambiguous though marginal warnings on the subject:

If therefore he thought about the matter at all [the merchant or the manufacturer] would formulate the problem of the formation of capital as follows: how can we account for the origin of capital on the supposition that prices are regulated by the average price, i.e. ultimately by the value of the commodities? I say 'ultimately' because average prices do not directly coincide with the values of commodities, as Adam Smith, Ricardo and others believe (Marx, 1867, p. 166 of 1961 edn; see also pp. 220 and 307).

But, if Marx manifestly knew that his theory of *value* does not provide us with prices directly, that a rather cumbersome 'transformation' process is necessary, why on earth should he have spent so much time on working out this difficult and apparently rather abstruse approach and why should he have so strongly stressed its importance in the Preface of *Capital*, book 1?

Is the theory of *value* a scientific proposition about social reality? Or is it a piece of metaphysics, a religious dogma or, to put it as Joan Robinson did, 'just a word'?

A few comments on methodology

In order to answer the above questions in a satisfactory manner, a thorough discussion of the 'meaning of meaning' would be required. This, however, is beyond the limits of the present article. Therefore I shall confine myself to outline some general considerations on methodology.

The scientific character of a proposition in theory should be mainly tested on the basis of its 'explanatory power' and of its logical consistency. By 'explanatory power' of a theory I mean its capability of representing the relations of the interdependence of the phenomena which constitute the objects of the investigation. Since social life is a process which goes on in history, a meaningful explanation of social reality should enable us to understand the

9. See Marx (1905–10, pp. 175, 181 and 190 of 1968 edn; 1939–41, p. 397 of 1967 edn) and Torr (1934, p. 106 of 1936 edn). This list is by no means exhaustive.

historical genesis and development of the observed events, what Marx would call their 'law of motion'.

Logical consistency, of course, *is* a necessary requisite of any good theory. The different hypotheses must not contradict each other and also it must be possible to move from the more abstract statements of the theory to those that represent a closer approximation to reality by logical and/or mathematical deductions.

In what follows I shall argue that Marx's theory of *value* possesses both these requisites. It has been a powerful analytical tool to understand a number of relevant social phenomena and, in particular, it has thrown light on the nature of profit under capitalism much more effectively than any other theory before or after it. Marx's theory of *value* naturally entails some necessary simplifications of reality but – as it will be seen in the next part – the introduction of further variables, while only adding complexity, does not invalidate the entire model.

What Marx meant by value

The next step in my investigation is to delineate the class of phenomena that Marx's theory of *value* deals with. This can be summarized as follows.

Men, as producers, carry on a social activity, that is, they perform a set of coordinated and interdependent operations, within a complex framework of interpersonal social relations, whether they be aware of it or not. Social relations have different levels of generality. Some of them are common to any *social* productive process; others belong to any economy based on the exchange of commodities; others are peculiar to a specific exchange economy, capitalism.

In Marx's view, capitalist economies have certain outstanding characteristics. First, the large majority of products of human activity are commodities; that is, they are produced to be sold; they are not simply useful objects – 'use-values' – but 'use-values for other people'. Commodities are bought and sold according to definite ratios which tend to be equal for any commodity throughout the market. Secondly, there are two main social groups sharply differentiated in respect to conditions of life, income, political power, behaviour, etc., namely, capitalists and labourers.

Marx thought that the controlling element was the different role that these two groups played in the process of production and the consequent different way in which they appropriated a part of social product. Therefore he focused his attention on this aspect of the question. In particular, Marx endeavoured to give a thorough answer to the question: why is the capitalist able to obtain a profit in proportion to his invested capital?

To each individual firm, profits appear as a simple difference between revenues and costs. But the origin of this difference was not fully understood by early nineteenth-century economists.

The theory that Marx was looking for had to delineate the process of formation of surplus within the historical context of capitalism. Whereas in a feudal society privileged classes appropriated a share of social product 'openly' by belonging to a special 'estate' or by direct coercion,

the bourgeoisie, whenever it has got the upper hand, has put an end to all feudal, patriarchal idyllic relations. It has pitilessly torn asunder the motley feudal ties that bound man to his 'natural superior', and has left no other nexus between man and man than naked self-interest, than callous 'cash payment' (Marx, see Feuer, 1959, p. 9).

Under capitalism, therefore, social relations take the semblance of market relations and profits accrue to capitalists as a result of the general mechanism of exchange of commodities. It follows that a good theory of profit must be consistent with a theory of relative prices which is a reasonable approximation to reality.

But, while any theory of profit lacking this requisite should be rejected as unable to explain a capitalist economy, a correct theory of prices may be built *without* any specific proposition on the origin and the nature of profit. The importance of this remark will become apparent in the following discussion of the relations between the Ricardian and Marxian views.

Broadly speaking, we can envisage two main explanations of profit. The first possibility is to conceive profit as withheld or as a residual from the net social product. The second possibility is to consider profit as the exchange equivalent of some specific contribution to the productive process and therefore to think of it as a 'real cost' – abstinence, waiting, etc. – like wages and the other expenses for means of production.

Of course, Marx took up the Ricardian view that profit was a residual, but criticized Ricardo for not having carried further the analysis, so as to show *how* such a residual originated and was appropriated by a special class of persons.

Ricardo never concerns himself about the origin of surplus-value. He treats it as a thing inherent in the capitalist mode of production, which mode, in his eyes, is the natural form of social production. Whenever he discusses the productiveness of labour, he seeks in it, not the cause of surplus-value but the cause which determines the magnitude of that value (Marx, 1867, pp. 515–16 of 1961 edn).

The theory of *value* is precisely the tool of analysis that Marx constructed to unmask the social relations behind seemingly autonomous market relations and to overcome the limits of the Ricardian analysis. It can be summarized in a few propositions:

1. The economic system can be analysed at two different levels of abstraction, the *value level* and the *price level*. We can move from the former to the latter in a formal logical way.

2. The central concept in *value analysis* is that of *abstract labour*. This is purposive human activity taken in abstraction from specific characteristics of different sorts of labour. Abstract labour is, by definition, the substance of *value*. Since the process of expenditure of abstract labour takes place over time, the magnitude of *value* is naturally measured in terms of abstract labour time. Dimensionally, we have therefore:

value = abstract labour time.

3. Within the context of *value analysis*, commodities are considered as *values*, i.e. as mere receptacles of human labour. Marx did not mean that the actual exchange of commodities is immediately and consciously an exchange of amounts of labour. He simply thought that his theoretical abstraction allowed him to isolate the aspects of exchange which were *relevant* in order to understand the problem at issue (Marx, 1867, p. 74 of 1961 edn). In particular *value analysis* enabled Marx to investigate the process of *formation of profits*, which belongs to the relationships between capitalists and labourers, neglecting as a first approximation the complications arising from the *equalization of the rate of profit* all over the system, which refers to the relationships among capitalists.

This point is stated very clearly in *Capital*, book 1:

From the foregoing investigation, the reader will see that this state-ment [i.e. that the starting point of analysis must be the exchange of *values*] only means that the formation of capital must be possible even though the price and value of a commodity be the same; for its forma-tion cannot be attributed to any derivation of the one from the other. If prices actually differ from values we must, first of all, reduce the former to the latter, in other words, treat the difference as accidental in order that the phenomena may be observed in their purity, and our observations not interfered with by disturbing circumstances that have nothing to do with the process in question (Marx, 1867, p. 166 of 1961 edn).

Marx's question can be, therefore, stated like this: how can we explain the emergence of a surplus, starting from the exchange of commodities as *values*?

The surplus cannot originate in the process of exchange itself because, by assumption, commodities are treated as *values*. It must originate instead in the process of productive consumption of commodities.

In order to be able to abstract value from the consumption of a com-modity, our friend, Moneybag, must be so lucky as to find, within the sphere of circulation, in the market, a commodity, whose use-value possesses the peculiar property of being a source of value, whose actual consumption, therefore, is itself an embodiment of labour and, consequently, a creation of value. The possessor of money does find on the market such a special commodity in capacity for labour or labour power (Marx, 1867, p. 167 of 1961 edn).

Labour power is the very human purposive activity reduced to a commodity that its owner – the labourer – sells to the capitalist. As for any other commodity, the *value* of labour power is measured by the total amount of labour expended in its pro-duction, namely, the labour embodied in food, clothing, housing and any other good which, in a specific situation, constitutes the necessaries for the labourer and his family.

What induces the capitalist to buy labour power is its ability to produce an amount of *value* larger than its own *value*. When the bargain between capitalist and labourer is executed both are entitled to use up the commodities just exchanged. The worker consumes his wage goods; the capitalist makes the labourer work beyond the time necessary to reproduce his wage goods. The result is: new commodities emerge which belong to the capitalist; the *value* of these commodities includes, besides the *value* of the capital advanced (means of production and wage goods) a *surplus-value*; the worker has maintained his labour power and is ready to sell it again.

Marx claims that a proper understanding of the *value relationships* is crucial for investigating the economic and social structure of capitalism. In particular, he maintains that 'The rate of profit [and the associated prices of production] is not a mystery, as soon as we know the laws of *surplus-value*. If we reverse the process, we cannot comprehend *ni l'un ni l'autre*' (Marx, 1867, p. 216 of 1961 edn).

The neo-Ricardian approach

In order to discuss these Marxian views it will be helpful first to consider for a while the reaction which followed the publication of Marx's works.

Bourgeois economists, even though they called Marx's theory an 'empty tautology', realized quite soon its distinctiveness and its danger to the ideological foundations of their social order. Neo-classical economics was to a large extent a theoretical reply – and a political antidote – to Marx's critique of capitalism. This anti-Marxian bias is particularly evident in the writings of Böhm-Bawerk – 'the bourgeois Marx'. He shared Marx's view that the first and most important question which a theory of value has to answer is: what is the cause of profit on capital[10] in an economy based upon commodity exchange? Therefore not only did he criticize the logical shortcomings of *Capital*, but he strived to develop an alternative theory of profit and capital.

I shall not elaborate here the shortcomings of neo-classical theory. I shall rather discuss a line of thought as old as the neo-classical but which has until recently been submerged by the latter and is now an object of revived interest, primarily because of Sraffa's influence. This line of thought I have referred to above as 'neo-Ricardian'.

10. Böhm-Bawerk would say 'interest on capital', but, as far as the present discussion is concerned, these two concepts can be considered equivalent.

Some basic premises of this approach can most clearly be ascertained by means of von Bortkievicz's discussion of Marx's theory of value. These same premises underline Sraffa and his school's work, but not nearly so explicitly.

Von Bortkievicz is known as the economist who gave a correct solution to the Marxian problem of the 'transformation of *values* into prices'. However, the relation between his work and Marx's is of a dialectical nature and he was a severe critic of Marx even though he accepted much of Marxian economic analysis. Since his well-known article 'Value and price in the Marxian system' contains a detailed discussion of the point in question, it seems worth quoting it at length.[11] At first von Bortkievicz seems to share the view expressed in the present article in regard to the role of Marx's theory of *value*.

If, however, there is any generally significant point on which Marx is to some extent superior to Ricardo, then it is the theory of the *origin of profit*.

Both take the view that profit, or speaking more generally, the gains of capital, originate in a withholding of some of the produce of labour. All efforts of the opponents of the 'theory of withholding', to show that Ricardo does not base himself on this theory, rest on an untenable interpretation of occasional remarks of his or on arbitrary additions to his ideas. We must, however, admit that the theory of withholding is not expressed in Ricardo as clearly as one might wish, whilst Marx succeeded in giving a pregnant and unequivocal expression to the view of the origin of profit which lies at the basis of this theory. . . . [Marx] does not permit even the germ of the idea that price calculation might be the cause of profit. Price calculation appears in Marx, on the contrary, as the necessary consequence of the fact that profit exists and that it reveals the well-known tendency towards equalization. To lift this veil [that is, the veil which in a capitalist economy enshrouds surplus labour] is the very purpose of 'value calculation' (von Bortkievicz, 1906–7, pp. 51–2 of 1952 trans.).

Immediately after, however, von Bortkievicz seems to minimize the importance of Marx's contribution.

11. See von Bortkievicz (1906–7). I want to make clear that I am not concerned here with von Bortkievicz's fully justified criticism of Marx's derivation of prices from *values*. The point in question is whether or not *value analysis* itself is analytically useful.

This device is indeed thoroughly useful, but when Marx presents matters as if the true nature of profit could not have been realized without it, then he overestimates his personal service to the theory of withholding (von Bortkievicz, 1906–7, p. 52 of 1952 trans.).

Von Bortkievicz eventually concludes his discussion reversing his previous opinion and arguing that Marx's *value analysis* 'does not form an essential stage in theory' but it makes more difficult, not easier, the investigation of the reciprocal relationships between prices, wages and the rate of profit. In his opinion the same objective can be reached with the ' "mathematical approach" . . . which reduces the complicated quantitative relationships involved to a set of equations, where the number of equations is equal to the number of unknowns' (p. 53 of 1952 trans.).

This problem was not satisfactorily solved either by Ricardo or by Marx, but since no basic difficulty is involved it *has* been given an exact solution, along the lines of von Bortkievicz's approach. With different degrees of generality, authors like von Bortkievicz himself, Dmitriev (1898) and, more recently, Schwartz (1961) and Sraffa (1960) have built analytical models that can determine simultaneously the rate of profit and relative prices, once the technical conditions *and* wages are given (or, alternatively, can determine wages and relative prices when the rate of profit is given).

Sraffa's and Schwartz's solutions have moreover the specific merit of showing that demand plays no role in determining the rate of profit and relative prices undermining the neo-classical theory of value and distribution based on the concept of demand and supply of commodities and of 'factors of production'. Sraffa and his school in particular have conclusively demonstrated the inconsistency of any theory of profit based on the concept of 'marginal productivity of capital'.

This is a very significant achievement. But does it exhaust the content of the Marxian theory of *value*? If we accept the 'operational' dogma that the object of a 'proper' theory of value is to study the quantitative relations between wages, rate of profit and relative prices, *value analysis* 'and the related concepts of *value* and *surplus-value* become an unnecessary detour and all the discussion about the 'transformation problem' is 'much ado about nothing'.[12] From this point of view the rather abstruse Marxian discourse turns out to be the simple statement that capitalists, in order to raise the rate of profit, must squeeze the share of wages in the net product.

But the derivation of prices from *values*, the solution of the 'transformation problem' is only subsidiary and a formal proof of consistency of Marx's theory of *value*. Even when this is worked out it remains to be explained how it is that profit exists at all. In a sense, the neo-Ricardian theory has pushed economic analysis back to a pre-Marxian stage – though in much more sophisticated and rigorous form. However, profit plays an essential role in a capitalist society and *some* theory of profit is required – just as in a State based upon apartheid some theory about race is necessary.

In this respect, Marx's theory of *surplus-value* is significant and still constitutes the only valid alternative to the neo-classical explanation of the origin and nature of capitalists' gains.

The concept of value *and the Marxian theory of exploitation*

In the following discussion I shall focus my attention on some analytically distinctive features of Marxian approach.

First of all, Marx's theory of *value* does not explain profit in terms of some 'general conditions of social life'. Of course he agrees with classical economists that the pre-condition for the existence of profit is that human labour is able to produce more than is required for its support. But to formulate a profit and wage economy many other conditions are requested.

The questions *why* are labourers ready to sell their labour power in the market and *why* do they actually work more than is necessary to support themselves are of no interest for bourgeois economists but they are the core of Marxian investigation. For 'one thing is clear – Nature does not produce on the one side owners of money or commodities and on the other side people possessing nothing but their own labour power' (Marx, 1867, p. 169 of 1961 edn). On the contrary, this is a result of a definite historical process which made the labourer 'free',

12. *This* is the reason why the neo-Ricardian theory, while providing the analytical tools for a correct solution of the 'transformation problem', at the same time denies its relevance.

free in the double sense, that as a free man he can dispose of his labour power as his own commodity, and that on the other hand he has no other commodity for sale, is short of everything necessary for the realization of his labour power (Marx, 1867, p. 169 of 1961 edn).

The significance of this point is by no means simply historical. Whatever the origin of the capitalist system may have been, once in existence it produces economic and social forces which tend to keep it working.

Capitalist production, therefore, under its aspect of continuous connected process, of a process of reproduction, produces not only commodities, not only surplus-value, but it also produces and reproduces the capitalist relations – on the one side capitalists, on the other side the wage labourer (Marx, 1867, p. 578 of 1961 edn).

The theory of *value* directs our attention both to the mechanism of capitalism itself and to the way in which capitalists maintain this basis. Not only are they maximizing their profits but they also strive to preserve the social framework which makes profits possible at all.

This point has far-reaching implications which are particularly manifested in the investigation of some problems that involve the inner structure of the economic and social order. One example will be sufficient to illustrate the case: unemployment.

Unemployment is not an accident in a capitalist economy. It has a function: keeping workers in their condition of 'freely' saleable commodity. As Kalecki wrote about thirty years ago, policies which guarantee *permanent* full employment are going to undermine 'discipline in the factories' and therefore 'political stability'. True, profits would probably be higher in such a situation than in a state of *laissez-faire* with insufficient effective demand. But if workers 'get out of hand' the profit-producing mechanism itself is threatened and this is far beyond the simpler question of the *level* of profits in different conditions (see Kalecki, 1943; also Baran, 1957, pp. 101–2 of 1967 edn.).

Unemployment, by the way, is a problem Marxian theory was able to deal with far more effectively than any 'scientific' theory before Keynes.

A second, distinctive feature of the theory of *value* should be mentioned. As von Bortkievicz himself recognized, looking at profit as *surplus-value*, it lays bare the relation between capitalists and labourers. In this context, labour time is *not* used simply to calculate the shares of profits and wages in terms of a unit of measure whose magnitude is independent of distribution of income. According to the theory of *value*, when the net social product is shared, what is being divided is the labourers' working day and this rules out any idea of a 'natural' or 'fair' distribution of income. On the contrary when we use the categories of 'profits on capital' and 'wages of labour', we have the false semblance of an association in which labourers and capitalists divide the net produce – or 'social surplus' – in proportion to the different elements which they respectively contribute towards its formation (see Marx, 1867, p. 533 of 1961 edn).

It is worth noticing here that a neo-Ricardian approach – in contrast to a Marxian one – to the problem of value and distribution *may* be associated with theories which attribute to profits some 'objective' social role.

A primary example of this is perhaps the 'macroeconomic theory of distribution'. Roughly speaking, it can be summarized as follows. There are two fundamental economic relationships which may be expressed in a formal way by two basic equations. The first equation tells us that wages and rate of profit are inversely related (the relation may be linear as in Sraffa's 'standard system' or not). The second equation tells us that, since investment originates mainly, or exclusively, from profits, the rate of accumulation is positively related to the rate of profit.

Now if the 'community' wants a given rate of accumulation – what 'community' would not? – it must be ready to accept a given rate of profit and therefore a corresponding level of wages. In this way the justification of profit as a premium for capitalists' social function, which is banished at the front door with the end of 'marginal productivity of capital', is unavowedly admitted at the back door.

There is no doubt that, in any given situation, one cannot 'eat the cake and have it' and, from this point of view, the above theory emphasizes an important feature of any economy based on scarcity. But the main shortcoming of the theory in question in explaining social reality is that it links in a definite way – and in its crudest form identifies – the allocation of net social product between consumption and investment with its distribution between profits and wages.

This is a further example of confusion between technical relations and social relations. The necessity of subtracting a portion of social product from immediate consumption in order to invest is obvious and any form of society will be facing this problem for quite some time. What is *not* obvious is that the decision about *how much* to invest and *which sort* of investment to carry on is performed by a special class of people who enjoy the privileges associated with that social role (income, power, prestige, etc.). The existence of such a class might have been justified in the past to 'develop forces of production'. There is no evidence that it is so today, especially as far as advanced capitalist countries are concerned.

Thus the theory in question rules out any conceivable possibility of a state of affairs in which 'profits' and 'wages' as such do not exist and still a share of social product is spent on aims different from immediate consumption. True, in that situation, labourers should work longer than the 'necessary' time but they could *decide* to do so – instead of *being forced* to. The difference at issue does not involve only the *quantitative* aspect of the question (more or less consumption and more or less investment), but also the crucial qualitative aspects of which sort of technique to employ and how to allocate saved resources (see Marx, 1867, p. 530 of 1961 edn).

A further argument must be briefly developed to show the specificity of the theory of *value*, as a theory of exploitation. Very often economists think that the only significant point is, in this respect, the inverse relation between wages and rate of profit. Now this is no doubt an important feature both of the Marxian and Ricardian approach, and Ricardo himself was accused of provoking class antagonism. But Marx's theory of exploitation and the associated political theory of class struggle has a much wider basis than the simple conflict between capitalists and labourer about who gets what slice of the cake.

Beyond 'purely economic' relations, the theory of *value* brings into the analysis a deeper and complex set of social contradictions. For the unique and specific character of capitalism is *not* that labourers do not have all the product of their labour. This has been true of any other previous society for thousands of years. The capitalist mode of appropriation of the surplus labour requires that labour – which is by its very nature an attribute of human personality – takes the form of a commodity that the labourer can separate from himself and sell to another person. Thus labour becomes wage labour, alienated life.

This fundamental feature of the capitalist mode of production shapes social behaviour patterns. It deeply affects the relationships of the worker to the products of his labour, to his own productive activity and to other individuals. I shall not discuss here Marx's theory of alienation. I should simply like to stress that alienation in Marx's analysis is not a pure psychological phenomenon, but has its roots in the fundamental *economic* mechanism of society. In this respect, the *surplus-value* theory of profit is the central element of a much wider theory of society.[13]

The theory of *value* performs a fourth important function within the Marxian analysis of capitalism. It links Marx's 'macroeconomic model', which shows the mechanism of the system setting some basic relationships between a limited number of variables, with his 'microeconomic model' of interindustry competitive relationships. Marx's argument runs as follows. In the long run, prices of production are regulated by the uniform rate of profit; the rate of profit, in its turn, is a function of two basic overall features of the economy, namely, a social factor, the rate of exploitation, and a technical factor, the methods of production. Both of these elements can be described in terms of the allocation of the (homogeneous) labour power among different sectors and can therefore be studied through *value analysis*.

The meaning of this will be fully appreciated when the derivation of prices of production from *values* (and some shortcomings of this part of the Marxian analysis) have been discussed.

The formal model
The 'transformation problem' and the 'average commodity'

In the first part of this article I have been dealing with the meaningfullness of Marx's theory of *value* as a scientific explanation of capitalist society. Now I am going to treat the problem of its self-

13. The relation between the Marxian theory of *value* and theory of alienation can be studied in Mészáros (1970).

consistency. Indeed Marx's analysis of profit cannot be fully accepted unless we are able to coordinate satisfactorily the highest level statements of the theory – those containing the terms *value* and *surplus-value* – with the lowest level statements – those referring to prices and profits.[14]

In this context, the first proposition due to Marx to be tested is that prices of production and the associated rate of profit can be fully determined as functions of *values* of commodities – including *value* of labour power.

First of all, I must discuss an important point as to the proper definition of the 'transformation problem'. Some authors (e.g. Oikisio, 1963, p. 297) maintain that prices and the rate of profit cannot be determined *only* by a knowledge of *values*, that is, *only* by a set of numbers which designate the amounts of labour time embodied in various commodities. Obviously, in these terms, the 'transformation problem' is not solvable. However, it seems to me clear that Marx always assumed that the technical conditions of production were a *datum* of the problem. As Leontief himself acknowledged, Marx's approach to the productive system, in book 2 of *Capital*, can be looked at as a rough example of input–output analysis in which the relevance of the interdependence of sectors is fully appreciated. Moreover, the very concept of 'socially necessary amount of labour embodied in a commodity' vanishes if we do not start from the knowledge of the stages of its production, whether in the form of a series of labour terms or in the form of a set of simultaneous input–output relations.[15]

The second Marxian proposition to be proved concerns the existence of an 'average' commodity whose price is equal to its *value* no matter what the uniform rate of profit may be:

The capital invested in some spheres of production has a mean, or average, composition, that is, it has the same, or almost the same,

14. In what follows I shall assume that the lowest level statements in Marxian theory are: (a) commodities are produced only by produced means of production and labour; (b) normal prices – 'prices of production' – tend to be such to cover costs and yield a uniform rate of profit. In the present article, therefore, I shall not discuss Marx's further approximations to reality, including rent, interest, monopoly, market fluctuations, etc.

15. It can also be argued that the detailed attention that Marx paid to the rate of turnover and its influence on the rate of profit supports my view (see Marx, 1894, pp. 70 ff. of 1959 edn).

composition as the average social capital. In these spheres the price of production is exactly the same as the value of the produced commodity. . . . If there were no other way of reaching a mathematical limit, this would be the one. . . . [The] average rate of profit . . . is the percentage of profit in that sphere of average composition (Marx, 1894, p. 173 of 1959 edn).

As is well known, Marx's treatment of these two points is by no means satisfactory. To what extent this depends on the state of incompleteness of *Capital*, book 3, is largely a matter of opinion. What is interesting is whether or not Marx's argument *may* be worked out correctly by a proper mathematical treatment. In my opinion some recent contributions on the subject, and especially Seton's, Morishima's and Sraffa's, support the basic soundness of Marx's insights.

Values and prices

Since the argument will be discussed in a rather formal way, I shall begin with some basic assumptions and definitions.

Consider an economy of n industries, designated by the subscript i ($i = 1, 2,..., n$), each of them producing a given amount of a single commodity A_i in a given time interval, let us say one year. The yearly output of the ith industry is taken to be the physical unit of measure of the ith commodity. Other notations are as follows:

c_{ij} = the amount of A_j ($j = 1, 2,..., n$) *used up* to produce a unit of A_i.

l_i = the amount of homogeneous labour time (man-year) required to produce a unit of A_i. Total labour time expended yearly is assumed to be equal to unity, i.e. $\Sigma_i l_i = 1$.

$(b_1, b_2,..., b_n)$ = the basket of consumption goods received by labourers per unit of labour time or, if you prefer, the (uniform) wage rate in terms of physical goods.

λ_i = amount of labour time directly and indirectly expended in the production of a unit of A_i, i.e. its *value*.

$k_{ij} = c_{ij} \lambda_j$. The matrix $K = (k_{ij})$ expresses the Marxian 'constant capital' in *value* terms.

$v_j = b_j \lambda_j$. The vector $(v_1, v_2,..., v_n)$ is the Marxian 'variable capital' in *value* terms.

σ = the rate of *surplus-value*, or rate of exploitation.

π = the rate of profit.

p_i = price, *per unit of labour embodied*, of a unit of A_i, i.e. the ratio between the price of a unit of A_i and its *value*.

ω_i = the organic composition of capital in the ith industry, that is, the ratio between constant and variable capital in *value* terms.

If we want our system to be in a self-replacing state we must add the assumption that $1 \geqslant (\Sigma_i c_{ij} + b_j)$ for any j. We assume also that the inequality holds true at least for one commodity.

From the relations just described we may readily determine the amount of labour time embodied in each commodity as follows:

$$\lambda_i = \sum_j c_{ij} \lambda_j + l_i \quad (i = 1, 2,..., n), \qquad\qquad 1$$
$$\sum_i l_i = 1$$

System **1** provides a fully determinate set of n positive λ_i under the usual assumptions about the input–output coefficients.[16] The economic meaning of these assumptions is that standard methods of production yield positive net outputs, which I have assumed.

The numbers $(\lambda_1, \lambda_2,..., \lambda_n)$ – the *values* of commodities – are sometimes interpreted as prices corresponding to a rate of profit equal to zero. It will be observed that we can determine them simply on the basis of technical conditions before making any statement about wages and profits. Knowledge of *values* of commodities *and* of physical wage rate $(b_1, b_2,..., b_n)$ enables us to determine the *surplus-value* – as a difference between the net *value* and the *value* of the wage goods – and the rate of *surplus-value* – as a ratio between the *surplus-value* and the *value* of wage goods.

Accordingly, we can write the following system of equations that I shall refer to as the *value system*:

$$\sum_j \{k_{ij} + l_i v_j (1 + \sigma_i)\} = \lambda_i \quad (i = 1, 2,..., n), \qquad\qquad 2$$
$$\text{where} \qquad \sigma_i = \frac{l_i - \sum_j l_i v_j}{\sum_j l_i v_j} = \frac{1 - \sum_j v_j}{\sum_j v_j}. \qquad\qquad 3$$

16. See Schwartz (1961, lecture 2, pp. 17–27) which provides the basis for the theorems which have been used in the second part of this article.

From **3** it appears that since the basket of wage goods $(v_1, v_2,..., v_n)$ per unit of labour time is the same in every industry, the rate of exploitation σ must be the same too.

The *value system* can be interpreted as a system of exchange ratios of an economy in which commodities are bought and sold according to the efforts required in producing them. But in a competitive capitalist economy every entrepreneur hires labourers to operate means of production and there are no barriers to investment in different sectors. In these conditions, the rate of profit – that is, the ratio between profits and total capital – will tend to be equal all over the system. Now a uniform rate of profit is consistent with exchange ratios corresponding to *values* only if the organic composition of capital is the same in every industry. If π_i is the rate of profit in the ith industry, we shall have from **2** and from the definition of ω_i:

$$\pi_i = \frac{\lambda_i - \sum_j (k_{ij} + l_i v_j)}{\sum_j (k_{ij} + l_i v_j)} = \frac{\sigma}{\omega_i + 1} \quad (i = 1, 2,..., n). \qquad 4$$

Since σ is uniform, it is evident that $\pi_1 = \pi_2 = ,..., = \pi_n$ only if $\omega_1 = \omega_2 = ,..., = \omega_n$. If we drop the unrealistic assumption that ω is uniform, exchange ratios of commodities which provide a uniform rate of profit will be determined according to the following system of equations which I shall refer to as the *price system*:

$$(1 + \pi) \sum_j (k_{ij} + l_i v_j) p_j = \lambda_i p_i \quad (i = 1, 2,..., n). \qquad 5$$

System **5** is linear and homogeneous in the variables $p_1, p_2,..., p_n$. If we assume that the non-negative matrix

$$G = (g_{ij}), \qquad g_{ij} = \frac{k_{ij} + l_i v_j}{\lambda_i}$$

is connected,[17] **5** will give us a positive rate of profit associated with a set of positive prices fully determined but for a scale factor as functions of *value* elements k_{ij}, l_i and v_j.[18]

17. From an economic point of view this means that every commodity is ultimately required for the production of every other commodity. See Schwartz (1961, lecture 2, pp. 17–27).

18. It should be stressed that the uniformity of the physical wage rate (and the following uniformity of σ) is by no means essential in order to solve the 'transformation problem'. If we drop that assumption the system of equations **5** will be modified as follows:

$$(1 + \pi) \sum_j (k_{ij} + v_{ij}) p_j = \lambda_i p_i \quad (i = 1, 2,..., n,) \qquad 5'$$

There is a last element of indeterminateness in the 'transformation problem'. As matter of fact, if prices are but 'transformed' *values* we should find *n absolute prices* instead of $(n-1)$ price ratios. From a formal point of view this amounts to adding a further equation to the system **5** which supplies the *numéraire* for the prices. Since we are dealing here with prices per unit of labour embodied, determining a *numéraire* corresponds to finding a commodity – or an aggregate of commodities – whose price is equal to its *value*.[19]

As we can easily see, this problem is quite the same as finding the Marxian 'average' commodity. The first step in this investigation is to understand what makes prices differ from *values*.[20] From equation **4** it follows that the reason why prices differ from *values* lies in the inequality of the organic composition of capital, ω_i. To see this let us suppose that starting from the *value system* capitalists try to obtain a uniform rate of profit on their capital, while commodities are exchanged to their *values*.

With a given σ, the amount of surplus produced in every industry depends upon *variable* capital, whereas what is needed to pay profits at the ruling π depends upon *total* capital.[21] In this situation for some industries – with a relatively high ω – total revenue will not be large enough to pay profits at the current π and therefore they will face a deficit. On the contrary, industries with a relatively low ω will realize a surplus. Since the different levels of ω depend upon technical circumstances, the only way of bringing into equilibrium all the industries is to modify the exchange ratios at which commodities are bought and sold.

---

where v_{ij} is the amount of the *j*th commodity eventually received by the labourers employed in the *i*th industry, measured in *value* terms. System **5'** will determine the rate of profit π and the $(n-1)$ price ratios as functions of the *value* elements k_{ij} and v_{ij}.

19. The best-known solutions of the 'transformation problem' include some sort of arbitrary 'invariance postulate' like: total *values* = total prices. For a discussion of this point see Seton (1957). In the following discussion it will be shown that even this last element of indeterminateness in the 'transformation problem' can be eliminated satisfactorily.

20. What follows is mainly based upon Sraffa (1960, ch. 3).

21. It does not matter at this stage which particular π will actually prevail in the system. See Sraffa (1960, p. 13).

In any given situation, we can conceive *a priori* of an industry with a peculiar ω^* which makes it the ideal limit between 'deficit' and 'surplus' industries. For this industry which I shall call the 'ω^*-industry' no necessity would arise to sell its product at a price different from its *value, providing other industries could do the same*. But the ω^*-industry uses as inputs commodities produced by industries which have not its equilibrium ω^* and whose products will not be sold at their *values*. Thus the ω^*-industry normally will have to 'transform' the *value* of its product as a consequence of the 'transformation' carried on in other industries.

However, let us imagine that the industries which produce the inputs for the ω^*-industry, taken as a whole, have the same organic composition of capital, ω^*, and the same is true for the industries which produce *their* inputs and so on without limit. In this case, no necessity – either direct or indirect – would arise for the ω^*-commodity of being sold at a price different from its *value*, whatever the uniform π may be. The ω^*-commodity is therefore the ideal *numéraire* we are looking for.

As matter of fact, the formal way of building up our ω^*-commodity is the same as that of Sraffa's 'standard commodity'. We have first to construct a composite commodity which is made up by the same commodities in the same proportions as its inputs taken as a whole. For this purpose, let us define a positive vector $(h_1, h_2, \ldots, h_n)$ such as:

$$\sum_i h_i(k_{ij} + l_i v_j) = a h_j \lambda_j \quad (j = 1, 2, \ldots, n), \qquad 6$$
$$\sum_i h_i l_i = \sum_i l_i = 1.$$

Where a is the eigenvalue and $(h_1, h_2, \ldots, h_n)$ is the eigenvector of the matrix

$$Q = (q_{ij}), \qquad q_{ji} = \frac{k_{ij} + l_i v_j}{\lambda_j}.$$

Since the matrix Q is non-negative and connected[22] the system 6

22. These properties of the matrix Q will appear self-evident if we consider that

$$q_{ij} = g_{ji} \frac{\lambda_j}{\lambda_i}.$$

The matrix Q can therefore simply be derived from the matrix G by the formula

$$Q = T^{-1} G' T$$

will provide us a unique and positive number a associated with a positive vector $(h_1, h_2,..., h_n)$.

Now let us multiply both sides of each equation i of the *value system* by the corresponding number h_i. We shall have the following *h-value system*.

$$h_i \sum_j \{k_{ij} + l_i v_j (1+\sigma)\} = h_i \lambda_i \quad (i = 1, 2,..., n). \qquad 7$$

Adding up, we obtain

$$\sum_i h_i \sum_j \{k_{ij} + l_i v_j (1+\sigma)\} = \sum_i h_i \lambda_i, \qquad 8$$

and therefore

$$\sigma = \frac{\sum_i h_i \lambda_i - \sum_i h_i \sum_j (k_{ij} + l_i v_j)}{\sum_j v_j} = \frac{1 - \sum_j v_j}{\sum_j v_j}. \qquad 9$$

That is the *surplus-value* and the rate of exploitation are the same both in the *value system* **2** and in the *h-value system* **7**.

Let us now multiply each equation of the *price system* by the corresponding number h_i. We shall have the following *h-price system*:[23]

$$h_i \{(1+\pi) \sum_j (k_{ij} + l_i v_j) p_j\} = h_i \lambda_i p_i \quad (i = 1, 2,..., n). \qquad 10$$

Adding up we obtain:

$$(1+\pi) \{\sum_i h_i \sum_j (k_{ij} + l_i v_j) p_j\} = \sum_i h_i \lambda_i p_i, \qquad 11$$

and therefore

$$\pi = \frac{\sum_i h_i \lambda_i p_i - \sum_i h_i \sum_j (k_{ij} + l_i v_j) p_j}{\sum_i h_i \sum_j (k_{ij} + l_i v_j) p_j}$$

$$= \frac{\sum_i h_i \lambda_i p_i}{\sum_i h_i \sum_j (k_{ij} + l_i v_j) p_j} - 1. \qquad 12$$

But from **6** we know that the aggregates $(\sum_i h_i \lambda_i)$ and $\{\sum_i h_i \sum_j (k_{ij} + l_i v_j)\}$ are identical but for a scale factor and their

---

where G' is the transpose of G and

$$T = (t_{ij}), \qquad t_{ij} = \lambda_i \delta_{ij}.$$

23. It should be stressed that since system **10** is derived from system **5** by simply multiplying both sides of each equation by a positive number, the values of π and $p_1, p_2,..., p_n$ which solve **10** solve **5**, too.

ratio is independent of prices of commodities which enter the aggregates themselves. We can write therefore:

$$\pi = \frac{\sum_i h_i \lambda_i}{\sum_i h_i \sum_j (k_{ij} + l_i v_j)} - 1, ^{24} \qquad \textbf{13}$$

and, from **9** and **13**,

$$\pi \sum_i h_i \sum_j (k_{ij} + l_i v_j) = 1 - \sum_j v_j. \qquad \textbf{14}$$

From **14**, letting ω^* be equal to $(\sum_i h_i \sum_j k_{ij} / \sum_j v_j)$ we have

$$\pi = \frac{1 - \sum_j v_j}{\sum_i h_i \sum_j (k_{ij} + l_i v_j)} = \frac{\sigma}{\omega^* + 1}. \qquad \textbf{15}$$

Let us consider now the aggregate output of the *h-system* as a composite commodity, whose equation of production is **11** and whose organic composition of capital is ω^*. It is easy to see that this ω^*-commodity is the *numéraire* we are looking for and has the two required requisites. First, we have from **14** that whatever the rate of profit which satisfies the *price system* may be, in the ω^*-industry profits paid on the *value* of total capital are equal to *surplus-value* produced in it. Secondly, the same holds true for the commodities which enter the total capital, taken as a whole, and so on throughout the various stages of production.[25] As matter of fact, these two properties reduce to one if we consider that both of them are functions of the vector $(h_1, h_2, \ldots, h_n)$ which solves the system **6**.

Therefore, as for the ω^*-commodity no necessity arises to be sold at a price different from its *value* and we can add to the system **5** the normalizing equation:

$$\sum_i h_i \lambda_i p_i = \sum_i h_i \lambda_i. \qquad \textbf{16}$$

Rate of surplus-value, *rate of profit and organic composition of capital*

The ω^*-commodity can also be used as 'representative' of the overall features of the economy. Since $(h_1, h_2, \ldots, h_n)$ is a unit sum vector, ω^* is the ratio between the weighted average of constant

24. From **13** and **6** it can be easily seen that $a = 1/(1+\pi)$.

25. This is evident since inputs and output of the *h-system* are in effect the same composite commodity taken in different amounts.

capitals and the weighted average of variable capitals of the entire system, measured in *value* terms. Equation **15**

$$\pi = \frac{1 - \sum_j v_j}{\sum_i h_i \sum_j (k_{ij} + l_i v_j)} = \frac{\sigma}{\omega^* + 1}$$

can therefore be taken as a summarizing expression of the functional relations between the rate of profit, the rate of *surplus-value* and the 'average' organic composition of capital.[26] From **15** we can derive the following conclusions:

1. $\pi > 0$ only if $\sigma > 0$; that is, a positive rate of exploitation is a necessary condition for the existence of a positive rate of profit.

2. $\pi < \sigma$ unless the matrix of constant capital $K = (k_{ij})$ is equal to zero.

3. π is a positive function of σ and a negative function of ω^*. Since both σ and ω^*, *ceteris paribus*, depend upon the vector $(v_1, v_2, ..., v_n)$, there is no straightforward way of saying in which direction π will move as a consequence of a change of wages. This is due to the twofold character of wages within the Marxian approach. As elements of variable capital, they belong, as it were, to the technical conditions of production and contribute to determine the 'average' organic composition of capital ω^*. As a share of total *value* added ($\sum_i l_i$) given to labourers, wages will determine the rate of exploitation σ.

Nevertheless, it can be demonstrated that the rate of profit π is inversely related to wages.

Since wages here are not expressed as a scalar but as a vector, I must define what I mean by an increase (or a decrease) of wages. Suppose that the bundle of wage goods changes from $(v_1, v_2, ..., v_n)$ to $(v'_1, v'_2, ..., v'_n)$. Then if $v'_j \geqslant v_j$, for all js ($j = 1, 2, ..., n$) and

26. In this sense, equation **15** is a rigorous version of the rather approximate equation of Marx in *Capital*, book 3, chapter 3:

$$p = s \frac{v}{c+v} = \frac{s}{(c/v)+1}$$

where p is the rate of profit, s the rate of surplus-value and c/v the organic composition of capital, measured as a ratio between *total* constant capital and *total* variable capital, in *value* terms (see Marx, 1894, pp. 49 ff. of 1959 edn).

$v'_j > v_j$ for some js, I will say that wages have increased, and vice versa.

As we know that the matrix $G = (g_{ij})$ is non-negative and connected, its eigenvalue $a = 1/(1+\pi)$ is a strictly positive and continuous function of each element of the matrix itself. Consequently any increase in some (or all) elements of the vector $(v_1, v_2, \ldots, v_n)$ – which means a decrease of σ – will decrease π, and vice versa.

Other things being equal, an increase of ω^* will affect π negatively. But to define an increase or a decrease of ω^* is much more difficult than it is for the simple ratio $(\Sigma_i \Sigma_j k_{ij}/\Sigma_j v_j)$. As a matter of fact, even if the ratio ω were increased by the same percentage in all sectors, the 'weights' attached to every vector – i.e. the elements of the vector $(h_1, h_2, \ldots, h_n)$ – would be altered and we could not be absolutely sure in which direction ω^* would move.

However, when changes in the different sectors are substantial and in the same direction it is very improbable that changes in 'weights' attached to different industries could reverse the general tendency. Therefore Marx's statement that a relative increase of the constant part of capital will cause a decrease of the rate of profit – with a given σ – seems to be a fair approximation (see Morishima and Seton, 1961, p. 209).

'Non-basics'

I have now to drop the assumption that the matrix $G = (g_{ij})$ is connected. The economic meaning of this is that some commodities exist which do not enter either as means of production or as wage goods in the production of other commodities. Following Sraffa's terminology, I shall call them 'non-basics'. Now it is readily seen that conditions of production of non-basic commodities play no role in determining π and the prices of 'basic' commodities. In order to show this, it will be sufficient to see that non-basic commodities do not enter the *h-price system*. Let us consider the non-basic commodity m and its equation within the system **6**, which defines the vector $(h_1, h_2, \ldots, h_n)$.

$$\sum_i h_i(k_{im}+l_i\,v_m) = ah_m\,\lambda_m. \qquad \textbf{17}$$

It is clear that since by definition both k_{im} and v_m are equal to zero, the only number h_m which satisfies the equation **17** is zero.[27]

27. We neglect here the case of $a = 0$ which is of no economic interest.

It follows that π and prices of basic commodities – which are fully determined by means of the *h-price system* – are not influenced *directly* by non-basics. Equilibrium in the production of *non-basic* commodities will be reached through an adjustment of their prices with respect to the prices of other commodities. An obvious consequence of the above discussion is that the organic composition of non-basic commodities does not play a part in determining the 'average' organic composition of capital, ω^*.

The Sraffian approach

The complexity of the functional relations between wages and the rate of profit can be simplified by taking Sraffa's approach. That is, wages will not be considered any longer as capital, advanced and physically specified. On the contrary, they will be treated as the quota of social surplus – the excess of gross output over means of production – which accrues to labourers. Accordingly, the rate of profit will be calculated only on the value of means of production.

Under these assumptions the price system will be modified as follows:

$$(1+\pi)(\sum_j k_{ij} p_j) + w l_i = \lambda_i p_i \quad (i = 1, 2, ..., n), \qquad 18$$

where w designates 'money' wages in terms of a unit of measure of prices. Given w, system **18** will determine π and $(n-1)$ price ratios or, alternatively, will determine w and the price ratios when π is given.

According to Sraffa's approach the *numéraire* for the system **18** will be constructed as follows. Let us start by defining the vector $(h_1^*, h_2^*, ..., h_n^*)$ which satisfies the system **6** when each element of the wage vector $(v_1, v_2, ..., v_n)$ is equal to zero. Let us then multiply each equation of the system **18** by the corresponding number h_i^*. We shall have:

$$h_i^*\{(1+\pi) \sum_j k_{ij} p_j + w l_i\} = h_i^* \lambda_i p_i \quad (i = 1, 2, ..., n), \qquad 19$$

which corresponds to Sraffa's 'standard system'.[28] The net

28. It should be noticed that: (a) as for commodities which do not enter the means of production, (i.e. non-basics), h^* is equal to zero. Therefore π and prices of commodities are fully determined independently of conditions of production of those goods. (b) π and prices of commodities which satisfy **18** will satisfy also the system **19**, providing that the unit of measure of wages and prices is the same in both systems.

product of the system **19**, the 'standard commodity', will be taken as a unit of measure of wages and prices, that is:

$$\sum_i h_i^* \lambda_i p_i - \sum_i h_i^* \sum_j k_{ij} p_j = 1. \tag{20}$$

The rate of profit π can be therefore expressed as follows:

$$\pi = \frac{(\sum_i h_i^* \lambda_i p_i - \sum_i h_i^* \sum_j k_{ij} p_j)(1-w)}{\sum_i h_i^* \sum_j k_{ij} p_j}$$

$$= \frac{1-w}{\sum_i h_i^* \sum_j k_{ij} p_j}. \tag{21}$$

But from **6** we know that the aggregates $(\sum_i h^* \lambda_i)$ and $(\sum_i h_i^* \sum_j k_{ij})$ are identical but for a scale factor. Their ratio is therefore independent of prices of commodities which enter the aggregates themselves. From **21** we can easily see that this ratio is equal to one plus the rate of profit corresponding to $w = 0$ that I shall designate by π_{max}.[29] We can then write:

$$\pi = \pi_{max}(1-w) \tag{22}$$

which is Sraffa's equation for the rate of profit.

The Sraffian equation **22** is the exact parallel of the Marxian equation **15**. Both of them express the rate of profit as a function of technical and social conditions. Unlike equation **15**, in **22** these two aspects are distinctly separated. The vector $(h_1^*, h_2^*,..., h_n^*)$ depends only upon the technique of production. On the contrary, w is a purely distributive element. It follows that the relation between π and w is not only inverse but also *linear*.

There is no doubt that the Sraffian approach is more straightforward and elegant. But is it also more significant?

As Sraffa points out, the drawback of treating wages as a share of the social net product is that it relegates 'subsistence' wage goods to non-basic products. But they are essentially 'basic' and changes in their methods of production should affect the rate of profit. The most rigorous way of dealing with this problem – in Sraffa's view – would be to separate 'subsistence' wage (specified in physical terms) and 'surplus' wages, treated as a variable. I am

29. From **21** and **6** it follows also that

$$\pi_{max} = \frac{1-a^*}{a^*}$$

where a^* is the value of a which satisfies the system **6** when $v_j = 0$ for all js.

not quite convinced that, for the problem at issue, the Sraffian approach is the most convenient. For one thing, it is hard to believe that the emergence of a 'surplus' wage leaves the 'subsistence' wage unchanged. As a matter of historical fact, it seems rather that the existence of a 'surplus' accruing to labourers over and above the customary necessaries has constituted a situation of transition to a new 'subsistence' wage level which includes larger amounts of some 'necessaries' and/or some additional goods that were considered before as luxuries.

True, the uniformity of 'money' wages (with homogeneous labour) seems a more realistic assumption than a uniform physical wage rate. However, this conceals a basic difference between capitalists' and labourers' attitudes. After all, capitalists as such want money to make more money; labourers want money to buy goods for final consumption. While a 'general rate of profit' is a perfectly meaningful concept, what is the rationale of a 'general level of wages' (and its modifications) unless some sort of general wage-goods basket is presupposed? When wages increase in terms of the 'standard commodity' they increase in terms of any other commodity, too – providing that no joint product enters into the picture. But if labourers' consumption patterns are different, the increase in some workers' purchasing power (in terms of their customary consumption goods) will be less than that for others. It will be a small consolation to be told that increases in 'standard wages' are exactly the same throughout the system.

In conclusion, in a model that deals with long-run conditions of equilibrium in a context of 'pure' competitive capitalism – two sharply distinctive social classes, capitalists and labourers, a uniform rate of profit, homogeneous labour – it seems more appropriate to keep the classical and Marxian view and to look at wages as a bundle of goods which actually represent labourers' standard of living under the prevailing circumstances.

Finally the Marxian approach to wages is more significant than the Sraffian one in the following respect. If we define the rate of exploitation as the ratio between the *surplus-value* and the *value* of wage goods, its economic and social meaning is unambiguous. Labourers have spent a part of their working day for themselves and the rest for capitalists. Certainly we can also call the expression $(1 - w/w)$ 'rate of exploitation'. But the 'standard wage' w has no special meaning except that of being measured in a peculiar 'money of account' which results in its relation to the rate of profit being linear.

Joan Robinson is right when she says that 'you can't put politics into an equation', but it would be certainly agreed that the choice between different formal descriptions of reality is by no means politically neutral.

Appendix. Fixed capital

Until now I have implicitly assumed that only circulating capital is used in the production of commodities.

To drop this assumption I shall substitute the matrix of the constant capital $K = (k_{ij})$ with a new matrix $\Theta = (\varphi_{ij})$, where φ_{ij} is the amount of the commodity A_j *tied up* in the production of a unit of the commodity A_i, measured in terms of labour embodied.[30] The matrix Θ includes both fixed and circulating capital. For simplicity's sake, I shall assume that no durable good is included in the bundle of wage goods $(v_1, v_2,..., v_n)$.

Let us now write the following system of equations:

$$(1+\pi) \sum_j (\varphi_{ij}+l_i v_j)p_j' = \lambda_i p_i' \quad (i = 1, 2,..., n), \qquad 23$$

where p_i' designates the *hire price*, per unit of labour embodied, of the commodity A_i, that is, the ratio between its *hire price* and its *value*. Of course, as for non-durable goods, *hire prices* and *prices* will coincide.

System 23 will determine π and the $(n-1)$ *hire price ratios* as functions of the *value* elements φ_{ij}, v_j and l_i. Once we know *hire prices* and the rate of profit, *prices* (per unit of labour embodied) can be determined, too. As is well known, in the simplest case of constant efficiency the relation between *hire price* and *price* of a durable good is the following:

$$p_i = p_i' \frac{(1+\pi)^{m_i}-1}{\pi(1+\pi)^{m_i}} \quad (i = 1, 2,..., n),$$

where m_i is the productive life of the ith good, measured in years.

30. With constant efficiency of durable productive goods, the system of equation **1**, which determines *values* of commodities will become

$$\lambda_i = \Sigma_j \frac{1}{m_j} \varphi_{ij} \lambda_j + l_i \quad (i = 1, 2,..., n), \qquad \mathbf{1'}$$

where m_j is the productive life of the jth good measured in years.

References

BARAN, P. A. (1957), *The Political Economy of Growth*, Monthly Review Press, 1967.

BÖHM-BAWERK, E. (1896), *Karl Marx and the Close of his System*, ed. P. M. Sweezy, Kelley, 1949.

DMITRIEV, V. K. (1898), *Essais economiques*, Editions du Centre National de la Recherche Scientifique, Paris, 1968.

DOBB, M. (1970), 'The Sraffa system and critique of the neo-classical theory of distribution', *De Economist*, vol. 118, pp. 347–62.

FELLNER, W. (1960), *Modern Economic Analysis*, McGraw-Hill.

FEUER, L. S. (ed.) (1959), *Karl Marx and Friedrich Engels: Basic Writings on Politics and Philosophy*, Anchor Books.

GORDON, D. F. (1959), 'What was the labor theory of value?', *Amer. econ. Rev.*, suppl., pp. 462–472.

GOTTLIEB, N. (1951), 'Marx's Mehrwert concept', *Rev. econ. Stud.*, vol. 18, pp. 164–78.

HARCOURT, G. C. (1969), 'Some Cambridge controversies in the theory of capital', *J. econ. Lit.*, vol. 7, pp. 369–405.

JOHANSEN, L. (1963), 'Labour theory of value and marginal utilities', *Econ. Plan.*, vol. 3, pp. 89–103.

KALECKI, M. (1943), 'Political aspects of full employment', *Polit. Q.*, vol. 14, pp. 322–31.

MARX, K. (1844), *Economic and Philosophic Manuscripts of 1844*, ed. D. Struik, Lawrence & Wishart, 1970.

MARX, K. (1847), *The Poverty of Philosophy*, Foreign Languages Publishing House, Moscow.

MARX, K. (1867), *Capital*, vol. 1, Foreign Languages Publishing House, Moscow, 1961.

MARX, K. (1894), *Capital*, vol. 3, Foreign Languages Publishing House, Moscow, 1959.

MARX, K. (1905–10), *Theories of Surplus Value*, Foreign Languages Publishing House, Moscow, 1968.

MARX, K. (1939–41), *Fondements de la critique de l'économie politique*, Editions Anthropos, Paris, 1967.

MAY, K. (1948), 'The structure of classical value theories', *Rev. econ. Stud.*, vol. 18, pp. 60–69.

MEEK, R. (1967), *Economics and Ideology*, Chapman & Hall.

MÉSZÁROS, I. (1970), *Marx's Theory of Alienation*, Merlin Press.

MILLS, C. W. (1962), *The Marxists*, Penguin.

MORISHIMA, M., and SETON, F. (1961), 'Aggregation in Leontief matrices and the labour theory of value', *Econometrica*, vol. 29, pp. 203–20.

NEWMAN, P. (1962), 'Production of commodities by means of commodities', *Revue Suisse d'économie politique et statistique*, vol. 98, pp. 58–75.

OIKISIO, N. (1963), 'A mathematical note on Marxian theorems', *Weltwirtschaftliches Archiv*, vol. 91, pp. 287–99.

ROBINSON, J. (1942), *An Essay on Marxian Economics*, Macmillan, 1966.

ROBINSON, J. (1953), *On Re-Reading Marx*, Cambridge University Press.

ROBINSON, J. (1954), 'The labor theory of value', *Sci. Soc.*, vol. 18, pp. 141–51.

ROBINSON, J. (1956), *The Accumulation of Capital*, Macmillan, 3rd edn, 1969.

ROBINSON, J. (1965), 'Piero Sraffa and the rate of exploitation', *New left Rev.*, vol. 31, pp. 28–34.

ROBINSON, J. (1968), *Economic Philosophy*, Penguin.

ROBINSON, J. (1969), 'The theory of value reconsidered', *Austral. econ. Pap.*, vol. 8, pp. 13–19.

ROGIN, L. (1956), *The Meaning and Validity of Economic Theory*, Harper & Row.

SCHWARTZ, J. T. (1961), *Lectures on the Mathematical Method in Analytical Economics*, Gordon & Breach.

SETON, F. (1957), 'The "transformation problem"', *Rev. econ. Stud.*, vol. 24, pp. 149–60.

SOWELL, T. (1963), 'Marxian value reconsidered', *Economica*, vol. 30, pp. 297–308.

SRAFFA, P. (1960), *Production of Commodities by Means of Commodities*, Cambridge University Press.

TORR, D. (ed.) (1934), *Karl Marx and Friedrich Engels: Selected Correspondence*, Lawrence & Wishart, 2nd edn, 1936.

VON BORTKIEVICZ, L. (1906–7), 'Value and price in the Marxian system', *Int. econ. Pap.*, no. 2, 1952.

14 Howard J. Sherman

Value and Market Allocation

Howard J. Sherman, 'The Marxist theory of value revisited', *Science and Society*, vol. 34, 1970, pp. 257–92. Specially condensed for this volume.

During Ricardo's lifetime, the labour theory of value ruled supreme, but soon after it was challenged by critics and weakened by 'supporters'. The process continued from the 1820s to the 1870s. John Stuart Mill in the 1840s and 1850s could be considered as a supporter of the labour theory only with a considerable stretch of imagination, for he identified cost of production with labour *plus* abstinence from consumption. Moreover, Mill strengthened the trend toward concentration on micro problems in a static analysis, quite alien to the classic attention to the evolution of the economy as a whole. The main neo-classical 'revolution', however, came in the 1870s with Jevons, Menger and Walras who emphasized the theory of marginal utility to the exclusion of almost all else. These marginalists saw the problem of economics as the optimizing of production and consumer satisfaction with given amounts of labour, resources and technology. Hence, they began with the psychological reaction of consumers to commodities and not with the relations of man to man, as Marx always did. In fact, several of them consciously aimed at replacing Marx's growing influence.[1]

Alfred Marshall (1890) was the first great economist to attempt a synthesis of the classical cost of production theory (related to the labour theory?) with the marginal utility theory of the early neo-classical writers. In the English-speaking countries, Marshall's was the definitive work followed in all details for many years, and it is still followed by all present-day neo-classical writers in most of the important and relevant points[2] (though he

1. See Meek (1956a, pp. 250–51). For a contrary view, see Bronfenbrenner (1967).

2. See any modern text on microeconomics, e.g. Samuelson (1948, see 1970 edn).

is now disputed in many details, and more sophisticated Western theorists rather trace their origins to Walras, 1874).

Marshall (1890, pp. 337–50 and 503 of 1953 edn) evolved the concepts of 'long-run' and 'short-run' time periods. In the short run, production is limited to present capacity because the time is too short for new investment to result in more available capital or greater capacity to produce. In the short run, therefore, the cost of increasing the limited supply and the intensity of the unsatisfied demand interact at the margin to determine price. The long run, on the other hand, is a long enough time for new investment to put more capital goods in place and expand the supply of output until it equals demand. In the long run, says Marshall, since demand is satisfied, the price is determined solely by the 'cost' of production (including an average profit on capital).

History of the debate on value

Soon after the third volume of Marx's *Capital* was published in 1894, important attacks were made on it by prominent economists. The most famous of all was the criticism by Böhm-Bawerk (1896). In his attack, Böhm-Bawerk claims that the marginal utility theory is the only valid theory of value; that the labour theory of value is contradicted by the facts of relative prices; and that Marx's qualifications to the labour theory (especially in the third volume of *Capital*, discussed below) are in complete conflict with his basic theory of value (stated in the first volume of *Capital*).

The fact that one of the first uses of neo-classical theory was in an overall attack on Marxism brought immediate Marxist attacks on it (e.g. Boudin, 1907). By the 1900s, when the two sides had crystallized, there was no chance for a fruitful discussion between them nor for any open-minded consideration of one by the other. It was this tradition which helped freeze the dogmatic Soviet position until very recently. The dogmatic Marxist answer admits nothing and challenges each of Böhm-Bawerk's arguments. On the one side, they argue that Marx's qualifications to the labour theory merely complicate, but do not contradict his basic theory of value; and that this theory is in very good accord with the economic reality.

On the other side, Marxists attack the marginal utility theory on many different grounds (see, e.g., Meek, 1956a, pp. 243–56). In the first place, they attack the motivations of its founders, claiming that its only reason for being is the refutation of Marx. Secondly, they criticize its social and ethical connotations and conclusions – that is, the defence of capitalism and private profit. (Though it is true that the early marginalists drew such conclusions, it is not so clear that these conclusions are a *necessary* result of their technical analysis.) Finally, the Marxists criticize the methodology of marginal utility economics. It is a subjective theory and lacks the objective measure of labour expended. It is very formal and technical, and far from the real problems of political economy. Conceding all of these criticisms, it should be noted that they do not amount to a refutation of the early marginal utility theory, much less to the modern formulations of it in conjunction with marginal productivity and long-run cost of production.

Contemporary views

Most conservative neo-classical economists continue to argue that Marxism is all wrong and in complete contradiction to neo-classical economics (see, e.g., Campbell, 1961). Similarly, most dogmatic Marxists continue to argue that neo-classical economics is all wrong and in complete contradiction to Marxist economics (see, e.g., Academy of Sciences of USSR, 1957).

Many liberal neo-classical economists argue that Marxist economics is a very special case within the framework of neo-classical economics, that its price theory agrees with neo-classical theory under very restricted assumptions.[3] On the other hand, most non-dogmatic Marxists consider neo-classical economics as a technical adjunct to Marxism, with a very restricted field of vision (tied to a faulty ideology) (see, e.g., Lange, 1935). These two views are not necessarily contradictory. One might consider that neo-classical price and allocation theory is a useful adjunct to the broader Marxist view of the political-economic evolution of capitalism. Yet we may still recognize that Marx's own statements on price theory represent a special and limited case within neo-classical price theory.

Neo-classical theory is best developed in the short-run, static

3. See, e.g., the brief but pithy comment by Dickinson (1963).

analysis of microeconomic problems; it studies the economics of maximization of output from given resources and may therefore be useful to factory managers in capitalism or socialism (or socialist planners). Marxist theory holds primarily as an analysis of the basic institutions and the dynamics of the economy as a whole; it is therefore most useful in understanding such macroeconomic problems as the business cycle and the long-run evolution of capitalism.

Marxist price theory as a special case of neo-classical price theory

Marx's labour theory of value states that individual prices are proportionate to the labour expended in the production of the product. This is a special case of neo-classical price theory utilizing certain basic assumptions. The assumptions and qualifications are as follows:

Pure competition

Marx began with the assumption of pure competition in order to investigate value and surplus value under these conditions. Under competition, commodities must sell at their value (including an average amount of profit) because a higher price will tend to increase the supply, while a lower price will tend to decrease the supply, thus bringing price back to value. The supply may be increased by competitors moving in or decreased by competitors moving out of the industry. But without competition this mechanism does not work. In that case, Marxist theory does not indicate the exact price, but only the direction in which it deviates from value.

Marx, like the classicals, knew that a higher degree of monopoly means more restriction of production and a *higher* price. Marx, however, presented no analytic tools for a more precise analysis. Thus, the labour theory of value is not too helpful in analysing any kind of monopoly price, whether it results from concentration and merger of capital, or from unique holdings such as a particular waterfall or a non-reproducible object such as a painting. The lack of precision became most obvious in Stalin's famous pronouncement that monopoly capitalism 'needs' the 'maximum' profit.[4] By contrast, the neo-

4. See Stalin (1952, pp. 31 ff.). Also see discussion in Meek (1956a, pp. 292–3).

classical theory is able to furnish a precise (but very unrealistic) analysis of monopoly price and output in terms of demand and supply (or marginal revenue and marginal cost).[5]

Yet Marx was the first major economist to predict the emergence of monopoly and economic concentration. He thoroughly explored its causes in terms of technological advance and the economies of large-scale enterprise. He further indicated the economic effects of monopoly on the distribution of income between classes, and the social and political effects of its vast power. Finally, Lenin made monopoly power the keystone of his theory of imperialism.

Long-run equilibrium

We have seen that in neo-classical analysis there is a sharp distinction between the 'short run', in which supply may change to meet demand only within the limits of present capacity, and the 'long run', in which the level of capacity itself may rise or fall so that supply may adjust to any demand (for this approximation, technology is fixed even in the 'long run'). In the short run, price is determined both by utility (and the distribution of income) as reflected in demand *and* by costs as reflected in supply conditions. In the long run, price is determined *only* by the 'cost' of supply, since demand affects only the amount of output sold. *If* all 'costs' may be resolved into labour cost (and if costs are constant over the relevant range), then the long-run case fits the Marxist argument that the value of any commodity is determined solely by the labour embodied in it.

Marx does not explicitly limit his value theory to the long-run time period, but it is taken for granted and implied in all that he says. He states very often that in his basic analysis he is only concerned with the situation where supply equals demand, and the context makes clear that this is long-run demand and supply. Marx is not interested in the details of competitive jockeying for position, but *begins* his analysis at the point where competition has equalized long-run supply and demand in each industry. Later on, as we shall see, Marx recognizes another qualification which transforms the value concept to the more realistic 'price of

5. More realistic neo-classical attempts began in the 1930s with Chamberlin (1933) and Robinson (1934).

production' concept (similar to Marshallian 'cost'). Here he explicitly states: 'The price of production includes the average profit ... it is in the long run a prerequisite of supply, of the reproduction of commodities in every individual sphere' (Marx, 1894, p. 233 of 1909 edn). In other words, if the long-run price is below this level, suppliers will not make the average profit and will move out of the industry. If, however, it is above that level, then profit is above average and more suppliers are attracted into the industry.

In the short run, the price according to the neo-classical analysis clearly rests on both demand and supply. Demand is determined by both income distribution and marginal utility. A large enough increase in demand must move production to a point of higher costs per unit because it eventually approaches the capacity limit (by definition). Of all this short-run theory of outputs and prices, Marx has nothing to say, unless one wishes to read some of it into his discussion of demand as an index of 'social necessity'. Even his meagre discussions of this point should rather be interpreted, however, as relating to those long-run or aggregate problems in which he was interested. Thus he explains that aggregate short-run price may be below aggregate value in depression or deflation, while it may be above aggregate value in inflation. Similarly, in discussing aggregate distribution, he considers how short-run wages may be temporarily above or below the value of the workers' labour power.

Socially necessary labour and technology

One of Marx's explicit qualifications to the labour theory of value was that it holds true only if the average prevailing technology is used. Suppose all other firms are producing watches by automated production, but one firm produces an identical product by an enormous expenditure of hand labour. Then the product of that firm will not have a higher exchange value than the others merely because it expends more labour. The reason is that the labour it expends is more than is 'socially necessary' at present.

Of course, in the more complex case where each of several firms has a somewhat different technology, it is not so clear how one would measure the deviation from the prevailing technology.

Marx merely says that 'the market' makes that calculation, but the ambiguity about measurement is not fully resolved.

Demand, utility and 'social necessity'

Marx seldom discussed the role of demand in determination of individual prices because (a) it plays no role in long-run price, where his interest lay; and (b) he left the discussion of monopoly price for a later stage of discussion. In discussions of unemployment Marx did give an extensive discussion of the role of *aggregate* demand in determining *aggregate* output and price levels.

It is well to emphasize that Marx does not deny the operation of demand (and utility to consumers) in determining prices and outputs. Marx carefully states that *a commodity must have some 'use-value'* (or utility), *or else it can have no exchange value in the market* (Marx, 1867, part 1). If there is no demand, the price will be zero.

In the long run, however, the *level* of demand – if it is above zero (and if costs per unit are constant) – can have no effect on the price, though it fixes the output and the allocation of resources.[6] In fact, the recognition by Marx that 'use-value' is a necessary condition for any value, combined with the usual Marxist statement that the aim of socialism is the production of use-values for the population, has been used by several East European economists as a justification for the widest use of supply and demand or (marginal) utility concepts in planning.[7]

In connection with long-run price, Marx shows the role of demand in the allocation of capital and labour. Thus Marx states that only 'socially necessary' labour expenditure gives rise to value. As we have seen, Marx uses the term 'socially necessary' in one sense to indicate that the exchange value is determined only by that labour which makes use of the average technology currently available to the society. Yet Marx also uses the term 'socially necessary' to indicate that the labour value is determined only by that labour which is used in producing

6. For Marshall's view of the role of demand in this case, see Marshall (1890, pp. 348–9 and 455–61 of 1953 edn).

7. See, e.g., Brus (1956). Also see the summary of Soviet views in Nove (1961, pp. 280–82).

products in the proportion demanded by society from each industry. Thus Marx (1894, pp. 745–6 of 1909 edn) writes:

If this division of labour among the different branches of production is proportional [to the demand], then the products of the various groups are sold at their values . . . or at prices which are modifications of their values . . . due to general laws. . . . Every commodity must contain the necessary quantity of labour, and at the same time only the proportional quantity of the total social labour time must have been spent on the various groups. For the use-value of things remains a prerequisite. The use-value of the individual commodities depends on the particular need which each satisfies. But the use-value of the social mass of products depends on the extent to which it satisfies in quantity a definite social need for every particular kind of product in an adequate manner, so that the labour is proportionately distributed among the different spheres in keeping with these social needs, which are definite in quantity.

It is apparent from the quote that the 'socially necessary' *allocation* of resources (though not the long-run *value* of products) is considered by Marx to be solely dependent on the pattern of demand, which is determined in part by the relative utilities to consumers. Sweezy (1942, p. 47) writing on this question in the 1940s, comments that, 'The competitive supply-and-demand theory of price determination is hence not only not inconsistent with the labor theory; rather it forms an integral, if sometimes unrecognized, part of the labor theory.' Sweezy admits that Marx did not further develop his theory of allocation according to consumer wants.

Marx did not further develop individual demand theory because he recognized that under capitalism effective demand is far more influenced by the distribution of income than by consumers' wants (see Marx, 1894, pp. 214 and 222–3 of 1909 edn). Secondly, Marx also neglected the theory of consumer wants because he was primarily interested in macroeconomic developments, for which investigation almost any economist takes consumer desires as relatively stable and unchanging, while changes in demand largely reflect changes in aggregate income or income distribution.

Skilled and unskilled labour

Marx reduced all costs to hours of average unskilled labour or multiples of that average working hour. For his purposes of aggregate analysis, this simplification is an acceptable abstraction.

Of course, in a more detailed micro analysis of relative wages and prices, we may wish to consider the effects of different grades of skilled labour or even different specific kinds of natural resources. In that case each relative cost depends greatly on the demand for that type of labour or resources. Thus:

The real influence of marginal utility comes in when we . . . admit non-homogeneous scarce natural resources, or non-homogeneous kinds of labour that cannot be produced in unlimited numbers by appropriate training. Thus, the rent of vine-bearing land is affected by the marginal utility of wine: the wages of skilled watchmakers (assuming there is some element of 'scarce' skill, i.e. of skill that cannot be conferred upon an average worker by suitable training) are affected by the marginal utility of watches (Dickinson, 1963, p. 239).

The transformation of value into the price of production

From the time of Adam Smith all economists (including Marx) have recognized that competition in the long run must result in a uniform rate of profit on capital in all industries. The reason is that capital will move from industries with lower profit rates to those with high profit rates, thus lowering supply of goods in the former and raising it in the latter. Hence prices (and profit rates) rise where they are lowest and fall where they are highest until profit rates tend to uniformity in all industries.

Yet the simplest version of the labour theory of value would not lead us to this result. Only living labour can produce surplus value or profit. The 'congealed labour' in capital goods, such as plant and equipment, is necessary to the production process, but does not produce a profit. Therefore, those industries using a high ratio of labour power to capital goods should show a higher rate of profit on capital. If two equal amounts of money capital are invested, we would expect the one spending more on living labour to also show a higher profit.

Of course, in the actual business world only a very small amount of capital is set aside to pay wages at any given time. Wage payments occur only periodically and capital is not kept in a money form between payments. Money for wages is normally taken from current revenue just before it is needed, so it is hard to isolate Marx's 'capital used to purchase labour power'. It is certainly *not* the same statistic as the total flow of wages paid in a given period, such as wages paid in a year. But this is an additional complication ignored in the rest of this discussion; it cannot change the conclusions in any way.

For Marx, the simplest version of the labour theory is only a first approximation (both logically and historically), so there is nothing contradictory in later modifying its conclusions to account for these additional facts (Marx, 1894, parts 1 and 2). When competition evens out the rate of profit, it causes profit or 'surplus-value' to flow from industries using a relatively high ratio of living labour (and producing relatively high profits) to those industries using a relatively low ratio of living labour (and producing relatively low profits). Competition does this by lowering high prices and raising low prices until there is a uniform rate of profit for all industries. The price in each industry then equals the 'cost' of production *plus* a uniform rate of profit on capital, where the cost includes the wages plus the value of the used-up plant, equipment and raw materials. This price is called the 'price of production'.

According to Marx, the price of production in each individual industry will equal the value of its product *only if* the ratio of the value of labour power expended to the value of the used-up capital goods happens to be identical to the average ratio for all industry. Marx calls this key ratio the 'organic composition of capital'. In every industry where this ratio happens to be different from the average ratio, the individual prices of production will differ from the individual values. However, Marx argues, the aggregate amount of value produced will still equal the sum of prices, and the aggregate surplus-value produced will still equal the sum of profits.

So long as the aggregate labour expended remains the same, the aggregate value and surplus-value produced do not change. Competition merely redistributes the surplus-value from one industry to another until there is a uniform rate of profit on capital. Thus, in Marx's own opinion, the labour theory of value and surplus-value holds only for the *aggregate* product (though he did believe that individual prices reflect and systematically deviate from values). The famous attack on Marx by Böhm-

Bawerk (1896) emphasizes that such an aggregate sum of values is meaningless because economic theory is concerned only with the relative value of commodities in exchange. Of course, Böhm-Bawerk was thinking only of price and allocation problems, and not of the whole range of Keynesian aggregate problems in which aggregate value is not only useful but necessary.

The aggregate equality of (a) values and prices, and the equality of (b) surplus-values and profits, rests on the grounds that all of the individual deviations above and below value must exactly cancel each other. This is necessarily true *only if* no commodity enters into the production of any other (see, e.g., Meek, 1956b). In the more general case we note that capital goods are used in the production of other goods, and that the individual prices of capital goods also deviate from *their* individual values. In this more difficult model we can prove only that one of the two equalities must hold, but that both will hold only under very special and accidental circumstances. Thus, if we wish to maintain the equality of aggregate surplus-value and aggregate profit, we must admit that the sum of prices may deviate from the aggregate value of all products.

The individual and even the aggregate deviation of prices from values does *not* invalidate the sophisticated version of the labour theory of value, though it certainly invalidates its simpler version.[8] Given the labour expenditure, the rate of surplus-value and the ratio of labour to used-up capital goods in each individual industry, the labour theory of value can still calculate all the individual prices and profits, as well as the aggregate amounts. If we are looking for a theory of relative individual prices, this qualification makes the labour theory vastly complicated and ridiculously clumsy for practical use. To the extent that we are concerned with Marx's aggregate economic conclusions, however, the whole issue is of such a small magnitude as to have no effect on the outcome.

Constant costs

Neo-classical theory considers three possible reactions of cost per unit to a rise in output in the long run: (a) rising costs, (b)

8. For perhaps the most sophisticated form of a labour theory, see Sraffa (1960).

constant costs and (c) falling costs. Marx, in his first approximation to value theory, almost always assumed the simplest case, the case of constant costs (or infinite elasticity of supply). Suppose there is an increase in demand for a product, caused perhaps by a change in consumer preference. With constant costs, the only result of the increase in demand is an increase in output, because with the same cost per unit of output, there is no change in the long-run price. Only in this case would Marshall join Marx in declaring that long-run price is completely unaffected by changes in demand and that it is governed solely by the 'cost' of supply (including an average 'profit').[9] Of course, the interpretation of 'cost' and 'profit' would differ greatly between Marx and Marshall.

It has been observed that *if* we assume constant costs and *if* 'cost' means the same as 'labour expended', then we may say that Marxian economics reaches (in a very roundabout manner) the same conclusions about long-run price and output as Marshallian neo-classical economics. The 'long run' here still assumes no technical progress. In a more general theory, however, it must be recognized that even in the long run there may be falling costs per unit (associated with a rising marginal product per worker) *or* rising costs per unit (associated with a falling marginal product per worker).

In either case a shift in demand from other products to this one, even though fully balanced by a shift in supply from other products to this one, will 'cause' a change in the price of this product as well as a rise in its output. (The change in price is due to the fact that at a higher level of output it may be technologically necessary to use more or less labour per unit of output.) Yet Marx in his theory of individual prices always implicitly assumes constant costs and makes no attempt to discuss these more general cases in his theory of value. The reason is that these issues, which are important practical questions for management, have little or no relevance to the evaluation of capitalism versus socialism (and are irrelevant to economic development issues

9. 'It is also to be recalled that Marshall tended to give primacy to the conditions of production as price determinants in the long run' (Nove, 1961, p. 278 n.). Also see Marshall (1890, pp. 337–50 and 503 of 1953 edn).

under any system). Marx does consider problems of rising or falling costs, but only within the very different context of the aggregate and dynamic problems of changes in population and technology.

We conclude from this analysis that Marxist price theory and neo-classical price theory are perfectly compatible. To analyse one actual set of prices, however, the Marxist would have to go through at least seven highly complicated approximations to take account of each of the qualifications mentioned above. Therefore, as a workable theory of relative individual prices, the Marxist theory is practically impossible to use, not because it is wrong, but because it is needlessly complex to a very high degree. The progressive Marxists conclude that the neo-classical price theory is a much more useful analytic tool for understanding how to set prices and allocate resources (though this is a practical issue only under central planning, and is not relevant to most of the analysis of the political-economic development of capitalism).

Neo-classical economics as a special case of Marxist economics

One modern American economist, Robert Campbell, contends that Marx made use of the classical theories of value up to the time of Ricardo, but that Marxists have missed the generalization and unification of value theory that came 'in the late nineteenth century with the concept of general equilibrium and the reduction of all explanations to the common denominator of utility' (Campbell, 1961, p. 403). Moreover, he believes, the 'new basic insight' of the utility school, that economics is 'the theory of allocation of scarce resources among competing ends' (p. 404), was never learned by Marxists. Therefore, he concludes, 'the bondage of a Marxist heritage in economic theory is not so much that the Marxist view is simply wrong in one particular (i.e. that it assumes that value is created only by labor) as that it does not comprehend the basic problem of economic theory' (p. 404).

Marx, of course, does *not* present a systematic theory of the allocation of scarce resources, though one may be *inferred* from his theory of value. He does often refer to the allocation of capital among industries according to the profitability of the different industries, which in turn would be a function of the given distribution of consumer demand. For the most part, though, it is true that Marx did not emphasize demand, let alone changes in demand; nor did he consider in detail the problems of producing proportionate to that demand; nor did he consider at all the related problems of choice among scarce resources and capital. In fact, Marx never did discuss in detail the marginal utility 'revolution' of the 1870s, which occurred late in his lifetime. His scathing references to the utility theories of the 'vulgar economists' concern the much earlier and superficial versions and do not relate to marginal utility theory. Engels did mention marginal utility in a critical vein a few times in the voluminous letters of his later years.[10]

Non-dogmatic Marxists nowadays admit that, with respect to the allocation of scarce resources, the neo-classical economists 'have developed a price theory which is more useful in this sphere than anything to be found in Marx or his followers' (Sweezy, 1942, p. 129). Yet the allocation of scarce resources on the basis of micro price theory is not the whole of economics, and certainly far from the whole of political economy.

Marx would never have agreed that allocation of scarce resources is *the* basic problem of economics (though it is related to the distribution of income and other basic problems). In capitalism, this problem appears mainly as a *technical*-economic problem for a single firm, a so-called micro-problem. Marx, however, was simply not interested in the technical micro-problems of the capitalist firm, such as where to invest, what technology to use, how much to produce or how many workers to hire. Marx was interested in the *political*-economic problems of the economy as a whole, so-called macro-problems of strategy for government or for whole economic classes.

What is it that makes people keep reading Marx while other economists gather dust on the shelves? Even in the abstruse subject of value, Marx sees human relations where other economists see statistics and graphs. Human beings make commodities; commodities do not make human beings (though it often feels that way in our upside-down, commodity-oriented society).

Suppose we ask a neo-classical economist what determines the price of a ton of steel? He will tell us about the demand in the

10. All of the scattered references of Marx and Engels to this subject are mentioned in Wiles (1964, pp. 50–51).

market, derived from the demand of consumers for pots and pans and so forth. He will tell us about the cost of supply in terms of the dollars and cents of each commodity and service going into the steel.

But if we ask Marx, he gives us an agonizingly real picture of the steel worker, stripped to the waist and dripping sweat, working at the furnace. If we ask about the cost of the furnace and other precision machinery, then he paints the picture of the painstakingly careful labour that went into its production. He will also call our attention to the miserable wages paid the steel worker and to the immense profits of the capitalist owner (who may be merely clipping coupons a long way from the steel plant). Thus Marx is concerned with the underlying *human* relations in the production process. It is in this sense that he thinks of the expenditure of human labour as underlying the value of goods. The important thing he gives to us is a view of human relationships, not a metaphysical statement about the determination of prices 'beyond supply and demand'. Unfortunately, many of his followers have lost the human insight and only retained the absolute, metaphysical statement about value when they try to state Marx in 'pure' economic language.

Marxism may use a crude price theory, but the scope of its political economy is unbelievably broader than the abstract and narrow world of neo-classical economics. Leaving aside social and political struggles for the moment, Marxist economics long ago criticized neo-classical and classical economics in the same way that Keynesians now do. Marx pointed out that capitalism faces a strange new problem unheard of in previous societies: not the scarcity of output and resources, but the excess of output and resources relative to the effective money demand for them. This problem opens up a whole new field of economics, the Alice-in-Wonderland economics of business cycles, general unemployment, depression and inflation, and lack of aggregate excess of demand. It is then apparent that the main body of neo-classical analysis is limited to the rare and accidental case of an exact full-employment equilibrium of aggregate supply and demand.

Furthermore, most neo-classical analysis limited itself to the activities of particular enterprises and their interactions. Very little neo-classical analysis is devoted to aggregate economic events, the area which Marx investigated in a very detailed and comprehensive manner. The few neo-classical concepts concerning aggregate economics, such as the celebrated Say's Law, have since been shown to be both superficial and inaccurate. These same concepts, as they existed in classical economics, were sarcastically dissected by Marx a hundred years ago.

Moreover, neo-classical price theory usually limits itself to a static picture, disregarding time. At best, it compares two such static pictures. Marx always concentrates on movement. He presents very detailed dynamic theories, both of short-run business cycle movements and of the long-run evolution of capitalism.

Further, neo-classical theory always remains at the level of *technical* economics, concerned with the price and production relationships between commodities (though it implies, usually in a devious and hidden manner, a very particular political ideology in defence of the *status quo*). Marx wrote openly on the vast problems of *political* economy, concerned with the social relationships between men; *for this purpose micro price theory is only a small and not too important tool.* Marx explores the basic institutions of capitalism, asking which class of men own the means of production and which class of men exert labour power and do the productive work? What are the economic links binding the two classes together? What human relationships are reflected in the value of commodities?

Neo-classical economics has nothing to say about the role of government, except the common belief that the economy will work automatically and well without any government (except to guard private property). Long before Keynes, Marx recognized the immense economic role played by governments in capitalism, in aiding the initial development of many industries as well as in measures to mitigate the business cycle. While Keynesian economics has a much more precise knowledge of the technical possibilities open to government intervention in capitalism, Marx goes further to discuss an aspect of government in capitalism which Keynes never recognized. Marx discussed the determination of government policy and structure by the nature of the economic relationships. In other words, Marxists emphasize that the technical possibilities apparently open to government are in reality drastically limited by the political and economic self-interest of the ruling capitalist class (both domestically and in the network of imperialist relationships abroad).

Finally, although neo-classical economics provides an accurate description of price movements, this theory is not useful – and is often made to serve in a deceptive ideological function – when applied to the distribution of income between labour and property owners. The fact that wages equal the 'marginal revenue product' of hiring workers does not prove the lack of exploitation, but is only a truism that holds because capitalists maximize profit by hiring to that point. The fact that interest equals the marginal cost of borrowing capital proves that financial capitalists and industrial capitalists are striking a realistic bargain, but does not prove that capital is 'productive' or that it 'produces' interest.

Marx would agree that the actual machines are a necessary or 'productive' part of the physical productive process; he would even agree to the importance of managerial labour. He would argue, however, that this productivity of physical capital goods (created by another labour process in the past) is quite different from the ability of capitalist owners to capture a certain portion of the product as interest or profit. 'It is, of course, true that materials and machinery can be said to be physically productive in the sense that labor working with them can turn out a larger product than labor working without them, but physical productivity in this sense must under no circumstances be confused with value productivity' (Sweezy, 1942, p. 61). In other words, 'Under capitalism "the productiveness of labor is made to ripen, as if in a hot-house". Whether we choose to say that capital is productive, or that capital is necessary to make labor productive, is not a matter of much importance.... What is important is to say that owning capital is not a productive activity' (Robinson, 1942, p. 18 of 1960 edn). This is clear in the case of a mere coupon-clipper (as most stock-owners are today). The fact that some of them may otherwise perform productive labour through their own managerial work is not in contradiction to the fact that they also make money by mere ownership of capital.

References

ACADEMY OF SCIENCES OF THE USSR, INSTITUTE OF ECONOMICS (1957), *Political Economy*, Lawrence & Wishart.

BÖHM-BAWERK, E. (1896), *Karl Marx and the Close of his System*, ed. P. M. Sweezy, Kelley, 1949.

BOUDIN, L. (1907), *The Theoretical System of Karl Marx*, Monthly Review Press, 1968.

BRONFENBRENNER, M. (1967), 'Marxian influence in "bourgeois" economics', *Amer. econ. Rev.*, vol. 57, pp. 624–35.

BRUS, W. (1956), 'Socialist production and the law of value', trans. in *Int. econ. Pap.*, no. 7, 1957, pp. 125–44.

CAMPBELL, R. (1961), 'Marx, Kantorovich and Novozhilov', *Slavic Rev.*, vol. 20, p. 403–4.

CHAMBERLIN, E. (1933), *The Theory of Monopolistic Competition*, Harvard University Press, 1950.

DICKINSON, H. D. (1963), 'Notes to article by L. Johansen "Labour theory of value and marginal utilities"', *Econ. Plan.*, vol. 3, pp. 239–40.

LANGE, O. (1935), 'Marxian economics and modern economic theory', *Rev. econ. Stud.*, vol. 2, pp. 189–201.

MARSHALL, A. (1890), *Principles of Economics*, Macmillan Co., 1953.

MARX, K. (1867), *Capital*, vol. 1. Charles H. Kerr, 1906.

MARX, K. (1894), *Capital*, vol. 3, Charles H. Kerr, 1909.

MEEK, R. (1956a), *Studies in the Labor Theory of Value*, International Publishers.

MEEK, R. (1956b), 'Some notes on the "transformation problem"', *Econ. J.*, vol. 66, pp. 94–107.

NOVE, A. (1961), *The Soviet Economy*, Praeger.

ROBINSON, J. (1934), *The Economics of Imperfect Competition*, Macmillan

ROBINSON, J. (1942), *An Essay on Marxian Economics*, St Martin's Press, 1960.

SAMUELSON, P. A. (1948), *Economics: An Introductory Analysis*, McGraw-Hill, 1970.

SRAFFA, P. (1960), *Production of Commodities by Means of Commodities*, Cambridge University Press.

STALIN, J. (1952), *Economic Problems of Socialism in the USSR*, International Publishers.

SWEEZY, P. M. (1942), *The Theory of Capitalist Development*, Oxford University Press Inc.

WALRAS, L. (1874), *Elements of Pure Theory*, Irwin, 1954.

WILES, P. J. D. (1964), *The Political Economy of Communism*, Harvard University Press.

Part Five
The Role of the State in
Monopoly Capitalism

In the orthodox tradition of economic theory, government has
a shadowy existence. When unemployment appears, or a
departure from Paretian optimality, such as an 'external
diseconomy of production or consumption', occurs (such a
departure is generally treated as an isolated occurrence in an
otherwise perfect world), the government becomes a *deus ex
machina* which restores the economic system to a state of bliss.
An aloof, neutral, impartial arbitrator that descends on the
scene, increases or decreases aggregate demand, enacts an
excise tax or gives a subsidy that re-creates full employment
and Paretian optimality.

In Reading 15 James O'Connor discusses the role of the
State in traditional microeconomic theory, macroeconomic
theory, public finance theory and in the theories of
'revisionists' such as J. K. Galbraith. He concludes with
Wicksell, that these theories proceed 'on the implicit and
unrecognized assumption that the society is ruled by a
benevolent despot'. Furthermore, O'Connor asserts that 'It
is only by taking the step toward the reconstruction of the
theory of the State and the State finances that we will have a
basis for a complete critique of bourgeois economic science.'

In Reading 16 Sumner M. Rosen discusses some of the
implications of military spending as the principal tool of
Keynesian fiscal policy. M. Kalecki, in a far-sighted article
written in 1943 (Reading 17), discusses the issue of whether
capitalists desire full employment and forecasts the 'political
business cycle' of post-war capitalist countries. D. M. Nuti
(Reading 18) argues that within the context of a capitalist
society 'incomes policy can be ineffective or even self-defeating,

and is always either an instrument for the preservation of the *status quo*, or outrightly iniquitous'. R. M. Goodwin (Reading 19) presents a model of a growth cycle which may help to explain why the trade union movement has been relatively ineffective in redistributing income. Finally, Bob Fitch (Reading 20) shows how J. K. Galbraith's liberal critique of capitalist society really contains a consistent ideological defence of that system.

15 James O'Connor

Scientific and Ideological Elements in the Economic
Theory of Government Policy

James O'Connor, 'Scientific and ideological elements in the economic
theory of government policy', *Science and Society*, vol. 33, 1969,
pp. 385–414.

In our time . . . faith in the manipulative omnipotence of the State
has all but displaced analysis of its social structure and understanding
of its political and economic functions (Paul A. Baran. 'On the political
economy of backwardness', in A. N. Agarwala and S. P. Singh, eds.
The Economics of Underdevelopment).

In no other field [than public finance] has the intrusion of metaphysics
done so much harm as here (Gunnar Myrdal, *The Political Element
in the Development of Economic Theory*).

There is a large and growing body of economic doctrine on the
subject of State expenditures and taxation which attempts to lay
down guidelines for State fiscal policy. 'Such studies', Peacock
and Wiseman (1961, p. 13) have written,

attempt to set up criteria for the size and nature of government expenditures and income by utilizing techniques usual in the study of market
economics. Starting from some concept of economic welfare, defined
in terms of individual choice, they attempt to specify the taxing and
spending activities of government that would conduce to the ideal
condition of such welfare.

The general questions which are raised are: how large should
the State budget be and how should budget expenditures be allocated between alternative ends? What should be the burden of
taxes on various groups? Put another way, what elements should
make up a normative theory of 'public finance'? Immediately we
can see that the conventional phrase 'public finance' reveals the
ideological content of bourgeois economic thought by prejudging
the question of the *real* purpose of State expenditures. In other
words, it remains to be shown just how 'public' are the real and
financial transactions that take place in the state economic sector.

Our first task is to develop as clearly as possible a statement of the two main lines of orthodox theory, one based upon neo-classical microeconomic theory, the second based on Keynesian macroeconomic theory. It should be said at the outset that although many bourgeois economists consider the analysis of public finance to be concrete, practical 'precepts for action', others are aware that the theory is devoid of any significant social and political content, and hence represents little more than a 'counsel of perfection'.

The second purpose of this paper is briefly to review the critique of orthodox microeconomic theory, or welfare economics, developed by orthodox economists themselves. This critique is based solely on the lack of internal consistency or logical clarity of the theory and in no way challenges its underlying assumptions. These underlying assumptions, as we shall see, are based on the criteria of competitive markets and welfare maximizing. In turn, these criteria take for granted the system of private ownership of the means of production and the economic, social and political institutions that go with private ownership. We believe that these criteria are based on a one-dimensional view of man and his real potentialities and, moreover, on a historically specific and short-lived system of political economy.

Thus our third purpose is to develop our own critique of orthodox public finance, one which challenges the assumptions of both micro and macro theory and goes beyond an attempt to reveal certain logical inconsistencies or contradictions implied by it. We do not, however, attempt to answer the question: what should the State do? We do not attempt to reconstruct the normative theory of State finance, because that would take us into a different subject altogether, the political economy of socialism. What State revenues and budgetary expenditures should be in a noncapitalist society would depend on the specific type of socialism to emerge from United States capitalism, the circumstances surrounding the struggle for socialism, the coalition of forces which lead the struggle, and so on. These questions would obviously take us well beyond the scope of our subject matter.

In its approach to the role of the State under capitalism, welfare economics, based on microeconomic analysis, adopts the principle of 'neutrality'. It is contended that the State (including State tax policy) should refrain from disturbing the pattern of resources allocation determined by private market relationships except in the event that the existing allocations are at odds with the competitive norm – the types of allocations which prevail in a regime of perfect competition – with 'welfare maximizing'.

The concept of ideal output is central to the normative theory of public finance. We have no intention of doing anything like full justice to the range and complexity of problems arising from and variations on the idea of ideal output, but rather make a simple and somewhat old-fashioned statement of it. Pigou (1920) defines ideal output as that composition of production such that 'no alternative output which could be obtained by means of reallocation among the various industries of the economy's resources would leave the community better off than before'. To put it differently:

any reallocation of the resources employed in producing the ideal output will so affect the various members of the economy that those who are better off as a result of the change will be unable to compensate those who are worse off as a result of the change and at the same time make a net gain for themselves.[1]

1. Formally: assume no externalities in production (a situation where a firm's costs of production depend not only on the size of the firm, but also on the size of the industry) and externalities in consumption (a situation where an individual's satisfaction depends not only on the quantity of a commodity he consumes, but also on the quantity of a commodity other individuals consume) and assume a constant income distribution and level of employment. What is the relationship between competitive and ideal outputs? One equilibrium condition under competition is $P_x/P_y = MPC_x/MPC_y$.

In the absence of externalities, private costs correspond to social costs, or $MPC_x = MSC_x$ and $MPC_y = MSC_y$. Next consider a transformation curve between x and y. The slope of the curve must be MSC_x/MSC_y, because MSC_x/MSC_y is equal to the decrease in the production of x associated with a given increase in the production of y (or vice versa). Competitive equilibrium thus requires that the output combination be one for which the slope of the transformation curve be equal to the slope of the price line. Ideal output is where the indifference and transformation curve are tangent. Thus ideal output corresponds with competitive output. If private market relationships lead to an output which departs from ideal, then the State's task is to encourage (or discourage) the production of commodities which are undersupplied (or oversupplied).

James O'Connor 369

The question next arises, when will private market relationships depart from ideal output or, to put it differently, when will the private market misallocate economic resources, thus providing the 'justification' for State intervention?

First, markets organized along monopolistic rather than competitive lines may lead to a misallocation of resources. Monopoly tends to keep prices higher and outputs lower than those prevailing under competition. Thus a tax to force the monopolist to lower the price, or a policy to restructure the market in order to bring the price down, is justified. In the event that the marginal social cost exceeds marginal private cost, however (the case of heroin production, for example), monopoly restrictions may improve the allocation of resources and an attack on the monopoly by the State would not be 'justified'.

Second, there is the more general case of the existence of externalities in production. The full-blown name for the concept is 'technological economies or diseconomies of scale', which arise in many industries where the costs facing the firm depend not only on the size and efficiency of the firm itself, but also on the size and efficiency of the industry in which the firm operates. Marshall was the first to formalize this concept and limit it to 'technological' (compared with pecuniary) economies and diseconomies.[2]

For example, in the fishing industry, the more operators are engaged in fishing, the higher will be the costs facing any individual operator. In this case, there are said to be external diseconomies of production. In this event, marginal social costs (MSC) will exceed marginal private costs (MPC). Thus the price of the commodity will be lower than it would be if the divergence between MSC and MPC were to be eliminated. In this event, orthodox theory argues that a tax is in order, to discourage private production and thus reduce social costs to the point where there is no disparity between social and private costs.

A good example of an industry in which there are considered to be external economies of scale is education. It is argued that social costs fall well below private costs because the educated in-

2. In classical economics, at least in Smith, Walras and Wicksell, there is no place for externalities, and even though Say and Mill recognized the possibility of their existence, they do not figure in their public policy recommendations.

dividual contributes more than the uneducated to capitalist society's growth and political stability. The same kind of argument is made regarding transportation facilities. In these cases State subsidies are in order, or even public ownership.

A third departure from ideal output is the presence of increasing returns to scale in the production of a commodity. If a commodity is produced under conditions of increasing returns (air transport, for example), then just as in any industry, marginal revenue should be set to marginal costs to maximize profits and hence welfare. But marginal costs will be below average costs because average costs by definition are declining. Thus in order to have an efficient resource allocation, the industry must be subsidized. Otherwise, the firm must restrict output to cover average costs and thus command a higher price. On the other hand, taxes should be imposed on decreasing return industries; in these sectors, a policy of pricing to cover costs will mean that marginal costs are higher than average costs, signifying a misallocation of resources.

The extreme example of decreasing costs or increasing returns is the case of the 'public good'. The public good is defined as an activity where the additional cost of extra use is zero, or to put it another way, where my consumption does not reduce what is available to you. Standard examples are radio and television programs, lighthouses and the Defense Department. Welfare economics teaches that for public goods price should be zero or near zero. With a price in excess of zero, ideal output exceeds actual output because more people could be better off and no one made worse off by an expansion of output.

It should be noted that the concept of a public good has little or nothing to do with whether the facility is owned by private capital or the State. Theoretically, private capital could own and manage lighthouses and the State could subsidize private capital so that prices could be set at zero and profits still made. To put it another way, lighthouses and television can be priced on the basis of private market principles; for example, radar could be placed on lighthouses to prevent free-riders by means of electronic scrambling of signals. And there is, of course, pay television. There is a category of public goods, however (military goods are given as the main example), in which the problem of 'revealed preferences' arises. One could choose whether or not to pay to see a television program. But in the case of a military establishment, it is thought that there would be a general tendency to underpay via voluntary contributions because once 'defense' is provided, everyone is 'protected' whether or not he wants the protection. It is not possible to bomb North Vietnam in the name of some Americans and not others. In these cases, private ownership of the means of production, in our example, the means of destruction, is not warranted because there is no entrepreneurial function provided. Thus public goods, no matter what their special character, should be either heavily subsidized or owned publicly.[3]

There is a fourth category of market imperfections which 'justify' State interference in the private economy. This is a catch-all category which includes the following special cases: first, the case of neighborhood effects or spillovers. To take one or two examples: my unwillingness to conform to quarantine laws or mosquito control will affect everyone in the community and thus it is justified for the State to coerce me to conform. Or, the existence of a public highway may raise property values locally. Thus the State is justified in paying transit deficits with property taxes. Or, situations where one firm affects the efficiency in the employment of resources by other firms. Suppose, for instance, that a farmer on a mountainside cuts down trees to cultivate his land, affecting adversely the ecological cycle by flooding the valley. These are not true technological externalities because the scale of the industry *per se* has nothing to do with the increase or decrease in the costs of the specific firm. Other examples come to mind in the capitalist labor market. For example, capitalists may have short-time horizons and hire workers with life-time horizons, such that work time is optimum in the short run but shortens a man's working life in the long run. Historically, hours laws can be traced to the irrationality of individual capitalists in the labor market and the need for the State to preserve the labor power for all capitalists from the depredations of individual capitalists.

A final case is a situation where external economies or positive

3. Is it any accident that orthodox economists tend to conclude from their surveys of current-day economic activity that on orthodox criteria the great bulk of such activity is 'justified'? For example, F. Bator (1960, p. 100) concludes that 96·8 per cent of public purchases are public or semipublic 'goods and services'. Bator is truly a Candide.

spillovers are so vast, and hence costs and prices under competition are so high, that the commodity does not even get produced. In this event, few people are even aware of the possible 'advantage' to society. Good examples are import-substitute activities in underdeveloped capitalist countries which may benefit the economy greatly in the long run but which are not begun in the absence of protective State policy.

We offer so many examples of cases which do not fit neatly into the standard orthodox categories only to emphasize the fact that faced with real concrete situations it is often possible to 'justify' any particular government interference after the fact – justify it in terms of orthodox criteria. Thus the idea of consumer sovereignty and welfare maximization (or ideal output) implies State intervention but offers few clear criteria. Because these criteria are so abstract, the dictum that taxes should be 'neutral' except in the event that they are consciously designed to improve resource allocation is somewhat empty. More important, there is nothing in normative theory to tell us whether or not the dictums are realistic in a political sense – or to suggest precisely what externalities the State can be expected to capture and which cannot be.

The traditional perspective on welfare maximizing and State policy has come under increasing fire from contemporary orthodox economists, not because there are so many cases which do not fit neatly into the increasing cost or externality categories where the 'correct' State policy is relatively straightforward and unambiguous, but rather because of the internal logic of the traditional view itself. Modern welfare economics rejects any partial analysis (an analysis restricted to one industry or branch of the economy) which purports to show that any given sector of the economy should be expanded to seize externalities in production. The arguments of contemporary welfare economists are highly mathematical and we will not reproduce them here. The gist of the main argument is that given external economies and necessary equilibrium conditions for the economy as a whole, it can be shown under certain assumptions no more or less arbitrary than those used by the traditional school that expanding sectors of the economy where there are no externalities may increase output even more than expanding sectors where there are. Further, there is the argument that there is no way to know whether a tax to correct an external diseconomy is better than some alternative measure, including the alternative of doing nothing (see, e.g., Baumol, 1964; Turvey, 1963).

One of the latest words on the subject has been said by Professor Baumol (1964), who wrote that if 'external economies are . . . strong . . . and persist, it will indeed pay society to increase all activity levels indefinitely'. Moreover, in the past decade there has been a sustained critique, again from an orthodox standpoint, of the theory of consumer behavior on which welfare economics is based (Graaff, 1957; Little, 1967).

Three major points have been made. First, consumers may not be consistent in their choices and thus it is not possible to say that they are better off in one situation rather than another. Second, externalities in consumption, or collective aspirations and well-being, have no place in traditional theory. Third, the argument is made that if the community is made up of one set of persons at one time and another at another time, how can it be said when and if the community is better off?

We can safely conclude from this brief review of the critics of traditional theory that welfare economics, even one based on the assumption that capitalism as a system is eternal, offers no firm criteria for State policy.

The reason is that the critics of traditional welfare economics, as well as its few remaining defenders, accept criteria based on values which are in turn derived from a system based on the domination of private capital. To put it another way, any notion of economic rationality which is independent of the 'rationality' of the competitive private market is still taboo.

For this reason, claims by some economic theorists that value judgements have no place in their analysis are without any real foundation. Many traditional and modern welfare economists may claim that they attempt merely to determine the circumstances in which people with given economic interests may pursue these interests more 'efficiently' by broadening the role of the State in the economy. But, at the same time, the theorist accepts these interests as valid – as worth defending and realizing. In the event that he rejected the given private interests, he would hardly waste time deducing from them implications for State action under varying sets of circumstances. It follows that the welfare economist ideologically supports the dominant private interests at the expense of the politically weakest private interests.

Another technical school of economics is the positive school. The positive economist views himself as a *technician* who rules out explicit normative theorizing and, finally, accepts the preferences of the 'authorities' as given. The customary role of the positive economist is either an adviser to the State or some private group, or a technician faced with a 'maximization' problem chosen by himself.

In the first case, the economist claims a certain neutrality with respect to the wisdom or lack of wisdom of some change proposed by the State and confines himself to formulating alternative means to a given end. Needless to say, the positive economist accepts without question the desired end and, moreover, ordinarily fails to consider *all* possible alternative means to this end. There are no economists, for example, currently employed to work out the economic implications of nationalizing the drug industry or the oil interests, even though on pure efficiency criteria alone many economists would be compelled to give these industries very low marks. Thus the economic technician is to one degree or another merely a normative economist in disguise.

This is not a surprising conclusion; what is surprising is the economists' claim that they are merely 'objective' analysts. If anything, the positive economist-technician adviser is less objective today than in the past. It can no longer be written as confidently that 'economists treating government influences on the economy have largely neglected the essential institutional and procedural aspects of government action. That is why their analyses and recommendations are often characterized as Utopian and unrealistic by the specialist in public finance' (Colm, 1948, p. 196). Today the 'objective' economist is more willing to dispense with independent critical judgements than in the past and, conversely, accept more constraints ('institutional and procedural aspects of government action') in his analysis.

In the second case, the economist analyses an economic maximization problem chosen by himself; for example, the 'optimum' investment in some new water resource. If all existing constraints –

physical, legal, administrative-budgetary, and so on – are incorporated in the analysis, then the economist is bound 'to exclude the interesting solution', to quote Otto Eckstein. What is meant by this is that a given market situation determines a certain set of prices, level of investment, and so on, and thus in order to put his apparatus to work, the economic technician must ignore at least one given political, property, financial or other given relationship. The choice of which constraint to 'assume away' is, of course, a normative judgement. Even here, the economist's values are in the center of his work.

The only important issues of State economic policy which the traditionalist does not refer to the welfare norm are the distribution of income, economic stabilization (including international stabilization) and economic growth. So far as the distribution of income is concerned, after many decades of debate, contemporary orthodox economists by and large reject the neo-classical fiction of 'tax justice'. The economist *qua* economist is powerless to make comparisons of 'interpersonal utility' and thus cannot justify a progressive tax structure, or any other tax structure, without reference to given legal norms, precedent, 'public opinion', and so on. Among orthodox economists the general consensus appears to be that the market distributes income more or less 'fairly' in advanced capitalist countries – even though there is some recognition that everyone does not have equal access to the capital market (e.g. higher education) – although the more sophisticated writers are fully aware that this is not a necessary attribute of the market. For example, Samuelson (1956, p. 328) rebuts those who accept the marginal productivity doctrine as a normative theory of income distribution between economic classes in the following way: 'Under appropriate conditions of demand and technology, a marginal productivity theory might impute 99 per cent of the national income away from labor, which would be exploitation enough in the eyes of radical agitators.'

Thus it would appear that contemporary economics has traveled a long way to go (admittedly) a very short distance, yet on one crucial question the subject remains in the Dark Ages. We refer to the tendency to separate the ('ethical') question of income distribution from the ('scientific' or 'objective') question of resource allocation and market efficiency. From the standpoint of formal *logic*, this separation is unobjectionable. However, an analysis of the political economy which ignores the actual connections between distribution and allocation is unreal. Clearly, economic efficiency depends on the distribution of output and income, and thus it is impossible to develop any fully satisfactory norms for resource allocation independent of the given distribution of income. Furthermore, it is not at all certain that a more equal income distribution would not automatically be accompanied by an increase in social consumption at the expense of private consumption as status symbols and material emulation in general would figure much less prominently in the social economy ('Review of the Month', 1959).

In a world of conspicuous consumption, for example, leveling income may greatly increase welfare. For another thing, if the satisfaction that one individual gets from his consumption depends in part on another individual's consumption, then changing the income distribution will change ideal output and hence welfare.

Lastly, in order to promote what *some* economic classes and groups consider to be an equitable distribution of income, it might be necessary to abandon the private market system altogether or, at the very least, modify it to the degree that its foundations are undermined. Needless to say, bourgeois economics defines 'ethical' and 'equitable' without reference to this alternative.

Complicating matters, the normative theory of State expenditure assumes that everyone benefits equally from a given expenditure (e.g., the police). The assumption is made that there is no link between the distribution of income and the welfare impact of State expenditures; for example, that individuals who cannot afford to travel benefit from highway expenditures as much as those who can. In the private market, bourgeois economists often justify inequalities in income distribution on the basis of 'preserving incentives'. No economist would ever dare say in public that inequalities in the welfare impact of 'public' expenditures are required to preserve incentives.

Next we turn to macroeconomic fiscal theory, again beginning with an exposition of the main lines of the theory. Macroeconomics, like economics generally, uses the postulate-deductive form of equilibrium theory which begins with a few simple axioms and combines them to form a group of concepts that are logically interrelated. These concepts provide the basic terms of the system and describe the primary general relations between them.

The purpose of macroeconomic, or income, theory is to analyse the determinants of aggregate or total spending on commodities. The elementary concept is the utility of objects for individuals; the general relation is the principle of maximization of utility for individuals and returns (profits) for firms. A million light years, however, separate individual utility and demand for commodities from aggregate demand for commodities, and in macroeconomic theorizing, individual utility is ordinarily lost sight of. This means that macroeconomics in no sense can be considered pure economic theory.

In the most simple macroeconomic model total income, or the value of total production (Y), is constituted by consumption spending (C), investment spending (I) and government spending (G) ($Y = C + I + G$). The level of employment is determined by the level of income or production [$E = E(Y)$]. The price level (P) is assumed to be unchanged up to the point of full employment. When full employment is reached, the price level is determined by the level of spending.

Macro theory does not independently investigate the determinants of consumption, which is made to depend on income via the 'marginal propensity to consume' (MPC). The simplest form of the consumption function is $C = a + bY$, where a is the volume of consumption when income is zero and b is the propensity to consume or the proportion of income consumed. Income itself, and hence employment and prices, are thus determined by investment spending and government spending.

There are almost as many theories of investment as there are investment theorists. The original Keynesian theory, a simple one, views investment as depending on the anticipated rate of profit (p), the money supply (M) and society's preference for holding assets in liquid (cash) form (LP). Government spending is determined by the political authorities and is not subject to economic laws.

The elementary functional relations of the system are: (a) The higher the *MPC*, the higher the level of income and employment; (b) The greater the stock of money, the lower the rate of interest, the higher the volume of investment and the higher the level of income and employment; (c) The weaker the preference for holding assets in the form of cash, the greater the demand for bonds, the higher the price of bonds, the lower the rate of interest, and the greater the level of investment, income and employment.

The system is said to be in equilibrium when the volume of production at current prices equals consumption, government spending and intended investment. Actual investment equals intended investment when inventories of commodities are no lower or greater today than capitalists expected them to be yesterday, i.e. when today's sales equal yesterday's production. In this event, the market is cleared; there is no excess demand or supply. The peculiar characteristic of the Keynesian model is that the system may be in equilibrium even though there may be a sizeable amount of unemployment (or, alternatively, inflation).

Thus to increase employment, income must be increased. Income may be increased directly by raising the propensity to consume (for example, by deflating the economy and increasing the real value of savings, and hence liberating savings for consumption), by raising investment (e.g. by subsidies to capitalists) and by government spending or tax reductions. Income may be increased indirectly by increasing the supply of money, lowering the rate of interest and hence raising the level of investment.

It should be obvious from this discussion that macro theory was formulated with an eye to macro policy – that in no sense can macro theory be considered pure theory, or value-free theory. The orientation of macro theory is toward the *control* of income, employment and prices via State economic policy. Thus macro theory, fiscal theory (the analysis of the effects of government spending, taxation and borrowing) and fiscal policy (applied fiscal theory) all boil down to fundamentally the same phenomenon – how to make capitalism a viable economic and social system by keeping unemployment and inflation within reasonable bounds.[4]

4. The foregoing are the elements of the theory of income and employment determination in the short run – when the capital stock, technology and the labor force are assumed to be unchanged. Neo-Keynesianism, or

It should also be obvious that macro theory (like microeconomics) is not a *social* science. It does not analyse the relations between men, but rather the relations between abstractions such as total income, the price level, etc.

Macro theory of the type discussed above, i.e. theory which places primary emphasis on demand, has been popular during two historical eras – during the later mercantilist period and today, the epoch of monopoly capitalism. In both periods the State plays a central role in the economy. During the era of *laissez-faire*, income theory was banished by the classical and neo-classical economists. Brought to life by Keynes, today it dominates economic thought in the advanced capitalist countries.

The main point is that macro theory is at one and the same time the science and ideology of the ruling class – or, more precisely, the dominant stratum of the ruling class, the corporate oligarchy. The corporate oligarchy has long ago accepted the inevitability and desirability of economic self-regulation – or what is euphemistically called government intervention in the economy. What is more, the corporate oligarchy is the only segment of the ruling class which is in a position to effectively *control* macrofiscal policy. I do not think that this assertion requires elaborate proof. There is a growing historical literature which describes the sources and development of a class consciousness on the part of

_____

growth theory (the theory of secular changes in income), bases itself on an analysis of the relationship between changes in income and spending and changes in the capital stock, or productive capacity. Put simply, neo-Keynesianism argues that if the addition to productive capacity due to yesterday's investment spending equals the change in total spending, the system will be in dynamic equilibrium. Put another way, the increment to spending from one period to another is just sufficient to absorb the extra commodities which yesterday's investment spending has made it possible to produce. If the increment to capacity is greater than the increment to spending, neo-Keynesian policy calls for State encouragement to consumption spending. If the increment to capacity is smaller than the increment to spending, neo-Keynesian policy calls for State encouragement to investment spending. For example, during the 1950s increments to income went to consumption and government spending. James Tobin and other neo-Keynesians thus convinced Kennedy to squeeze consumption and push investment, in order to keep increases in productive capacity in line with increases in consumer income and spending.

the corporate rich, and there is a sociological literature which describes the modes of control by the corporations of the quasi-private planning and policy organizations such as CED and the process of ideology formation in which these organizations play a decisive role. Even if such a literature did not exist, it is easy to understand why fiscal policy *must* be formulated in the interests of the hundred or so dominant corporations, because the health of the economy depends almost exclusively on the health of these giants.

Income theory, then, is a *technical* science to the degree that it has practical value to the corporations. To put it another way, income theory is scientific in so far as it is useful to preserve and extend monopoly capitalism as a system and perpetuate class divisions and class rule. On this criterion, for example, neo-Keynesian theory is more scientific than Keynes's original doctrines. A fiscal policy for growth is more practical than one for economic stabilization because of its bias in favor of investment and hence profits.

On the other hand, income theory is not a *critical* science because it constitutes itself on the given economic and legal foundations of capitalism. It fails to make the foundations of capitalism themselves a subject for analysis. At best, then, income theory offers only a description of the *mechanics of operation* of advanced capitalist economies. A critical science is not a science of mechanics, but of real causes, historical causes; the variables are not abstractions such as the interest rate, or supply of money, but rather they are *human* agents.

Thus over the past thirty years there has developed an elaborate analysis of the determinants of income, employment and production – an analysis which has proven to have great practical value in helping the State underwrite business investments and business losses – or to use the long-current euphemism, in helping the government to stabilize the economy and encourage it to grow. What is more, its practical value to the corporations and business in general is greatly enhanced by the fact that business increasingly takes it for granted that income theory *is* an accurate description of the economy.

On the other hand, few would place much confidence in the explanations of the ultimate causes of fluctuation and growth which are integral to income theory. These explanations run in terms of individual psychological motivations and responses and abstract completely from the ever-changing, concrete socio-economic setting which decisively conditions consumer and business behavior. The concepts of 'propensities', 'preferences', 'anticipations and expectations' seem to Marxist economists to be very fragile foundations for such an elaborate structure as income theory. The alternative, and correct, path, in my view, is to submit consumption, investment and government spending to a *structural* determination, i.e. to deduce the implications for the volume of and changes in investment (or consumption) in the context of the *actual* behavior of large corporations operating in oligopolistic markets.

Perhaps an analogy will be useful at this stage. A good one is the relationship between medicine, on the one hand, and biochemistry, biophysics and other sciences which attempt to understand the body as a whole, on the other. To a surprising degree, there is frequently a great gulf separating medicine from the body sciences. The diagnosis and treatment of some diseases – a good example is mental illness – often remain unchanged when the body scientists advance their understanding of the causes of illness, for the simple reason that medicine remains an excellent description of the mechanics of the body. In fact, it is well known that in psychotherapy *a priori* statements about which technique will produce results with any given patient are very hard to come by. Often, the therapist is not even aware of why he has achieved results. One could make the same statement about some economic policymakers.

Income theory is neither right nor wrong – in the sense of being close to or distant from the real causes of economic change – because income theory does not pretend to investigate real causes. It is only more or less useful – more useful if the mechanics of operation of the economy are accurately specified, less useful if not. The main criterion of success is *results*.

Income theory can achieve good results even though its theoretical foundations may be weak. But it could get better results if it were scientifically based on real causes, as we will suggest below. The point which needs emphasis, however, is that it is impossible for an economic theory which exists to maintain capitalism and class rule to be based on real causes. The reason is that a causal science is a critical science, one which subjects the foundations of capitalism – as well as the transitory economic manifestations of these foundations – to analysis. Clearly, a theory which is designed to perpetuate the social and economic relations (and indirectly the taboos and superstitions) of capitalism will be of little value to anyone who wishes to question these relations and taboos and superstitions.[5]

If the economic theory questioned its own assumptions, it would negate itself; and since income theory is first and foremost ruling-class theory, a critical theory would imply that the ruling class would have to question itself, its own right to rule, or negate itself. Let me illustrate with a simple example in the form of a hypothesis: suppose that inflation is caused by the groups or classes which benefit from inflation; suppose further that anti-inflation policy is in the hands of those who caused the inflation. The anti-inflation policy will leave some groups or classes worse off and some better off. Among those who will be better off, will be the group which was the prime mover behind the inflation, the original beneficiaries. Now suppose that the ruling class employs economists to study inflation – indeed, not only study inflation, but find acceptable ways to cause inflation. Clearly, a critical science of inflation would require that economists study not only their employers but themselves.

The economics profession adamantly refuses to do this – to consider itself a part of the experimental field. But it is obvious that economics as a technical science is a *social* phenomenon – and it may be true that only economists are in a position to comprehend their own social role. In fact, we believe it can be shown that the economist's tools have made it possible to have a little unemployment and a little inflation, an optimal situation for the corporations. For example, two famous economists, Paul Samuelson and Robert Solow, wrote an article entitled, 'Our menu of policy choices', in which 'we' are given the 'choice' of a

5. Conversely, an individual interested in supporting capitalism could not in his theorizing admit its real causes. Once real causes are comprehended – that economic growth requires alienation of labor, fragmentation of the personality, mutilation of the spirit – the theorist would see *himself* as another victim and hence would oppose the system.

little unemployment and a little inflation or, alternatively, a little inflation and a little unemployment! Abolishing both unemployment and inflation is impossible given the fact (for bourgeois economists, the eternal fact) that employment depends on the growth of income, which in turn depends on investment, which in turn requires at least a slight profit inflation (that is, prices rising faster than money wages).

In short, income theory does not seek to remove the extremes of society – unemployment and inflation (and capital and labor, rich and poor, privileged and underprivileged, rulers and ruled) – but rather, to quote Marx, it attempts to 'weaken their antagonisms and transform them into a harmonious whole'. Marxists believe this to be impossible. And hence a critical bourgeois social science, including income theory, is for this reason impossible.

Let us now turn to the treatment which public finance affords the relationship between budgetary policy and economic growth. 'Growth models in their present form', Peacock and Wiseman write, 'cannot be treated as anything more than exercises in a technique of arrangement.' The basic reason that income and growth theory is unrealistic is the failure to include a theory of State expenditures. Evsey Domar once noted that government expenditures can be dealt with in one of three ways: they can be assumed to be 'exogenous' to the system, they can be merged with consumption expenditures or they can be assumed 'away altogether'. The latter alternative is completely unsatisfactory and to assume that government expenditures are determined by 'outside' forces is tantamount to an admission that they are beyond the realm of comprehension. Merging all government spending with private consumption merely substitutes fiction for fact.

Paradoxically, government spending is increasingly placed in the middle of discussions of growth and stagnation. Most economists view the State as a kind of *deus ex machina* and assume that government spending not only can but should make up the difference between the actual volume of private expenditures and the level of spending which will keep unemployment down to a politically tolerable minimum. State expenditures in this way are incorporated into models of fluctuations and growth. However, the *actual* determinants of government spending are not considered; rather, what is considered is the volume of spending and taxation necessary to achieve certain goals given certain assumptions and characteristics of the given model.

The reason why economists do not know the actual determinants of government expenditure is not hard to find. There are no markets for most goods and services provided by the State and hence it is not possible to lean on the doctrine of revealed preferences. Thus a theory of State expenditures requires an examination of the forces influencing and conditioning demand. But utility theory forbids any inquiry into these forces – putting aside statistical explanations such as the age-mix of the population, climatic conditions and the like.[6]

This line of thinking leads to the conclusion that before fiscal theory can lay claim to being a critical science, the laws which govern the determination of the volume and composition of State expenditures, and the relation between expenditures and taxes, must be uncovered. This means that fiscal theory must have a clear notion of the character of the State under monopoly capitalism – fiscal theory is then a branch of the theory of the State.

Space does not permit any but the briefest discussion of the elements which truly scientific fiscal theory must contain.

First of all, a clear distinction must be made between socially necessary costs and economic surplus – a distinction between the value of total output and the costs of producing that output. The concept of 'necessary costs' is value-free in the sense that it has meaning independently of any given economic system. Necessary costs are outlays required to maintain the economy's productive capacity and labor force in their given state of productivity or efficiency. The difference between total output and necessary costs constitutes economic surplus. Further, a distinction must be made between what may be called discretionary uses of the surplus by the State and nondiscretionary spending. Without these distinctions, it is not possible to evaluate the role of State expenditure in the determination of aggregate demand and economic growth.

To the degree that State expenditure constitutes necessary costs,

6. The logical reason is that an equilibrium model must assume that demand is independent of supply. Thus it is forbidden to raise the question: how does supply or production condition demand?

State outlays merely substitute for private outlays – and hence do not have any independent effect on aggregate demand. The only difference is that taxpayers as a whole, rather than as a specific industry or branch of the economy, are charged with the costs. An example is education outlays required to maintain the labor force in its given state of productivity.

To the degree that State expenditures comprise economic surplus and to the degree that the surplus consists of nondiscretionary spending (e.g., education outlays required to raise the skill level of a labor force in accordance with advancing technology), State outlays again substitute for private spending – and aggregate demand remains unchanged. In our view, nondiscretionary spending is made up of two main categories: first, a large part of collective consumption – expenditures on social amenities laid out more or less voluntarily by residents in a given community; second, what might be called complementary investments, a special form of private investment the costs of which are borne by the taxpayer, and without which private investment would be unprofitable. Water investments in agricultural districts would be a good example.

Additional demand, and hence economic surplus, *is* generated, first, by wasteful and destructive outlays (the main example being military spending) and, second, by discretionary investments, or State investments made to encourage future private accumulation (e.g. industrial development parks). In this case, there is an increment to demand and surplus because private capital would otherwise not have made the expenditure. Here the rise in government spending will be financed largely out of taxes and thus at the expense of private consumption. The State will in this event create more surplus (or savings) than it absorbs.[7]

Finally, transfer payments (e.g. debt interest and farm payments) generate more surplus than they absorb because they alter the distribution of personal income in the direction of greater inequality.

Whether or not the fiscal policy can be a viable instrument for maintaining a respectable volume of demand depends on whether

7. For example, if the State spends an extra $1 million, financed from income taxes, private spending will be reduced by only $900,000 ($MPC = 0.9$), and therefore $100,000 of surplus will be created.

or not total State spending generates more surplus than it absorbs. If so, then the State budget must continuously increase for the economy to remain in the same place. If not, then State expenditures cannot be considered in any sense autonomous and, correspondingly, the State cannot be considered to be able to act independently of the specific interests of specific firms, industries or other segments of the ruling class. Of course the truth lies somewhere in between these extremes – exactly where we do not know. But often it is more scientific to admit to an area of ignorance than to confidently predict that capitalism can or cannot save itself by the utilization of budgetary policy.

One important tributary of both the micro and macro theories of the State finances is budgetary planning. The outlines for an 'optimal' budget plan have been presented by Musgrave (1959, chs. 1–2) and others. It is assumed that the scale of social wants is predetermined and that the State is responsible to the 'people'. The need for 'national planning' arises from the historical expansion of the role of the State in the economy and the growing recognition of the need to establish economic objectives as an essential basis for the formulation of economic and fiscal government programs. Musgrave's 'optimal' budget is the logical extension of this position.

Musgrave assumes that the State has three main economic functions: the improvement of the allocation of resources, income redistribution and economic stabilization. From this it follows that there should not be one budget but three: an allocation budget which is formulated such that traditional welfare goals are realized; a distribution budget which distills 'society's' idea of equity into a concrete set of transfer payments; and a stabilization budget which insures an appropriate level of aggregate spending or effective demand.

These are the 'real' budgets; the consolidated budget should be merely considered as an administrative device. 'Consolidation [of the budget]', Musgrave writes, 'to be sure, presents no dangers in our imaginary model of efficient budgeting. It is . . . an uninteresting clerical operation undertaken after each of the sub-budgets has been formulated on its own merits.' But Musgrave is concerned that 'in the real world the matter is regarded differently [since] there the tendency is to view the budget in consolidated terms from the outset and thus confuse the underlying issues in the planning stage'. Musgrave of course refers to the underlying issues as defined by policymakers oriented to the needs of the large corporations. From the standpoint of small businessmen or the working class, the absolute size of the budget may itself be an 'underlying issue'.

What is more, it would seem to confuse the issue to formulate the sub-budgets 'on [their] own merits', for the reason that for the 'loser' the redistribution budget, to take an instance, has no merits. And even accepting Musgrave's own terms of reference, it is difficult to see how the sub-budgets can be formulated on their own merits because of the interrelationships between them. For example, an income distribution which Musgrave might consider to be 'fair' with full employment may be considered by him to be 'unfair' with a substantial unemployment rate.

Finally, it should be pointed out that when Musgrave says these are the three 'functions' of the State there is the implication that these are *real* functions and not merely Musgrave's opinion of what the State should have as functions. To be sure, the State may affect the allocation of resources, income distribution and aggregate demand, but these may be the indirect effects of the *real* functions.

It is safe to conclude that traditional economics offers no important criteria for State economic policy independent of the welfare norm other than the precept, 'a little unemployment, a little inflation'. Inevitably, even some bourgeois economists have been unhappy with this state of affairs. The most articulate spokesman of the bourgeois 'revisionists' is John Kenneth Galbraith, whose *The Affluent Society* (1958) attempts to develop a concept of economic rationality which is partly independent of market rationality. Galbraith's writings represent a sharp break from the traditionalist school in that he *emphasizes* sources of waste under capitalism which cannot be taxed out of existence and sources of gain which subsidies to private interests will fail to bring into being. Not that traditional welfare economics is unaware that these kinds of waste – two favorite examples are the resources used to form a cartel and to circumvent tax laws – arise under capitalism, but they are considered to be 'exceptional' or 'off the beaten track'. What distinguishes the Galbraithian school is the single-minded focus on one source of irrationality – namely, the 'artificial' creation of wants by private producers, together with a generalized ideological and financial bias against the public sector and State-provided goods and services.[8]

Put briefly, Galbraith reasons as follows: the demand for public goods in advanced capitalist economies increases more rapidly than the supply of public goods and, given the absence of a price mechanism, there is no tendency for demand and supply to ever reach an equilibrium. Put another way, there is perpetual shortage growing ever more severe, of public goods and services.

The sources of expansion of demand are located in the growth of urbanization, the social and industrial division of labor in a complex economy, the rise in average income, and so on. These tendencies all add up to an increase in the *per capita* demand for roads, schools, public health facilities, utility services, urban planning, and the like. On the other hand, there are three related drags on the supply of public goods. First, a general ideological bias against 'government' limits the expansion of the public sector, the 'conventional wisdom' in the past held that State activities were inherently unproductive and that the need for rapid capital accumulation was first and foremost on the economic agenda. Present thinking about the public sector is irrational because it is conditioned by the prevalence of economic scarcity in the past.[9] Second and third, the operation of markets for private goods under advanced capitalism leans heavily on selling costs to 'synthesize' or artificially create demand and thus prevents the accumulation of taxable surpluses by consumers. Private production and consumption is pushed beyond a rational level because it is 'the process of satisfying wants that creates wants'.

8. Several well-known policy economists accept Galbraith's main theses. For example, see Rostow (1960).

9. The truth of this proposition is a historical question which it is inappropriate to fully consider here. Galbraith is in fact quite wide of the mark; in the past the propertied interests feared the State and therefore forbade the State to acquire productive assets. For this reason, the working class either resented or was indifferent to the State because the State was physically and financially unable to meet working-class economic needs and demands.

The process places consumers in a financial bind (i.e. deep in debt) which in turn sharply limits State expenditures.

Galbraith's opponents fall naturally into one of two camps – critics from the right and critics from the left. Henry Wallich (1961) and F. A. von Hayek (1961) can be cited as representative of the former. Wallich is an exponent of a more or less undiluted form of traditional normative theory. Referring to actual changes in various types of private and public spending, he shows, for example, that both private *and* collective savings for old age have risen more rapidly than total output. Of total expenditures on health and medical care, more than three-quarters were private in 1960. Even in the sphere of education, about one-fifth of total outlays on education were nongovernmental. From these and other data, Wallich asserts that public needs have not been necessarily neglected, nor are they necessarily intrinsically public in character. What may be required, he concludes, is better *private* spending, rather than more public spending; the aim of the State should be to encourage private business to seize objective opportunities to provide social needs, thus retaining free choice in the marketplace. For bourgeois economists this position – close at home to the competitive norm as it is – has a certain security and familiarity to recommend it. But it hardly comes to grips with Galbraith's main point – economic waste caused by synthesizing demand.

The same complaint cannot be made about von Hayek's critique, which purports to meet Galbraith's argument head on. The gist of von Hayek's position is that it does not prove the small value of something merely because people do not feel the need for it until it is produced. Readers of novels could hardly be aware that they would enjoy *Crime and Punishment* until it was actually written. If Galbraith believes that wants are 'passively' created by the production process by which they are satisfied, then his thesis is no more than a truism; if he claims that wants are 'deliberately' (Galbraith uses both words) created, then he might have a case but, in this event, he displays little understanding of the nature of the market system. Individual producers cannot influence wants, von Hayek reminds us, much as they may try, because they are faced with competition from others trying to do the same thing.

What escapes von Hayek is that it is precisely the inability of any producer to influence his consumers which gives the characteristic of *necessity* to the whole process. It is the net effect of the process of want synthesization (or the selling system) that is important – not the gains and costs to any given producer of advertising and other sales efforts. Put another way, the point is not that the wants which are created are those which any specific producer desires to create, but merely that in general wants are 'deliberately' created. To the extent that books and paintings, for example, are transformed into commodities, wants are 'deliberately' created in the above sense; the art world is governed by necessity (that is, is not subject to conscious human control). The question whether a writer or painter himself 'deliberately creates wants' is an altogether different, and for our present discussion, mainly irrelevant, matter. Thus we can safely conclude that von Hayek's criticism is wide of the mark, given the fact that producers purposefully synthesize wants in order to sell commodities in general, not necessarily the product of their own work.

Galbraith's critics from the left rest their case on two fundamental points (Baran, 1960; 'Review of the Month',1959). First, it is readily conceded that there exists a 'conventional wisdom' which throws up a bias against the public sector (or at least certain activities of the public sector), but that this masks private material *interests*, which are as powerful now as in the past. Thus an expansion of the public sector requires far more than the popularization of a new *idea*; it is required to curtail the power of those whose interest it is to maintain the old ideas. But Galbraith fails to propose any means of accomplishing this. Clearly, people must be educated to the need for public services; simultaneously attempts by private producers to instill ever greater desires for private goods must be thwarted. On this question, as well, Galbraith is silent, although it is only fair to point out that other liberals use the cold war as a crutch for arguments in favor of 'structural changes' in the economy in order to pursue a more 'effective' foreign policy (Bazelon, 1965).

Putting this possibility aside, the editors of *Monthly Review* correctly write:

It would seem that there is nothing left for liberals to do but take their pens in hand and go forward to do battle for the public mind against capitalism's growing army of open and hidden persuaders. We wish them luck but fear that the contest is an unequal one. It is not that liberals can expect no success . . . [but] under capitalism liberal reform is a labor of Sisyphus. It never ends, and relative to needs and possibilities it makes little if any progress.

The second main point refers to the sources of financing of an expanded public sector. There are three broad possibilities: first, the bill can be shifted to the working classes, but it is precisely their interests the enlargement of the public sector is designed to serve; second, although it is theoretically feasible to appropriate the private product of the propertied classes, public services would then grow at the expense of profits, meeting with dogged resistance on the part of private interests. What would increase resistance of private business even more is the idea of taxing itself in order to subsidize its own competition (e.g. State insurance, public housing, etc.); third, a larger public sector can be financed out of economic growth, and a subsequent expansion and rationalization of federal subsidies to State and local governments. This latter possibility is in fact foremost in the thinking of most contemporary students of public finance, chiefly because of the fatal drawbacks of the other two approaches. Yet it is not as politically 'neutral' an approach as would appear at first glance. It places the burden of promoting economic growth on the State, which, however, is forbidden to acquire and reproduce productive assets. Thus State economic policy is necessarily directed toward promoting *private capital accumulation* and hence raising the profit share of national income; in effect, we are told that the distribution of income must be worsened before it is possible to correct the imbalance between private and public goods and services. Actually, one main task of the capitalist State has *always* been to promote private accumulation and therefore it is readily understandable why the 'growth school' of public finance is so popular among bourgeois economists.

To this critique, we add two observations. First, Galbraith, as well as the traditionalists, lacks any theory of the *distribution* of public goods and services. It can be shown that in middle-class communities there is an approximation of an 'optimal' bundle of private and public goods, but not in urban working-class communities. Thus, what Galbraith (together with some Marxist writers) mistakes for a generalized shortage of public goods are often in fact inequalities in their distribution.

Second, Galbraith does not tell us whether we should correct overcrowded highways by building more highways, or developing mass transit, or both. In general, he fails to provide any criteria for public spending, excepting impressionistic references to 'unsatisfied public needs'. The problem is not that the values of the economists figure in their scientific work; quite the opposite. The problem is that they fail to have any strongly felt values and hence substitute the ruling values for their own.

The 'revisionists', of which we take Galbraith as the key representative, depart from the traditional school in two fundamental and related respects: first, as we have seen, Galbraith locates *important* irrationalities in advanced capitalism which do not fit easily into traditional externality concepts; second, Galbraith is led by this position to introduce the State as a *deus ex machina*; the State 'solves problems' when they arise without reference to the source or nature of the problem. Between the two varieties of bourgeois thought, then, there is a quite different assessment of the possibilities of social and economic change in a capitalist society. The traditional school, represented by Baumol, describes individual needs and desires as they are transfigured by a voting process into State economic activity. The State economy is reduced to the totality of personal needs; therefore, assuming that individual behavior is rational and well informed, what is possible is what exists; today's allocation of resources within and between the 'private' and 'public' sectors is in general the only possible one.

Galbraith's State, on the other hand, is the creation of objective reason – as opposed to the rationality of the market – and submits to reasoned argument by enlightened citizens. But as to how the State attained the independence to play the role assigned it, and as to how the role is played concretely, we are left in the dark.[10]

10. In his earlier work on 'countervailing power', Galbraith also assigns the State a certain mysterious independence. It should not surprise us that Keynes and his followers share a similar perspective. Keynes looked to the State 'not to do things which individuals are doing already, and to do

One reason that both the traditional and Galbraithian schools offer no concrete independent criteria to guide State policy is attributable to the lack of any coherent theory of the capitalist State.[11] As Buchanan (1960, p. 4) has put it, neither school has made 'explicit their assumptions concerning the form of the

_____

them a little better or a little worse; but to do those things which at present are not done at all' (quoted in Robbins, 1952, p. 99 of 1962 edn).

Walter Heller advances a closely related view. To paraphrase his position very roughly: the role of the economist in government is to rationally blend the service, stabilization and income-transfer 'functions' of government. We must note the assumption that these are truly 'functions' and that the State with the right advice can and will correct irrationalities and inequities.

11. John Due (1954) is a well-known student of public finance and the author of the leading basic textbook in the field. He is also a man who not only cannot separate science from ideology or fact from value, but also is not even aware of the difference.

In chapter 1 of his text, *Government Finance*, his purpose is a 'preliminary review of the reasons *why* the governments have undertaken various forms of economic activity' (p. 3, italics added). He thus poses a scientific question: e.g., why do military, education and highway expenditure make up the vast share of government spending? On page 6, this scientific perspective becomes less sharp. An explanation of the trend of increasing State activity 'must be based upon a consideration of the extent to which a free market society attains or fails to attain the goals of economic welfare which are accepted by society'. Note too that he *assumes* certain 'goals' which are 'accepted by society'.

But immediately a certain ambiguity creeps in: '*To the extent that* the undertaking of economic activity by government is based upon the desires of the community, it reflects dissatisfaction with the adequacy of the market economy in obtaining optimum welfare' (italics added). But he does not describe the conditions under which the government will *not* undertake economic activity based on the desires of the community.

Pages 7 to 13 are devoted to an analysis of the *reasons* for State economic activity. The 'reasons' are taken out of the pages of the books of *normative* economists! Thus science for Due consists of the following steps: first, hypothesize a competitive economy with welfare maximizing as 'society's goal' (as if the average person either knew or cared about the precepts or counsels of normative economics!); second, 'explain' State economic activity on the basis of departures from these idealized goals (e.g. externalities, public goods, internal economies of scales, monopoly, a 'fair' income distribution, high employment without inflation, etc.). That is, Due makes a very unsubtle shift from positive science to normative economics.

His choice of language is one clue. He frequently uses the expression 'the task of the government is to. . . '. This obscures his real meaning. If he stuck to the scientific question, he would write, 'the government *does* such polity'.[12] Wicksell caught the problem from almost the right perspective when he wrote that 'much of the discussion in fiscal theory proceeds on the implicit and unrecognized assumption that the society is ruled by a benevolent despot'. It is probably more accurate to say that one welfare theorist's benevolent despot is another's arbitrary dictator.

We conclude with the reminder that few modern orthodox economists concern themselves very much with the question of the real relationships between the private and public sectors. The public sector 'exists' on the basis of *a priori* reasoning, or it is assumed to exist in a vacuum. One exception to the rule is Buchanan, who appreciates that 'any approach to a complete or satisfactory treatment of the public economy must examine as a central feature the way in which collective decisions are made', but he himself does not attempt to reconstruct economics along these lines. It is clear from the above analysis, however, that the important questions revolve around the real functions of the State under monopoly capitalism. It is only by taking the step toward a reconstruction of the theory of the State and the State finances that we will have a basis for a complete critique of bourgeois economic science.

References

BARAN, P. (1960), 'Discussion', *Amer. econ. Rev., Pap. Proc.*, vol. 50, pp. 119–23.

BATOR, F. (1960), *The Question of Government Spending*, Harper & Row.

BAUMOL, W. (1964), 'External economies and second-order optimality conditions', *Amer. econ. Rev.*, vol. 54, pp. 358–72.

---

and such *because. . . .* '. If he were honest (or, to be fair, if he understood the difference between science and economic game playing) he would write, 'the government *should* do such and such because. . . '.

In chapter 2 he switches gears altogether, admitting the irrelevance of the criteria of normative economics. The government is no longer the embodied will of 'society', but rather the interpreter of this will. 'The task of determining community consensus about the desirability of the various degrees of attainment of the goals, and thus of the relative importance attached by society to the activities, rests upon the government.'

12. Even Buchanan, who among bourgeois economists is one of the most aware of the need for some solid sociological foundations for public finance theory, fails in these essays to go beyond a critique and to reconstruct the theory. When he attempts to do so in a book co-authored by Gordon Tullock, he cannot give up the traditional extreme utilitarian assumptions.

BAZELON, D. (1965), *The Paper Economy*, Random House.

BUCHANAN, J. B. (1960), *Fiscal Theory and Political Economy*, University of North Carolina Press.

COLM, G. (1948), 'Why public finance?', *Nat. Tax J.*, vol. 1, pp. 193–206.

DUE, J. (1954), *Government Finance*, Irwin.

GALBRAITH, J. K. (1958), *The Affluent Society*, Houghton Mifflin.

GRAAFF, J. de V. (1957), *Theoretical Welfare Economics*, Cambridge University Press.

LITTLE, I. M. D. (1967), *A Critique of Welfare Economics*, Clarendon Press.

MUSGRAVE, R. (1959), *The Theory of Public Finance*, McGraw-Hill.

PEACOCK, A. T., and WISEMAN, J. (1961), *The Growth of Public Expenditures in the United Kingdom*, Princeton University Press.

PIGOU, A. C. (1920), *The Economics of Welfare*, Macmillan, 4th edn, 1932.

'REVIEW OF THE MONTH' (1959), *Monthly Review*, vol. 10, pp. 337–44.

ROBBINS, L. (1952), 'The economic functions of the state in English classical political economy', in E. S. Phelps (ed.), *Private Wants and Public Needs*, Norton, 1962.

ROSTOW, W. W. (1960), 'The problem of achieving and maintaining a high rate of growth', *Amer. econ. Rev.*, *Pap. Proc.*, vol. 50, pp. 106–18.

SAMUELSON, P. A. (1956), 'Economic theory and wages', in D. M. Wright (ed.), *The Impact of the Union*, Kelley.

SAMUELSON, P. A., and SOLOW, R. (1960), 'Our menu of policy choices', *Amer. econ. Rev.*, *Pap. Proc.*, vol. 50, pp. 177–94.

TURVEY, R. (1963), 'On divergencies between social cost and private cost', *Economica*, vol. 30, pp. 309–13.

VON HAYEK, F. A. (1961), 'The non sequitur of the "dependence effect"', *South. econ. J.*, vol. 27, pp. 346–8.

WALLICH, H. C. (1961), 'Public versus private: could Galbraith be wrong?', *Harper's Mag.*, October.

16 Sumner M. Rosen

Keynes Without Gadflies

Sumner M. Rosen, 'Keynes without gadflies', in T. Roszak (ed.), *The Dissenting Academy*, Vintage, 1968, pp. 62–91.

Economists have never exactly been wildcats or outcasts, but neither have they ever been as domesticated as they are today. The number of economists has probably never been larger nor have they ever found their services as welcome – and as well paid – in so many institutions of society as is now the case.

This agreeable state of affairs holds true for the work of both academic and nonacademic economists. For if it was once true that university economists carried on a species of scholastic discourse which had little in common with the work of practical men of affairs in the United States Treasury, the Federal Reserve System or the import–export firms, this separation is no longer true. Beginning with the New Deal and more so still during the Second World War, economists in increasing numbers found themselves advising or working full time in federal agencies. The Employment Act of 1946 formalized the permanent importance of economic analysis in public affairs; since that time there has been a continuing interchange of academic and governmental duties on the part of large numbers of professional economists. Business firms and labor unions, as well as nonprofit agencies, have employed more and more professional economists, until at last the Kennedy years were the high-water mark in the reliance of government on academic economists. Today there are few men teaching economics who have not served, or will not serve, a stint in government, business or subsidized research on practical questions at home or abroad. The nature of economics and of the work of economists as it is treated in these pages applies, with all the strengths and weaknesses which that application implies, inside as well as out of the universities. Almost nowhere – except for such strongholds of conservative tradition as the University of Chicago – are there intellectual centers where a creative and reflective minority can serve as the conscience or gadfly to the profession as a whole. A justified inference from this analysis is that such centers are badly needed, but there are yet no signs of their being provided. Nor are they likely to be until more economists begin to state their own dissatisfactions with the state of the art they practice and to call for higher standards of relevance, independence and creativity.

One clue to the current state of American economics can be gained through a perusal of a volume issued in 1966 marking – celebrating, rather – the 'Twentieth anniversary of the Employment Act of 1946' (Joint Economic Committee, 89th Congress and Session, 23 February 1966). The anniversary took the form of a symposium under the sponsorship of the Joint Economic Committee. A distinguished list of speakers addressed a distinguished audience, which also heard messages from three living presidents, under whom that famous statute has been administered. Those who came were celebrating not an anniversary but a victory, the triumph of the 'new economics'. All who had served as chairmen of the Council of Economic Advisers, established in the law, took part as speakers or panelists. Among them was Walter Heller, Mr Kennedy's economic chief of staff, who deserves much of the credit for managing the widespread acceptance of Keynesian ideas which may mark the most significant permanent achievement of the Kennedy years. In his luncheon address, Mr Heller remarked:

In commenting on the so-called policy revolution of the past five years, I have sometimes said that the nation has simply pressed into public service the economics taught in its classrooms for twenty years and accepted as orthodox by 80 to 90 per cent of its economists.

Except for remarks of characteristic bite and dissent by Leon Keyserling (not, strictly speaking, an economist) there were virtually no quarrels with the substance of this comment by any speaker, despite the low growth rates and high unemployment of the Kennedy years. The event was a celebration of a revolution well fought and finally secured, a revolution in the thinking of a nation and in the willingness of its leaders to act in accord with the new doctrines.

The Employment Act is a monument both to the effectiveness of the change in thinking which Keynes initiated and to the deep and widely felt fear that the end of the Second World War might well bring back the conditions of the 1930s unless safeguards were adopted. Even so, the policy directives in the law were, in the words of Congressman George Outland, 'much emasculated'.

What had been conceived of as a full-employment bill, 'the most constructive single piece of legislation in the history of this nation' in the words of Congressman Wright Patman, underwent a long process of modification and compromise. The result, hardly digestible as a piece of prose, much less policy, reads:

Declaration of policy
The Congress hereby declares that it is the continuing policy and responsibility of the Federal Government to use all practicable means consistent with its needs and obligations and other essential considerations of national policy, with the assistance and cooperation of industry, agriculture, labor and State and local governments, to coordinate and utilize all its plans, functions and resources for the purpose of creating and maintaining, in a manner calculated to foster and promote free competitive enterprise and the general welfare, conditions under which there will be afforded useful employment opportunities, including self-employment, for those able, willing and seeking to work, and to promote maximum employment, production and purchasing power (Public Law 304, 79th Congress).

What, one is tempted to ask, was the cheering about?

Economists have spent the past thirty years bringing to fruition what we might call, to use Lawrence Klein's phrase, the 'Keynesian Revolution'. The process has three important aspects. One is that the revolution turned out to be substantially less extensive than its enthusiasts claim. Unemployment had not been solved; steady growth in response to the right fiscal and monetary stimuli had not been achieved; inflation has remained a periodic threat. A second is that the revolution preempted nearly all the professional energies available and dominated the development of economic studies – and of economists – throughout most of this period. A third aspect is that its apparent triumph, however important – and it *is* important – has tended to cultivate among economists and their public a complacency about the adequacy of our arsenal of policies for dealing with economic problems. But urgent problems exist about which Keynes and Keynesianism have little to tell us. The result is a disturbing vacuum.

More perhaps than that of any other of the great economists, Keynes's work had direct and important meaning for policy and policymakers. This, more than the depth or originality of his analysis, explains the continuing degree of controversy about it. Keynes argued forcefully that the successful preservation of capitalism requires that the State intervene in the economy. The major purpose of this intervention is to secure or maintain a level of activity adequate to assure a high level of employment. Since this will not happen automatically, the State must act deliberately to make it happen.

Most economists accepted Keynes's conclusions quickly. This in itself was a new phenomenon in a field where authority has always yielded only slowly to new ideas. One reason was the deep and almost complete degree of frustration which economists had experienced in attempting to deal with the depression of the 1930s. It was an unprecedented catastrophe, wholly inconsistent, in its depth and duration, with anything in the accepted arsenal of ideas. Another reason was the essential moderation of Keynes's viewpoint. Keynes was a capitalist and his theory was designed to restore and preserve the vigor of capitalism. He cherished its major institutions and mechanisms: prices, profits, consumer choice, free markets. He prescribed intervention as the necessary price to pay for this preservation, and economists – never a radical group – were saved the necessity of coming to grips with more radical solutions. A final reason for the success of Keynesianism was its novelty and freshness, after many decades of aridity and intellectual decay. Economists responded eagerly and gratefully to this offer of rescue, rejuvenation and restoration to the contemporary world and its issues. The most distinguished of today's economists, Paul A. Samuelson, has described his response and that of his contemporaries as like 'the unexpected virulence of a disease first attacking and then decimating an isolated tribe of South Sea Islanders'. Keynes was the prophet come to save his people from that worst of afflictions: irrelevance. And he provided not a nostrum or a simple set of slogans, but an intellectual system worthy of study, ready to challenge the old system on its own ground.

With zeal, the disciples set out to complete Keynes's work. This undertaking had three aspects. The first was to bring order out of the suggestive, fragmentary and unfinished character of much of the *General Theory*. Men like Hicks, Harrod, Meade and Kaldor in England undertook this work, soon joined by many Americans, preeminently Alvin Hansen, Seymour Harris and their colleagues and students. In virtually any issue of any of the important economic journals, as well as in many books on economics published each year, this work still goes on. These men and others have devoted much of their lives to the elaboration, completion and, in some cases, the correction of the original Keynesian insights. Other things have been built on to the essentially short-run Keynesian analysis, one of the most important being the integration of the original short-run analysis of the full-employment problem with an analysis of the balance between investment and the growth of the labor force required to assure full employment over long periods of time. This work, plus the elaboration of the key elements of the Keynesian analysis – consumption, savings, investment, interest, money, employment – and their interaction, has been the mainstream of economic analysis throughout most of the thirty years since the *General Theory* appeared. The work has been well done and has made us all Keynesians.

The second task was to bring the message to a wider public. This task fell, as it happened, primarily to one man. In this way, the first edition of Samuelson's *Economics: An Introductory Analysis* (1948) created a stir comparable to that of the *General Theory*. It represented as drastic and refreshing a departure from the textbooks of the previous generations as did the work of Keynes, the exposition of whose work forms its heart. It was in addition brash, irreverent, lively and contemporary. It has now gone through seven editions, sold over two million copies in the United States, plus many more in translation abroad and continues to dominate the textbook market in introductory courses in economics. Virtually every college graduate who has taken a course in economics in the past twenty years has come under the influence of this book and its imitators.

Among the ideas which this book articulated were that a rate of inflation of 5 per cent a year 'need not cause too great concern', that monetary measures are relatively ineffective in influencing the level of total spending and that 'a positive fiscal policy' is both possible and necessary to avoid cyclical swings and to help secure 'a progressive, high-employment economy free from excessive inflation or deflation'. Taxes are evaluated, not by their alleged effects on incentives to work, but by their progressiveness, including their redistributive effects, and the 'burden' of the public debt is shown to lie more in its effects on income distribution than in any deleterious result of simply continuing to grow; in fact, Samuelson argues that a growing national debt, if required to maintain steady high employment, is perfectly acceptable and very convenient for the monetary managers. Virtually nothing is said in defense of profits and the traditional 'incentives' of a free-enterprise economy.

If one recalls the orthodox ideas on which previous generations had been raised, this is a catalogue of heresies. Their acceptance has by no means been instantaneous or universal. Successive editions have hedged on some of the more unqualified of these statements, and more importantly, later editions (like the third edition of 1955) introduced the concept of a 'neo-classical synthesis', bringing together the Keynesian and classical systems of analysis. Keynes and the classics were merged, a mainstream of thought mapped and continuity achieved. In the process, a good deal of the boldness, originality and activism of the early Keynesians has been modified or abandoned altogether.

There remained a third task: to bring Keynesian ideas to the center of effective policy making. The early impact of these ideas outside of the academy was not great. This was largely because of their novelty and because the urgency of the problems out of which they had arisen began to abate and, before long, to disappear completely. It was difficult at first even to imagine what might be involved in the deliberate use of State instruments to influence the overall behavior of the economy. The techniques needed to measure and define the need were lacking and had to be constructed. The skepticism, conservatism and ignorance of important men would not yield readily to the complex and radical proposals of an intellectual and a foreigner to boot. All this would take time. Even as these ideas were beginning to make their impact, however, the economy began to respond to the preparations for war and support of the allies. A pragmatic proof of the effects of government expenditures on the level of economic activity furnished the first demonstration that Keynes was right. As American entry into the Second World War grew near, the burden of depressed conditions began to be lifted. Within a few years, the entire picture had been transformed; full and overfull employment came, maximum production was the major goal, economic techniques were required not for stimulus but mainly to suppress inflationary pressures and ration scarce commodities and resources.

In 1941, the final report of the Temporary National Economic Committee was submitted. This was a different kind of intellectual investment, stemming from earlier traditional distrust of monopolies and of 'bigness'. TNEC was virtually its last serious effort. A major impact of the depression was to revitalize this tradition and to bring new attention to the structural features of modern American capitalism. From the time of Veblen, Ripley and Commons, some economists had directed their attention to the key institutions which emerged in the late nineteenth century as dominating elements in economic life, primarily the investment banks and the large industrial corporations. The depression was widely interpreted as a failure of the business system. It became increasingly widespread doctrine that something fundamental had gone awry with the workings of that system, that a serious reconstruction of its structural elements was required.

TNEC conducted the only serious and broad-scale study of the structure of the economy and its defects that has ever been made. A distinguished committee, composed of senators, congressmen and laymen, TNEC was charged by President Roosevelt to make a searching analysis of the economy. Many economists wrote monographs for TNEC, some of them still the best studies of their kind. Others, like Arthur R. Burns, were stimulated to research and writing. Responding to the insights of Piero Sraffa, Edward Chamberlin and Joan Robinson broke new ground in the analysis of more realistic models of competitive behavior than those which assumed no imperfections, selling costs or irrationalities on the part of buyers. These books were major efforts to integrate a more realistic view of market behavior with conventional economic theory. But they were not successful in focusing economic thought in any serious study of structural problems and their consequences. Chamberlin and Robinson did not really deal with these questions, while Burns, Corwin, Edwards and others who wrote were not ready to extend this analysis, or to undertake the proselytizing effort needed to give their work visibility and momentum. As for TNEC, it was a victim of changing times and concerns. By 1941, when the final report was ready, Americans had lost interest. Wholly new problems had arisen, the old ones were rapidly vanishing and the only crusade to follow was that against the Axis powers. The one significant piece of legislation which TNEC produced was the 1950 amendment to the Clayton Act, closing a thirty-six-year-old loophole. This 'Celler-Kefauver' amendment forbids mergers which reduce competition consummated by the direct acquisition of assets; the original law was confined to the acquisition of stock. This law has been used effectively in some important cases, but it has operated less to undo past acts of merger than to prevent proposed or prospective mergers. Moreover, it came very late in the day; the concentrated structure of American industry was the dominant fact when TNEC began its inquiry and remains the dominant fact today. Credit for passage of the Celler-Kefauver amendment belongs to the persistence and skill of a handful of crusading public servants and economists who gathered around the Kefauver antimonopoly subcommittee and worked closely with it from positions in the Federal Trade Commission and the Antitrust Division of the Department of Justice. They were few and so were their victories. Since Kefauver's death, the small band has dwindled even further; we are unlikely to see any sequel to the investigation of the drug industry which the subcommittee conducted in 1959–60. But even here the legislative results focused primarily on industrial *practices*; no alterations in the *structure* of the industry and the concentration of market power growing out of that structure were seriously proposed.

TNEC left a scholarly legacy, but little else. The inquiries which it began have not been continued; more important, the assumption underlying the work of the Commission – that the structure of industry required a searching look and whatever alterations that look made necessary – has been abandoned by economists, almost without exception. That is one reason why, when latterday radicals raised the 'power structure' to the status of a keynote in the litany of the movements for racial justice and peace, the economists could offer no guidance or insight to give the slogan flesh and to direct the attention of political activists to the central targets for any meaningful reform of the economic system. Antitrust is the closest we come in the United States to an ideology of economic power, but it has little meaning or relevance to those who suffer most from the use and abuse of concentrated economic power in the hands of large corporations, whether as consumers, workers or citizens.

One of the few groups of economists whose work still derives from a concern with important issues of public policy are those who specialize in employment and labor-market matters. Theirs is a somewhat different tradition, more engaged and problem-oriented in its very origins. The study of labor problems had its serious beginnings with Professor Frank Commons and his associates at the University of Wisconsin. It was rooted in Commons's commitment to the close study of economic institutions as the key to understanding. It grew during periods of struggle, often intense and dramatic, between employers and unions seeking recognition, status and effectiveness. In the hands of Commons and his successors, the study of labor economics has remained responsive to the realities of labor–management relations. These scholars have followed closely and on the whole accurately the phases which characterize the evolution of the labor movement and the present pattern of industrial relations. Some have sought to write more generalized studies,[1] but these efforts have remained reasonably close to the reality they sought to describe. In this they follow the example of such earlier writers as Selig Perlman, Robert Hoxie and Frank Tannenbaum.

These studies avoid both the aridity and the unreality of the theoretical economists, and the sweeping inferences of many Continental writers for whom labor problems have traditionally offered a basis for speculation on the larger issues of class and ideology. They have an American pragmatism at their root. But they also reflect another tradition which has grown stronger in the past two decades. This is the view that speculation on large

1. Recent examples include Dunlop (1959), Kerr, Dunlop, Harbison and Myers (1960) and Lester (1958).

questions is not simply dangerous but unseemly as well. The view that a scholar may in good conscience grind a political or ideological ax is anathema to most American intellectuals. It may be overstating the case to argue that we all serve what Louis Hartz calls the 'liberal tradition', but the work of most scholars who study labor–management relations is influenced by certain unstated premises which are consistent with Hartz's brilliantly stated thesis. These might be articulated this way:

1. Conflict is never about basic principles and is, therefore, never irreconcilable.

2. Pragmatic compromise without total dedication to an ideological program is characteristically American; therefore,

3. Those institutions which have achieved permanence and success in the United States have done so because they understood and adapted to these conditions. The American labor movement, and the system of settling industrial conflict which it has helped to create, exemplify these characteristics; in the American setting, they are positive virtues.

It is no accident that Daniel Bell, who has announced 'the end of ideology', has worked for many years in the industrial-relations area and served as labor editor of *Fortune* magazine. Seymour Martin Lipset, a central molder of the anti-ideology school, has a similar background; his study of the International Typographical Union (Lipset, Trow and Coleman, 1956) served as a laboratory for the development of many of the ideas which flow from the writings of these and other men. For them, values – democracy, participation, autonomy, choice – must be defined in terms of the institutional social structure in which men find themselves. Relativism is the keynote; the scholar's job is to explicate the structures in order to clarify their effects on the people who inhabit them. This is important work and these men have done it well. But it is devoid of normative standards. It summons the scholar to no issue. He observes, comments, reflects, but he does not take part or take sides. He remains strictly outside politics. I do not mean party or electoral politics, at which many scholars play with enthusiasm. I mean *issue* politics, in which deep vested interests collide or in which serious questions of social justice are at stake.

Labor economists have helped to deal with important policy questions. When high levels of unemployment began to appear and to persist in the face of high levels of economic activity, from 1956 onward, serious efforts were made to clarify the causes. The result was the celebrated 'structural-aggregate' controversy. One school led by economists close to the White House, whose spokesman was Walter Heller, argued that unemployment required more Keynesian treatment in the form of measures to stimulate business investment and raise the level of consumer spending. The structuralists, a minority though an able one, argued that the labor market has imperfections so deeply rooted as to require direct and special treatment without which no amount of aggregate demand stimulus can be expected to reduce unemployment sufficiently or quickly enough. The depreciation and tax-credit provisions of the Kennedy administration, and the 1964 tax cut, represent a policy victory for the majority. Such legislative measures as the Area Redevelopment Act of 1961, the Manpower Development and Training Act of 1962, the Appalachia and Regional Development Act of 1965 and the Economic Opportunity Act of 1964 were structuralist measures, though only the first reflects any serious prior work by economists.

Keynesian remedies are consistent with a wide range of political and ideological positions; the same is true of structural ones. It is a mistake to assume, as many conservatives do, that Keynesians inevitably advocate larger public deficits, higher levels of public spending and social welfare measures. The stereotype no longer fits, if it ever did. This is in part sophistication, in part a retreat on the part of the Keynesians from the identification with these measures which was attributed to them during the depression, when unemployment was the problem and stagnation a specter which seemed to face a mature American economy. The most deliberate application of Keynesian measures to the economy, which occurred in the 1962–6 period, involved no significant new measures of public spending. The only really important area of nonmilitary public spending which has been greatly expanded since the Second World War has been highway construction, hardly a piece of social innovation. Instead economic stimulation has taken the form of tax cuts, stimuli to business investment and manipulation of interest rates. What Robert Lekachman has recently called 'commercial Keynesianism' has, like the tamed and domesticated versions of Freud which dominate psycho-analysis, come to mean all that we do now mean by Keynesian remedies. Perhaps the most ironic aspect of this trend has been the Heller proposal to dispose of prospective surpluses in federal revenues by sharing them with State governments. This proposal, made in the name of reinvigorating the States, would strengthen some of the most socially regressive tendencies in American political life. In effect, it is an abdication of any federal responsibility for creating and legitimatizing new areas of public expenditure. Even economists of the center, like John Kenneth Galbraith, reject these proposals and their implications. Yet Heller and his colleagues are the men who presided over and managed so well the conversion of Keynesian doctrine into one which almost every segment of opinion, including many of the most important business groups, finds acceptable, desirable, even indispensable.

As for the structural approach, it too fits a variety of political philosophies. The ranking Republican member of the Joint Economic Committee, Congressman Thomas B. Curtis of Missouri, has long argued that because structural imperfections explain much of our unemployment problem, we need no expansion of federal spending to solve it. Monetary and banking men, particularly those close to the Federal Reserve System, argue structural theories in order to justify their anti-inflationary bias against expansionist measures. Aggregative proponents accuse the structuralists of strengthening the case against increasing the level of demand. But those who see structural problems as important also include people who seek much higher levels of activity and expenditure in raising literacy, improving the mobility of workers, strengthening the effectiveness of the United States Employment Service, mounting effective campaigns against racial discrimination in employment, vastly improving the quality of academic and vocational education, helping to bring more economic activity into 'depressed areas', etc. It is unfortunately true that, outside of the spokesmen for the AFL–CIO (American Federation of Labor, Congress of Industrial Organization) and a handful of others, few of these people are professional economists. But those few deserve recognition.

When one reviews the list of problems just mentioned, one is struck by the extent to which they were brought to public attention not by economists but by journalists, politicians and sociologists, among others. The attack on depressed areas was largely organized and directed by a coalition led by the Textile Workers Union, whose leadership was alarmed by the effect on their traditional base in New England of the large-scale migration of the industry in the 1940s and 1950s. Poverty came to the fore as a result of the famous book *The Other America* (1962), by Michael Harrington – socialist and journalist – and public discussion was dominated thereafter by such writers as Dwight Macdonald, Mollie Orshansky of the Social Security Administration, Oscar Lewis, Paul Jacobs and others. Economists have contributed virtually nothing of importance to the formation of public opinion or public policy on poverty. When the profession finally got around to discussing it at their annual meeting in 1965, little was said to indicate any urgency or to bring any special insight to bear. Galbraith's famous book *The Affluent Society* (1958), perhaps the most influential since Keynes, treats poverty as the unfinished business of a rich society, requiring only attention and some easily prescribed remedies, especially the education of the children of the poor. The tone is complacent, the treatment routine. Four years later, Harrington's book appeared and the entire tone of the discussion changed, though the facts were the same.

The structural school deserve credit for their concern with these problems, but they did little to develop the implications of this concern in ways which would effectively change public opinion, alter political priorities or even pose an effective intellectual challenge to their professional colleagues. The best study of the problem of unemployment which has yet appeared (Gilpatrick, 1966) makes a scholarly and persuasive case that structural unemployment is a fundamental fact and that its victims are clearly identifiable groups in the society, including farm workers, unskilled laborers, young people, old workers, women and particularly Negroes. Where these categories overlap, serious and persistent unemployment exists regardless of the level of overall demand. But every single one of these groups has found its principal spokesmen coming almost entirely from outside the ranks of the professional economists (see Becker, 1957). The development of public policy and – even more important – the discussion and critique of those policies which have been adopted in recent years in these problem areas have not benefited perceptibly from the attention of the economists. Others have borne the burden in an era of unprecedented change in economic life. In the one case where economists have been appealed to – the case of automation – they have tended to deprecate the issue without furnishing the kind of hard evidence which would make this attitude credible, particularly to working men and women. It is one thing – and worth doing – to point out that the real world is complicated; it is another to seem to argue, as many economists do, that automation is so much like previous technological factors that it is not likely to alter long-term trends in growth or employment. Perhaps this is so, but the evidence is far from persuasive. Arguments which try to mollify the fears which automation arouses are, to say the least, premature.

Most of the other major issues of our time, some of them newly emerging and others familiar from the past, have not attracted the attention of many economists. The crises which this society and others are likely to face in future decades involve such forces as the impact of science, the nature and dominance of media of information, population pressures, urbanization and – perhaps most important of all – the long-term relationship between 'haves' and 'have-nots', both within the society and in the world at large. On most of these, the economists have little to say, or when they speak, nothing of real significance or intellectual distinction.

These issues do not here require elaborate description. Some are squarely within the presumed competence of the economist; others are more peripheral. In the first group fall those questions which directly affect economic welfare and relationships. A brief listing will indicate how these have fared at the hands of the professionals.

Economic development

Problems of the 'emerging nations' and their economic future have generated a large volume of economic studies and a substantial group of professional economists taking this as their major concern. This is one of the larger groups in the National Science Foundation listing, but numbers less than one thousand – 7 per cent of the total. After some twenty or more years of intensive work, some of it excellent, we still lack a theoretical framework comparable to those which exist in such well-trod areas as monetary theory, price theory, international trade or aggregative economics. In fact, the key components of such a theory have yet to be agreed upon; some writers stress capital accumulation and the mobilization of savings, others the creation of entrepreneurial elites, still others the central role of planning. What passes in the United States as the leading candidate for an overall framework is Walt W. Rostow's *Stages of Economic Growth* (1961), a mélange of historical and statistical generalizations of doubtful validity and of little use to serious students or practitioners dealing with hard questions. The most important theoretical contributions have been the work of men outside the United States or outside the central tradition, like Paul Baran, Gunnar Myrdal and Raul Prebisch. What the work of these men has in common, something almost wholly lacking in the bulk of serious American work, is the central role which they assign to the industrialized nations in determining the future of the underdeveloped majority of nations. Whether from Baran's Marxist perspective, Myrdal's melancholy pessimism or Prebisch's salty and direct challenge from his position as a leading Latin American economist and spokesman, these writers assign a major share of historical responsibility for the sharp and perilous division of the world's economic units to the dominance of the Western European powers and the United States. They argue, correctly and persuasively in this writer's view, that the handful of rich countries, the United States foremost among them, will by their actions determine the possibility of ending that division short of a cataclysmic upheaval. This is putting the major responsibility where it belongs.

Most American writers, by contrast, tend to stress the importance of actions required in the developing economy, from political reform to the creation of effective capital markets. Few deal seriously with the larger issues of altering the domestic balance of power in those areas where it is concentrated in the hands of landholding or commercial oligarchies, and almost all have either ignored or denied the central role of the forces on which this handful of outsiders have focused. One result has been that American public opinion has hardly been touched with any deepening of its sense of responsibility for the future of the underdeveloped world, and American policy has scarcely altered from the improvised beginnings of the early days of foreign aid.

Wealth and income

Except for Robert J. Lampman's pioneering studies (1960; 1962), economists have scarcely concerned themselves with the question of wealth and its ownership, particularly from any broad perspective related to considerations of social welfare. Studies of income distribution have been more frequent, but tend to concentrate on one of two questions, that of 'relative shares' – i.e. the share of income going to 'labor', 'ownership', 'agriculture', etc. – or that of the share of income going to the top 1 to 5 per cent of income receivers. The prevailing view tends to echo that of Simon Kuznets (1950), who has studied the latter question most carefully, and is expressed by Galbraith (1958, p. 85):

there has been a modest reduction in the proportion of disposable income going to those in the very highest income brackets and a very large increase in the proportion accruing to people in the middle and lower brackets.

This widely celebrated 'income revolution' of the period since the First World War has been effectively challenged and demolished, not by economists but by a historian (Kolko, 1962) and a statistician of the Bureau of the Census (Miller, 1964). These works have not received a fraction of the attention paid to less important but less disturbing works.

Similarly, the first effective treatment of the income tax system from the point of view of its equity to different population groups, classes and categories of income was by Philip M. Stern in his *Great Treasury Raid* (1964). A fairly rich and lively vein of economic discussion of tax policy has generally neglected welfare and equity concerns in favor of concentration on the 'disincentive' effects of sharply progressive rates, the relationship of the rate structure of stabilization policies and the effects of taxes on the efficient allocation of resources. Economists generally support the principles of progressiveness and of equal treatment, but except for such notorious loopholes as the depletion allowance, have not scrutinized the prevailing tax system from the point of view of this criterion with anything like the depth or rigor required.

If we turn to such questions as the economic effects – costs, benefits and policy requirements – in areas such as resource conservation, urban growth, the role of advertising and of mass media in affecting economic attitudes as well as economic behavior, and the effect of the dramatic expansion of research and development on economic growth, economists have little to teach us so far. On the question of population growth and its meaning, the vein is somewhat richer, but here too the major work is done by demographers.

Arms and the economy

We can conclude this survey with the most important abdication of any by the economists. This is a failure which applies across the board; the theoreticians, the institutionalists and the aggregative economists alike have virtually ignored the most important single force in the American economy of the past twenty-five years, war and preparation for war.

Economists have sometimes been willing to discuss the question of the economy's ability to deal with the consequences of important cutbacks in military spending, but the discussion has acquired no structure or continuity, engendered no schools or positions to be debated. The level of attention has been episodic and the intensity of involvement tepid at best. Those economists who have taken the trouble to deal with the question have, in most instances, been content to write an article for the press or to grant an interview. These normally follow a standard pattern: the economy is sound, arms spending is a small proportion of the gross national product, appropriate stabilizing measures are available to meet any likely degree of arms reduction. Most of these writers treat arms spending as an unwelcome burden, the ending of which would free resources for constructive purposes. A few scholars have gone deeper, primarily in studying regional impacts and assessing the structural problems which arms reduction would impose. Only a handful have sought seriously to deal with the major issues which disarmament would raise.[2] Most of this discussion has taken place outside of the mainstream of economics and only a handful of professional economists have been involved. The discussion has had virtually no impact. The Joint Economic Committee has never held hearings on the question and the official agencies of the United States government have issued reports only reluctantly and in response to pressures emanating from the peace movement and international agencies. This is astonishing on its face. Despite disclaimers and apologetics, the essence of the situation is as Robert Heilbroner (1960, p. 133) describes it:

a central aspect of our growth experience of the past two decades is one which few spokesmen for the future candidly discuss. This is the fact that our great boom did not begin until the onset of the Second World War and that its continuance since then has consistently been tied to a military rather than to a purely civilian economic demand.

Unlike economists, business firms and the periodicals which serve them – *Fortune*, *Business Week*, the *Wall Street Journal* – pay assiduous attention to defense spending. Its vital role in economic life is acknowledged by high government officials, when they are asked, though they do singularly little on their own initiative to give this sector the attention it deserves. The chairman of the Council of Economic Advisers, Gardner Ackley, told a *Wall Street Journal* reporter on 19 October 1966, that 'almost to the hour' one could date the rapid rise in GNP to the press conference on 28 June 1965, when President Johnson announced a doubling of draft calls and the imminent despatch of 50,000 American soldiers to Vietnam. He went on to say: 'If the war hadn't speeded up last year, I expect we would have been looking around for further measures to stimulate the economy.' But a perusal of the report of the cabinet-level committee which Mr Ackley chaired in 1964–5 on the need for government planning to cope with arms reductions was characterized by a high degree of confidence, bordering on complacency.[3]

2. An example of the first category is Harris (1959, pp. 20 ff.). The second category includes articles such as Peterson and Tiebout (1964). The major contribution to the third category is Benoit and Boulding (1963).

3. *Report of the Committee on the Economic Impact of Defense and Disarmament.* See the discussion of this report in Rosen (1965).

This neglect would seem to fly in the face of facts of enormous magnitude and to denote almost complete lack of responsibility. But the scholars and teachers are not consciously evading or avoiding a duty which they know in their hearts must be faced. Rather, they are conforming to a point of view about the economy and about their own role and responsibility which they find both bearable and honorable. It is part of a more general view of scholarship which effectively molds all but a handful of men, and casts that handful into the role of peripheral figures, cranks or monomaniacs. This is at root an ahistorical, a technical or mechanical, a nonpolitical view of what the economy is and how it works. It is seen as a system with stable structural characteristics, operating within parameters which will not change. The major elements in it – consumers, banks, business firms, labor unions, farmers, government agencies – are treated as stable subsystems, to be studied so that they can be more effectively managed and their strengths and attitudes more accurately predicted. Virtually all debates among economists about economic policy are disagreements about the meaning of this kind of analysis. Most of the participants, however, agree that, given accurate studies and predictions, the policy tools available to government are more than adequate, in strength and sophistication to deal with any problems that may rise.

This approach totally neglects what seems to one observer to be the major role of arms spending in shaping the economy and the society throughout the past twenty-five years. These effects include the role of arms spending in the degree of industrial concentration, its effects on the supply and use of scientific and engineering talent, its effects on the location of economic activity – e.g. in the growth of California, with all that implies about the pattern of our national politics – its shaping of patterns of educational investment and activity, its stimulation of a close partnership between the major contractors and the Department of Defense – the well-known but little understood 'military-industrial complex' and, perhaps the most important to intellectuals, its success in blunting the interest of economics in probing the roots and basic structural characteristics of our economic system. Nothing succeeds like success and the economy has been successful enough to suggest that basic questions are no longer as relevant as they seemed to be in the postdepression years. It has been a comforting and comfortable time.

The arms economy has been the major Keynesian instrument of our times. But its use has been cloaked as 'national interest', its effects have been largely unexamined, its international consequences largely deleterious and destabilizing, its importance making for uncritical acceptance and dependence by large segments of the society, its long-run effects hardly glanced at. The arms economy has done much more than distort the use of scarce creative scientific and engineering talent, as Seymour Melman (1965) and others have correctly charged. It has forced us to neglect a whole range of urgent social priorities, the consequences of which threaten the fabric of our society. A backlog of needs for schools, housing, urban facilities, clean air and water, transportation, hospitals and a long list of other essentials cry out for attention and fail to get it. In 1966 it was necessary once more for the President to say 'wait' to these and other claims long overdue, with Vietnam as the excuse. The arms economy is the major obstacle to any meaningful use of public funds for these needs and no other funds can begin to do the job. This is the central fact; from it stem important consequences.

One is that those sectors of society whose rights, dignity and opportunity are blocked or stunted by these social defects have a direct and vital stake in the future of the arms economy. While it preempts national energies and federal funds, their claims will not be met. Another is that those who claim to see deeper and to know more – the economists – have failed the most important test: that of relevance to major issues. A third is that our international position, dependent in the long run on our contribution to the eradication of backwardness and social injustice, cannot fundamentally improve while our international policies are shaped and dominated by our military position. Nowhere in the world has the United States or the industrial nations as a whole altered the balance of forces between growth and stagnation, poverty and and hope, except where we have literally lifted a military ally with massive infusions of economic support, as in Taiwan and South Korea. Economists who correctly call for far larger American contributions to the cause of economic growth and development have not yet learned that their call must be accompanied by a far deeper concern with our military preoccupations and priorities. There are choices to be made and economists are specialists in analysing choices. But they have failed to perceive this one, let alone deal with it.

Long ago, economists opted for a separation of their studies from fundamentals. In so doing they adopted a prevailing American view that the fundamentals are not in question. The older fashion of joining economic and political concerns into political economy passed from the scene. Economists found new roles, some of them exciting and useful, but there were no new departures to be made. Even the major intellectual figures of the recent past – Schumpeter, Keynes, Kuznets, Hansen, Commons, Mitchell – did not cultivate or stimulate a fresh look at fundamentals,[4] and their students and disciples have seldom strayed from well-worn paths of inquiry. The major innovations of recent years have been in quantitative methods, highly useful for problem-oriented research and for practical use. Here men like Leontief and Samuelson have led the way toward what may be called scientism.

The long-cherished wish of the economists to function on a level of precision and complexity comparable to that of the chemists, physicists and biologists now seems to have been achieved in the hands of these men. But the physicists and the others deal with fundamental questions at the heart of their field of knowledge; the mathematical economists and econometricians, by contrast, function at two other extremes – that of systematic abstraction in the one case and of data manipulation in the other.

Economists have historically worked on a foundation consisting of the central issues of their era and the central values of the writer. Adam Smith valued liberty, Ricardo productivity and progress, Marx the elimination of exploitation, Keynes the achievement of full employment. These provided the normative tests by which they judged the economic systems about which they wrote (or dreamed), and on them they built their recommended solutions. Even when writing abstractly, economists imply, presuppose, a system and a set of values by which they judge and invite judge-

4. 'No doubt there were differences in the ideologies of Alvin Hansen and Henry Simons. I doubt that they would impress a Marxist or Buddhist' (Dewey, 1960, p. 7).

ment. The economic ideologies derive from these roots.

The stress on scientism is itself a kind of ideology; it suggests the central values of the economic tradition in the West – free markets, efficiency, growth – are sufficiently valid for our time to require no further serious scrutiny. Rather, they are the accepted base on which to build more effective techniques for achieving them.

There are, of course, areas of inquiry where quantitative methods are necessary and appropriate; these tend to be those areas where the fundamentals are well established and where quantity has always been the essence of the question. Examples include monetary theory and international trade.

In these areas, Keynes's additions have been assimilated, but in a 'revisionist' adjustment to accommodate the American institutional structure and distribution of power. We have had enormous increases in the quantity and quality of economic information and much of this has involved the invention of new kinds of economic measuring devices. And as noted earlier, the students of industrial relations – many of whom are only formally economists – have been diligent in studying and analysing conflict, though they have been singularly unwilling to apply their rich insight to the field of international relations, where it might save us all.

One is left with the disappointing, indeed depressing, conclusion that economists have largely failed to meet their obligations to the society of which they are a part. Instead they have found a place – or places – in that society at a price, the sacrifice of independence and of dedication to relevance.

Long ago and in other places, this was not true. 'Rightly or wrongly, economists have always dealt with policy. From Adam Smith to J. M. Keynes, each of the masters has addressed himself to the issues of his time' (Wilcox, 1960, p. 28). A series of forces have combined over the past twenty-five years to change this by concealing from view the existence of major issues which require attention. It is a sobering but inescapable conclusion that until this sense of crisis returns, the economists will not respond to the challenges of our society and our world. The tragic possibility is that when this happens there may not be time to think, and without thought, action cannot save us.

References

BECKER, G. S. (1957), *The Economics of Discrimination*, University of Chicago Press.

BENOIT, E., and BOULDING, K. E. (eds.) (1963), *Disarmament and the Economy*, Harper & Row.

DEWEY, D. J. (1960), 'Changing standards of economic performance', *Amer. econ. Rev., Pap. Proc.*, vol. 50, pp. 1–12.

DUNLOP, J. T. (1959), *Industrial Relations Systems*, Holt, Rinehart & Winston.

GALBRAITH, J. K. (1958), *The Affluent Society*, Houghton Mifflin.

GILPATRICK, E. G. (1966), *Structural Unemployment and Aggregate Demand*, Johns Hopkins Press.

HARRIS, S. (1959), 'Can we prosper without arms?', *New York Times Mag.*, 8 November.

HEILBRONER, R. (1960), *The Future as History*, Harper & Row.

KERR, C., DUNLOP, J. T., HARBISON, F., and MYERS, C. A. (1960), *Industrialism and Industrial Man*, Harvard University Press.

KOLKO, G. (1962), *Wealth and Power in America*, Praeger.

KUZNETS, S. (1950), *Shares of Upper Income Groups in Income and Saving*, National Bureau of Economic Research.

LAMPMAN, R. J. (1960), *Changes in the Share of Wealth Held by Top Wealth-Holders, 1922–1956*, National Bureau of Economic Research.

LAMPMAN, R. J. (1962), *The Share of Top Wealth-Holders in National Wealth*, Princeton University Press.

LESTER, R. A. (1958), *As Unions Mature*, Princeton University Press.

LIPSET, S. M., TROW, M., and COLEMAN, J. (1956), *Union Democracy*, Princeton University Press.

MELMAN, S. (1965), *Our Depleted Society*, Holt, Rinehart & Winston.

MILLER, H. (1964), *Rich Man, Poor Man*, Thomas Y. Crowell Co.

PETERSON, R. S., and TIEBOUT, C. M. (1964), 'Measuring the impact of regional defense-space expenditures', *Rev. Econ. Stat.*, vol. 47, pp. 421–8.

ROSEN, S. M. (1965), 'The new orthodoxy on disarmament economics' *Correspondent*, pp. 61–9.

WILCOX, C. (1960), 'From economic theory to public policy', *Amer. econ. Rev., Pap. Proc.*, vol. 50, pp. 27–35.

17 M. Kalecki

Political Aspects of Full Employment

M. Kalecki, 'Political aspects of full employment', *Political Quarterly*, vol. 14, 1943, pp. 322–31.

A solid majority of economists is now of the opinion that, even in a capitalist system, full employment may be secured by a government spending programme, provided there is in existence adequate plant to employ all existing labour power and provided adequate supplies of necessary foreign raw materials may be obtained in exchange for exports.

If the government undertakes public investment (e.g., builds schools, hospitals and highways) or subsidizes mass consumption (by family allowances, reduction of indirect taxation, or subsidies to keep down the prices of necessities), if, moreover, this expenditure is financed by borrowing and not by taxation (which could affect adversely private investment and consumption), the effective demand for goods and services may be increased up to a point where full employment is achieved. Such government expenditure increases employment, be it noted, not only directly but indirectly as well, since the higher incomes caused by it result in a secondary increase in demand for consumption and investment goods.

It may be asked where the public will get the money to lend to the government if they do not curtail their investment and consumption. To understand this process it is best, I think, to imagine for a moment that the government pays its suppliers in government securities. The suppliers will, in general, not retain these securities but put them into circulation while buying other goods and services, and so on until finally these securities will reach persons or firms which retain them as interest-yielding assets. In any period of time the total increase in government securities in the possession (transitory or final) of persons and firms will be equal to the goods and services sold to the government. Thus what the economy lends to the government are goods and services whose production is 'financed' by government securities. In reality the government pays for the services not in securities but in cash, but it simultaneously issues securities and so drains the cash off; and this is equivalent to the imaginary process described above.

What happens, however, if the public is unwilling to absorb all the increase in government securities? It will offer them finally to banks to get cash (notes or deposits) in exchange. If the banks accept these offers, the rate of interest will be maintained. If not, the prices of securities will fall, which means a rise in the rate of interest, and this will encourage the public to hold more securities in relation to deposits. It follows that the rate of interest depends on banking policy, in particular on that of the Central Bank. If this policy aims at maintaining the rate of interest at a certain level that may be easily achieved, however large the amount of government borrowing. Such was and is the position in the present war. In spite of astronomical budget deficits, the rate of interest has shown no rise since the beginning of 1940.

It may be objected that government expenditure financed by borrowing will cause inflation. To this may be replied that the effective demand created by the government acts like any other increase in demand. If labour, plant and foreign raw materials are in ample supply, the increase in demand is met by an increase in production. But if the point of full employment of resources is reached and effective demand continues to increase, prices will rise so as to equilibrate the demand for and the supply of goods and services. (In the state of overemployment of resources such as we witness at present in the war economy, an inflationary rise in prices has been avoided only to the extent to which effective demand for consumption goods has been curtailed by rationing and direct taxation.) It follows that if the government intervention aims at achieving full employment but stops short of increasing effective demand over the full employment mark, there is no need to be afraid of inflation.[1]

1. Another problem of a more technical nature is that of the National Debt. If full employment is maintained by government spending financed by borrowing, the National Debt will continuously increase. This need not, however, involve any disturbances in output and employment, if interest on

The above is a very crude and incomplete statement of the economic doctrine of full employment. But, I think, it is sufficient to acquaint the reader with the essence of the doctrine and so enable him to follow the subsequent discussion of the *political* problems involved in the achievement of full employment.

It should be first stated that although most economists are now agreed that full employment may be achieved by government spending, this was by no means the case even in the recent past. Among the opposers of this doctrine there were (and still are) prominent so-called 'economic experts' closely connected with banking and industry. This suggests that there is a political background in the opposition to the full employment doctrine even though the arguments advanced are economic. That is not to say that people who advance them do not believe in their economics, poor though these are. But obstinate ignorance is usually a manifestation of underlying political motives.

There are, however, even more direct indications that a first class political issue is at stake here. In the great depression in the thirties, big business opposed consistently experiments for increasing employment by government spending in all countries, except Nazi Germany. This was to be clearly seen in the USA (opposition to the New Deal), in France (Blum experiment) and also in Germany before Hitler. The attitude is not easy to explain. Clearly higher output and employment benefits not only workers, but entrepreneurs as well, because their profits rise. And the policy of full employment outlined above does not encroach upon profits because it does not involve any additional

---

the Debt is financed by an annual capital tax. The current income after payment of capital tax of some capitalists will be lower and of some higher than if the National Debt had not increased, but their aggregate income will remain unaltered and their aggregate consumption will not be likely to change significantly. Further, the inducement to invest in fixed capital is not affected by a capital tax because it is paid on any type of wealth. Whether an amount is held in cash or government securities or invested in building a factory, the same capital tax is paid on it and thus the comparative advantage is unchanged. And if investment is financed by loans it is clearly not affected by a capital tax because it does not mean an increase in wealth of the investing entrepreneur. Thus neither capitalists' consumption nor investment is affected by the rise in the National Debt if interest on it is financed by an annual capital tax.

taxation. The entrepreneurs in the slump are longing for a boom; why do not they accept gladly the 'synthetic' boom which the government is able to offer them? It is this difficult and fascinating question with which we intend to deal in this article.

The reasons for the opposition of the 'industrial leaders' to full employment achieved by government spending may be subdivided into three categories: (a) the dislike of government interference in the problem of employment as such; (b) the dislike of the direction of government spending (public investment and subsidizing consumption); (c) dislike of the social and political changes resulting from the *maintenance* of full employment. We shall examine each of these three categories of objections to the government expansion policy in detail.

We shall deal first with the reluctance of the 'captains of industry' to accept government intervention in the matter of employment. Every widening of State activity is looked upon by 'business' with suspicion, but the creation of employment by government spending has a special aspect which makes the opposition particularly intense. Under a *laissez-faire* system the level of employment depends to a great extent on the so-called state of confidence. If this deteriorates, private investment declines, which results in a fall of output and employment (both directly and through the secondary effect of the fall in incomes upon consumption and investment). This gives to the capitalists a powerful indirect control over government policy: everything which may shake the state of confidence must be carefully avoided because it would cause an economic crisis. But once the government learns the trick of increasing employment by its own purchases, this powerful controlling device loses its effectiveness. Hence budget deficits necessary to carry out government intervention must be regarded as perilous. The social function of the doctrine of 'sound finance' is to make the level of employment dependent on the 'state of confidence'.

The dislike of the business leaders for a government spending policy grows even more acute when they come to consider the objects on which the money would be spent: public investment and subsidizing mass consumption.

The economic principles of government intervention require that public investment should be confined to objects which do not compete with the equipment of private business (e.g. hospitals, schools, highways, etc.). Otherwise the profitability of private investment might be impaired and the positive effect of public investment upon employment offset by the negative effect of the decline in private investment. This conception suits the businessmen very well. But the scope of public investment of this type is rather narrow and there is a danger that the government, in pursuing this policy, may eventually be tempted to nationalize transport or public utilities so as to gain a new sphere in which to carry out investment.[2]

One might therefore expect business leaders and their experts to be more in favour of subsidizing mass consumption (by means of family allowances, subsidies to keep down the prices of necessities, etc.) than of public investment; for by subsidizing consumption the government would not be embarking on any sort of 'enterprise'. In practice, however, this is not the case. Indeed, subsidizing mass consumption is much more violently opposed by these 'experts' than public investment. For here a 'moral' principle of the highest importance is at stake. The fundamentals of capitalist ethics require that 'You shall earn your bread in sweat' – unless you happen to have private means.

We have considered the political reasons for the opposition against the policy of creating employment by government spending. But even if this opposition were overcome – as it may well be under the pressure of the masses – the *maintenance* of full employment would cause social and political changes which would give a new impetus to the opposition of the business leaders. Indeed, under a regime of permanent full employment, 'the sack' would cease to play its role as a disciplinary measure. The social position of the boss would be undermined and the self-assurance and class consciousness of the working class would grow. Strikes for wage increases and improvements in conditions of work would create political tension. It is true that profits would be higher under a regime of full employment than they are on the

2. It should be noticed here that investment in a nationalized industry can contribute to the solution of the problem of unemployment only if it is undertaken on principles different from those of private enterprise. The government must be satisfied with a lower net rate of return than private enterprise, or it must deliberately time its investment so as to mitigate slumps.

average under *laissez-faire*; and even the rise in wage rates result-ing from the stronger bargaining power of the workers is less likely to reduce profits than to increase prices, and thus affects adversely only the *rentier* interests. But 'discipline in the factories' and 'political stability' are more appreciated by the business leaders than profits. Their class instinct tells them that lasting full employment is unsound from their point of view and that unemployment is an integral part of the 'normal' capitalist system.

One of the important functions of fascism, as typified by the Nazi system, was to remove the capitalist objections to full employment.

The dislike of government spending policy as such is overcome under fascism by the fact that the State machinery is under the direct control of a partnership of big business with fascist up-starts. The necessity for the myth of 'sound finance', which served to prevent the government from offsetting a confidence crisis by spending, is removed. In a democracy one does not know what the next government will be like. Under fascism there is no next government.

The dislike of government spending, whether on public in-vestment or consumption, is overcome by concentrating govern-ment expenditure on armaments. Finally, 'discipline in the factories' and 'political stability' under full employment are maintained by the 'new order', which ranges from the sup-pression of the trade unions to the concentration camp. Political pressure replaces the economic pressure of unemployment.

The fact that armaments are the backbone of the policy of fascist full employment has a profound influence upon its economic character. Large-scale armaments are inseparable from the expansion of the armed forces and the preparation of plans for a war of conquest. They also induce competitive re-armament of other countries. This causes the main aim of the spending to shift gradually from full employment to securing the maximum effect of rearmament. As a result employment becomes 'overfull'; not only is unemployment abolished but an acute scarcity of labour prevails. Bottlenecks arise in every sphere and these must be dealt with by creation of a number of controls. Such an economy has many features of a 'planned economy' and is sometimes compared, rather ignorantly, with socialism. However, this type of 'planning' is bound to appear whenever an economy puts itself a certain high target of production in a particular sphere, when it becomes a 'target economy' of which the 'armament economy' is a special case. An 'armament economy' involves in particular the curtailment of consumption as compared with what it could have been under full employment.

The fascist system starts from the overcoming of unemployment, develops into an 'armament economy' of scarcity and ends inevitably in war.

What will be the practical outcome of the opposition to 'full employment by government spending' in a capitalist democracy? We shall try to answer this question on the basis of the analysis of the reasons for this opposition given in the second section. We argued that we may expect the opposition of the 'leaders of industry' on three planes: (a) the opposition on principle against government spending based on a budget deficit; (b) the opposition against this spending being directed either towards public investment – which may foreshadow the intrusion of the State into the new spheres of economic activity – or towards subsidizing mass consumption; (c) the opposition against *maintaining* full employment and not merely preventing deep and prolonged slumps.

Now, it must be recognized that the stage in which the 'business leaders' could afford to be opposed to *any* kind of government interventions to alleviate a slump is rather a matter of the past. Three factors have contributed to this: (a) very full employment during the present war; (b) the development of the economic doctrine of full employment; (c) partly as a result of these two factors the slogan 'Unemployment never again' is now deeply rooted in the consciousness of the masses. This position is reflected in the recent pronouncements of the 'captains of industry' and their experts. The necessity that 'something must be done in the slump' is agreed to; but the fight continues, firstly, as to '*what* should be done in the slump' (i.e. what should be the direction of government intervention) and, secondly, that 'it should be done *only* in the slump' (i.e. merely to alleviate slumps rather than to secure permanent full employment).

In the current discussions of these problems there emerges time and again the conception of counteracting the slump by stimulating *private* investment. This may be done by lowering the rate of interest, by the reduction of income tax or by subsidizing private investment directly in this or another form. That such a scheme should be attractive to 'business' is not surprising. The entrepreneur remains the medium through which the intervention is conducted. If he does not feel confidence in the political situation he will not be bribed into investment. And the intervention does not involve the government either in 'playing with' (public) investment or 'wasting money' on subsidizing consumption.

It may be shown, however, that the stimulation of private investment does not provide an adequate method for preventing mass unemployment. There are two alternatives to be considered here.

1. The rate of interest or income tax (or both) is reduced sharply in the slump and increased in the boom. In this case both the period and the amplitude of the business cycle will be reduced, but employment not only in the slump but even in the boom may be far from full, i.e. the average unemployment may be considerable, although its fluctuations will be less marked.

2. The rate of interest or income tax is reduced in a slump but *not* increased in the subsequent boom. In this case the boom will last longer but it must end in a new slump: one reduction in the rate of interest or income tax does not, of course, eliminate the forces which cause cyclical fluctuations in a capitalist economy. In the new slump it will be necessary to reduce the rate of interest or income tax again, and so on. Thus in not too remote a time the rate of interest would have to be negative and income tax would have to be replaced by an income subsidy. The same would arise if it were attempted to *maintain* full employment by stimulating private investment: the rate of interest and income tax would have to be reduced continuously.[3]

3. A rigorous demonstration of this is given in my article to be published in *Oxford Economic Papers*.

In addition to this fundamental weakness of combating unemployment by stimulating private investment, there is a practical difficulty. The reaction of the entrepreneurs to the measures described is uncertain. If the down-swing is sharp, they may take a very pessimistic view of the future and the reduction of the rate of interest or income tax may then for a long time have little or no effect upon investment, and thus upon the level of output and employment.

Even those who advocate stimulating private investment to counteract the slump frequently do not rely on it exclusively but envisage that it should be associated with public investment. It looks at present as if 'business leaders' and their experts (at least part of them) would tend to accept as a *pis aller* public investment financed by borrowing as a means of alleviating slumps. They seem, however, still to be consistently opposed to creating employment by subsidizing consumption and to *maintaining* full employment.

This state of affairs is perhaps symptomatic of the future economic regime of capitalist democracies. In the slump, either under the pressure of the masses or even without it, public investment financed by borrowing will be undertaken to prevent large-scale unemployment. But if attempts are made to apply this method in order to maintain the high level of employment reached in the subsequent boom a strong opposition of 'business leaders' is likely to be encountered. As has already been argued, lasting full employment is not at all to their liking. The workers would 'get out of hand' and the 'captains of industry' would be anxious to 'teach them a lesson'. Moreover, the price increase in the up-swing is to the disadvantage of small and big *rentiers* and makes them 'boom tired'.

In this situation a powerful block is likely to be formed between big business and the *rentier* interests, and they would probably find more than one economist to declare that the situation was manifestly unsound. The pressure of all these forces, and in particular of big business – as a rule influential in government departments – would most probably induce the government to return to the orthodox policy of cutting down the budget deficit. A slump would follow in which government spending policy would come again into its own.

This pattern of a 'political business cycle' is not entirely conjectural; something very much like that happened in the USA in 1937–8. The breakdown of the boom in the second half of 1937 was actually due to the drastic reduction of the budget deficit. On the other hand, in the acute slump that followed, the government promptly reverted to a spending policy.

The regime of the 'political business cycle' would be an artificial restoration of the position as it existed in nineteenth-century capitalism. Full employment would be reached only at the top of the boom, but slumps would be relatively mild and short lived.

Should a progressive be satisfied with a regime of the 'political business cycle' as described in the preceding section? I think he should oppose it on two grounds: (a) that it does not assure lasting full employment; (b) that government intervention is tied down to public investment and does not embrace subsidizing consumption. What the masses now ask for is not the mitigation of slumps but their total abolition. Nor should the resulting fuller utilization of resources be applied to unwanted public investment merely in order to provide work. The government spending programme should be devoted to public investment only to the extent to which such investment is *actually needed*. The rest of government spending necessary to maintain full employment should be used to subsidize consumption (through family allowances, old age pensions, reduction in indirect taxation, subsidizing of prices of necessities). The opposers of such government spending say that the government will then have nothing to show for their money. The reply is that the counterpart of this spending will be the higher standard of living of the masses. Is not this the purpose of all economic activity?

'Full employment capitalism' will have, of course, to develop new social and political institutions which will reflect the increased power of the working class. If capitalism can adjust itself to full employment a fundamental reform will have been incorporated in it. If not, it will show itself an outmoded system which must be scrapped.

But perhaps the fight for full employment may lead to fascism? Perhaps capitalism will adjust itself to full employment in *this* way? This seems extremely unlikely. Fascism sprang up in Germany against a background of tremendous unemployment and maintained itself in power through securing full employment while capitalist democracy failed to do so. The fight of the progressive forces for full employment is at the same time a way of *preventing* the recurrence of fascism.

18 D. M. Nuti

On Incomes Policy [1]

D. M. Nuti, 'On incomes policy', *Science and Society*, vol. 33, 1969, pp. 415-25.

The framework

One of the main features of advanced capitalist countries in the 1960s is that the level of income and employment of labor has not been limited by effective demand, but by the necessity of keeping the balance of payments in equilibrium. Western governments have learned their Keynesian lesson -- there can be no doubt about it, since Keynes made the front cover of *Time* magazine – and know how to manage aggregate demand through monetary and fiscal policy. With a few exceptions, however, they have been prevented from fully utilizing this newly acquired skill by their inability to control – with the same instruments of economic policy – the behavior of the balance of payments. At a fixed foreign exchange rate, the full employment level of real income and the (uncontrolled) price level associated with it require imports which, given government and private expenditure overseas, are too high with respect to the exports corresponding to that price level. In the attempt to obtain simultaneously full employment of labor and external equilibrium, Western governments have been relying more and more heavily, in recent years, on a crude form of direct control, rather than on monetary and fiscal policy. This is direct control of incomes (wages, rents, dividends) and prices, which has become known as *incomes and prices* policy. Sometimes prices are not controlled and we have *incomes policy*; sometimes only wages are controlled and we have *wages policy*.

1. Mario Nuti's analysis based on British 'incomes policy' is directly relevant to the current government program in the United States to meet the 'inflation problem' by fiscal policies to reduce public and private expenditures, and raise the official unemployment rate back to an 'acceptable' 4 per cent (*Eds.* of *Science and Society*).

The *aim* of all possible versions of an incomes policy is that of obtaining a given rate of change of the level of internal prices, possibly zero, either to obtain price stability for its own sake, or more probably to obtain a level of internal prices consistent with the maintenance of external equilibrium at full employment.

The *instrument* of incomes policy is the direct control of the relation between the rates of increase of money wages and average productivity of labor. This relation, together with the target rate of price change, implies a (spoken or unspoken) government policy with regard to income distribution, and a set of assumptions about other economic variables. The purpose of these notes is to analyse the mode of operation of incomes policy, in some of its possible versions, and its assumptions and limitations.

The target price level

The target price level is determined by the import and export functions and by the target level of the balance of payments surplus, the level of income, the foreign exchange rate, government expenditure overseas and net private investment overseas.

The balance of payments surplus can be defined as:

$$B = rpE - p_i M - G - F \qquad\qquad 1$$

where: B = balance of payments surplus (in \$)
      E = volume of exports
      M = volume of imports
      p = internal price level
      p_i = international price level (in \$)
      r = rate of foreign exchange (\$ per £1)
      G = net government expenditure overseas (military expenditure, economic aid, etc., in \$)
      F = private net investment overseas (in \$)

The import function can be written as:

$$M = M\left(\frac{rp}{p_i}, X\right), \qquad \frac{\delta M}{\delta r} = \frac{p}{r}\frac{\delta M}{\delta p} > 0;$$

$\frac{\delta M}{\delta X} > 0$ where X = real income.   2

The export function can be written as:

$$E = E\left(\frac{rp}{p_i}, Q\right), \qquad \frac{\delta E}{\delta r} = \frac{p}{r}\frac{\delta E}{\delta p} < 0;$$

$$\frac{\delta E}{\delta Q} > 0 \quad \text{where } Q = \text{volume of world trade.} \qquad\qquad \textbf{3}$$

The assumptions of incomes policy are:

1. The balance of payments should be in equilibrium, i.e. $B = 0$; or the deficit should not exceed the international borrowing power of the country, $\bar{B}$, i.e. $B \geqslant -\bar{B}$; or be positive to build up reserves, $B > 0$. Call B^* the surplus aimed at.

2. Real income X should be at the full employment rate X^*.

3. The foreign exchange rate r is fixed at the level $\bar{r}$ (e.g.: £1 = \$2.40) and must remain such.

4. Private investment overseas, i.e. the acquisition or sale of national holdings of foreign assets, is not to be controlled. The magnitude of F is whatever private capitalists choose it to be, $\bar{F}$.

5. Government net expenditure overseas is also given, $\bar{G}$. Since the volume of world trade Q and the international price level p_i are largely outside government control and can be considered as exogenous, the equation

$$\bar{r}p E\left(\frac{\bar{r}p}{\bar{p}_i}, \bar{Q}\right) - \bar{p}_i M\left(\frac{\bar{r}p}{\bar{p}_i}, X^*\right) - \bar{G} - \bar{F} - B^* = 0 \qquad\qquad \textbf{4}$$

determines the level of prices p consistent with external balance. Call $\dot{p}/p$ the percentage rate of change of the price level in time ($\dot{p} = dp/dt, t = \text{time}$). There might be an institutional constraint on $\dot{p}/p$, $a \leqslant \dot{p}/p$. Most probably, $\dot{p}/p \geqslant 0$. Only if equation **4** has no solution for p, or no solution satisfying $\dot{p}/p \geqslant a$ will the government consider revising one or more of the five assumptions listed above, and accept one or more of the following policies: (a) a lower target surplus (or a higher deficit) in the balance of payments; (b) less than full employment income; (c) devaluation or floating of the national currency; (d) control of private investment overseas; (e) reduction of government expenditure overseas. It should be noticed here that since p appears in equation **4** always in the form (pr), the conditions necessary to improve the trade balance by a lower internal price level are the same as those necessary to improve the trade balance by lowering the rate of exchange. In other words, whenever incomes policy is expected to be successful in maintaining external equilibrium, devaluation would be equally capable of producing the same result. These conditions are often expressed in terms of price elasticities of imports and exports: at full employment income X^* and given p_i and Q:

$$\eta_E + \frac{p_i M}{r p E} \eta_M > 1 \quad \text{where } \eta_E = -\frac{p}{E} \frac{\delta E}{\delta p} \text{ and } \eta_M = \frac{p}{M} \frac{\delta M}{\delta p}. \qquad 5$$

This holds of course provided the elasticities of supply of imports and exports is infinite (at full employment, this means that domestic demand is compressed enough to make room for exports).

Money wages, productivity, the price level and income shares

The control of the relation between money wages and the productivity of labor, together with the target rate of price change, determine the change of the relative shares of wages and profits in the national income.

Let us define Y = money income = Xp, W = the wage bill = wL, where w = average money wage, L = employment; x = average productivity of labor = X/L; z = the share of wages in the national income.

By definition $z = (wL/pxL)$, i.e. $w = zpx$ from which:

$$\frac{\dot{w}}{w} = \frac{\dot{z}}{z} + \frac{\dot{p}}{p} + \frac{\dot{x}}{x}. \qquad 6$$

This is the necessary relation between the percentage rates of change of money wages, prices, productivity and the share of wages. The target rate of increase of prices is given by equation 4. The rate of increase of productivity can be taken as exogenous in the short run – given by the development of technology and the attitude of management to innovation and technical change. The actual relation between the rates of increase of money wages and productivity will depend on $\dot{z}/z$, i.e. the rate of change of the share of labor in the national income. This is where possible forms of incomes policy vary and we can think of three possible versions.

Versions I and II lay emphasis on the cost side of the determination of the price level, version III on the demand side.

Three versions of incomes policy

Version I: Money wages increase at the same percentage rates as productivity: $\dot{w}/w = \dot{x}/x$. This implies $\dot{z}/z = -(\dot{p}/p)$: the share of labor falls in the same proportion as prices rise. This is the most common way people think of incomes policy.

Version II: Income shares are frozen: $\dot{z}/z = 0$. From this we have $\dot{w}/w = \dot{x}/x + \dot{p}/p$. This is a slight variation of version I and is more favorable to the workers whenever the target price change is positive. If $\dot{p}/p = 0$, versions I and II coincide. If productivity remains unchanged, it takes the form $\dot{w}/w = \dot{p}/p$: this implies the stabilization of the real wage rate and is perhaps the oldest form of wages policy, advocated by trade unions. As a rule, for a defensive policy employers try to link wages to productivity, and workers try to link wages to the price level.

Version III: Income shares are such that the volume of profits is sufficient to finance the desired level of investment.

Define k as (real) investment per man; $v = k/x$ investment per unit of output; $s =$ propensity to save of profit earners, $s > 0$ (propensity to save of wage earners $= 0$); $I =$ (real) investment; $\Pi =$ total profits; $\pi = \Pi/X$ the share of profits. The required level of profits is:

$$\Pi = \frac{1}{s} I. \qquad\qquad 7$$

The required share of investment depends on the rate of growth of real income $g = \dot{X}/X$

$$\frac{I}{X} = vg. \qquad\qquad 8$$

from which:

$$\pi = \frac{1}{s} \frac{k}{x} g \qquad\qquad 9$$

and $\quad \dfrac{\dot{\pi}}{\pi} = \dfrac{\dot{k}}{k} + \dfrac{\dot{g}}{g} - \dfrac{\dot{s}}{s} - \dfrac{\dot{x}}{x}. \qquad\qquad 10$

On the other hand $\pi = 1 - z$, and therefore

$$\frac{\dot{\pi}}{\pi} = -\frac{\dot{z}}{z}\frac{z}{\pi}. \qquad\qquad 11$$

From **6**, **10** and **11**:

$$\frac{\dot{w}}{w} = \frac{\dot{p}}{p} + \frac{\dot{x}}{x}\left(1 + \frac{\pi}{z}\right) + \frac{\pi}{z}\left(\frac{\dot{s}}{s} - \frac{\dot{g}}{g} - \frac{\dot{k}}{k}\right) \qquad 12$$

which is the wage rule for version III. This implies

$$\frac{\dot{z}}{z} = \frac{\pi}{z}\left(\frac{\dot{s}}{s} + \frac{\dot{x}}{x} - \frac{\dot{k}}{k} - \frac{\dot{g}}{g}\right). \qquad\qquad 13$$

If technical change is neutral, i.e. $\dot{k}/k = \dot{x}/x$, and if saving propensity of profit-earners s and growth rate g are constant, version III is the same as version II, and if in addition $\dot{p}/p = 0$, it is the same as version I. This version of incomes policy embodies the only economic argument in favor of a particular income distribution and is implicit for instance in the spirit of incomes policy in the United Kingdom today.

These three rules refer to macroeconomic variables, which are aggregates of sectoral variables. Since prices, wages and productivity vary at different rates in different sectors of the economy, the basic macroeconomic rule selected has to be translated into a set of sectoral rules.

In each sector i of the economy, the wage rate is linked to productivity by a particular relation

$$\frac{\dot{w}_i}{w_i} = f_i\left(\frac{\dot{x}_i}{x_i}\right). \qquad\qquad 14$$

In the sectors where productivity of labor increases at a rate faster than the average, wages should rise at a rate lower than that of productivity in that sector and the prices of the product ought to fall. Conversely, in the sectors where productivity of labor increases at a rate lower than the average, wages should rise at a rate higher than that of productivity in that sector and the price of the product should rise. The exact relationship between wage and productivity in each industry will depend on the values of the elasticity and cross elasticities of demand with respect to prices, and on the extent to which mobility of labor among sectors depends on wage differentials. (If it does not, incomes policy can be used also to modify the structure of wages as well as their average level.) These relations are complex and have been investigated in the simple case of a two-sector economy by Lancaster (1958). It has also been suggested that the rate of price change in each sector should be such as to preserve the profit margins necessary to finance the economic growth of each sector (Marris, 1964): this is the same principle embodied in version III at the national level and implies that expansion occurs through the growth of the firms already operating in an industry, rather than through the increase of the number of firms; the principle therefore seems more appropriate to the economy as a whole than to each single sector. The determination of the set of rules relating wages and productivity in each sector ought to be consistent with the stabilization of a chosen price index at a level p such that

$$\frac{\dot{p}}{p} = \sum b_i \frac{\dot{p}_i}{p_i} \quad \text{where } b_i \text{ are the appropriate weights.}$$

The change in the share of income going to wages should be

$$\frac{\dot{z}}{z} = \sum b_i \frac{\dot{z}_i}{z_i}.$$

The rate of increase of wages in a particular sector is often determined by 'productivity bargaining': a basic increase is stipulated, geared to expected productivity increases in the sector or in the economy, but above-norm wages are granted in case of above-norm productivity increases.

Implications of incomes policy

Let us suppose that incomes policy is successful in controlling whatever is meant to be controlled: wages, or incomes or incomes and prices. These are the implications of incomes policy:

1. If incomes are controlled but prices are not, and the actual price increase is greater than the target price increase, the actual share of profits is higher than the target share of profits. Incomes policy is ineffective to maintain external equilibrium, but entrepreneurs are rewarded for failing to keep their part of the bargain, i.e. for failing to hold prices at the internationally competitive level (the same thing happens if, after a devaluation,

firms fail to reduce accordingly their export prices expressed in foreign currency, i.e. if they raise their prices expressed in national currency).

2. Whenever this is the case, profits will swell and even if dividends are controlled, capitalists will get their reward under the form of capital appreciation of their stock holdings.

3. If, under any of the three versions examined, the rate of change of wages is equal to the rate of change of productivity plus the rate of increase of prices, incomes policy is an instrument of preserving present distribution. Workers do not sacrifice their share but forfeit their chance of improving their share. Yet there is no reason why workers should have to trade their bargaining power in exchange for full employment. There is no inherent 'fairness' in any given distribution of income at full employment. The only economic argument which can be put forward in defense of a particular income distribution is that it is adequate to finance further economic growth (on this, see the following point).

4. Whenever the rate of change of wages is lower than the rate of change of productivity plus the rate of increase of prices, the share of wages in the national income falls. Under version I, it falls for no specified reason. Under version III the government accepts as a given, unchangeable institutional datum the saving habits of the capitalists and strives to preserve profit margins and adjust them to a changing technology, so that capitalists' consumption is not interfered with, whereas the share of workers is adjusted to whatever level is consistent with the equilibrium of aggregate demand. If consumption was compressed by means of taxation and the State used its tax revenue to finance investment either by lending to private companies or by purchasing their shares, the workers would benefit indirectly through the higher future State income. If the State instead guarantees profit margins consistent with investment requirements, by means of wages and prices control, effectively a part of the product is 'nationalized' and simply handed over by the government to the capitalists, whose only claim to it is their belonging to the propertied classes. A temporary disequilibrium in the balance of payments is prevented by a forcible transfer of wealth from one class to another of the population: one section of the community

is compelled to restrict its consumption to make room for accumulation, but has no rights in the ensuing accumulation of capital. If workers are made to accept a given level of consumption in the name of the requirements of national growth, the least they should obtain in return is that a corresponding fraction of the national capital should be put under their control, either through nationalization or through popular shareholding.

5. If wages are linked to productivity in each sector, as under productivity bargaining at the firms' level, the introduction of new techniques with higher labor productivity will raise the ruling wage rate. This may deter entrepreneurs from introducing labor-saving innovations and paradoxically productivity of labor may well be lower than it would have been otherwise, defeating the very logic of incomes policy.

6. Finally, in all the versions of incomes policy the standard of living of workers depends on circumstances over which they have no control: productivity does not depend on hard work as much as on the type and age of equipment in use, and this is decided by managers. If the link between money wages and productivity is institutionalized, the choice of techniques of production at the firm's level ought to be put under some form of workers' control.

The alternatives

Incomes policy can be ineffective or even self-defeating and is always either an instrument for the preservation of the *status quo* or outrightly iniquitous. In the current experience of advanced capitalist countries, the striking class connotations of incomes policy are hidden under the guise of appeals to the 'national interest', so that opposing incomes policy comes to be regarded as morally despicable or at any rate antisocial. To add insult to injury, this kind of policy can only be enforced and is being enforced by governments commanding popular and union support, e.g. the social democratic government of this country and others in Western Europe.

Those economists who, instead of uncovering the real nature of this policy, cooperate with their government and wrap the package in academic respectability, are responsible for the continuance and growth of gross forms of social inequality. In so far as they conceal the political and social meaning of their recommendations, they fail the ethics of their profession.

There are two main alternatives to incomes policy. The first, lying within the framework of modern capitalism, consists in the rejection of one or more of the assumptions underlying incomes policy, i.e. the acceptance of one or more of the following propositions:

1. A level of employment lower than full employment. This not only will reduce import requirements given the lower level of real income, but will presumably weaken the bargaining power of trade unions and make wage control either unnecessary or more easily enforceable. This is the thesis advocated in the United Kingdom by Professor Paish and by the Governor of the Bank of England. To accept less than full employment of labor would be an open admission of the failure of economic policy, because it would involve deliberate inefficiency: more commodities could be produced by existing resources, but the system of economic relations and decision-making rules prevents the economy from reaching its full potential. This is an inefficient policy, but has the advantage of being openly reactionary, so that it can be assessed on its own merits.

2. Direct or indirect control of net private investment overseas (ranging from disincentives to the nationalization of national holdings of foreign assets).

3. Cuts in government expenditure overseas (much of this expenditure is due to military commitments linked with the existence of national investments overseas).

4. The abandoning of a fixed exchange rate and the introduction of a floating exchange rate or a 'crawling peg'.

5. An increase of international monetary cooperation, such that countries can be allowed to run larger deficits for longer periods without precipitating national and international crises.

The second alternative is that of a society where the means of production are owned by the State. The proportion of income which is not paid out in wages and is called profits does not go to another section of the community, the class of capitalists, but goes back to the whole community in the form of collective consumption and capital accumulation, owned and controlled by the community. In that context, incomes policy as the deliberate aiming at some productivity–wage ratio in each sector and in the economy as a whole becomes a perfectly straightforward instrument of national planning and indeed has been used in the socialist countries of Eastern Europe, especially in the postwar period, with increasing frequency. In that context, incomes policy is not ineffective because prices are controlled; is not conservative nor iniquitous because in a sense the share of workers in the product is always equal to unity, since real consumption depends solely on the accumulation policy of the State, and is more equally shared than under capitalism; does not hinder productivity because bonuses of managers and workers in addition to wages are linked to productivity not only of labor but of all other resources as well.

Incomes policy can be acceptable only after the replacement of capitalism with a socialist society.

References

LANCASTER, K. (1958), 'Productivity-geared wage policies', *Economica*, vol. 25, pp. 199–212.
MARRIS, R. L. (1964), 'Incomes policy and the rate of profit in industry', *Trans. Manch. Stat. Soc.*, December, pp. 1–28.

19 R. M. Goodwin

A Growth Cycle

R. M. Goodwin, 'A growth cycle', in C. H. Feinstein (ed.), *Capitalism and Economic Growth*, Cambridge University Press, 1967, pp. 54–8. Specially revised and enlarged for this volume.

Since its first appearance capitalism has been characterized by alternating ups and downs. This paper attempts to give more precise form to an idea of Marx's – that it can be explained by the dynamic interaction of profits, wages and unemployment. My thesis is that the very structure of capitalism constitutes a homeostatic mechanism which functions by means of variations in distributive shares but does so in such a way as to keep them constant in the long run. If real wages go up, profits go down: if profits go down, saving and investment lag, thus slowing up the creation of new jobs. But the labour force is continually growing both through natural increase and through men 'released' by technological progress. The reserve army of labour grows, wages lag behind the growth of productivity, profits rise and accumulation is accelerated back up to a high level. This in turn gradually reduces unemployment, wages rise, and so it goes on, indefinitely. The structure of such a system is somewhat more complex than might appear and therefore it seemed advisable to use some mathematics to check that the quantitative logic does indeed confirm the conclusions. Also it enables us to get some further results which are not quite obvious, for example, that the mechanism implies a long-run constancy of relative shares of wages and of profits. This suggests an explanation of the paradox that every trade unionist feels he can and is certain that he has, in fact, raised wages at the expense of profits, whereas the scanty evidence suggests that this distribution has not changed significantly during a century of growing trade union power.

Presented here is a starkly schematized and hence quite unrealistic model of cycles in growth rates. This type of formulation now seems to me to have better prospects than the more usual treatment of growth theory or of cycle theory, separately or in combination. Many of the bits of reasoning are common to both, but in the present paper they are put together in a different way.

The following assumptions are made for convenience:

1. Steady technical progress (disembodied).

2. Steady growth in the labour force.

3. Only two factors of production, labour and 'capital' (plant and equipment), both homogeneous and non-specific.

4. All quantities real and net.

5. All wages consumed, all profits saved and invested.

These assumptions are of a more empirical, and disputable, sort:

6. A constant capital–output ratio.

7. A real wage rate which rises in the neighbourhood of full employment.

Number 5 could be altered to constant proportional savings, thus changing the numbers but not the logic of the system. Number 6 could be softened but it would mean a serious complicating of the structure of the model.

These assumptions are too simple and too crude to represent reality; they are not, however, arbitrarily or frivolously chosen. They were chosen because they represent, in my opinion, the most essential dynamic aspects of capitalism; furthermore, they are factually based, to the order of accuracy implicit in such a model. Number 6 should be a result and not an assumption, in which case it need only be roughly true over time. Number 7 should run in terms of money, not real, wages, which, with allowance for inflation, would achieve the same sort of result but at a cost of considerable complication. Any Marxist-inclined economist should ask: why analyse an unreal, idealized system? The answer is that to show the logic and plausibility of a type of behaviour and of its analysis, it is essential to get it clearly and simply stated. If and when such an analysis finds wider acceptance, then it is not too difficult to make the model more realistic by incorporating additional, empirically valid assumptions.

Symbols used are:

q is output;

k is capital;

w is wage rate;

$a = a_0 e^{at}$ is labour productivity, α constant;

σ is capital–output ratio (inverse of capital productivity);

w/a is workers' share of product, $(1-w/a)$ capitalists';

Surplus = profit = savings = investment = $(1-w/a)q = \dot{k}$;

Profit rate = $\dot{k}/k = \dot{q}/q = (1-w/a)/\sigma$;

$n = n_0 e^{\beta t}$ is labour supply, β constant;

$l = q/a$ is employment.

Writing $(\dot{q}/l)$ for $d/dt(q/l)$, we have

$$\frac{(\dot{q}/l)}{q/l} = \frac{\dot{q}}{q} - \frac{\dot{l}}{l} = \alpha,$$

so that $\quad \dfrac{\dot{l}}{l} = \dfrac{1-w/a}{\sigma} - \alpha \cdot$

Call $\quad u = \dfrac{w}{a}, \qquad v = \dfrac{l}{n},$

so that $\quad \dfrac{\dot{v}}{v} = \dfrac{1-u}{\sigma} - (\alpha + \beta) \cdot$

Assumption 7 may be written as

$$\frac{\dot{w}}{w} = f(v)$$

as shown in Figure 1.

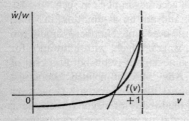

Figure 1

The following analysis can be carried out using such an $f(v)$, with a change in degree but not in kind of results. Instead, in the interest of lucidity and ease of analysis, I shall take a linear approximation (as shown in Figure 1),

$$\frac{\dot{w}}{w} = -\gamma + \rho v$$

and this does quite satisfactorily for moderate movements of v near the point $+1$. Both γ and ρ must be large. Since

$$\frac{\dot{u}}{u} = \frac{\dot{w}}{w} - \alpha,$$

$$\frac{\dot{u}}{u} = -(\alpha + \gamma) + \rho v.$$

From this and the equation above for v, we have a convenient statement of our model.

$$\dot{v} = \left[\left\{ \frac{1}{\sigma} - (\alpha + \beta) \right\} - \frac{u}{\sigma} \right] v. \qquad\qquad 1$$

$$\dot{u} = \{ -(\alpha + \gamma) + \rho v \} u. \qquad\qquad 2$$

In this form we recognize the Volterra (1931) case of prey and predator. To some extent the similarity is purely formal, but not entirely so. It has long seemed to me that Volterra's problem of the symbiosis of two populations – partly complementary, partly hostile – is helpful in the understanding of the dynamical contradictions of capitalism, especially when stated in a more or less Marxian form.

This Golden Goose Egg Theory of capitalism seems to me to fit actual working-class experience and trade union strategy better than the straight Marxian one. Thus it may help to explain some of the lack of success of Marxism in the unions. It also helps to explain, and in some measure to forgive, the fatuity and pusillanimity of social democracy.

Eliminating time and performing a first integration we get

$$\frac{1}{\sigma} u + \rho v - \left[\frac{1}{\sigma} - (\alpha + \rho) \right] \log u - (\gamma + \alpha) \log v = \text{constant}.$$

Letting $\theta_1 = \frac{1}{\sigma};$ $\eta_1 = \frac{1}{\sigma} - (\alpha + \beta),$

   $\theta_2 = \rho;$ $\eta_2 = \gamma + \alpha,$

we can transform this into

$$\varphi(u) = u^{\eta_1} e^{-\theta_1 u} = H v^{-\eta_2} e^{\theta_2 v} = H \psi(v),$$ 3

where H is an arbitrary constant, depending on initial conditions; since $1/\sigma > (\alpha + \beta)$, all coefficients are positive. By differentiating,

$$\frac{d\varphi}{du} = \left(-\theta_1 + \frac{\eta_1}{u}\right)\varphi,$$

$$\frac{d\psi}{dv} = \left(\theta_2 - \frac{\eta_2}{v}\right)\psi,$$

so that we can see that these functions have the sorts of slopes given in Figure 2.

Our problem as stated in 3 is to equate $\varphi(u)$ to $\psi(v)$ multiplied by a constant H. This can be done neatly in the four quadrant positive diagram in Figure 3. We draw through the origin a

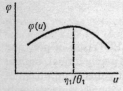
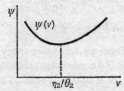

Figure 2

straight line, A, with the slope $\varphi/\psi = H$ (arbitrary since dependent on the given initial condition). Then in symmetrical quadrants we place the two curves φ and ψ and equating these two through the constant of proportionality gives a possible pair of values for u and v. All possible pairs of u and v constitute a solution, which may be plotted in the remaining quadrant. It can be shown, and indeed is quite obvious, that these solution points lie on a closed, positive curve, B, in u, v space. By going back to equations 1 and 2 we can find in what order the points succeed each other and hence in what direction we traverse curve B, as indicated by arrows in Figure 3. A second integration will yield u and v as functions of time, thus allowing us to determine the second arbitrary factor, the point on B at which we start. By varying the slope of A we can generate a family of closed curves broadly similar to B, thus yielding all the possible solutions. One initial condition selects the curve, a second fixes the starting point, and then we traverse some particular curve B in the direction of the arrows for ever, in the absence of given outside changes. There remains only to spell out the meaning of the motion.

Hence we may classify our model as a non-linear conservative oscillator of, fortunately, a soluble type. Since it is non-linear, the solution would not be essentially altered by replacing $-\gamma+\rho v$ with $f(v)$; it would still be a conservative (closed orbit) oscillator. However, more cumbersome, graphical methods become necessary in place of Volterra's elegant analytic ones. As the representative point travels around the closed curve B, u vibrates between ξ_1 and ξ_2, and v between ζ_1 and ζ_2. Both u and r must be positive and v must, by definition, be less than unity; u normally will be also but may, exceptionally, be greater than unity (wages and consumption greater than total product by virtue of losses and disinvestment). Over the stretch 0 to $+1$ on the u axis, the point u indicates the distribution of income, workers' share to the left, capitalists' to the right. The capitalists' share, multiplied by a constant, $1/\sigma$, gives us the profit rate

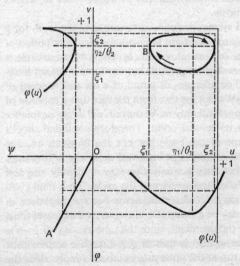

Figure 3

and the rate of growth in output, $\dot{q}/q$. When profit is greatest, $u = \xi_1$, employment is average, $v = \eta_2/\theta_2$, and the high growth rate pushes employment to its maximum ξ_2 which squeezes the profit rate to its average value η_1/θ_1. The deceleration in growth lowers employment (relative) to its average value again, where profit and growth are again at their nadir ξ_2. This low growth rate leads to a fall in output and employment to well below full employment, thus restoring profitability to its average value because productivity is now rising faster than wage rates. This is, I believe, essentially what Marx meant by the contradiction of capitalism and its transitory resolution in booms and slumps. It is, however, un-Marxian in asserting that profitability is restored not (necessarily) by a fall in real wages but rather by their failing to rise with productivity. Real wages must fall in relation to productivity; they may fall absolutely as well, depending on the severity of the cycle. The improved profitability carries the seed of its own destruction by engendering a too vigorous expansion of output and employment, thus destroying the reserve army of labour and strengthening labour's bargaining power. This inherent conflict and complementarity of workers and capitalists is typical of symbiosis.

An undisturbed system has constant average values η_1/θ_1 for u and η_2/θ_2 for v, hence a constant long-run average distribution of income and degree of unemployment. Much more remarkable is the fact that a *disturbed* system still has the same constant long-run values. The time averages of u and of v are independent of initial conditions. We can see this from the fact that a rotation of A (an outside change) will only make the curve B larger or smaller but will not alter its central point. Therefore continual shocks will alter the shape of the cycle but not the long-run average values. Output and employment both will show alternating rates of growth. Whether they actually decrease or merely rise less rapidly will depend on the severity of the cycle. For a mild cycle the growth rate may decrease but never become negative; in other cases there may be a sharp fall. However, the increases must predominate over the decreases, since the time average of $1 - u$ is positive and hence so also is that of $\dot{q}/q$. Likewise employment grows in the long run at the same rate as labour supply, since the time average of v is constant. Similarly the equality of the growth rate in wages to that in productivity follows from the constancy of u. By contrast the profit rate is equal to $1-u$ and therefore tends to constancy. We may look at this as standing Ricardo (and Marx) on his head. Progress first accrues as profits but profits lead to expansion and expansion forces wages up and profits down. Therefore we have a Malthusian Iron Law of Profits. This is because of the tendency of capital, though not capitalists, to breed excessively. By contrast labour is something of a rent good since the supply, though variable, does not seem to be a function of wages. Hence it is the sole ultimate beneficiary from technical progress. By now there would, I suppose, be considerable agreement that what happened in history is: wage rates went up; profit rates stayed down. It is to the explanation of this that the present paper is addressed.

Reference

VOLTERRA, V. (1931), *Théorie mathématique de la lutte pour la vie*, Gauthier-Villars, Paris.

20 Bob Fitch

A Galbraith Reappraisal: The Ideologue as Gadfly

Bob Fitch, 'A Galbraith reappraisal: the ideologue as gadfly',
Ramparts, May 1968, pp. 73–84.

Perhaps it is now time, when America has come to face the complexities of empire, that her best minds begin to shed their innocence. It was all there, in embryo, with our nineteenth-century novelists: the innocent, naïve, goodhearted chap up against the slippery European sophisticates. Perhaps in those days it didn't much matter; the sensitive American plopped back, exhausted, uncomprehending of the new forces which faced him. More than a little of Henry Adams's bemusement prevails even today.

But today the United States carries out *la mission civilatrice* in every part of the globe. The sun never sets on her network of military bases or her multinational corporations. There are revolts, too, on the far frontiers. The generals need troops immediately; more taxes must be raised; the children of the intellectuals – the sensitive ones – will have to put down their books and learn to fire a mortar. The rat-bitten ghetto children will have to wait their turn; the peasants will have to tighten their belts. The social machine is not working well. There's a harsh clatter and roar from the engine room. So many problems. So much misery. So many needs. How can it be changed? Who can even describe it?

There is at least one man among us who feels qualified to describe the way things work. Professor John Kenneth Galbraith's credentials are impressive indeed: he is chairman of the Americans for Democratic Action (ADA), former ambassador to India, professor of economics at Harvard, former head of the Office of Price Administration, a Far Eastern art expert and a novelist both satiric and nostalgic. And Professor Galbraith does not lack prominent backers and admirers. The former editor of *Encounter*, Irving Kristol, presently of *The Public Interest*, compares Galbraith with Ralph Waldo Emerson, to the former's advantage. Galbraith, according to Kristol, goes beyond liberal reformism: he 'ingeniously combines the tradition of moral-analysis'.

Arthur Schlesinger Jr chummily praises Galbraith's militancy in fighting 'unremitting guerrilla warfare in support of the public sector'. President John Kennedy, also an admirer of guerrilla warfare, thought highly enough of Galbraith's *The Affluent Society* (1958) to make it an explicit issue in the 1960 presidential campaign. And a recent Time cover story (1968) found Galbraith a most quotable and possibly the most influential critic of US society.

Chosen by Air Force Secretary Thomas K. Finletter in 1952 to participate in a small Stevenson brain trust, Galbraith was the first prominent Stevensonian to switch to Kennedy in 1960. He remained in the Kennedy entourage until the assassination, serving successively as a member of the task force on foreign economic development, as ambassador to India and as a top speech writer ('let us never negotiate out of fear; but let us never fear to negotiate').

After Kennedy's death, Galbraith's adjustment to the new Johnsonian order may have been a little too quick even for the 'Irish mafia'. William Manchester reports that 'Galbraith outraged everyone within earshot by announcing that he had written "a very good draft overnight" for the new President.' Galbraith himself has described this *contretemps* as a reflection of the division between the Kennedy loyalists and the Kennedy 'realists', in which camp he remained until after the Johnson–Goldwater campaign. At any rate, Galbraith now holds a portfolio in Senator Robert Kennedy's shadow cabinet.

This is a mighty good record for an economics professor, certainly good enough to make his academic peers gnash their teeth, for Galbraith is successful in a thousand ways that they cannot be (and he writes *novels* too). But his colleagues might ask just *what* an American intellectual gets when he gets 'power'. They would learn that it is little indeed. Without an independent base in the trade unions or in the ethnic communities, without a private fortune or control of a political machine, the intellectuals who sniff after power are forced to follow in the camp of any political army which has even a slight chance of seizing Washington with a minimum of bloodshed and looting.

In fact, the sole asset of men like Galbraith (unless they are willing to fill a bureaucratic pigeonhole) is their ability to develop ideology and present it as social criticism. Republicans don't care much for this sort of thing and they even hate it when it's stood on its head – that is, when social criticism gets developed into ideology – so intellectuals, willy-nilly, get to be Democrats.

And how well we have learned that the structure of the Democratic Party means that any attempt at ideology will produce a monstrosity. At the Party's base is the familiar trade union, black, Jewish, Mexican–American, urban coalition. And at the top are bankers, corporation presidents, oilmen, defense contractors and plantation owners. What sort of Solomon could write a program reflecting the needs of both the share-cropper and the plantation owner, the draft-eligible graduate student and the defense contractor, the automobile manufacturer and the auto worker? It is as if the British Liberal Party, *Action Française*, the Italian Christian Democrats and the South African Nationalist Party had all gone mad and declared a merger.

From his ivy-covered podium Galbraith is supposed to ideologize for this monstrosity. His job seems to be to design attractive ideological grillwork that will mask the fundamental mismatch between the base of the party and the controlling powers. Specifically, he must satisfy both the constituencies that demand reform and those from whom the reforms are demanded.

Since the beginning of his labors as an ideologist in 1952 with *American Capitalism*, Galbraith has had something for everyone. He has aimed simultaneously at the oilman, the Democratic Party boss, the college sophomore and the ordinary middle-class citizen. Each of them worries from his own perspective about Vietnam, guerrilla warfare in the ghettos, Haight-Ashbury and De Gaulle. They want to know where the roots of the problems lie and they are beginning to wonder whether there is something about the way this country goes about getting its living – its complex apparatus of production, consumption and distribution – that explains what's going on.

Galbraith is the only significant producer in a growing market.

But the market's product specifications are devilishly narrow. With a stroke of a pen, Galbraith must open the wound and dress it again, titilate the conscience and sooth it. At the end of each paragraph the oilman, the boss, the sophomore and the ordinary citizen must each be able to say: 'Ah yes, I see how it works. Now if we will all try a little harder together. . . .'

Paragraph after mellifluous paragraph the magic seems to work. The reader is left with the simultaneous convictions that the *status quo* is really very decent and that there is also an urgent need for 'change'. Throughout the entire performance, the reader has the feeling that the author somehow combats all the selfish moguls and ideological troglodytes in Christendom.

But a close inspection of the texts shows no advocacy of a more equal income distribution, no plea for full employment, not even a program for closing tax loopholes. What Galbraith does attack are ugly billboards, dirty air, water pollution, insufficient funds for public education and he says we ought to spend more to see that these problems get solved. This program may put him somewhat to the left of Ladybird, but it is certainly not honest-to-God reformism.

Decent reformism admits, at a minimum, that conflicts of interest exist in society and that consequently the poor and unorganized will have to present a political challenge to the rich and the powerful if they are ever going to achieve their demands. Galbraith, on this fundamental question of power, takes the Democratic Party line: no basic conflicts of interest exist because State power is legitimate and is being exercised for the benefit of all.

Galbraith's special pre-eminence in high Democratic Party circles stems from his chief ideological discovery: that big business can be beautiful. Prior to Galbraith's popular work, corporate giantism was the dirty little secret of many radicals and a few academic economists. Monopolistic corporations created more embarrassment at the university than the last thirty pages of *Ulysses*; professors admitted their existence, but preferred to discuss the matter after class. Academic economics is still busy extolling unrestricted competition, free trade, the profit motive and the anarchy of production and distribution. But this world of *laissez-faire* economics, as Galbraith often points out, has pretty well disappeared. It is the wrong apology for the wrong century for the wrong system. Galbraith has a much more salable product.

The theme of monopolistic predominance and its essential benignity carries through all of Galbraith's major work. Most everything else is ancillary. *American Capitalism*, the book which first established Galbraith as an outstanding *advocatus de fide*, argued that political stability in the US was a product of the stalemate between big business and big labor. This was one side of the famous theory of countervailing power. The other side spoke out for the 'right' of monopolies to engage in price discrimination. As Galbraith put it: 'To achieve price discrimination – to use bargaining power to get a differentially lower price – is the very essence of the exercise of countervailing power.'

Galbraith's next important book was the pre-Watts classic, *The Affluent Society*, which showed that political stability in the US had been achieved because the problems of economic equality and insecurity had been largely eliminated. In *The Affluent Society*, Galbraith admitted that monopolized industry tended to produce less than competitive industry, but he side-stepped the issue by righteously pointing out that the US had an unhealthy obsession with production anyway.

In Galbraith's most recent work, *The New Industrial State* (1967), several of the key hypotheses of the prior works have been abandoned, but the defense of monopoly and monopoly power remains as firm as ever. Today the US is stable, Galbraith argues, *despite* the existence of poverty and insecurity (they're 'outside' the industrial system) and *because* 'big' labor has accepted a subaltern role. (Whatever happened to 'countervailing power'?)

It is belief in the permanence of an ideal rather than logical consistency that gives Galbraith's work its unity. In this light, *The New Industrial State* can be seen as volume three of a larger opus entitled 'Monopoly Without Tears'. The overarching theme of the 'trilogy' is the endless viability, plasticity and, above all, the desirability (given a few moderate improvements) of the present economic and social order.

The conclusion that General Motors is good for you (and could be better), and in any case will never die, will sound familiar to many students of American corporate-liberal thought. And thus there will be a tendency among those who resist the message to overlook the political and doctrinal ingenuity that went into *The New Industrial State*.

This would be a mistake. To dismiss Galbraith simply as 'another Establishment apologist' not only greatly overestimates the craftsmanship of his peers, but it also overlooks what can be learned from observing America's premier 'monophile' at work.

Could the monopoly structure of US heavy industry be at the root of persistent unemployment, urban poverty, huge arms budgets and the never-ending crusade against 'communism'? Decidedly not, says Galbraith. He admits that some of these ills are consistent with both Marxian-socialist and Smithian-capitalist predications on the consequences of monopoly. But this is precisely why he calls those ideas 'the conventional wisdom'. For generations the conventional wisdom held that competition was a good thing and monopoly a bad thing. Now that we are living under monopoly capitalism we see how groundless the fears of monopoly were. Monopoly – which Galbraith calls 'modern industrialism' – is efficient and humane. Competition is the real villain of the piece.

The New Industrial State acknowledges all the defects of the old system of competitive free-enterprise capitalism. Yes indeed, the author muses, those old-time capitalists – the Fords, Morgans, Mellons and Rockefellers – they were tough old bastards. Union busting, sweating labor, buying up competition, maintaining a vested interest in unemployment – all this was consistent with their solitary goal in life, the accumulation of capital through the pursuit of maximum profits. Galbraith is glad they've all died off and that new men are in power.

Who are the new men of power, who, according to Galbraith, run the modern corporation? They are called the 'technostructure'. The technostructure is not the top managerial elite, the men whose salaries are set by the ebb and flow of corporate profits. The technostructure is different, and better. First of all it's a lot larger and that makes an immediate step toward democracy. It's made up of all the engineers and middle-echelon bureaucrats: everyone who brings 'specialized knowledge, talent or experience to group decision making'. Second, and most important, since it can't get any of the profits the corporation makes, it doesn't have the old 'profit *über alles*' obsession. In fact it seems to be worried mainly about security – the corporation's and its own.

According to Galbraith, now that the technostructure has taken charge and eliminated the profit motive as the single goal of corporate enterprise, it's possible to relax and enjoy 'industrialism'. The corporations no longer compete against each other: they divide the market and allow everyone to prosper. Nor do they try to hold workers' wages down. Instead, they give the workers a reasonable share of what they want and pass on the increased wage bill to the consumer. This ends the anarchy of the system. The corporations can plan their production schedules with the knowledge that prices will remain constant. And the workers no longer have to fear layoffs. The market is replaced by 'planning'. We leave the realm of competitive necessity and enter the kingdom of monopolistic 'freedom': the Great Post-Keynesian No-Hassle State.

Before we can settle back and enjoy Galbraith's New Order, however, there remains a small problem. Why do corporations and unions still behave very much as they did when the capitalists and their hired managers held sway? Why, to cite only the most obvious example, did 1967 see the highest number of strikes in fourteen years? How can 'planning' and the demise of the market be reconciled with persistent balance of payments deficits and the export of capital during periods of high unemployment? Or with the go-go mutual funds and the great speculative booms on the stock exchanges?

There are two possible explanations. One is that trade unionists and corporations have not yet learned their Galbraith: they are still burdened with the 'conventional wisdom'. The other is that *The New Industrial State* represents as faithful a portrayal of America's corporate economy as *Gone With the Wind* did the Southern slave system. Let's examine the latter possibility.

How did the 'technostructure' take control of the corporations away from the capitalists in the first place? Galbraith's explanation is that technostructures supply information and capitalists supply capital; and that in a century in which information is scarcer than capital, the technostructure was able to seize power.

It's true, of course, that there is a lot of capital around these days, a lot more than in the nineteenth century. But big blocs of capital like the $800 million TWA borrowed through the investment banking houses in 1967 aren't to be found in everyone's cookie jar, as the record interest rates indicate. Technical information, on the other hand, while highly prized, is not scarce in the same sense. Nor are the men who provide it. To take an obvious example, in the aerospace industry, which employs over half of all US engineers and scientists, layoffs and unemployment are quite common because of volatility and the competition for government contracts. In fact, technology is changing so rapidly that many engineers are becoming obsolete.

Far from constituting the corporate ruling class as Galbraith thinks they do, technicians, according to many experts, are developing into a kind of *lumpenproletariat*. Stanley Hawkins, training coordinator at Lockheed Missile and Space Company says, 'The problem of the unemployed engineer is with us now – the problem of the *unemployable* engineer is approaching with frightening rapidity.' Now the technostructure may be as humane and rational as Galbraith thinks it is, but at the moment the technocrats seem to be taking orders from the top, collecting unemployment checks and stretching their coffee breaks, just like the rest of the working class.

If the technostructure doesn't run the corporations, who does? Could it be small groups of rich businessmen similar to those that ran them in the past? Galbraith tries to show that individual wealth no longer plays a role and that the predominance of outside monied interests has vanished. He cites the thirty-five-year-old analysis of 'the separation of ownership from control' by Adolph A. Berle Jr, together with a couple of more recent studies by writers equally unable to discover any outside forces controlling corporate management.

Several recent investigators, however, have discovered the outside centers of power that Berle, Galbraith & Company were unable to locate. For example, in 1965 the anti-trust subcommittee of the House Judiciary Committee published a study of seventy-four important industrial-commercial companies; in this handful of firms 1480 officers and directors held a total of 4428 positions. The report concluded that interlocking directorates are as prevalent today as in 1914 when the Clayton Act, prohibiting interlocking directorates, was passed.

More recently, *Fortune* reported that in 1966, controlling ownership of 150 of the 500 largest US corporations rested in the hands of an individual or of the members of a single family. And this was admittedly a 'very conservatively' drawn estimate, excluding cases in which businessmen – who are known to wield great influence – own less than 10 per cent of the voting stock. In practice, Wall Street experts maintain that the holders of 5 to 10 per cent of the stock can prevail over the unorganized mass of stockholders.

With the technostructure back in its accustomed position of supplying technical information to profit-maximizing businessmen, the rest of the corporate landscape also falls back into proper perspective. Corporate 'planning' – comfortably eulogized by Galbraith in *The New Industrial State* as a kind of rich man's socialism – instead of replacing the jolts and kicks of the market becomes a series of short-run responses to it.

Take the labor market for example. In *The New Industrial State* wage demands don't lead to bitter class struggles because price increases can always be passed on to the consumer and because labor basically has it made. Within this framework, how can we fit the eight-month-old national copper strike involving nearly 50,000 miners? According to A. H. Raskin, labor editor of the *New York Times*, the chief grievance of the miners is the work schedule: 'For three years the standard work schedule in all branches was twenty-six consecutive days without a single day off. Then would come two days to recuperate, followed by another twenty-six-day stint, and so on for three years.'

The deadlock over these primitive conditions comes in an industry which is dominated by a few giants – Anaconda, Kennecott and Phelps Dodge: Galbraith's 'mature corporations', i.e. oligopolists. They represent his *nouvelle vague* of flexible, noncompetitive corporations. Why don't they give in to the miners' demand for a less than twenty-six-day work 'week'? It would amount to an increase of only about four cents a pound in the cost of copper. Why don't they simply pass this on to the consumer?

The reason is that the consumer in this case is not unorganized American housewifery but such firms as AT&T, GE and Westinghouse who are able to choose between aluminum and copper. And aluminum is already about 13 cents a pound cheaper than copper. It is no wonder that these 'mature corporations' are acting so immaturely.

In the Galbraithian wonderland of corporate planning, the corporations needn't pay attention to what goes on in the capital market either. The mature corporation has its own 'source of capital, derived from its own earnings, that is wholly under its own control. No banker can attach conditions as to how retained earnings are to be used.' Were it otherwise, Galbraith admits, bankers would hold the strings of the corporation and tell the technostructure what to do.

In the real world of the American economy, something like this is exactly what does happen. In 1966, for example, about *half* of all the new funds used by corporations for growth came from external sources. In this year alone, bond issues and bank loans were equal to about two-thirds of undistributed profits. And although the figures are not yet available, 1967 appears to have dwarfed 1966 in this respect, creating what *Fortune* describes as 'an epic corporate bond binge'. Standard Oil of New Jersey, General Electric, Westinghouse, Texaco, Union Carbide – mature corporations all – paid their respects to the bond market to the tune of $200 million or more. Leading all other investment bankers, with $3·8 billion worth of issues, was the old dinosaur of capitalist enterprise, Morgan Stanley. Some of his clients included General Motors, Mobil Oil, US Steel and IBM.

When the investment bankers manage a big bond issue for a corporation, or extend other kinds of credit, they increasingly earn the right to intervene on matters like mergers, financing, granting of stock options, dividends and even advertising campaigns. And with so much emphasis these days upon the stock market 'performance', the pressure exerted by the banks for higher profits and dividends grows continually greater.

But even if outside financial interests weren't prodding the corporation to increase its rate of profit; even if the labor market were always stable; and even if one firm's prices weren't another firm's costs, the whole notion of corporate planning 'replacing' the market in the US would still be absurd on its face. It is like saying that because two nations' armies follow their respective battle plans and their troops follow orders that the resulting war between them is 'planned'.

This kind of *post facto* reconciliation of conflicting social forces begins to smell very familiar to the reader with a nose for the ranker side of historical analogy. The 'principle of consistency' which Galbraith proclaims from his Procter and Gamble soapbox – 'As always reality is in harmony with itself' – smells suspiciously like Hegel's excuse for Frederick William IV: 'What is real is rational.' And, as Montesquieu pointed out, the Jesuits' apologies for the counterreformation had the same fetid odor: 'The Society of Jesus may pride itself on the fact that it was the first to prove to the world that religion and humanity are compatible' (*Esprit des Lois*).

Galbraith is surely in the forefront of those who would do for monopoly capitalism what the Jesuits did for Catholicism – establish its compatibility with humanity. But like all really first-rate ideologists he comes down to earth finally with a political program.

First he disposes of the main alternative system. It's not that socialism is wicked, it's merely *passé*, says Galbraith. The development of technology took control away from the capitalists. Similarly, it is the 'technical complexity and planning and associated scale of operations' that has made things too complex for democratic control over the means of production to be exercised today. How could an elective body run a steel factory? It would be impossible. Consequently, socialism is a 'spent slogan'; it would result in 'social control without success'; it no longer seems 'worth the struggle'.

So here we are: we can't go forward to socialism; and we can't go backward to competitive capitalism. Monopoly capitalism is all there is.

How, then, can the liberal intellectual face the future? With Maharishi Mahesh Yogi? A prefrontal lobotomy? The answer Galbraith gives is to go into politics – especially university politics – and try to 'change things'. But not very much. The Galbraithian corporation is basically decent – just a bit insensitive and overimpressed by technology and growth. What it needs is a little couth.

Galbraith sees this as a ready-made opportunity for the 'Educational and Scientific Estate'. Atomic scientists should use their influence for atomic restraint; artists and poets should try to beautify the cities; educators should try to elevate the overall cultural tone of American life. All these factions within the 'Educational and Scientific Estate' should try to work together to get control over the university budget and thus reassert an area of independence from government and corporate control, at least within their own area of specialization. (It might be pointed out that in this political program, the problems of racism, unemployment, economic imperialism and poverty have not even been raised. But perhaps the strategy is not to fight on all fronts at once.)

And thus, as the E&S Estate broadens its base and hardens its cadre through protracted struggle, it might very well succeed in winning the one off-campus reform that Professor Galbraith considers urgent enough to mention: creation of an American 'BBC'.

Perhaps the professor will permit another vision to those who find his account of Utopia a bit spare: a socialist America in which the 'corporate ruling elite' will be the overwhelming majority of Americans working in their factories and offices; where the only ghettos will be those displayed as plastic models in historical museums and where the word 'unemployment' sends young men to the dictionary instead of the relief office. Perhaps then, on a television program emanating from one of our hundreds of 'BBCs', a panel of historians, sociologists and psychologists can analyse how the human imagination became narrow and inverted to the point of functional blindness among precisely the most brilliant and favored of America's citizens during the late period of its defunct global empire.

References

GALBRAITH, J. K. (1952), *American Capitalism*, Houghton Mifflin.
GALBRAITH, J. K. (1958), *The Affluent Society*, Houghton Mifflin.
GALBRAITH, J. K. (1967), *The New Industrial State*, Houghton Mifflin.
Time (1968), 'The all-purpose critic', *Time*, 16 February.

Further Reading

Dear Reader,
The critique of academic economics presupposes a mastery of academic economics. *Das Kapital*, for example, is a painstaking work on a vast amount of material. Marx read just about every economics text and traced the historical development of each basic proposition of the conventional economics of his day.

We have listed below a few of the more outstanding works dealing with the themes of each section. The task of learning and unlearning and dialectically transcending is up to you.

Historical descriptions of the rise of the neo-classical school

M. Dobb, 'On some recent tendencies in modern economic theory' in *On Economic Theory and Socialism*, Routledge & Kegan Paul, 1955.

L. Rogin, *The Meaning and Validity of Economic Theory*, Harper & Row, 1956.

E. K. Hunt, *Property and Prophets*, Harper & Row, 1972.

Mystification and the evasion of social reality: criticisms of conventional academic economic theory

I. Mészáros, *Marx's Theory of Alienation*, Merlin Press, 1970.

P. Anderson, 'Components of the national culture', *New left Rev.*, vol. 50, 1968, pp. 3–57.

G. Lukács, *History and Class Consciousness*, trans. R. Livingstone, Merlin Press, 1971.

K. Marx, *Economic and Philosophic Manuscripts of 1844*, ed. D. J. Struick, trans. M. Milligan, Lawrence and Wishart, 1970.

S. K. Nath, *A Reappraisal of Welfare Economics*, Kelley, 1969.

The capital controversy and income distribution

P. Sraffa, *Production of Commodities by Means of Commodities*, Cambridge University Press, 1960.

J. Robinson, *Economic Heresies: Some Old-Fashioned Questions in Economic Theory*, Basic Books, 1971.

G. C. Harcourt, 'Some Cambridge controversies in the theory of capital', *J. econ. Lit.*, vol. 7, 1969, pp. 369–405.

'Paradoxes in capital theory: a symposium', *Q. J. Econ.*, vol. 80, pp. 503–83.

Value, prices and profit in commodity society

E. Böhm-Bawerk, 'Karl Marx and the close of his system', R. Hilferding, 'Böhm-Bawerk's criticism of Marx', L. von Bortkievicz, 'Transformation of values into prices of production in the Marxian System,' all in *Karl Marx and the Close of his System*, ed. P. M. Sweezy, Kelley, 1966.

E. Mandel, *The Formation of the Economic Thought of Karl Marx*, trans. B. Pearce, New Left Books, 1971.

R. Meek, *Studies in the Labor Theory of Value*, International Publishers, 1956.

H. J. Sherman, *Radical Political Economy: Capitalism and Socialism from a Marxist Humanist Perspective*, Basic Books, 1971.

The role of the State in monopoly capitalism

J. Steindl, *Maturity and Stagnation in American Capitalism*, Oxford Institute of Statistics, 1952.

M. Kalecki, *Theory of Economic Dynamics: An Essay on Cyclical and Long-Run Changes in Capitalist Economy*, Allen & Unwin, 1954.

P. Mattick, *Marx and Keynes: The Limits of the Mixed Economy*, Porter Sargent, Boston, 1969.

P. M. Sweezy, *Theory of Capitalist Development*, Monthly Review Press, 1942.

G. W. Domhoff, *The Higher Circles: The Governing Class in America*, Random House, 1970.

Acknowledgements

Permission to reproduce the Readings in this volume is acknowledged from the following sources:

1 Routledge & Kegan Paul
2 Lawrence and Wishart
3 UK & Commonwealth rights: Lawrence and Wishart
  USA and Canada rights: International Publishers
4 The Merlin Press
5 *Quarterly Journal of Economics*
6 Monthly Review Press
7 Basil Blackwell
8 *De Economist*
9 *De Economist*
10 *Canadian Journal of Economics*
11 *Review of Economic Studies*
12 Economics of Planning
13 Dr Alfredo Medio
14 *Science and Society*
15 *Science and Society*
16 USA and Canada rights: Random House Inc
   UK and Commonwealth: Chatto and Windus
17 *The Political Quarterly*
18 *Science and Society*
19 Cambridge University Press
20 *Ramparts Magazine Inc*

Author Index

Subject Index

Penguin Modern Economics Readings

Theory of the Firm
Edited by G. C. Archibald

This collection of Readings brings together papers representing the main work being done in the field. Key methodological as well as theoretical problems are tackled in depth. In neo-classical equilibrium theory, firms are described according to their production function. Thus the aim of Part One is to estimate both production functions and the firm's long-run costs. The remaining Parts consider the various types of market structure, pricing policies and income distribution. Also included, is an alternative to the profit maximization theory; Baumol's sales maximization hypothesis. The final Part considers the relatively new topic of linear programming and its relation with conventional economic analysis.

G. C. Archibald is Professor of Economics at the University of Essex.

Other titles available in this series:

Capital and Growth
Edited by G. C. Harcourt and N. F. Laing

Two groups are at present debating the controversial theory of capital. They are loosely referred to as the neo-Keynesian and the neo-neo-classical. The editors of the volume believe the debate is founded upon post-war interest in problems of economic growth and income distribution over time, together with the clash of rival ideologies as to how these problems are best tackled, both in developing and developed economies.

G. C. Harcourt is Professor of Economics at the University of Adelaide; N. F. Laing is Reader in Economics at the same university.